Photorealism and Ray Tracing in C

Photorealism and Ray Tracing in C

Christopher D. Watkins,
Stephen B. Coy,
and Mark Finlay

M&T Books
A Division of MIS:Press, Inc.
A Subsidiary of Henry Holt and Company, Inc.
115 West 18th Street
New York, New York, 10011

Library of Congress Cataloging-in-Publication Data

Watkins, Christopher
     Photorealism & ray tracing in C / Christopher Watkins, Stephen Coy, & Mark Finlay
         p. cm.
     Includes bibliographical references and index.
     ISBN 1-55851-247-0
     1. C (Computer program language) 2. Computer graphics. I. Coy, Stephen. II. Finlay, Mark. III. Title. IV. Title: Photorealism and ray tracing in C.
QA76.73.C15W38   1992
006.6'765--dc20

92-26419
CIP

95   94   4 3

Project Editor: Sarah Wadsworth
Acquisitions Editor: Christine de Chutkowski
Technical Editor: Ray Valdés
Developmental/Copy Editor: Kevin Shafer

Cover Design: Lauren Smith Design
Art Director: Margaret Horoszko
Production Supervisor: Cynthia Williams
Color Image Production: Jeremy F. Mende

Contents

Acknowledgements

The outline for this book and all of the code were written by Christopher D. Watkins and Stephen B. Coy. The code is based on Stephen B. Coy's original shareware Vivid 2.0 ray-tracer, Mark VandeWettering's public domain MTV ray-tracer, and Christopher D. Watkins' Proteus Algorithm ray-tracer. Vivid is a trademark of Vivid Software. Bill Tolhurst contributed the modeling software and the chapter on the modeler (Chapter 14). Thanks to Mike Thompson for his contributions to the ray tracer and to some of the software tools. Thanks also to Addison Rose of DM Productions for some Pascal to C code translation.

The text of this book was written by Christopher D. Watkins, Stephen B. Coy, and Mark Finlay and edited by Christopher D. Watkins and Mark Finlay. Christina N. Noland also contributed to the text editing.

The color plates in this book were generated by Christopher D. Watkins and Stephen B. Coy.

3-D models of a helicopter, a dinosaur, a duck, an F117, a heart, a hotrod, a telephone, a skull, a Venus, and a Corvette were supplied by Seth Jarvis of Mira Imaging, Inc., 2257 South 1100 East, Suite 1A, Salt Lake City, Utah 84106.

Highly detailed 3-D models of an '82 Porsche 911SC, an '83 Camero, an '83 Honda 110 ATC, a bust of Beethoven, a cow, a dump truck, a foot, a galleon, a low-top tennis shoe, a P51 Mustang, a Bell Ranger helicopter, and a triceratops were supplied by John Mellor of Viewpoint Animation Engineering, 870 West Center, Orem, Utah 84057.

The ice cube model was built by Ron Lloyd, and the chess piece models are copyright Randy Brown at UNC/Chapel Hill. Our thanks to Eric Haines for ideas on some of the procedural objects and the teapot database.

Thanks also to David Palermo for his contribution of "Sculpture" found in the Gallery plate.

The BGI graphics driver is copyright Jordan Hargrave, and text fonts were produced by VVFONT15, written by B. J. Traylor.

All of the software in this book was written in C using Borland C++ version 3.1 and WATCOM C version 9.0. The Borland C++ software was furnished by Borland International, 1800 Green Hills Road, Scotts Valley, California 95066. The WATCOM C software was furnished by WATCOM, 415 Phillip Street, Ontario, Canada, N2L 3X2.

The 640 x 480-pixel 24-bit color computer graphics displays were produced on the Cardinal 7000 graphics card. Eight-bit color displays were produced on both the Cardinal 7000 and STB Powergraph ERGO-VGA boards with 1 megabyte of memory. The boards were furnished by Fred Hermanson of Cardinal Technologies, Inc., 1827 Freedom Road, Lancaster, Pennsylvania 17601 and by Gary Keller of STB Systems, Inc., 1651 N. Glenville, Suite 210, Richardson, Texas 75081.

Thanks to Ken Welton and Michael Glaser of Lavista Systems, 3776 Lavista Road, Suite 100, Tucker, Georgia 30084, for supplying extra equipment for development and image generation.

A special thanks to Andy Maglione, Jr. and Harold Gessford of the Outer Banks Radio Shack, Kitty Hawk, North Carolina for the supply of equipment and software tools needed to complete the book when our equipment failed at the remote location.

Thanks also to Jack Brady of Southeastern Digital Images, 4900 Frammons Court, Atlanta, Georgia 30338, for acting as a sounding board for ideas.

Special thanks to our parents who supplied us the tools and inspiration for learning at an early age.

And much thanks to Jolt Cola Company for keeping us up long enough to complete the software and text.

Algorithm, Inc. of 3776 Lavista Road, Suite 100A, Atlanta, Georgia 30084 supplied the CCD captured images of the Andromeda Galaxy, the Dumbbell Nebula and Earth's moon.

Algorithm, Inc. is an Atlanta based scientific research and engineering company that produces custom software and turn-key systems primarily for medical imaging and visualization, photo-realistic rendering and animation. Algorithm, Inc. has produced other tools for ray tracing, volume rendering, 3-D modeling, animation, image processing and interactive image warping and morphing. Most applications are DOS or Microsoft Windows and are portable. Contact us at the above address or call (404 634-0920 for more information regarding our products.

Why This Book is for You

Many of today's movies use computer graphics to create special effects and to reduce production costs. Movies like *Terminator II* and *Beauty and the Beast*, for example, are full of complex computer-generated imagery. The textured marble columns and chandelier in *Beauty and the Beast* would have been a production company's nightmare without the aid of computer graphics. The movie would have cost the production company much more in time, money, and effort without this technology.

This book is for people who wish to produce similar images on an inexpensive PC but have been frustrated by a lack of basic programming tools. The programs and libraries in this book will enable you to produce high-quality photorealistic computer renderings using both a common VGA and a more advanced 24-bit color graphics card. The software is modular enough that you should be able to adapt it to a variety of environments.

❖ In Part I, you will learn about the tools needed to handle the vector mathematics and matrix algebra required by computer graphics. The use of these tools is illustrated through sample programs.

❖ Part II discusses the production and use of a ray tracer. Actual C code in the text accompanies the explanations. This section also provides conceptual theory on ray tracing and on illumination models for shading objects.

❖ Part III addresses procedurally defined objects, covering such objects as fractal land formations, quaternion slices, three-dimensional Julia and Mandelbrot sets, and solids of revolution.

1

❖ Part IV discusses the production of a three-dimensional modeling tool used to build object databases. You will see the wire-frame outline of the primitive objects that comprise your new object move from left to right, up to down, and far to near as you use the three-dimensional cursor keys.

❖ In Part V you will find methods for improving image quality after the image has been produced. A color-reduction method is given for reducing the 24-bit color data to 8-bit color data for display on a common VGA.

❖ Part VI describes the graphical display devices and explains how to use them to display the images that you have generated.

❖ Part VII talks about work beyond this text, discussing issues like animation, complex ray tracing, radiosity, and stereo images.

Two 1.2 MB 5 ¼" floppy disks contain all of the graphics software referenced in this book, including the modeling and rendering software and the color-reduction software. The disks also contain some of the image files and all of the scene files required to render the images found in the center of this book.

Introduction

Just about everyone has seen the beautiful and engaging three-dimensional computer-generated imagery that is produced for movies, television, and magazines. This book is for those who wish to produce such images on low-cost PC equipment, but have been frustrated by the lack of the basic programming tools required to do so. The programs and libraries in this book enable you to produce high-quality photorealistic computer renderings using both the common VGA and the more advanced 24-bit color graphics hardware. Specifically, graphics drivers are provided for the STB Powergraph ERGO VGA and the Cardinal 7000 24-bit color graphics cards. The software is modular enough that you should be able to adapt it to a variety of other environments.

Rendering complex three-dimensional scenes is analogous to producing a movie. You assume the role of director and must coordinate all of the various components. The actors (objects in the environment), the script (what the objects will do during an animation and how the camera will move), art direction (specifying how the scene will be lit and how all of the elements of the scene will look), the camera work (controlling camera motion, focus, depth of field, and so forth), and assorted supporting roles all contribute to making the final image on the screen. This book provides all the software necessary to allow you to create scenes of startling realism as well as environments that could never exist outside a computer-generated world.

Organization of the Book

The book is divided into eight logical parts, each of which addresses a particular aspect of computer-image generation. Each chapter of the book is comprehensive, building from the previous chapters in order to produce more complex imagery. Basic three-dimensional graphics and mathematics, the basic building blocks around which most of the other programs are written, are examined, as well as a scene-rendering technique known as *ray tracing*. Methods for procedurally and manually creating objects for the ray tracer are also discussed. Techniques for exploiting the VGA display hardware to produce optimal images are given.

Part I covers the conventions used for labeling variables, procedures, and other entities in the programs and pseudo-code. This approach makes the code easier to understand. Also included are the tools needed to handle the vector mathematics and matrix algebra required in computer graphics. These are organized in an easy-to-use and functionally obvious fashion. Graphics commands are developed here in Borland C++ in such a way as to be universal, thus allowing you to use the compiler of your choice. Some notable compilers are the Watcom C version 9.0 and the Borland C++ version 3.1.

Part II discusses ray tracing. The explanations are given by pseudo-code and are associated with actual C code in the text. Included in Part II are theory on ray-object intersection testing, object surface normal calculation, shadow calculation, Kay-Kajiya bounding slabs for increased ray tracing speed, illumination models, and the basic physics of light. You will learn practical methods for texturing objects both procedurally and from maps that have been scanned into your computer. You will see how super-sampling the scene with rays and averaging the results acts as an effective anti-aliasing method to remove the jagged edges of objects, thus making objects appear more realistic. You also will gain an understanding of light reflection and refraction as you trace rays from reflective objects and through glass and water. You will see the way light plays on diffuse and specular surfaces. A special technique is also developed for the surface normals of objects that are created with facets (small planar surfaces like triangular patches) to smooth the object and make it appear solid.

Part III teaches you how to create some fantastic databases to ray trace. Fractal images generated as z-buffers (such as mountain ranges, three-dimensional Julia and Mandelbrot Sets) are brought to life. Hamiltonian/Norton quaternions are ray traced as z-buffer approximations. Methods for creating broken tiled surfaces (such as pools and table tops) are shown along with routines for generation of realistic clouds through turbulence techniques. Summed sinusoids are used to create some beautiful and realistic water scenes.

Part IV covers the development of a simple three-dimensional CAD wire-frame editor that allows you to build up objects for the ray tracer. Here you will interactively build up letters and other objects by translating, rotating, and scaling such primitive objects as spheres, cones, cylinders, boxes, and pyramids.

Part V describes techniques for improving the image once it has been generated. Methods such as filtering are discussed. Histogram and median-cut methods are shown to accommodate the VGA hardware (only 256 colors), since the ray tracer computes 24-bit color (16,777,216 colors). Floyd-Steinberg dithering is given to improve image quality by diffusing the error in color reduction. Ordered dithering is also discussed.

Part VI contains the drivers for the particular graphics hardware discussed. Information on the STB PowerGraph ERGO VGA (1024 x 768-256 color) and on the Cardinal 7000 (640 x 480-16,777,216 color) hardware is given. General programming information and display programs for these cards are included.

Part VII carries you beyond this text by discussing such topics as computer animation and production, advanced rendering techniques such as radiosity and the role ray tracing has there, other ray tracing methods, and stereoscopic techniques.

Part I

Chapter 1 describes the organizational standards adopted for the software found in this book. Naming conventions for functions, variables, and macros are described here, and you will find a general discussion of C as it pertains to graphics.

The mathematics module

Chapter 2 describes the mathematical functions commonly required for computer graphics. These functions are at the heart of most of the programs found throughout the book. These are the routines that provide straightforward manipulation of three-dimensional objects and their environments. All mathematical operations on three-dimensional vectors and matrices are handled here.

Transformations including translation (moving a point in space), scaling (changing the length of a vector), and rotation (rotating a point around a coordinate axis) are represented as matrices. One of the nicest features of these types of transformations is that any combination of them may be expressed as a single affine transformation. This allows for a compact and efficient means of expressing the motion of an object or of the camera. This is also convenient for the modeling of light sources, since you will express the interaction of light with a surface by a three-dimensional vector from the light to the surface. This module also includes a pseudo-random number generator for use in procedural modeling and texturing. Since you control the seed, the random-number generator causes any software relying on this function to generate the same results each time it is invoked.

The graphics interface module

Chapter 3 contains a number of useful graphics routines required for the software in this book. Basic plotting, color palette manipulation, circle and line generation, and graphics mode selection all are included here. These routines call Base routines that address specific graphics hardware and compilers. A description of three-dimensional theory and orthographic versus perspective projection of three-dimensional points onto the two-dimensional screen also are covered. Wire-frame drawing routines are included to draw contours of models rather than drawing solid models.

Using the modules

Chapter 4 is where the fun begins. Here you learn how to use the tools developed in Chapters 1 through 3.

The first program generates a two-dimensional fractal crystal growth. The growth looks something like silver with many seemingly random branches. This chapter also teaches you how to grow two-dimensional grass, bushes, and coral. Plants will grow until the sunlight from above is blocked by another growth. A three-dimensional starfield program creates the sensation of flying through space. The last program produces a computer simulation of three particles orbiting in three-dimensional space.

Part II

Chapter 5 introduces ray tracing theory and the ray tracing program. This chapter examines the mathematics modules that are specific to the functioning of the ray tracing program.

Ray tracing theory

Chapter 6 discusses ray tracing theory and the classic ray tracing algorithm. Conceptual understanding of the ray tracing program and the primary recursive ray tracing function occurs here.

The ray tracing program

Chapter 7 discusses the functioning of the main program section of the ray tracer. Anti-aliasing, projection, camera model, and backgrounds are discussed here.

Ray-object intersection tests

Chapter 8 provides an understanding of how reverse light rays leaving your eyes pass through a pixel of the screen and mathematically "hit" the objects you want to view. Spheres, cones, and other primitive geometric shapes are examined.

Chapter 8 introduces a special case of a triangular patch that knows something about its neighbor patches. If an object is made of these patches, the object can be made to look smooth, as opposed to appearing as a "collection" of triangular patches. This chapter also discusses clipping, where you create an object by throwing away parts of a larger object. Bounding schemes for increased ray tracing efficiency also are covered. Here objects are surrounded by larger objects, so if you hit the larger object, you check for intersection with the smaller ones inside it.

Shading, texturing, and lighting

Chapter 9 teaches you how to shade objects so they look photorealistic. The chapter begins with a mathematical understanding of the objects' surface normals. The surface normal is important because it tells you how a ray of light will bounce off of an object or refract through an object. A shading model incorporates effects of ambient, diffuse, and specular light reflection, as well as transparency and reflectivity (shine).

Chapter 9 also discusses texturing, which is of supreme importance in creating the photorealistic effect. Textures based on mathematical functions (these are called procedural textures) are used to obtain wood grains, marble, and clouds. Water and other textures are obtained by perturbing the object's surface normal with a mathematical function, thus perturbing the shading calculation. You will learn how to add atmospheric effects like fog and haze to ocean scenes and late-night street scenes. And finally, Chapter 9 discusses shadows, an effect that is important in producing photorealistic imagery.

The ray tracer code in review

Chapter 10 describes the functioning of all of the modules of the ray tracer. An overall understanding of the program takes form here.

How to use the ray tracer

Chapter 11 tells you how to use the ray tracing program. You will produce an ASCII file that holds a virtual world to render. Positions and orientations of light sources, the camera and objects of the scene, and their material descriptions are initialized here.

Part III

Chapter 12 begins Part III, where procedural object database generation is presented. You will learn about a tile puzzle constructed from primitive objects (like spheres, cylinders, and planes) and a fractal tree made of spheres and cylinders. These objects and others are created from primitive objects by mathematically defining the object. Positions and orientations of the primitive objects are calculated using a mathematical expression.

Chapter 13 introduces another form of procedural database called a z-buffer object database. Here, a two-dimensional array holds a value that represents the height at a given location. This type of database lends itself to terrain and ocean objects. Mandelbrot and Julia sets are computed the classic way, except you will use the iteration count for determination of height and not color.

Part IV

Chapter 14, which is Part IV, discusses the production and use of a three-dimensional object modeling tool called Ed. This tool helps you produce special objects for the ray tracer and set up scenes. Objects are created from the primitive objects (spheres, cones, rings, and so forth) and are written out to an

ASCII file for integration into your scene or for direct rendering. Chapter 11 describes this integration process.

Part V

Chapter 15, which is Part V, introduces color processing. Here is where the 16,777,216 colors (24-bit color) that are calculated (256 intensity levels for each of red, green, and blue) by the ray-tracing program are reduced down to the VGA-displayable 256 colors (8-bit color). One method of color reduction is called the *color histogram with a least-squares fit*. A color histogram is created of all of the colors. The most commonly used colors are kept, while the least used are discarded. Also discussed is the median-cut method of color reduction. This function normalizes colors that are too far outside a certain range. Dithering algorithms are discussed. Basic image processing functions like filtering are also introduced. These functions apply not only to the reduced images, but to the 24-bit color images as well.

Part VI

Information about the graphics hardware and the compiler-specific and hardware-specific functions appears in Chapter 16, which is Part VI. The STB ERGO PowerGraph VGA and the Cardinal 7000 24-bit color cards are discussed. A table of statistics for each of the graphics cards is given, which shows modes, resolutions, colors and other useful information. Also presented are image-display programs that take advantage of the features of each of these cards and display either the image-processed or original images.

Part VII

Chapter 17 (Part VII) is the general-interest section of the book. This chapter discusses more complex models, the actual production of animation, and advanced technologies like radiosity for photorealistic rendering. Stereo images for a true three-dimensional effect are also presented here.

Hardware and Software Required

The software for this book was developed on Watcom C version 9.0 and Borland C++ 3.1 and written in a standard C convention to allow it to be ported easily to other compilers and machines. With minimal modifications, the software should be capable of being compiled on Microsoft C. It should be an easy task to modify the software to run on the Turbo C++ compiler. The only change that must be made for this task is to examine the different ways the compilers implement standard functions. These programs may also run on earlier versions of the compiler with minimal modification.

If you are using a version of C different from the versions used in this book, you should obtain a copy of Watcom C 9.0 or Borland C++ 3.1. Borland International has a good upgrade policy, enabling you to get the latest version of Borland C++ at a reduced price. If you are a beginning C programmer, you should use Borland C++ because its integrated environment makes programming an easy process. For the more advanced programmer, you should use Watcom C. The code that is generated by this compiler runs substantially faster than Borland C++. Those who elect to use a compiler other than these will experience messy compilation errors. It is true that you can get around these errors by production of your own routines to handle the incompatibilities, but this will take you longer to get the software up and running.

All of the software on the program disks and in the book should run on any IBM PC or compatible 386 with coprocessor and 8 megabytes of RAM that has a VGA card and monitor or better. Graphics modes 46 (640 x 480 x 256) and 56 (1024 x 768 x 256) are used in the book. You can also use the Cardinal 7000 24-bit color mode (640 x 480 x 16,777,216). The STB System's PowerGraph ERGO VGA and the Cardinal Technologies' Cardinal 7000 24-bit color card (both of which can handle the super VGA 1024 x 768 x 256-color mode) are supported. Both of these boards use the Tseng 4000 chip. Since techniques for driving super-VGA cards have not been standardized, the drivers in this book are guaranteed to drive these graphics cards (and probably most other graphics cards using the Tseng 4000 chip). If you can obtain the necessary addressing and port information from your graphics card company, you can rewrite the software graphics drivers in this book for your specific graphics card.

Most of the software presented in this book will run on any IBM PC or compatible with 2 megabytes of RAM, but the faster the machine and the more memory, the better off you are. All of the programs are computationally intensive.

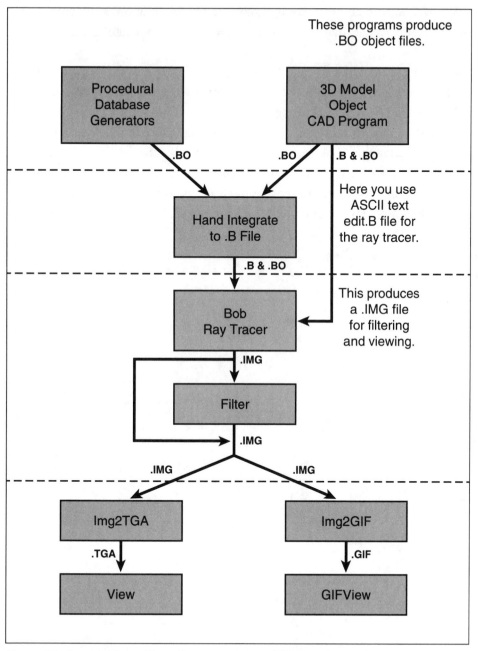

Figure I-1. An overview of how the programs and files work together

A 386 with a math co-processor or a 486, are suggested in order to generate the high-resolution single-frame renderings in a reasonable amount of time.

Summing it all Up

If you are like the majority of personal computer programmers, you may not realize the true power of your computing system to produce high-quality three-dimensional graphics, especially photorealistic graphics like the ones in movies. After completing this book, you should be able to take the programs in the book and improve upon them. You should be able to generate more complex scenes and add features to the ray tracer and modeler, as well as use the mathematics and graphics modules for a multitude of other personal programming projects.

PART I

Standards and Universal Modules

CHAPTER 1

Standards and the C Language

This chapter provides both a primer on the C language and a description of the kind of programming style used in the writing of this code. For those who are already familiar with C, you can move onto Chapter 2 to get into the ray tracing program directly.

Since the code in this book has been developed by many people over several years, the style of each module is a little different, and thus inconsistent with other modules. Unfortunately, this is inevitable in any creative and time-consuming project. The goal in this book is to develop certain programming practices that make the project progress more smoothly. This chapter is not intended to preach to you about what constitutes good programming style. Instead, it points out why we chose C as a programming language, and how certain feats are accomplished using C.

Why C ?

The C language has become the language of choice for the development of complex computer graphics programs and scientific simulations programming. It is a language that is classified as a high-level language, but it still allows an engineer the ability to produce code that has an efficiency approaching that of assembly language for real-time applications. The C language is also available on just about every machine and operating system, and has been for some time.

The C language has significant advantages over Pascal and FORTRAN. The portability of C between machines of both the UNIX and MS-DOS platforms makes it appealing to researchers who must work on a variety of hardware. Because of their inherent mobility, the C data structures are well-suited to graphics programming. The availability of fast, efficient compilers, debuggers, and other development tools makes C much more desirable for large projects. The C language is constructed to encourage development of general library routines that can be used as the building blocks for many graphics programs.

The C code is much quicker and easier to develop than the equivalent assembly code. With a little effort, C code efficiency can approach that of equivalent assembly code. Additionally, programming in assembly language may take days of preparation and coding, whereas the same program might take half an hour in C. The added performance of assembly language over C is usually not worth the extra development time. In many instances, C and assembly language are mixed in the same program (Borland C++ allows in-line assembly code, for instance). These hybrid programs usually have the main program and human interface written in C, and any routines (like mathematics modules and graphics modules) that are computationally expensive written in assembly.

The Concept of a Programming Language

The fundamental purpose of a programming language is to provide a means of expressing an algorithm that can then be executed by a computer. A programming language must have the following five basic elements in order to conform to this definition:

1. A methodology for organizing data (*data* refers to "datatypes" and variables)

2. A methodology for describing operations (these are operators)

3. A methodology for controlling operations based on previous operations (this is called *program control*)

4. A methodology for structuring the data and operations so that a sequence of program statements can be executed from any location within the program (these are *data structures* and *functions*)

5. A methodology for moving data between the program and the outside world (referred to as *I/O*, input/output)

Listing 1-1 is a simple C program that contains each of these five elements.

```
main()
{
   float addnums();    // declare functions

   int added,numb;     // declare variables
   int index, i;
   float numarray[50];
   float    total;

   printf("\n\nNumber of numbers to add? ");
   scanf("%d", &numb);

   printf("\n\nEnter numbers to add?\n ");
   for(index=0; index<numb; index++) {
     i = scanf("%f", &numarray[index]);
      if (i != 1) break;
   }

   total = addnums(numarray, numb);

printf("\n\nTotal is %f", total);
}

float addnums(array, arraysize)
   float array[];
   int arraysize;
{
   int i;
   float sum=0.0;
   for(i=0;i<arraysize;i++)
     sum=sum+array[i];
   return(sum);
}
```

Listing 1-1. A simple C program

The first line of Listing 1-1 begins the *main()* function. This declares that a program which has no arguments will be defined after the left brace ({ found on the next line), and up to the line just before the next function, called *addnums*. The *main* program is the main control of the program. It is the first part of the program that is executed.

The next line declares the functions that are called throughout the main program. The function *addnums* sums the elements of an array called *array* of length *arraysize* and returns this value. This corresponds to goal 1, which is to provide a means of organizing data (in this case, using the *array* data construct). Notice the use of "//" for comments. In addition, "/*" and "*/" can be used to define multiple line comments on all compilers. Notice next that variables such as *added* and *numb* are declared.

Input is then taken regarding the number of numbers that you wish to add together (goal 5, which is to interact with the outside world). The program then prompts you to enter the actual numbers into an array for later addition. The function *addnums* is then called to actually add the numbers found in the array and return the value to a variable called *total*. The provision for functions and operators satisfies goal 4. Within *addnums*, a "for" loop is used to cycle through the array and add all of the elements together. This corresponds to goal 3, which is to gain program execution control. The provision of operators like + and - satisfies goal 2. The result from *addnums()* is subsequently displayed on your terminal.

Variables and Data Types

All computer programs manipulate information that is represented in some digital format. A variable in C is defined by declaration of an alphanumeric group of characters. This group will recall the number assigned to it for any other reference to that variable. Note that this variable name (*identifier*) must start with a letter or an underscore and cannot be the same as the standard or compiler-specific C key words. Note that C is case-sensitive. "AddNums" is different from "addnums" and "Addnums".

The C language contains many different number types. Figure 1-1 shows some of the standard types and how they are represented internally.

Variable declaration	32-bit size	32 bit range		
char	8	-128	->	127
unsigned char	8	0	->	255
int	32	-2.1e9	->	2.1e9
unsigned int	32	0	->	4.3e9
short	16	-32768	->	32767
unsigned short	16	0	->	65535
long	32	-2.1e9	->	2.1e9
unsigned long	32	0	->	4.3e9
float	32	-1e-38	->	1e38
double	64	-1e-308	->	1e308

Figure 1-1. Variables in C for a 32-bit machine

Most high-level languages allow for the definition of indexed lists, more commonly referred to as *arrays*. Arrays can also be multidimensional. In C, multidimensional arrays are implemented as an array of arrays. An element of such an array can be accessed as follows:

```
type arrayname[size1][size2]...[sizeN];
```

This example shows an N-dimensional array of a generic type. The available types are those listed in Figure 1-1 (that is, int, double, and so on). Notice that in C, the size for each dimension is held in brackets, whereas in many languages the sizes of each dimension are separated by commas.

Text data types such as *char* actually define 8-bit numbers that represent an alphanumeric character (that is, ASCII). Note that strings in C are terminated with a NULL (ASCII 0) character, so a 35-character message actually occupies 36 bytes (characters) of data. Some handy special characters are as follows:

\\ ....defines a backslash

\' ....defines an apostrophe

\" ....defines a quote

\n ....defines a carriage-return line feed

\xhhh ....defines a hexadecimal ASCII character

The Operators

The methods used to manipulate variables and actually produce some sort of useful result are called *operators*. The C language has a seemingly endless set of operators to perform both mathematical and logical operations. The C++ language compounds this immensely by allowing you to define your own operators on your own data types. Some of the more common types of operators are as follows:

❖ *Assignment operators* assign a value to a variable. The equals sign (-) is the assignment operator.

❖ *Arithmetic and bitwise operators* are used to perform multiplication, division, addition, subtraction, and modulus (integer remainder after division). The modulus operator works only on integer-typed variables, whereas all of the other operators work with all variable types. In C, the three unary arithmetic operators are the unary minus (-), an increment (++), and a decrement (--). The increment and decrement are usually used with *pointers* (data addresses).

❖ *Binary bitwise operations* are performed on integer operands using the "&" symbol for AND, the "|" symbol for OR, the "^" symbol for bitwise exclusive OR (XOR), the "<<" symbols for the arithmetic shift left, and the ">>" symbols for the arithmetic shift right. The number of bits is the operand for the arithmetic shifts. The unary bitwise NOT operator will invert all of the bits in the operand. The symbol for this is "~".

Operators can be combined using the assignment operator and any of the arithmetic operators. The following are a few examples:

a=a+b;	a += b;	a=a-b;	a -= b;
a=a*b;	a *= b;	a=a/b;	a /= b;
a=a%b;	a %= b;	a=a&b;	a &= b;
a=a|b;	a |= b;	a=a^b;	a ^= b;
a=a<<b;	a <<= b;	a=a>>b;	a >>= b;

For readability of code during development, many programmers do not use the combined operators. If you have some kind of complicated pointer expression instead of the variable *a,* though, they can be most useful. In this case, you are not required to enter it on both sides of the expression and the meaning is somewhat clearer.

❖ *Logical operators* are operators that yield an absolute (true or false) response. They are commonly used to control loops and to perform machine-level coding. The "==" operator is used to determine the equality of two arguments. Do not confuse this with the "=" assignment operator. The "<" symbol is the "less than" comparison operator. The "<=" symbol is the "less than or equal to" comparison operator. The ">=" and ">" logical operators are "greater than or equal to" and "equal to" logical comparisons. The "!=" symbol is the "not equal" to logical operator. The last three logical operators are "&&" for AND, "||" for OR, and "!" for NOT.

❖ *Operator precedence* is the order in which multiple operations will be performed in the absence of parentheses to clarify the expression. The following is a list of operators in decreasing precedence:

```
++ --...................increment, decrement
-..........................unary minus
* / % ................multiplication, division, modulus
+ -.....................addition, subtraction
<< >>................shift left, shift right
< <= >= >.........comparison with "less than" or "greater than"
== !=.................equal, not equal
& ^ |..................bitwise AND, XOR, OR
&& ||..................logical AND, OR
```

Note a couple of rules regarding C and the conversion of types. First, if an operation involves two types, the one of higher rank takes precedence. The ranking from highest to lowest is *double, float, long, int, short,* and *char. Unsigned* outranks *signed*. For example, if you add a *float* and a *double* together, the *float* is promoted to type *double* and then added to the *double* variable. The result is then converted to the type of variable on the left-hand side of the assignment. In an assignment statement, the result is converted to the type of the variable being assigned.

Program Control

This section discusses the ability to control the conditional execution or repetition of certain statements based on the results of certain expressions.

Conditional execution means the "if-else" statement is used to execute a series of statements conditionally based on the results of some expression. Its format is as follows:

```
if(integer_value) {
        first statements
}
else {
        second statements
}
```

If integer_value is nonzero, then the first statements are executed. Otherwise, the second statements are executed. Note that compound statements can be created with the "if-else" statement by using brackets to enclose certain statements.

The *switch* statement is another useful tool to use when more than four alternatives are chosen for a situation. An example of the *switch* statement is as follows:

```
switch(integer_expression)
{
case constant1:
statements; break;

case constant2:
statements; break;

case constant3:
statements; break;

case constant4:
statements; break;
```

```
default:
statements;
}
```

The C language also supports a single-line conditional expression that allows you to express a single "if-else" statement in one line. The form for this expression (known as the *ternary operator*) is

```
expression1 ? expression2 : expression3.
```

If expression1 is nonzero, then the whole conditional expression has the value of expression2. If expression1 is 0, then the whole expression has the value of expression3. Some programmers think that this type of expression should never be used directly in your code. However, it is often used to define an efficiently executing macro. For example, to define a macro to find the maximum of two variables, you would use

```
#define MAX(a,b)  ( (a) > (b) ? (a) : (b) )
```

The C language supports this type of expression because the expression usually can be implemented efficiently by the compiler. Since macros are often in-line substitutions, the MAX function in the previous example is efficiently performed.

The C language uses three loop types for program control; the "while" loop, the "do-while" loop, and the "for" loop. The "while" loop takes the form

```
while(expression)
    statements;
```

The "while" loop repeats the statements until the expression becomes 0. The decision to pass through the loop is made at the beginning, so you may never pass through it.

The "do-while" loop takes the form:

```
do { }
while(expression);
```

The "do-while" loop repeats the statements until the expression becomes 0. Note that the decision to pass through this loop is made at the end of the loop, therefore you always pass through this loop at least once. The "for" loop is a more general form of a FORTRAN "do" loop. The "for" loop takes the form:

```
for(initial condition; test condition; modify)
   statements;
```

The "for" loop is commonly used for indexing arrays. It is an infinite loop if no bounds are set (that is, if you omit the test condition). The initial condition is the initial value for a variable. The test condition may be any logical expression, but is usually a comparison of the loop variable to some ending value (such as, i < 10). The loop variable is usually altered by the modify expression (such as, i++).

The C language provides three additional control statements: *break, continue,* and *goto.* Note that these statements can make a complex program difficult to follow, but are often quite handy. As shown previously, the *break* statement can be used to exit a *switch* statement, or any other type of loop. The *continue* statement, on the other hand, tells the program to skip to the end of the loop and proceed with the next iteration. The *goto* statement is a statement that carries you to any other place in the program and aborts any loop that you might be in at the time.

Functions

All C programs consist of one or more functions. Even *main()* is considered a function. A function has a type, a name, a pair of parentheses containing an optional argument list, and a pair of braces containing an optional list of executable statements. The format is as follows:

```
type name(argument list)
declarations for arguments in argument list {
body of function (statements) }
```

The type is that of the value the function returns. The C language provides *void,* a special data type for functions that do not return a value. The types for the arguments in the argument list are located in the second line of the function. Within the function body, the return statement is used to return a number back as the value of the function. Many recently released compilers allow the declarations for the arguments in the argument list to be included in the parentheses. This type of declaration corresponds to the ANSI standard version of C, as well as to C++.

The C language extensively uses *header files* (traditionally having the file extension .H) to define data structures and to declare functions. The ANSI standard supports the use of *function prototypes* to define not only the return value of a function, but also the data types of its arguments. Note that for C, function prototypes are optional, whereas C++ requires them. Function prototypes allow the compiler to do much more extensive error checking during the compilation of your code. Calling a function with the wrong number or the wrong type of arguments is common. If the function has a prototype, the compiler can check each of your calls to see that you have the correct number and type of variables passed to the function. This can greatly reduce the number of mystifying bugs in a program. A typical prototype in a header file is as follows:

```
extern void thefunction(int)
```

Macros

Two of the most appealing aspects of the C language are macros and the C preprocessor. The ability to compile program segments conditionally, create aliases of any text in the program, and to create user-defined macros make C a powerful language. But "powerful" can also translate to "confusing."

A short example of a macro is one that finds the maximum number of two numbers. When using a macro that has arguments, always put the arguments in parentheses. This ensures that if an expression is passed to the macro, the expression is evaluated before the rest of the macro is processed. Without this convention, you can create some of the most irritating and subtle bugs imaginable.

Pointers and Arrays

Pointers are variables that hold addresses of some data, rather than the data itself. Pointers primarily access different data elements within an array to allow for dynamic memory allocation. Pointers access different locations in a data structure and also pass structures as arguments. The C language uses the *call-by-value* convention for argument passing. This means that C passes a copy of the data to the function, not the data itself. If you want the function to modify the actual variable, you must pass a pointer to that variable. If you want to pass some huge structure to a function, you pass the pointer. Otherwise, the program copies the entire structure each time the function is called.

The three pointer operators in C are "*", "&", and "->". The "*" pointer operator is called the *indirection operator*. Use the indirection operator whenever the data stored at the address pointed to by a pointer is required (thus, indirect addressing). The "&" pointer operator fetches the address of the variable to which it is applied. For example, *&a* is the address of *a*. The "->" pointer operator is the member-access operator. If *s* is a pointer to a structure, then *s->member* is the element member of that particular structure.

Memory

Unlike FORTRAN, C fully supports dynamic memory allocation. The C language uses four standard functions to manipulate memory. The first function is *malloc()*, which allocates a chunk of memory of whatever size (in bytes) you pass it and returns a pointer to this newly allocated memory. The *calloc()* function does the same thing, except it sets all of the memory to 0 as well. The *free()* function returns the memory allocated by *malloc()* or *calloc()* back to the system, making it available for other uses. The *realloc()* function essentially performs a *free()* followed by another *malloc()*. It recognizes instances where you may want less memory than was already allocated, so it can just give you back the memory you already had. It is more efficient in some cases than using *free()* and *malloc()* separately.

The following are examples of these functions:

```
int *pointer;
pointer = (int *) malloc(sizeof(int));

int *array;
array = (int *) calloc(100, sizeof(int));
```

Note the use of the *sizeof()* function. This function returns the size of data types in bytes, which can be used to make your code system-independent. For example, an *int* on a PC is usually 16-bits long, whereas on a workstation it may be 32-bits long.

Structures

One of the most useful features of C is the *structure* data type. Structures enable you to group data types together into a convenient packet. Unlike arrays, data types can be mixed and matched freely in whatever fashion you need. For example, you could define a light source as

```
struct lightsource
{
  float red, grn, blu;
  float falloff; int
  lighttype
}
```

To declare a structure called light, you would use the following:

```
struct lightsource cyanlight;
```

In this example, *cyanlight* becomes a structure of type *lightsource*. You can now initialize and access the data in the structure as follows:

```
cyanlight.red       = 0.0;
cyanlight.grn       = 1.0;
cyanlight.blu       = 1.0;
cyanlight.falloff   = 0.0;
cyanlight.lighttype = 1;
```

You could also declare a pointer to such a structure as

```
struct lightsource *light_ptr;

light_ptr = &cyanlight;

light_ptr->red       = 0.0
light_ptr->grn       = 1.0;
light_ptr->blu       = 1.0;
light_ptr->falloff   = 0.0;
light_ptr->lighttype = 1;
```

Now all of the data for a light source can be passed around in one easy-to-use package, rather than as separate arrays with complicated indices.

typedef

The C language essentially enables you to define your own data types by using the *typedef* statement. You declare one name to be equivalent to some other name, usually a structure definition. You may then use this equivalent name just as any other data type declaration (such as *int* or *char*). For instance, if you want another way to express the *lightsource* structure template, you can create the *LIGHTSOURCE* type.

```
typedef struct lightsource LIGHTSOURCE;
```

Basically, this statement replaces all occurrences of *LIGHTSOURCE* with the *struct lightsource* declaration. You can now declare the light to be

```
LIGHTSOURCE cyanlight;
```

Input and Output (I/O)

Two of the basic I/O functions in the C programming language are *scanf* and *printf*. Much like the FORTRAN *read* statement, the *scanf* function parses a line entered by the user and places this data into a variable (or variables). The *printf* function displays variables on the console in a program-specified format by using a format string. A *printf* statement might look something like this:

```
printf("\n\nNumber of Light Sources = %d", NumLgtSrc);
```

Some of the format specifiers are as follows:

%5d ....signed integer with width 5

%16p ....pointer value with width 16

%5.4f............floating-point number with width 5 and 4 places past the
decimal point

%5.4e............floating-point number in exponential format with width
5 and 4 places past the decimal point

%c................single character

%s................string

%8x ....integer in hexadecimal format with width 8

A few of the special escape sequences in the format string are

\\ ....print a single backslash
%% ....print a single percent sign (%)
\n...................carriage return and line feed

The *scanf* function is similar to the *printf* function. For example,

```
scanf("%d %f", integernumber, floatingpointnumber);
```

File I/O

The C language contains numerous standard disk I/O functions. Most C file access is sequential (that is, the file is read until you reach the end of the file). A file may be read character-by-character using the functions *getc()* and *putc()*. The functions *fprintf()*, *fscanf()*, *fgets()*, and *fputs()* allow you to treat a file as a buffered stream of text. To access a binary file randomly, use *fread()*, *fwrite()*, and *fseek()*. A conventional way of handling a file might be as follows:

```
FILE *file_pointer;

file_pointer =
fopen("the_filename","the_filetype_string")

fclose(file_pointer);
```

This routine first opens a file called "the_filename" by using the options specified in "the_filetype_string". The available filetype strings are

"r" ....open file for reading
"w"...............create new file or overwrite old file
"a" ....append existing file or create new file
"r++"............open existing file for reading and writing
"w++" ....create a new file for reading and writing
"a++" ....append an existing file for reading and writing

Also, an "a" or a "b" can be appended to these strings to select either ASCII file format ("a") or binary format ("b"). You will find that UNIX systems will not require this distinction, but MS-DOS computers do require the distinction.

Programming Style

Programming in the C language requires a great deal of practice, patience, and understanding. Many subtle tricks and nuances must be seen and tried before they can be used effectively. While pointers allow great program flexibility, they can also cause considerable grief. Typical examples are the use of uninitialized global pointers or freeing the wrong chunk of memory. These kinds of problems are also difficult to track down.

The ray tracing code in this book is fairly modular and straightforward. *Modular* code means keeping such things as file I/O limited to one small set of routines. Try not to put disk I/O calls throughout your code. Instead, make one set of routines to read and write each file type that you support.

Other References

For further information on programming in C, you should read some of the references presented in the bibliography. In particular, Kernighan and Ritchie's *The C Programming Language* is the virtual bible of C programming style and convention.

Ray Tracing, Ho!

The following chapters describe some of the utility modules used by the ray tracer for vector manipulation, three-dimensional projections, and other low-level graphics routines. These modules are used in some simple example programs in Chapter 4. Part II describes Bob, the ray tracer *par excellence*.

CHAPTER 2

The Mathematics Module

Before discussing computer graphics, you must first understand the basic building blocks required to run the program presented in this book. These components include routines that perform special mathematical functions as well as those that handle the interface to your computer's graphics hardware. This chapter describes the header files required for compiling the mathematics module, as well as the contents of the mathematics module itself. These header files contain declarations of the datatypes and global variables used by both the mathematics and graphics modules found in this chapter and in Chapter 3. This chapter discusses how the various functions in the modules work, and why they are of importance to computer graphics. Chapter 4 carries you through example programs that use many of the functions found in these modules.

The remainder of this book assumes you have a basic working knowledge of the C programming language, in particular the use of defined types (*typedef*), structures, and pointers. Knowledge of basic aspects of the PC platform, such as segmented memory and the VGA architecture, is also assumed.

The Header Files

The header files (those with an .H file extension) contain *typedefs* and declarations of global variables used by the mathematics and graphics interface modules. None of the other modules in this book will compile correctly without all of these header files. The header files are very short, but they contain important information which allows the modules to be compiled and linked separately. The four header files are BkDefs.H and BkMath.H (discussed in this chapter), and BkGlobs.H and BkGraph.H (discussed in Chapter 3, which presents the graphics module).

The BkDefs.H header file

The BkDefs.H header file contains defined constants as well as datatype declarations. Several variable types have been redefined for easier recognition and understanding. For instance, an *unsigned char* is now called a *Byte* and an *unsigned int* is now a *Word*. These are the most commonly found names for each variable type. The preprocessor definitions specify constants used by the mathematics and graphics interface modules. An example of this is the constant that represents the irrational number *pi*. Listing 2-1 shows the complete BkDefs.H header file.

```
/*
```

```
        BkDefs.H = Defines Header File for Modules
        Copyright 1988, 1992 Christopher D. Watkins and
        Stephen B. Coy (Contributions by Larry Sharp)
                    ALL RIGHTS RESERVED
```

```
*/

typedef unsigned char        Byte;

typedef unsigned int         Word;

typedef unsigned long        DWord;

typedef enum {false, true} Boolean;

typedef char Name[80];

typedef struct
{
  Byte Red;
  Byte Grn;
  Byte Blu;
} RGB;

typedef RGB    Palette_Register[256];

typedef float TDA[3];

typedef int    TDIA[3];
typedef float FDA[4];
```

```
typedef float Matx4x4[4][4];


#define MaxCol     7
#define MaxInten 35

#define Ln10        2.30258509299405E+000
#define OneOverLn10 0.43429448190325E+000
#define Pi          3.1415927
#define PiOver180   1.74532925199433E-002
#define PiUnder180  5.72957795130823E+001
```

Listing 2-1. Program Listing of BkDefs.H

The BkMath.H header file

The BkMath.H header file contains the function prototypes for the routines in the mathematics module. The function prototypes specify the names and arguments for all the functions found in the mathematics module and the arguments (passed data) that these functions require. Listing 2-2 shows the complete BkMath.H header file. Note that these prototype lists make a great table of commands, since all of the functions contained in the module are listed here.

```
/*
```

```
            BkMath.H = Header File for Math Module
                   Prototypes for BkMath.C
        Copyright 1988, 1992 Christopher D. Watkins and
        Stephen B. Coy (Contributions by Larry Sharp)
                    ALL RIGHTS RESERVED
```

```
*/
extern int   Round(double x);
extern float Frac(double x);
extern int   Trunc(double x);
extern float SqrFP(float x);
extern int   Sqr(int x);
extern float Radians(float Angle);
extern float Degrees(float Angle);
extern float CosD(float Angle);
```

```
extern float SinD(float Angle);
extern float Power(float Base, int Exponent);
extern float Log(float x);
extern float Exp10(float x);
extern float Sign(float x);
extern int   IntSign(int x);
extern int   IntSqrt(int x);
extern int   IntPower(int Base, int Exponent);
extern float MIN(float a, float b);
extern float MAX(float a, float b);
extern float MIN3(float a, float b, float c);
extern float MAX3(float a, float b, float c);
extern float MIN4(float a, float b, float c, float d);
extern float MAX4(float a, float b, float c, float d);
extern void  Vec(float r, float s, float t, TDA A);
extern void  VecInt(int r, int s, int t, TDIA A);
extern void  UnVec(TDA A, float *r, float *s, float *t);
extern void  UnVecInt(TDIA A, int *r, int *s, int *t);
extern float VecDot(TDA A, TDA B);
extern void  VecCross(TDA A, TDA B, TDA C);
extern float VecLen(TDA A);
extern void  VecNormalize(TDA A);
extern void  VecMatxMult(FDA A, Matx4x4 Matrix, FDA B);
extern void  VecSub(TDA A, TDA B, TDA C);
extern void  VecSubInt(TDIA A, TDIA B, TDA C);
extern void  VecAdd(TDA A, TDA B, TDA C);
extern void  VecAdd3(TDA A, TDA B, TDA C, TDA D);
extern void  VecCopy(TDA A, TDA B);
extern void  VecCopyInt(TDIA A, TDIA B);
extern void  VecLinComb(float r, TDA A, float s, TDA B, TDA C);
extern void  VecScalMult(float r, TDA A, TDA B);
extern void  VecScalMultI(float r, TDIA A, TDA B);
extern void  VecScalMultInt(float r, TDA A, TDIA B);
extern void  VecAddScalMult(float r, TDA A, TDA B, TDA C);
extern void  VecNull(TDA A);
extern void  VecNullInt(TDIA A);
extern void  VecElemMult(float r, TDA A, TDA B, TDA C);
extern void  VecNegate(TDA A);
extern void  VecMin(TDA a, TDA b, TDA c);
extern void  VecMax(TDA a, TDA b, TDA c);
extern void  VecNegate(TDA A);
extern void  ZeroMatrix(Matx4x4 A);
extern void  Translate3D(float tx, float ty, float tz,
                 Matx4x4 A);
extern void  Scale3D(float sx, float sy, float sz, Matx4x4 A);
extern void  Rotate3D(int m, float Theta, Matx4x4 A);
extern void  Multiply3DMatrices(Matx4x4 A, Matx4x4 B,
```

```
                   Matx4x4 C);
   extern void  MatCopy(Matx4x4 a, Matx4x4 b);
   extern void  PrepareMatrix(float Tx, float Ty, float Tz,
                   float Sx, float Sy, float Sz, float Rx,
                   float Ry, float Rz, Matx4x4 XForm);
   extern void  PrepareInvMatrix(float Tx, float Ty, float Tz,
                   float Sx, float Sy, float Sz, float Rx,
                   float Ry, float Rz, Matx4x4 XForm);
   extern void  Transform(TDA A, Matx4x4 M, TDA B);
   extern void  InitRand(float Seed);
   extern int   RandInt(Word Range);
   extern float Rand();
```

Listing 2-2. Program Listing of BkMath.H

Compiling the Modules

The header files are used to compile and link the modules separately. To reduce total compilation time, you link all of your other graphics software with the already compiled mathematics and graphics modules. In order to compile these modules, all of the header files must be present in your working directory. If any of the header files are missing, a compilation error occurs. The best way to use this software is to set up Turbo C/C++ project files (.PRJ files) (or Make files, if you are using the Watcom compiler).

First, compile each of these modules; you can then compile your graphics program (or any of the later ones in this book). Once the modules are compiled, you simply link all the resulting object files (files with the .OBJ extension for most compilers). To compile using Borland's interactive development environment (IDE) which comes with the Borland compiler, you start the IDE and then load each module into the IDE separately; then type ALT-C C for each module. Next press ALT-P. When you are prompted for the name of the project file, type in the name of the program (such as EXAMPLE). Now press ALT-A, and add the appropriate .OBJ files (the ones you just compiled) to the project list. When you have entered all of them, you can link the .OBJ files together by pressing ALT-C L. Remember, all of this software must be compiled using the **LARGE MEMORY MODEL.**

The BkMath.C Program

Before you can learn to produce images, you must become familiar with the various program support modules. These modules form the basis for most of the graphics programs in this book. The remainder of this chapter describes the mathematics module contained in the BkMath.C file. Most of the functions in this module manipulate two- and three-dimensional vectors by using the basic techniques of linear algebra. Vectors describe all of the geometry of the three-dimensional world, including both the positions and orientations of all objects, the viewer, and light sources. The routines described here provide an efficient and elegant means of manipulating vectors to perform functions such as rotation, scaling, and translation of objects, as well as light-intensity calculations. The routines in this module may also be used by any other applications that require various sorts of vector manipulation.

Remember that the header files are required for proper compilation of the mathematics and graphics modules. These header files contain type definitions and global data used by all of the modules. To ensure proper operation, BkMath.C should be compiled separately and linked into the programs that require it.

The following three types of routines are found in the mathematics module: numerical functions, vector and matrix functions, and affine transformation functions. The numerical functions are single-valued functions that take a single number as input and compute some function of that number. Functions like sine and cosine fall into this category. This module also contains the definitions of common mathematical constants such as π and e.

The vector and matrix functions create and manipulate vectors. For the purposes of this discussion, a *vector* is a collection of numbers (normally two or three) that represents either a point on a plane (X,Y) or in three-dimensional space (X,Y,Z). Vectors are also used to define directions, such as in which direction a surface is facing. All of the standard vector operations (such as the vector dot and cross products) can be found here. Several transformation routines are provided, since you will often need to transform vectors when performing such operations as rotating an object. To transform a vector, you multiply the vector coordinates by a single four-by-four matrix. One of the most convenient aspects of vector transformations is that each type of transformation (rotation, scaling, and translation) can be represented by one four-by-four matrix. You can then combine multiple transformations into a single matrix using vector multiplication. The result represents all of the desired transformation operations (rotation, scaling, and translation). With operations such as these, you can construct complex objects from primitive objects (like triangles and parallelograms) and place them into a virtual context.

The sections that follow discuss all the functions found in the mathematics interface module and some of their uses. These discussions should be used as a reference guide for the more complicated graphics routines presented later.

```
/*
```

```
    Radians     - converts degrees to radians
    Degrees     - converts radians to degrees
    CosD        - cosine in degrees
    SinD        - sine in degrees
    Power       - power a^n
    Log         - log base 10
    Exp10       - exp base 10
    Sign        - negative=-1  positive=1  null=0
    IntSign     - negative=-1  positive=1  null=0
    IntSqrt     - integer square root
    IntPower    - integer power a^n
*/

#include "stdio.h"
#include "stdlib.h"
#include "math.h"
#include "BkDefs.h"
#include "BkMath.h"

int Round(double x)
{
  return((int)(x+0.5));
}

int Trunc(double x)
{
  return((int)(x));
```

```
    }

    float Frac(double x)
    {
      int y;

      y=((int)(x));
      return(x-(float)y);
    }

    float SqrFP(float x)
    {
      return(x*x);
    }

    int Sqr(int x)
    {
      return(x*x);
    }

    float Radians(float Angle)
    {
      return(Angle*PiOver180);
    }

    float Degrees(float Angle)
    {
      return(Angle*PiUnder180);
    }

    float CosD(float Angle)
    {
      return(cos(Radians(Angle)));
    }

    float SinD(float Angle)
    {
      return(sin(Radians(Angle)));
    }

    float Power(float Base, int Exponent)
    {
      float BPower;
      int   t;

      if(Exponent==0)
        return(1);
```

```
  else
  {
    BPower=1.0;
    for(t=1; t<=Exponent; t++)
    {
      BPower*=Base;
    }
    return(BPower);
  }
}

float Log(float x)
{
  return(log(x)*OneOverLn10);
}

float Exp10(float x)
{
  return(exp(x*Ln10));
}

float Sign(float x)
{
  if(x<0)
    return(-1);
  else
  {
    if(x>0)
      return(1);
    else
    {
      return(0);
    }
  }
}

int IntSign(int x)
{
  if(x<0)
    return(-1);
  else
  {
    if(x>0)
      return(1);
    else
    {
      return(0);
```

```
      }
    }
}

int IntSqrt(int x)
{
  int OddInt, OldArg, FirstSqrt;

  OddInt=1;
  OldArg=x;
  while(x>=0)
  {
    x-=OddInt;
    OddInt+=2;
  }
  FirstSqrt=OddInt >> 1;
  if(Sqr(FirstSqrt)-FirstSqrt+1 > OldArg)
    return(FirstSqrt-1);
  else
    return(FirstSqrt);
}

int IntPower(int Base, int Exponent)
{
  if(Exponent==0)
    return(1);
  else
    return(Base*IntPower(Base, Exponent-1));
}

float MIN(float a, float b)
{
  if(a<b)
    return(a);
  else
    return(b);
}

float MAX(float a, float b)
{
  if(a>b)
    return(a);
  else
    return(b);
}

float MIN3(float a, float b, float c)
```

```
{
  float t;

  t=MIN(a, b);
  return(MIN(t, c));
}

float MAX3(float a, float b, float c)
{
  float t;

  t=MAX(a, b);
  return(MAX(t, c));
}

float MIN4(float a, float b, float c, float d)
{
  float t;

  t=MIN3(a, b, c);
  return(MIN(t, d));
}

float MAX4(float a, float b, float c, float d)
{
  float t;

  t=MAX3(a, b, c);
  return(MAX(t, d));
}


    /*
```

```
            Vector and Matrix Routines
```

```
    Vec        - Make Vector
    VecInt     - Make Integer Vector
    UnVec      - Get Components of vector
    UnVecInt   - Get Components of Integer Vector
    VecDot     - Vector Dot Product
    VecCross   - Vector Cross Product
```

```
            VecLenVector         - Length
            VecNormalize         - Vector Normalize
            VecMatxMult          - Vector Matrix Multiply
            VecSubVector         - Subtraction
            VecSubVector         - Subtraction Integer
            VecAddVector         - Addition
            VecAdd3Vector        - Addition
            VecCopyVector        - Copy
            VecLinComb           - Vector Linear Combination
            VecScalMult          - Vector Scalar Multiple
            VecScalMultI         - Vector Scalar Multiple
            VecScalMultInt       - Vector Scalar Multiple and Rounding
            VecAddScalMult       - Vector Add Scalar Multiple
            VecNull              - Vector Null
            VecNullInt           - Vector Null Integer
            VecElemMult          - Vector Element Multiply
*/

void Vec(float r, float s, float t, TDA A)
{
  A[0]=r;
  A[1]=s;
  A[2]=t;
}

void VecInt(int r, int s, int t, TDIA A)
{
  A[0]=r;
  A[1]=s;
  A[2]=t;
}

void UnVec(TDA A, float *r, float *s, float *t)
{
  *r=A[0];
  *s=A[1];
  *t=A[2];
}

void UnVecInt(TDIA A, int *r, int *s, int *t)
{
  *r=A[0];
  *s=A[1];
  *t=A[2];
}

float VecDot(TDA A, TDA B)
```

```
{
  return(A[0]*B[0] + A[1]*B[1] + A[2]*B[2]);
}

void VecCross(TDA A, TDA B, TDA C)
{
  C[0]=A[1]*B[2] - A[2]*B[1];
  C[1]=A[2]*B[0] - A[0]*B[2];
  C[2]=A[0]*B[1] - A[1]*B[0];
}

float VecLen(TDA A)
{
  return(sqrt(SqrFP(A[0])+SqrFP(A[1])+SqrFP(A[2])));
}

void VecNormalize(TDA A)
{
  float dist,invdist;

  dist=VecLen(A);
  if(!(dist==0.0))
  {
    invdist=1.0/dist;
    A[0]*=invdist;
    A[1]*=invdist;
    A[2]*=invdist;
  }
  else
  {
    puts("Zero-Length Vectors cannot be Normalized");
    exit(1);
  }
}

void VecMatxMult(FDA A, Matx4x4 Matrix, FDA B)
{
  int mRow, mCol;

  for(mCol=0; mCol<4; mCol++)
  {
    B[mCol]=0;
    for(mRow=0; mRow<4; mRow++)
      B[mCol]+=A[mRow]*Matrix[mRow][mCol];
  }
}
```

```
void VecSub(TDA A, TDA B, TDA C)
{
  C[0]=A[0]-B[0];
  C[1]=A[1]-B[1];
  C[2]=A[2]-B[2];
}

void VecSubInt(TDIA A, TDIA B, TDA C)
{
  C[0]=(float)(A[0]-B[0]);
  C[1]=(float)(A[1]-B[1]);
  C[2]=(float)(A[2]-B[2]);
}

void VecAdd(TDA A, TDA B, TDA C)
{
  C[0]=A[0]+B[0];
  C[1]=A[1]+B[1];
  C[2]=A[2]+B[2];
}

void VecAdd3(TDA A, TDA B, TDA C, TDA D)
{
  D[0]=A[0]+B[0]+C[0];
  D[1]=A[1]+B[1]+C[1];
  D[2]=A[2]+B[2]+C[2];
}

void VecCopy(TDA A, TDA B)
{
  B[0]=0.0+A[0];
  B[1]=0.0+A[1];
  B[2]=0.0+A[2];
}

void VecCopyInt(TDIA A, TDIA B)
{
  B[0]=A[0];
  B[1]=A[1];
  B[2]=A[2];
}

void VecLinComb(float r, TDA A, float s, TDA B, TDA C)
{
  C[0]=r*A[0]+s*B[0];
  C[1]=r*A[1]+s*B[1];
  C[2]=r*A[2]+s*B[2];
```

```
}

void VecScalMult(float r, TDA A, TDA B)
{
  B[0]=r*A[0];
  B[1]=r*A[1];
  B[2]=r*A[2];
}

void VecScalMultI(float r, TDIA A, TDA B)
{
  B[0]=r*(float)A[0];
  B[1]=r*(float)A[1];
  B[2]=r*(float)A[2];
}

void VecScalMultInt(float r, TDA A, TDIA B)
{
  B[0]=Round(r*A[0]);
  B[1]=Round(r*A[1]);
  B[2]=Round(r*A[2]);
}

void VecAddScalMult(float r, TDA A, TDA B, TDA C)
{
  C[0]=r*A[0]+B[0];
  C[1]=r*A[1]+B[1];
  C[2]=r*A[2]+B[2];
}

void VecNull(TDA A)
{
  A[0]=0.0;
  A[1]=0.0;
  A[2]=0.0;
}

void VecNullInt(TDIA A)
{
  A[0]=0;
  A[1]=0;
  A[2]=0;
}

void VecElemMult(float r, TDA A, TDA B, TDA C)
{
```

```
    C[0]=r*A[0]*B[0];
    C[1]=r*A[1]*B[1];
    C[2]=r*A[2]*B[2];
}

void VecMin(TDA a, TDA b, TDA c)
{
    if(a[0]<b[0])
      c[0]=a[0];
    else
      c[0]=b[0];
    if(a[1]<b[1])
      c[1]=a[1];
    else
      c[1]=b[1];
    if(a[2]<b[2])
      c[2]=a[2];
    else
      c[2]=b[2];
}

void VecMax(TDA a, TDA b, TDA c)
{
    if(a[0]>b[0])
      c[0]=a[0];
    else
      c[0]=b[0];
    if(a[1]>b[1])
      c[1]=a[1];
    else
      c[1]=b[1];
    if(a[2]>b[2])
      c[2]=a[2];
    else
      c[2]=b[2];
}

void VecNegate(TDA A)
{
  A[0]=-A[0];
  A[1]=-A[1];
  A[2]=-A[2];
}

/*
```

```
┌──────────────────────────────────────────────────┐
│                                                    │
│           Affine Transformation Routines           │
│                                                    │
└──────────────────────────────────────────────────┘
```

```
ZeroMatrix          - zeros the elements of a 4x4 matrix
Translate3D         - make translation matrix
Scale3D             - make scaling matrix
Rotate3D            - make rotation matrix
ZeroAllMatrices     - zeros all matrices used in
                      transformation
Multiply3DMatrices  - multiply 2 4x4 matrices
PrepareMatrix       - prepare the transformation matrix
                      (Tm=S*R*T)
PrepareInvMatrix    - prepare the inverse transformation
                      matrix
Transform           - multipy a vertex by the transformation
                      matrix
  */

  void ZeroMatrix(Matx4x4 A)
  {
    int i, j;

    for(i=0; i<4; i++)
    {
      for(j=0; j<4; j++)
        A[i][j]=0.0;
    }
  }

  void Translate3D(float tx, float ty, float tz, Matx4x4 A)    {
    int i;

    ZeroMatrix(A);
    for(i=0; i<4; i++)
      A[i][i]=1.0;
    A[0][3]=-tx;
    A[1][3]=-ty;
    A[2][3]=-tz;
  }

  void Scale3D(float sx, float sy, float sz, Matx4x4 A)
  {
    ZeroMatrix(A);
    A[0][0]=sx;
    A[1][1]=sy;
    A[2][2]=sz;
```

```
  A[3][3]=1.0;
}

void Rotate3D(int m, float Theta, Matx4x4 A)
{
  int    m1, m2;
  float c, s;

  ZeroMatrix(A);
  A[m-1][m-1]=1.0;
  A[3][3]=1.0;
  m1=(m % 3)+1;
  m2=(m1 % 3);
  m1-=1;
  c=CosD(Theta);
  s=SinD(Theta);
  A[m1][m1]=c;
  A[m1][m2]=s;
  A[m2][m2]=c;
  A[m2][m1]=-s;
}

void Multiply3DMatrices(Matx4x4 A, Matx4x4 B, Matx4x4 C)    {

  int    i, j, k;
  float ab;

  for(i=0; i<4; i++)
  {
    for(j=0; j<4; j++)
    {
      ab=0;
      for(k=0; k<4; k++) ab=A[i][k]*B[k][j];
      C[i][j]=ab;
    }
  }
}

void MatCopy(Matx4x4 a, Matx4x4 b)
{
  Byte i, j;

  for(i=0; i<4; i++)
  {
    for(j=0; j<4; j++)
      b[i][j]=a[i][j];
```

```
      }
}

void PrepareMatrix(float Tx, float Ty, float Tz,
         float Sx, float Sy, float Sz,
         float Rx, float Ry, float Rz,
         Matx4x4 XForm)
{
  Matx4x4 M1, M2, M3, M4, M5, M6, M7, M8, M9;

  Scale3D(Sx, Sy, Sz, M1);
  Rotate3D(1, Rx, M2);
  Rotate3D(2, Ry, M3);
  Rotate3D(3, Rz, M4);
  Translate3D(Tx, Ty, Tz, M5);
  Multiply3DMatrices(M2, M1, M6);
  Multiply3DMatrices(M3, M6, M7);
  Multiply3DMatrices(M4, M7, M8);
  Multiply3DMatrices(M5, M8, M9);
  MatCopy(M9, XForm);
}

void PrepareInvMatrix(float Tx, float Ty, float Tz,
       float Sx, float Sy, float Sz,
       float Rx, float Ry, float Rz,
       Matx4x4 XForm)
{
  Matx4x4 M1, M2, M3, M4, M5, M6, M7, M8, M9;

  Scale3D(Sx, Sy, Sz, M1);
  Rotate3D(1, Rx, M2);
  Rotate3D(2, Ry, M3);
  Rotate3D(3, Rz, M4);
  Translate3D(Tx, Ty, Tz, M5);
  Multiply3DMatrices(M4, M5, M6);
  Multiply3DMatrices(M3, M6, M7);
  Multiply3DMatrices(M2, M7, M8);
  Multiply3DMatrices(M1, M8, M9);
  MatCopy(M9, XForm);
}

void Transform(TDA A, Matx4x4 M, TDA B)
{
  B[0]=M[0][0]*A[0]+M[0][1]*A[1]+M[0][2]*A[2]+M[0][3];
  B[1]=M[1][0]*A[0]+M[1][1]*A[1]+M[1][2]*A[2]+M[1][3];
  B[2]=M[2][0]*A[0]+M[2][1]*A[1]+M[2][2]*A[2]+M[2][3];
}
```

```
/*
┌────────────────────────────────────────────────────────────────┐
│                                                                  │
│                 Pseudo-Random Number Generator                   │
│                                                                  │
└────────────────────────────────────────────────────────────────┘

*/

double OldRand;

void InitRand(float Seed)
{
  OldRand=Seed;
}

int RandInt(Word Range)
{
  float sigma=423.1966;

  OldRand=Frac(sigma * OldRand);
  return(Trunc(OldRand * (float)Range));
}

float Rand()
{
  float sigma=423.1966;

  OldRand=Frac(sigma * OldRand);
  return(OldRand);
}
```

Listing 2-3. Program Listing of BkMath.C

Basic Math Functions

The following notational conventions are used throughout the rest of this chapter and in Chapter 3. All integer variables (or function arguments) will begin with "i," all floating-point variables with "x,", and all vectors with "v."

The mathematics module contains the following numerical conversion functions:

Function   **Description**

Round(x) ....Returns the nearest integer to *x*

If $x > 0$, $Round(x) = Trunc(x + 0.5)$

If $x < 0$, $Round(x) = Trunc(x - 0.5)$

Trunc(x) ....Returns the integer part of *x*, truncating the fractional part

Frac(x)..............Returns the fractional part of *x*

If $x > 0$, $Frac(x) = x - Trunc(x)$

Sqr(i)................Returns *i*i*

SqrFP(x) ....Returns *x*x*

All of these routines can be expressed in terms of C code rather than the routines presented here (that is, N*=N is the same as N=Sqr(N)). These routines are presented in such a way as to make the code more accessible to people who are considering converting the software to other languages.

The *Radians* and *Degrees* functions

These functions are most useful when manipulating data based on angles. Much of the software in this book requires these routines for proper calculation of lighting and viewing vectors. Most of the time, you must manipulate angles represented as radians ($2*pi$ radians = 360 degrees). However, you'll want to enter and express angles as degrees. These routines provide an easy conversion between the two units. The functions make use of the *PiOver180* and *PiUnder180* constants, as shown here:

Function   **Description**

Radians(x) ....Returns *x* expressed in radians

$Radians(x) = x * PiOver180$

Degrees(x) ....Returns *x* expressed in degrees

$Degrees(x) = x * PiUnder180$

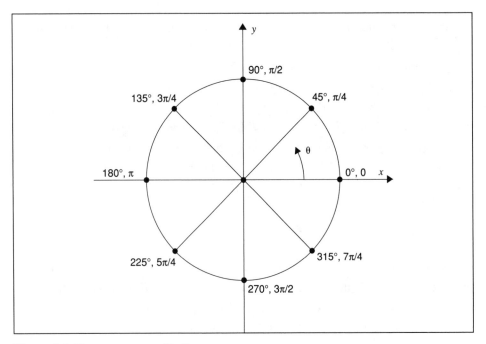

Figure 2-1. Degrees versus Radians

Figure 2-1 shows the correspondence of radian measure to degree measure.

The *CosD* and *SinD* functions

These functions make use of the C math library's trigonometric functions *cos* (cosine) and *sin* (sine). These functions also use the function *Radians*, as shown here:

Function	Description
CosD(x)	*CosD(x)* = cos(*Radians(x)*)
SinD(x)	*SinD(x)* = sin(*Radians(x)*)

Our functions perform the same operation as the corresponding functions in the C library except that they take their arguments as angles expressed in degrees. These functions are particularly useful for generating an animation sequence where repeating motion is required. These functions walk you around the periphery of a circle as the angles in their arguments are increased, so they are ideal for repeating motion.

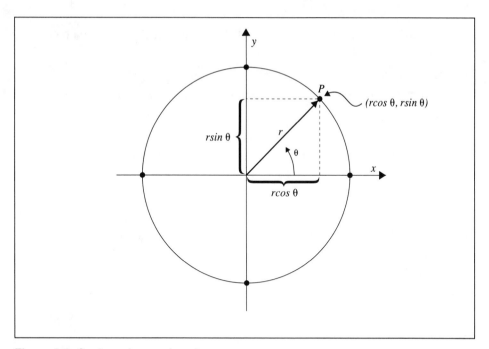

Figure 2-2. Cosine, sine, and vectors

Figure 2-2 shows how these functions relate to a circle of radius r. Later these functions will be used to create procedurally defined databases.

The *Power* function

This function has two arguments: a base value and an integer exponent. The value the *Power* function returns is derived by raising the base to the exponent (that is, base ^ exponent). Essentially, the base is multiplied by itself Exponent number of times, as shown here:

Function   **Description**
Power(x,i) ....Raises *x* to the power *i*.
$$Power(x,i) = x^i$$

If the exponent is equal to 0, the function returns a value of 1.0, since any number raised to the power of 0 is 1. Otherwise, the variable *BPower* is initialized to 1.0, and a loop from 1 to the value of exponent begins. *BPower* is multiplied by Base each iteration of the loop. After the loop has ended, the value in *BPower* is returned.

The *Log* function

This function finds the base 10 logarithm of a number, as shown here:

Function	Description
Log(x)	Computes the base 10 logarithm of *x*.

$$Log(x) = \log(x) / Ln10$$

The C *log* function computes the natural logarithm of the number and then divides this value by the constant *Ln*10 (the natural logarithm of 10). The real-valued result is then returned.

The *Exp10* function

This function finds the value of 10.0 raised to the power of a floating point number, as shown here:

Function	Description
Exp10(x)	Raises 10 to the power *x*.

$$Exp10(x) = exp(x*Ln10)$$

First, the value passed to the function is multiplied by the constant *Ln10*. By using the C *exp* function, you calculate the natural logarithm of the new value. The result of this operation is returned.

The *Sign* and *IntSign* functions

These functions are used to find the sign of a floating-point number and the sign of an integer number, as shown here:

Function	Description	
Sign(x)	*Sign(x)*	$= 1, x > 0$
		$= -1, x < 0$
		$= 0, x == 0$
IntSign(i)	Same as for *Sign*, except integer argument	

Both functions return a value of -1 if the number is less than 0, 0 if the number is equal to 0, or 1 if the number is greater than 0.

The *IntSqrt* function

This function computes the nearest integer to the square root of its integer argument, as shown here:

Function   **Description**

IntSqrt(i)...............Finds the integer nearest the square root of its argument.

$$IntSqrt(i) = Round(sqrt((float)i)))$$

This function may seem complex, but consider the following example. A value is passed to *x*, *OddInt* is initialized to 1, and *OldArg* is set to equal *x*. With these values set, a "while" loop begins. With each iteration of the loop, *OddInt* is subtracted from *x* and the value of 2 is added to *OddInt*. This continues until *x* is less than 0. After the termination of the loop, *OddInt* is divided by 2 and the value is stored in the variable *FirstSqrt*.

At this point, *FirstSqrt* either contains the integer square root or the integer square root plus 1. An "if-else" statement then checks to see if the value in *First-Sqrt* needs to be decremented or not. The appropriate action is taken, if necessary, and the value in *FirstSqrt* is returned.

This routine is included because for simple square root calculations, it is faster than the built-in square root function on some compilers.

The *IntPower* function

IntPower is a recursive function that raises an integer value to an integer power, as shown here:

Function   **Description**

IntPower(i,j) ....Same as power, but for integer arguments only.

$$IntPower(i,j) = i^j$$

Recursion implies that a function calls itself. Like the *Power* function, if the exponent is equal to 0, a value of 1 is returned. Otherwise, the exponent is decremented and the function calls itself. Once the exponent is 0 through successive calls to itself, a value of 1 is returned to the previous call. The value 1 is then multiplied by Base and returned to the next previous call and so on until the highest level is reached. The power of the integer is returned.

The *MIN* and *MAX* functions

These functions return the minimum and maximum number of two floating-point numbers, respectively, as shown here:

Function	Description
MIN(x,y)	minimum of (*x,y*)
MAX(x,y)	maximum of (*x,y*)
MIN3(x,y,z)	minimum of (*x,y,z*)
MAX3(x,y,z)	maximum of (*x,y,z*)
MIN4(x,y,z,a)	minimum of (*x,y,z,a*)
MAX4(x,y,z,a)	maximum of (*x,y,z,a*)

The *MIN3* and *MAX3* functions return the minimum and maximum number of three floating-point numbers, respectively. The *MIN4* and *MAX4* functions return the minimum and maximum numbers of four floating point numbers, respectively.

The minimum and maximum routines are useful for finding the boundaries of an object (often referred to as the *extent* of the object). By running through the list of points that make up an object (such as vertices of its sides) and computing maximum and minimum found so far, you can determine the maximum and minimum values for each dimension.

For example, a three-dimensional object requires three tests for each point (usually a vertex) that comprises the object. A bounding box can then be defined by two points: the minimum value in each of X, Y, and Z and the maximum value. This is discussed in more detail when bounding objects and the Kay-Kajiya method are examined in the ray tracing section of this book.

Vector and Matrix Routines

This section discusses the vector and matrix types used extensively throughout most computer graphics applications. This set of modules allows you to move objects around in space, derive their projections onto a two-dimensional display, and perform most standard vector operations.

In order to facilitate this, several new datatypes must be defined. The *TDA* datatype is an array of three floating-point numbers representing the components of a three-dimensional vector. Each number represents the coordinate in the X, Y, and Z directions, respectively. In accordance with the normal mathematical notation for vectors, the three standard unit vectors i, j, and k are used. These unit vectors are simply vectors of length 1 that point along the positive x-, y-, and z-axes. They are defined as follows:

```
i   (1, 0, 0)
j   (0, 1, 0)
k   (0, 0, 1)
```

These standard unit vectors may be manipulated as any other vector. Any vector V (X,Y,Z) may be represented as the sum of the vectors i, j, k, as shown here:

```
V = Xi + Yj + Zk
```

This is useful in understanding some of the other vector operations, such as rotation and scaling.

Figure 2-3 shows a three-dimensional vector that begins at point P_1 and terminates at point P_2. Notice that points P_1 and P_2 are three-dimensional points, having x, y, and z components.

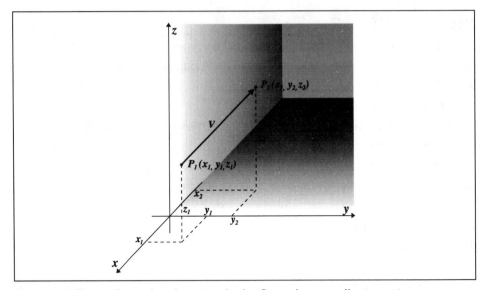

Figure 2-3. Three-dimensional vectors in the Cartesian coordinate system

For computational efficiency, the *TDIA* variable type is the same as type *TDA* type except that it uses three integer values rather than floating-point values. The *FDA* type is a four-dimensional vector of floating-point numbers. Four-dimensional vectors compactly express the translation operation. For the purposes of this book, the fourth element is almost always 0.0 or 1.0.

Finally, the *Matx4x4* type represents a four-by-four element matrix of floating-point values. This type expresses all vector transformation functions as explained later in this chapter.

The *Vec* and *VecInt* functions

These functions are used for the actual creation of vectors. The *Vec* function takes three floating-point numbers and stores them in a *TDA* type that it creates. The *VecInt* function does the same, except that it stores three integers into a *TDIA*. This is a very efficient means of working with vectors. The code now passes a pointer to the *TDA* structure representing the vector, rather than having to pass all three values as separate arguments.

The *UnVec* and *UnVecInt* functions

These functions do exactly the opposite of the *Vec* and *VecInt* functions. *UnVec* extracts the three values stored in a *TDA*, and places them into three separate floating-point variables. *UnVecInt* extracts them into integer variables.

The *VecDot* function

This routine computes one of the singularly most useful geometric functions of two vectors: their dot product. The dot product of two vectors *A* and *B* is defined as

```
VecDot(A,B) = VecLen(A) * VecLen(B) * cos(θ)
```

where VecLen computes the magnitude (or length) of the vector and θ is the angle between the two vectors. This is the same as simply multiplying each element of *A* by the corresponding element in *B* and summing all of the products together. The value of the dot product is

```
A•B = ab cos x
```

VecDot is the floating-point number returned. The variables *a* and *b* are the magnitude of vectors *A* and *B*. The variable *x* is the angle between the two vectors.

This function has a number of interesting properties, including:

❖ If *VecDot* = 0, then the vectors are perpendicular to each other.
❖ If *VecDot* = *VecLen*(A) * *VecLen*(B), then the two vectors have exactly the same direction.
❖ If *VecDot* = -(*VecLen*(A) * *VecLen*(B)), then the two vectors point in exactly opposite directions.

Figure 2-4 shows the dot product of v_1 and v_2. Notice the angle between the two vectors.

59

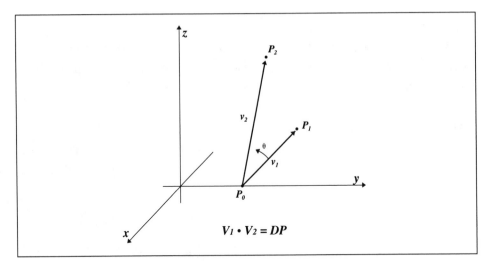

Figure 2-4. The vector dot product

One important use of this function in computer graphics is to determine whether you are facing a particular facet of an object. If the surface normal of the facet (the *surface normal* is the direction the surface is facing) is dotted with the viewing direction and the resulting number is negative, then you can see the facet since the vectors are pointing opposite to each other (the face is pointing in your general direction). If the resulting number is positive, then the vectors are pointing in the same general direction and you cannot see the face (that is, the object is turned away from you).

The *VecCross* function

This routine finds the cross product of two vectors. The cross product generates a third vector that is perpendicular to the plane defined by the two vectors used in the computation. The vector cross product has a length of

```
| A x B | =  ab sin x
```

where A and B are vectors, a and b are the magnitudes of the two vectors, and x is the angle between them. *VecCross* is the resulting vector.

The two argument vectors define a plane (if they are not the same vector). *VecCross* is, therefore, useful in determining the surface normal of an object facet. For example, you can use two of the edges of a facet as vectors, compute their cross product, and then have a vector representing the direction the surface faces (surface normal). Subsequently, this surface normal is used in the shading of the facet lying in that plane. (This is discussed in more detail in the modeling and ray tracing sections of this book.)

The vector cross product is computed as follows :

```
A x B = (Ay Bz - Az By, Az Bx - Ax Bz, Ax By - Ay Bx)
```

Note that the directions *i*, *j*, and *k* refer to the *x*-, *y*-, and *z*- axes, respectively. As a simple example, note that *k* is the cross product of *i* and *j*. Also note that the order of the two vectors is important. *VecCross*(v_2, v_1) is a vector pointing in the exact opposite direction (180 degrees) of *VecCross*(v_1, v_2).

In Figure 2-5, vector CP is the cross product of v_1 and v_2, and this vector CP is perpendicular to the plane defined by vectors v_1 and v_2.

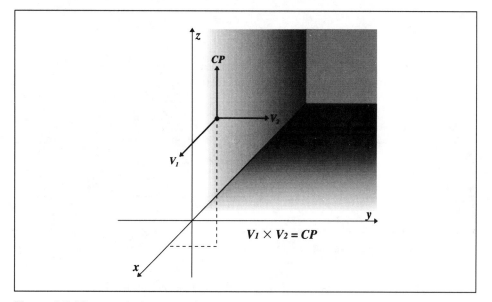

Figure 2-5. The vector cross product

The *VecLen* function

This function finds the magnitude (or length) of a vector. The *VecLen* function is basically a three-dimensional extension of the Pythagorean theorem. The length is the square root of the sum of the squares of the component values, as shown here:

```
VecLen(v) = sqrt(x*x + y*y + z*z)
```

This function may also be used to find the distance between two points in three-dimensional space. The vector would contain the differences between each component of the two desired points.

The *VecNormalize* function

A *normalized vector* is one that has the same direction as a given vector, but has unit length or magnitude (that is, its length equals 1). Note in Figure 2-6 that v_2 is the normalization of v_1, pointing in the same direction, but with length 1. This function is used quite often in the computation of the surface normal for a facet, described previously. The *VecCross* function computes a vector pointing in the right direction, but the lighting model, for example, needs a vector of unit length. *VecNormalize* fills this need by normalizing the vector, thus giving it unit length.

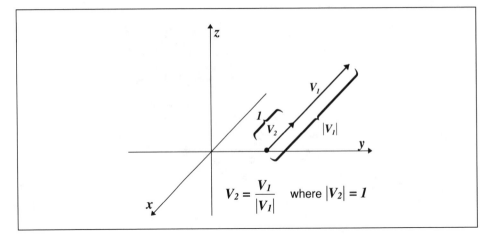

Figure 2-6. Normalized vector

The first thing the *VecNormalize* function does is to find the length of the vector passed to it. Next it checks to see if the length is 0 and if so, prints an error message and exits. The reason for this is that a vector with a length of 0 has no direction, and therefore, cannot be normalized. Once you have determined that a vector is usable, you can determine the inverse distance by computing 1.0 / length. Next, multiply each element in the vector by the inverse distance, to produce the normalized vector.

Note that the vectors you pass to this function (and several others in this module) perform their operations in-place—that is, they modify the vector passed to it. In other words, the *VecNormalize* function is called by reference rather than by value. This means that if you need to save your original vector, pass a temporary vector to this function and use the *VecCopy* function to store the new values into your destination vector.

The *VecMatxMult* function

This function is the fundamental vector-transformation function. It multiplies the elements of a 4-element *FDA* by the elements of a 16-element *Matx4x4* matrix using the standard mathematical definition. This function allows you to transform a vector by rotating, scaling, and translating it in one operation.

The operation is accomplished with two "for" loops, each ranging from 0 to 3. This allows you to cover all 16 elements of the matrix, as well as the 4 elements of the *FDA*. The results are stored in a separate *FDA*.

The *VecSub* and *VecSubInt* functions

These two functions perform the subtraction of two vectors (A - B) placing the result into a third (C). They are provided for both the *TDA* and *TDIA* types. Notice in Figure 2-7 that the subtracted vector v_3 points to v_2, since $v_3 = v_2 - v_1$.

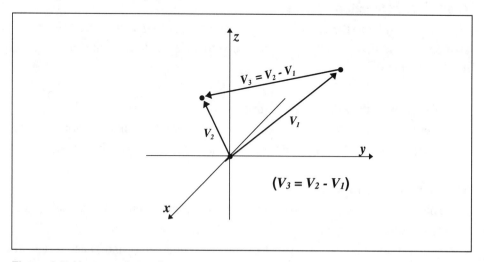

Figure 2-7. Vector subtraction

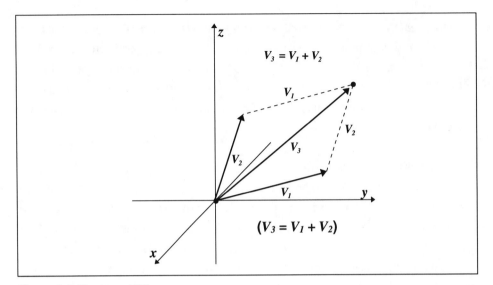

Figure 2-8. Vector addition

The *VecAdd* function

This function performs almost the same operation as *VecSub* except that the vector components are added instead of subtracted. Notice in Figure 2-8 that vector v_2 slides up to the end of vector v_1 when added.

The *VecAdd3* function

This is similar to the *VecAdd* function, except that four vectors are passed. The elements of the first three vectors are added together and the results are stored in the fourth vector.

The *VecCopy* and *VecCopyInt* functions

These functions copy the elements of one vector into another vector. The *VecCopy* function is for floating-point numbers and the *VecCopyInt* integer numbers.

The *VecLinComb* function

This function computes a linear combination of two vectors A and B and places the result into a third vector C.

Four variables are passed, two floating-point numbers(r and s) and three vectors (A, B, and C). The elements of A are multiplied by r and the elements of B are multiplied by *s*. The results are added and stored into the vector *C*. The operation is as follows:

```
C = rA + sB
```

Note that *VecAdd* is equivalent to *VecLinComb*(1.0, A, 1.0, B, C) and *VecSub* is equivalent to *VecLinComb*(1.0, A, -1.0, B, C).

The *VecScalMult, VecScalMultI,* and *VecScalMultInt* functions

These functions scale a vector by multiplying each element of the passed vector times a given floating-point number and storing the result into a new vector. This operation keeps the vector direction the same but changes its length. *VecScalMultI* uses type-casting to convert the integers in the passed *TDIA* to floating-point before multiplying. Both *VecScalMult* and *VecScalMultI* return floating-point *TDA* vectors. The VecScalMultInt function returns an integer TDIA vector. Figure 2-9 shows that multiplying vector v_1 by 2 yields a vector twice as long.

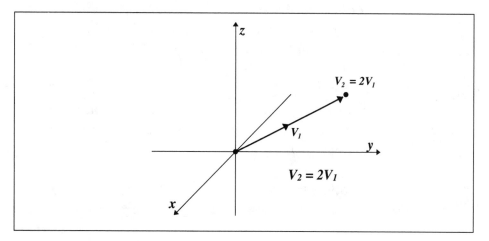

Figure 2-9. VectorScalar multiplication

The *VecAddScalMult* function

This function is a convenient function for combining several operations into one call. It performs a *VecAdd* function on the input vectors *A* and *B*, followed by a *VecScalMult* function that uses the argument r. The result is stored in C. The operation is as follows:

```
C = rA + B
```

The *VecNull* and *VecNullInt* functions

The *VecNull* function simply sets all elements in a *TDA* to 0. Similarly, the *VecNullInt* function sets all elements in a *TDIA* to 0.

The *VecElemMult* function

This function accepts a floating-point number and three *TDA*'s as input (r, A, B, and C, respectively). The elements of vector A are multiplied by the elements of vector B and the resulting vector is then multiplied by r. The results are stored in the vector C.

```
C = (rAxBx, rAyBy, rAzBz )
```

The *VecMin* and *VecMax* functions

The *VecMin* function finds the minimum component of a vector and the *VecMax* function finds the maximum component.

The *VecNegate* function

This function negates the elements of a given vector by changing the sign of each element. This function effectively reverses the direction of a vector, making it point in the opposite direction.

Affine Transformation Routines

The affine transformation is the heart of all the geometric manipulations of vectors. The affine transformation provides a means to express concisely all the graphics transformations you need to perform on objects, including translation (moving the object in space), scaling (changing the size of the object), and rotation (changing an object's orientation).

You may question the use of a four-by-four matrix when all the vectors used in this book are three-dimensional. The reason is to incorporate translation into a single matrix transformation. Therefore, the *TDA* (or *TDIA*) types are converted to the *FDA* type by setting the last element to 1.0. The first column of the four-by-four matrix then represents the translation of the vector using standard matrix multiplication, as shown here:

$$\begin{bmatrix} b_0 \\ b_1 \\ b_2 \\ b_3 \end{bmatrix} = \begin{bmatrix} a_0 \\ a_1 \\ a_2 \\ a_3 \end{bmatrix} \times \begin{bmatrix} m_{00} & m_{01} & m_{02} & m_{03} \\ m_{10} & m_{11} & m_{12} & m_{13} \\ m_{20} & m_{21} & m_{22} & m_{23} \\ m_{30} & m_{31} & m_{32} & m_{33} \end{bmatrix}$$

In most of the examples in this book, $a_3 = 1.0$, and (a_0, a_1, a_2) represents a three-dimensional input vector. In addition, $m_{33} = 1.0$, and $m_{03} = m_{13} = m_{23} = 0.0$ for most matrices, so that b_0 also equals 1.0 after the transformation.

The routines presented in this section create matrices for scaling, rotation, and translation; combine these matrices into a single transformation matrix; and perform various mathematical operations using these matrices. All of the matrix operations use the *Matx4x4* type.

The *ZeroMatrix* function

This function zeroes out all of the elements in a given matrix.

The *Translate3D* function

This function creates the linear translation matrix to translate a vector to a new location in space. Technically speaking, only points can be manipulated in this manner, since a vector is always assumed to have reference to the origin. For the purpose of this book, however, points and vectors are interchangeable.

This matrix consists of a diagonal of 1's (referred to as the *identity matrix* since it leaves a vector unchanged when applied as a transformation), with the first elements of the last three rows set to the negative of the three translation parameters passed to the function. This results in the following matrix:

$$T = \begin{bmatrix} 1 & 0 & 0 & 0 \\ -t_x & 1 & 0 & 0 \\ -t_y & 0 & 1 & 0 \\ -t_z & 0 & 0 & 1 \end{bmatrix}$$

Figure 2-10 shows a vector (point) translation.

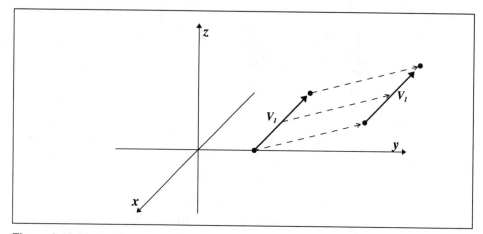

Figure 2-10. Vector (point) translation

The *Scale3D* function

This function creates a scaling matrix to scale each component of a vector. The diagonal consists of the three scaling parameters passed to the procedure and a 1.0 in the first position. Only the scale of the vector will be changed by this transformation and not the origin of a three-dimensional vector. If all three scale factors are the same, the result will be the same as using *VecScaleMult*, leaving the direction unchanged. If they are different, then both the direction and length of the vector may change. The scaling matrix is

$$S = \begin{bmatrix} S_x & 0 & 0 & 0 \\ 0 & S_y & 0 & 0 \\ 0 & 0 & S_z & 0 \\ 0 & 0 & 0 & 1 \end{bmatrix}$$

Note that scaling is similar to that of *VecScalMult*.

The *Rotate3D* function

This function creates the matrix to rotate a vector in space about either of the x-, y-, or z-axis. This function requires an integer that indicates about which axis to rotate (1 for the x-axis, 2 for the y-axis, and 3 for the z-axis) and a real number that represents the rotation angle in degrees. The function first sets the matrix to the identity matrix. Then the cosine and sine of the angle are placed into certain matrix elements, depending on the axis chosen.

The matrix for rotation about the x-axis is:

$$R_x = \begin{bmatrix} 1 & 0 & 0 & 0 \\ 0 & \cos\theta & \sin\theta & 0 \\ 0 & -\sin\theta & -\cos\theta & 0 \\ 0 & 0 & 0 & 1 \end{bmatrix}$$

The matrix for rotation about the y-axis is:

$$R_y = \begin{bmatrix} \cos\theta & 0 & -\sin\theta & 0 \\ 0 & 1 & 0 & 0 \\ -\sin\theta & 0 & \cos\theta & 0 \\ 0 & 0 & 0 & 1 \end{bmatrix}$$

The matrix for rotation about the z-axis is:

$$R_z = \begin{bmatrix} \cos\theta & \sin\theta & 0 & 0 \\ -\sin\theta & \cos\theta & 0 & 0 \\ 0 & 0 & 1 & 0 \\ 0 & 0 & 0 & 1 \end{bmatrix}$$

Figure 2-11 shows a vector rotation about the y-axis.

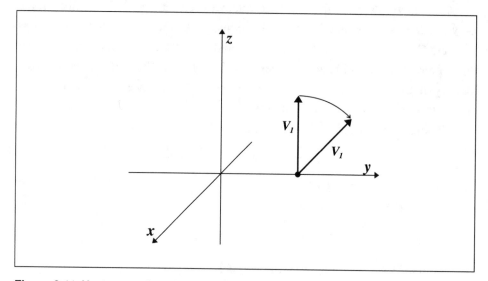

Figure 2-11. Vector rotation about the y-axis

The *Multiply3DMatrices* function

This function performs the multiplication of two real number, four-by-four matrices, or effectively combining two separate transformations into one. By chaining together all transformations, you produce the single composite transformation that represents all rotations, scaling, and translation for each axis.

You generate the composite transformation by first setting it equal to the identity matrix (all 1.0 in the diagonal elements, 0.0 everywhere else). You then compute each transformation (rotation, scaling, translation) separately and combine the transformation with the composite matrix by using *Multiply3DMatrices*. The net result will be a matrix that represents all the transformation operations, which may then be applied to points or vectors as needed. Note that the order of matrix composition is crucial. A different order of multiplication can produce entirely different and unexpected results.

Since each object in a scene may be moved separately, you may need different composite matrices for each object. As discussed later, all these transformations are generated by using this same procedure.

The *MatCopy* function

This function simply copies a given matrix into another matrix.

The *PrepareMatrix* function

This function generates a complete affine transformation matrix that handles translation, scaling, and rotation of a point in space. The function calls *Scale3D* to create the scaling matrix, *Rotate3D* for each of the three axes (x, y, and z) to create the rotation matrices, and *Translate3D* to create the translation matrix. *Multiply3DMatrices* is then called numerous times to build up the final total transformation matrix as a composite of the translation, scaling, and rotation matrices. This transformation matrix is returned.

The *PrepareInvMatrix* function

This function creates a matrix that is the inverse of the one generated by *PrepareMatrix*. An *inverse matrix* "undoes" the transformations of its complementary matrix. For example, if you transform a point, you can apply the inverse matrix to the transformed point to get back the original point. This routine computes the inverse matrix for each individual operation of translation, rotation, and scaling by using the negative values of the translation coefficients, the negative rotation angles, and the inverse (1.0 /) scaling coefficients. The final inverse matrix is then computed by combining the component matrices in the reverse order that *PrepareMatrix* uses. The reverse order is necessary so that each component will precisely cancel its corresponding transformation in *PrepareMatrix*.

The *Transform* function

This function performs the multiplication of a real three-dimensional vector (*TDA*) by a real four-by-four matrix (*Matx4x4*). The resulting vector is the one corresponding to the various transformations represented by the passed matrix.

Pseudo-Random Number Generation

These routines create pseudo-random numbers by using the power-residue sequence approach for positive pseudo-random-number generation. *Pseudo-random* means that the sequence only appears to be random and can be regenerated exactly on initialization by passing the same "seed value" to the routine. In addition, the sequence is only approximately uniformly distributed in the interval 0.0 - 1.0.

The pseudo-random-number generator starts by initialization with an arbitrary floating-point number (the *seed value*). New numbers are generated by multiplying a constant (σ) with the seed value and returning the fractional part, thus guaranteeing that the result is between 0 and 1. Every time the routine is called, a new number in the sequence is generated based on the previous value and, indirectly, the seed. Therefore, it guarantees that any sequence can always be regenerated, if you know the seed. Therefore, if your program generates an image that you like and the program uses the random number generator (such as the fractal mountain and plant generators), you can regenerate the same image as long as you know the seed value.

The *InitRand* function

This function initializes the random number generator with a real number. *OldSeed* is set to the passed seed value. *InitRand* must be called for usage of both the *Rand* and *RandInt* functions. Any time the same value is passed to *InitRand*, the same sequence will be generated by *Rand* and *RandInt*.

The *Rand* function

This function returns a positive real-typed random number between 0.0 and 1.0. *OldRand* takes on the fractional part of *OldRand* times the constant σ. *OldRand* is then the returned value. Note that *InitRand* must be called prior to any use of *Rand*.

The *RandInt* function

This function returns a positive integer-typed random number from a word-type range argument, or a value from 0 - (Range-1). You get the next value from *Rand()*, which is always in the range 0.0 - 1.0, multiply this by *Range*, and return *Trunc()* of the result.

With a basic understanding of the functions available in the mathematics module, you are ready to learn about the graphics module and its capabilities.

CHAPTER 3

The Graphics Interface Module

Chapter 2 discussed the functions found in the mathematics module and some of their possible uses. This chapter describes several low-level and utility graphics functions used by the software in this book. These functions can be found in the BkGraph.C graphics interface module. They cover a wide variety of operations — from setting a graphics mode on an SVGA graphics card to three-dimensional plotting. Chapter 4 discusses the methods for using the modules presented in Chapter 2 and this chapter.

The graphics routines found in BkGraph.C are intended primarily for an STB ERGO Powergraph SVGA graphics card. With proper programming information (normally included with your graphics card) you should be able to make these routines work with your graphics card. Only SVGA 256-color modes are supported by this graphics driver. Chapter 16 discusses the Cardinal Technologies, Inc. 7000 graphics card and other 24-bit color drivers. These drivers create a 24-bit color display program.

To begin the examination of the graphics module, we will first consider the header file required by the graphics module. Note that the header files BkDefs.H, BkMath.H, and files related to the mathematics module were discussed in Chapter 2.

The BkGlobs.H Header File

The BkGlobs.H header file instantiates the global variables for the mathematics and graphical interface modules. These variables are shared by all of the modules and main program code. The variables found here pertain mainly to image resolution and to the three-dimensional graphics routines. Listing 3-1 contains the BkGlobs.H header file.

```
/*
```

```
          BkGlobs.H = globals for the BkGraph.C modules
            Copyright 1988, 1992 Christopher D. Watkins
          and Stephen B. Coy (Contributions by Larry Sharp)
                      ALL RIGHTS RESERVED
```

```
*/
```

```
int      XRes, YRes;
Word     MaxXRes, MaxYRes;
Word     MaxX, MaxY;
float    Asp;
Boolean  PerspectivePlot;
float    Mx, My, Mz, ds;
Boolean  Draw_Axis_And_Palette;
int      Angl, Tilt;
```

Listing 3-1. Program Listing of BkGlobs.H

The BkGraph.H Header File

The header file BkGraph.H contains the function prototypes found in the graphical interface module. Much like BkMath.H, these prototypes specify all the functions found in the graphics interface module along with the arguments that they require. Listing 3-2 shows the BkGraph.H header file.

```
/*
```

```
            BkGraph.H = prototypes for BkGraph.C
            Copyright 1988, 1992 Christopher D. Watkins
          and Stephen B. Coy (Contributions by Larry Sharp)
                      ALL RIGHTS RESERVED
```

```
*/
extern int  XRes, YRes;
extern int  CentreX, CentreY;
extern Word MaxXRes, MaxYRes;
extern Word MaxX, MaxY;
```

```
extern float Asp;
extern Boolean PerspectivePlot;
extern float   Mx, My, Mz, ds;
extern int   Angl, Tilt;
extern Boolean Draw_Axis_And_Palette;
extern void Set_Mode(int Mode);
extern void Pre_Calc();
extern void Init_Palette(Palette_Register Color);
extern void Init_Palette_2(Palette_Register Color);
extern void Cycle_Palette(Palette_Register Hue);

extern int MinI (int A, int B);
extern int MaxI (int A, int B);

extern void Swap(int *first, int *second);
extern void Circle(Word x, Word y, Word radius, Byte color);
extern void Set_Graphics_Mode(Word xRes, Word yRes);
extern void Wait_For_Key();
extern void Exit_Graphics();
extern void Title();
extern void Init_Plotting(float Ang, float Tlt);
extern void Init_Perspective(Boolean Perspective,
                  float x, float y, float z, float m);
extern void Map_Coordinates(float X, float Y, float Z, int *Xp, int
    *Yp);
extern void Cartesian_Plot_3D(float X, float Y, float Z, Byte
    Color);
extern void Cylindrical_Plot_3D(float Rho, float Theta, float Z,
    Byte Color);
extern void Spherical_Plot_3D(float R, float Theta, float Phi, Byte
    Color);
extern void Draw_Line_3D(TDA Pnt1, TDA Pnt2, Byte Color);
extern void Put_Pixel(int x, int y, Byte Color, Byte Intensity);
extern void Put_Axis_And_Palette(Boolean PlaceOnScreen);
extern void Display_Axis();
extern void Display_Palette();
extern void Axis_And_Palette();
extern void Set_Palette(Palette_Register Hue);
extern void Line(int x1, int y1, int x2, int y2, Byte Color);
extern void Plot(Word x, Word y, Byte color);
extern Byte Get_Pixel(Word x, Word y);
extern void Init_Graphics(Byte mode);
```

Listing 3-2. Program Listing of BkGraph.H

The BkGraph.C Program

With an understanding of the header files required for the graphics module, you are now ready to examine the graphics module itself, called BkGraph.C. A listing of this module is presented in Listing 3-3. The discussion of this program begins with an examination of some of the low-level graphics functions.

```
/*
```

```
        BkGraph.C = the graphics module
   Dependencies = BkDefs.H, BkMath.H and BkGraph.H
        Copyright 1988, 1992 Christopher D. Watkins
    and Stephen B. Coy (Contributions by Larry Sharp)
                ALL RIGHTS RESERVED
```

```
*/
```

```
/*
    Plot          - place pixel to screen
    Set_Palette   - set palette register
    Init_Palette  - 64 levels of gray, red, green, and blue
    Init_Palette2 - 7 colors with 35 intensities each - use with
                    Pixel
    Cycle_Palette - cycle through palette
    Circle        - circle draw routine
    Draw          - line draw routine
    Init_Graphics - initialize graphics
    Wait_For_Key  - wait for key press
    Exit_Graphics - sound and wait for key press before exiting
                    graphics
    Title         - set up text screen colors
*/
#include <stdio.h>
#include <stdlib.h>
#include <dos.h>
#include <conio.h>
#include <math.h>
#include <malloc.h>
#include <graphics.h>

#include "BkDefs.H"
#include "BkMath.H"
#include "BkGraph.H"
```

```c
Word    X_Off, Y_Off;
static Byte Res;

#define Low_Res     1
#define Medium_Res  2
#define High_Res    3


void Plot(Word x, Word y, Byte color)
{
  if((x<XRes) && (y<YRes))
      putpixel(x, y, color);
}


static Palette_Register Color;

void Set_Palette(Palette_Register Hue) {
     int subi;

     for (subi=0; subi<256; subi++) {
          setrgbpalette (subi, Hue[subi].Red, Hue[subi].Grn,
            Hue[subi].Blu);
     }
}

void Init_Palette(Palette_Register Color)
{
  Word i;

  for(i=0; i<64; i++)
  {
     Color[i].Red=i << 2;
     Color[i].Grn=i << 2;
     Color[i].Blu=i << 2;
  }
  for(i=64; i<128; i++)
  {
     Color[i].Red=(i-64) << 2;
     Color[i].Grn=0;
     Color[i].Blu=0;
  }
  for(i=128; i<192; i++)
  {
     Color[i].Red=0;
     Color[i].Grn=(i-128) << 2;
```

```
        Color[i].Blu=0;
    }
  for(i=192; i<=255; i++)
  {
      Color[i].Red=0;
      Color[i].Grn=0;
      Color[i].Blu=(i-192) << 2;
  }
}

void Init_Palette_2(Palette_Register Color)
{
  Word i;

  for(i=0; i<36; i++)
  {
      Color[i].Red=0;
      Color[i].Grn=0;
      Color[i].Blu=(Round(1.8*i)) << 2;
  }
  for(i=36; i<72; i++)
  {
      Color[i].Red=0;
      Color[i].Grn=(Round(1.8*(i-36))) << 2;
      Color[i].Blu=0;
  }
  for(i=72; i<108; i++)
  {
      Color[i].Red=0;
      Color[i].Grn=(Round(1.8*(i-72))) << 2;
      Color[i].Blu=(Round(1.8*(i-72))) << 2;
  }
  for(i=108; i<144; i++)
  {
      Color[i].Red=(Round(1.8*(i-108))) << 2;
      Color[i].Grn=0;
      Color[i].Blu=0;
  }
  for(i=144; i<180; i++)
  {
      Color[i].Red=(Round(1.8*(i-144))) << 2;
      Color[i].Grn=0;
      Color[i].Blu=(Round(1.8*(i-144))) << 2;
  }
  for(i=180; i<216; i++)
  {
```

```
        Color[i].Red=(Round(1.8*(i-180))) << 2;
        Color[i].Grn=(Round(1.8*(i-180))) << 2;
        Color[i].Blu=0;
    }
  for(i=216; i<252; i++)
    {
        Color[i].Red=(Round(1.8*(i-216))) << 2;
        Color[i].Grn=(Round(1.8*(i-216))) << 2;
        Color[i].Blu=(Round(1.8*(i-216))) << 2;
    }
}

void Cycle_Palette(Palette_Register Hue)
{
  Word i;
  RGB  tmp;

  tmp=Hue[0];
  memcpy(&Hue[0], &Hue[1], 765);
  Hue[255]=tmp;
  Set_Palette(Hue);
}

void Swap(int *first, int *second)
{
  int temp;

  temp=*first;
  *first=*second;
  *second=temp;
}

void Circle(Word x, Word y, Word radius, Byte color)
{
  int a, af, b, bf, target, r2, asp;

  if(Res==High_Res)
    asp=100;
  else
      asp=120;
    target=0;
    a=radius;
    b=0;
    r2=Sqr(radius);
    while(a>=b)
    {
```

```
    b=Round(sqrt(r2-Sqr(a)));
    Swap(&target,&b);
      while(b<target)
    {
      af=(asp*a)/100;
      bf=(asp*b)/100;
          Plot(x+af, y+b, color);
          Plot(x+bf, y+a, color);
          Plot(x-af, y+b, color);
          Plot(x-bf, y+a, color);
          Plot(x-af, y-b, color);
          Plot(x-bf, y-a, color);
          Plot(x+af, y-b, color);
      Plot(x+bf, y-a, color);
      ++b;
      }
    —a;
  }
}


int MinI (int A, int B) {

    if (A < B) return (A);
    else return (B);
}


int MaxI (int A, int B) {

    if (A > B) return (A);
    else return (B);
}

int Trivial_Reject (int *x1, int *y1, int *x2, int *y2) {

    if (MaxI (*x1, *x2) < 0) return (true);
    if (MinI (*x1, *x2) >= XRes) return (true);
    if (MaxI (*y1, *y2) <0) return (true);
    if (MinI (*y1, *y2) >= YRes) return (true);

    return (false);

}


int Clip_To_Screen (int *x1, int *y1, int *x2, int *y2) {
```

```
    int SegmentVisible = true;

    if (Trivial_Reject( x1, y1, x2, y2)) {
        SegmentVisible = false;
    }

    return (SegmentVisible);
}


void Line(int x1, int y1, int x2, int y2, Byte Color)
{
    if ( (x1 == x2) && (y1 == y2)) {
        /* Do Nothing. Line is actually a point */
    }

    else {
        if (Clip_To_Screen(&x1, &y1, &x2, &y2)) {
            setcolor(Color);
            line(x1, y1, x2, y2);
        }
    }
}

int   CentreX, CentreY;


Byte G_Mode;

int huge Detect()
{
  return(G_Mode);
}

int gdriver=DETECT, gmode, errorcode;

void Init_Graphics(Byte mode)
{
  G_Mode=mode;
  printf("\nEntering Graphics Mode: %d", mode);
  installuserdriver("SVGA256", Detect);
  initgraph(&gdriver, &gmode, "");
  errorcode=graphresult();
  if(errorcode!=grOk)
  {
      printf("Graphics error: %s\n", grapherrormsg(errorcode));
      getch();
```

```c
        exit(1);
    }
  XRes=getmaxx();
  YRes=getmaxy();
  CentreX = XRes / 2;
  CentreY = YRes / 2;
}


void Set_Graphics_Mode(Word xRes, Word yRes)
{
  XRes=xRes;
  YRes=yRes;
  if((XRes<321) && (YRes<201))
      Init_Graphics(0);
  else if((XRes<641) && (YRes<401))
      Init_Graphics(1);
  else if((XRes<641) && (YRes<481))
      Init_Graphics(2);
  else if((XRes<801) && (YRes<601))
      Init_Graphics(3);
  else
      Init_Graphics(4);
}

void Wait_For_Key()
{
  char k;

  while(!(k=getch()));
}

void Exit_Graphics()
{
  sound(1000);
  delay(500);
  nosound();
  Wait_For_Key();
  closegraph();
}

void Title()
{
  textcolor(YELLOW);
  textbackground(BLUE);
  clrscr();
}
```

```
/*
```

```
┌─────────────────────────────────────────────────┐
│  ┌───────────────────────────────────────────┐  │
│  │     Three Dimensional Plotting Routines     │  │
│  └───────────────────────────────────────────┘  │
└─────────────────────────────────────────────────┘
```

```
        InitPlotting        - rotation and tilt angles
        InitPerspective     - observer location and distances
        MapCoordinates      - maps 3D space onto the 2D screen
        CartesianPlot       - plot a Cartesian system point
        CylindricalPlot3D   - plot a cylindrical system point
        SphericalPlot3D     - plot a spherical system point
        DrawLine3D          - plot a line from 3D coordinates
*/

float CosA, SinA;
float CosB, SinB;
float CosACosB, SinASinB;
float CosASinB, SinACosB;

void Init_Plotting(float Ang, float Tlt)
{
  CentreX=XRes/2;
  CentreY=YRes/2;
  Angl= (int) Ang;
  Tilt= (int) Tlt;
  CosA=CosD(Ang);
  SinA=SinD(Ang);
  CosB=CosD(Tlt);
  SinB=SinD(Tlt);
  CosACosB=CosA*CosB;
  SinASinB=SinA*SinB;
  CosASinB=CosA*SinB;
  SinACosB=SinA*CosB;
}

void Init_Perspective(Boolean Perspective, float x, float y, float
  z, float m)
{
  PerspectivePlot=Perspective;
  Mx=x;
  My=y;
  Mz=z;
  ds=m;
}
```

```
void Map_Coordinates(float X, float Y, float Z, int *Xp, int *Yp)
{
  float Xt, Yt, Zt;
  float OneOverZt;

  Xt=(Mx+X*CosA-Y*SinA);
  Yt=(My+X*SinASinB+Y*CosASinB+Z*CosB);
  if(PerspectivePlot)
  {
      Zt=Mz+X*SinACosB+Y*CosACosB-Z*SinB;
      OneOverZt=1.0/Zt;
      *Xp=CentreX+Round(ds*Xt*OneOverZt);
      if(Res!=Low_Res)
          *Yp=CentreY-Round(ds*Yt*OneOverZt);
      else
          *Yp=CentreY-Round(ds*Yt*OneOverZt*Asp);
  }
  else
  {
      *Xp=CentreX+Round(Xt);
      if(Res!=Low_Res)
          *Yp=CentreY-Round(Yt);
    else
      *Yp=CentreY-Round(Yt*Asp);
  }
}

void Cartesian_Plot_3D(float X, float Y, float Z, Byte Color)
{
  int Xp, Yp;

  Map_Coordinates(X, Y, Z, &Xp, &Yp);
  Plot(Xp, Yp, Color);
}

void Cylindrical_Plot_3D(float Rho, float Theta, float Z, Byte
  Color)
{
  float X, Y;

  Theta=Radians(Theta);
  X=Rho*cos(Theta);
  Y=Rho*sin(Theta);
  Cartesian_Plot_3D(X, Y, Z, Color);
}
void Spherical_Plot_3D(float R, float Theta, float Phi, Byte Color)
{
```

```
  float X, Y, Z;

  Theta=Radians(Theta);
  Phi=Radians(Phi);
  X=R*sin(Theta)*cos(Phi);
  Y=R*sin(Theta)*sin(Phi);
  Z=R*cos(Theta);
  Cartesian_Plot_3D(X, Y, Z, Color);
}

void Draw_Line_3D(TDA Pnt1, TDA Pnt2, Byte Color)
{
  int   Xp1, Yp1;
  int   Xp2, Yp2;
  float x1, y1, z1;
  float x2, y2, z2;

  UnVec(Pnt1, &x1, &y1, &z1);
  UnVec(Pnt2, &x2, &y2, &z2);
  Map_Coordinates(x1, y1, z1, &Xp1, &Yp1);
  Map_Coordinates(x2, y2, z2, &Xp2, &Yp2);
  Line(Xp1, Yp1, Xp2, Yp2, Color);
}

  /*
```

```
┌─────────────────────────────────────────────────┐
│                                                   │
│                      Pixel                        │
│                                                   │
└─────────────────────────────────────────────────┘
```

```
    PutPixel - plots pixel
     GetPixel - gets pixel

    Color 1 - Blue
          2 - Green
          3 - Cyan
          4 - Red
          5 - Magenta
          6 - Brown/Yellow
          7 - Gray Scale

      Intensity levels (0..35) for each color
*/

void Put_Pixel(int x, int y, Byte Color, Byte Intensity)
{
  Byte Col;
```

```
    if(Intensity>MaxInten)
        exit(1);
    Col=((MaxInten+1)*(Color-1)+Intensity) & 255;
    Plot(x, y, Col);
}



Byte Get_Pixel(Word x, Word y)
{
  if((x<XRes) && (y<YRes))
      return(getpixel(x, y));
  else
    return(0);
}


/*
```

```
               Setup of Coordinate Axes and Color Palette
```

```
    PutAxisAndPalette - toggle for Axis and Palette
    AxisAndPalette    - places Axis and Color Palette on screen
*/

void Put_Axis_And_Palette(Boolean PlaceOnScreen)
{
  if(PlaceOnScreen)
    Draw_Axis_And_Palette=true;
  else
    Draw_Axis_And_Palette=false;
}

void Display_Axis()
{
  int x, y, z, sx, sy;

  sx=XRes/320;
  sy=YRes/200;
  for(x=-100*sx; x<101*sx; x++)
  {
      Cartesian_Plot_3D(x, 0, 0, 35);
    Cartesian_Plot_3D(100*sx, 0, 0, 251);
  }
  for(y=-100*sy; y<101*sy; y++)
  {
```

```
      Cartesian_Plot_3D(0, y, 0, 71);
      Cartesian_Plot_3D(0, 100*sy, 0,251);
    }
  for(z=-100*sx; z<101*sx; z++)
  {
      Cartesian_Plot_3D(0, 0, z, 107);
      Cartesian_Plot_3D(0, 0, 100*sx, 251);
    }
}

void Display_Palette()
{
  int  X, Y, sx, sy;
  Byte Color;
  Byte Intensity;

  sx=XRes/320;
  sy=YRes/200;
  for(Color=1; Color<=MaxCol; Color++)
  {
    for(Intensity=0; Intensity<=MaxInten; Intensity++)
    {
      for(X=0; X<4*sx; X++)
      {
      for(Y=0; Y<4*sy; Y++)
        Put_Pixel(X+(5*sx)*Color,
              (190*sy)-Y-(5*sy)*Intensity,
                Color,
              Intensity);
      }
    }
  }
}

void Axis_And_Palette()
{
  if(Draw_Axis_And_Palette)
  {
    Display_Axis();
      Display_Palette();
  }
}
```

Listing 3-3. Program Listing of BkGraph.C

The *Plot* function

The primary purpose of this routine is to plot a pixel of a given color to the specified (X,Y) location on the screen. This function accomplishes this through a call to the .BGI driver plot function. Note that the .BGI routine is called only when the plotting coordinates fall within the screen boundaries.

The *Clear_Palette* function

This function takes a predefined variable type called *Palette_Register* and zeroes it out. These variables contain the red, green, and blue components of the colors (one for each color). The *Palette* determines how each color value (0 - 255) is displayed on the screen.

The *Set_Palette* function

This function sets the *Palette* using the passed *Palette_Register* array address.We use the BGI driver *setrgbpalette* to store the appropriate 256-color palette to the graphics card a color palette entry at a time. Our palette is now set.

The *Init_Palette* function

This function sets up a standard palette containing 64 levels of gray, red, green, and blue. First calculate the gray by making the first 64 R, G, and B (red, green, and blue) components of the palette equal. Equal shades of red, green, and blue produce a gray shade. For the next 64 components, set only the red values, and zero out the green and blue components. Do the same for green and blue and your palette is complete.

The *Init_Palette_2* function

This *Palette* consists of seven colors, each having 35 intensities. The colors of the palette are blue, green, cyan, red, magenta, brown, and gray. To accomplish this, seven "for" loops are used, each ranging from 0 to 35.

The first loop sets up blue colors by setting red and green to 0 and calculating 35 shades of blue. Be sure to scale out the levels of blue so that the brightest blue has an intensity of 63. Next, set up green by setting red and blue to 0 and calculating 35 shades of green. For the cyan, zero out the red component, and then make the 35 green and blue components equal. Set up the red colors by setting the green and blue values to 0 and calculating 35 shades of red.

Calculate the magenta by setting the green to 0 and giving equal values to the 35 red and blue components. Calculate the 35 brown colors by making the blue values 0 and giving equal values to the red and green components. Set the 35 gray shades by giving equal values to the red, green, and blue components. The remaining palette entries are left at 0.

The *Cycle_Palette* function

This is a simple animation technique that can be used in many different ways. Basically, it performs a circular rotation of the current palette, moving the first entry (for pixel value 0) to the last (for pixel value 255). Save the first palette entry in a temporary variable, then shift the remaining 255 entries down by 1. Next, replace the last entry with the entry stored in the temporary variable. Finally, call *Set_Palette* to set up the new palette of colors.

The *Swap* function

This function simply swaps two integer values. The first is stored in a temporary variable. The second is placed into the first and the temporary is placed into the second, thus swapping the two integers. This function is used by the *Circle* function described next.

The *Circle* function

This function draws a circle onto a screen with the correct aspect ratio for the given resolution. The routine requires a position (x, y), a radius, and a color number. Since a circle is symmetrical, eight points are plotted at once. The only difference in the eight points is the sign of the x and y components for the points. Therefore, you only need to span one-eighth of the circle to draw the complete circle. Note that aspect correction is also handled in the routine. The aspect ratio comes into play because, in certain resolutions, a pixel may not be square (that is, equal size on the monitor). For the Powergraph ERGO SVGA card, the 1024 x 768 and 640 x 480 modes have square pixels and thus an aspect ratio of 1. The 320 x 200 VGA mode has an aspect ratio of 1.2 (1 over (1024 / 768) * (*YRes* / *XRes*)). To perform the aspect correction, the x or y components are multiplied by this ratio for the current graphics card.

Computations for the circle are as follows. One offset starts with the value of the radius, the second offset is 1. The target value is also set to 1. Loop until the second offset is less than the first, thus indicating that one-eighth of the circle has been traversed. Within this loop, the function computes the value of the second offset (using the equation for a circle) and then swaps it with the target value. A new loop is entered, which iterates until the value of the second offset is greater than or equal to the target value. For each iteration, the computation of the x offsets is completed (including computation for aspect ratio) and eight symmetric points plotted. The second offset is then incremented by 1. This second loop guarantees that pixels are filled in where there is little change in the second offset. When this loop finishes, the first offset is decremented by 1 and then another iteration of the first loop begins. This process yields a circle with just enough points for the given resolution.

The *Line* function

This routine draws a line from one point to another point, using a specified color number. Note that the .BGI line-drawing routine is used, and that only lines whose points both fall into the screen are plotted through use of the *Clip_To_Screen* function (described below). Figure 3-1 shows an example of the *Line* function.

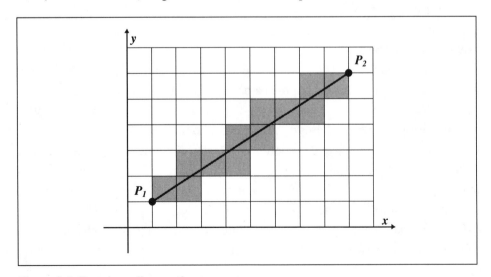

Figure 3-1. Drawing a line on the screen

The *MinI* and *MaxI* functions

These functions find the minimum and maximum values of two integer numbers and return an integer number.

The *Trivial_Reject* function

This function is used by the *Line* function to reject drawing lines whose endpoints both fall outside of the screen coordinates.

The *Clip_To_Screen* function

This function is used to clip a line that falls outside of the screen coordinates. It is called by *Line*.

The *Init_Graphics* function

This function must be called prior to calling any other graphics routines. It performs basic initialization for all graphics operations and sets the graphics mode by using the passed argument.

This function first checks to see which graphics mode is being requested. If the mode is illegal, an error message is printed and the program tells you to press a key to exit. Otherwise, appropriate variables are initialized. Bounding variables are used in clipping operations. Next, give *XRes* and *YRes* the maximum values for the resolution. Then calculate *CentreX* and *CentreY* to define the center pixel of the display. Notice the use of the .BGI driver function *InitGraph()*.

The *Set_Graphics_Mode* function

This function enables you to set up a graphics window of any size (up to 1024 x 768). You pass the *X-Resolution* and the *Y-Resolution* to this function and *Set_Graphics_Mode* calculates the best possible graphics mode for this window. This function calls *Init_Graphics* to determine appropriate offsets for the center of the screen and other set-up procedures.

The *Wait_For_Key* function

This function allows your program to wait for any keystroke before continuing.

The *Exit_Graphics* function

This function is called when your program has finished using the graphics display. The *Exit_Graphics* function starts by sounding a beep and calling *Wait_For_Key*. The screen is put back into normal DOS text mode.

The *Title* function

This routine sets the text screen colors to a blue background with yellow text and clears the screen. It is useful for initial display screens and data-display screens.

Three-Dimensional Plotting Routines

With a basic understanding of some of the low-level graphics functions, you can now examine some of the more advanced three-dimensional plotting concepts. The following routines are useful for creating three-dimensional computer displays. The routines cover initiating perspective, mapping three-dimensional space onto a two-dimensional surface (namely your computer screen), displaying an axis and a palette, and general graphics support.

The *Init_Plotting* function

This routine initializes variables that are used in three-dimensional plotting and have any dependence on the rotation and tilt angles (*Angl* and *Tilt*). *Angl* specifies the Z-rotation angle (location of the viewer with respect to the origin of the three-dimensional coordinate system), and *Tilt* specifies the pitch of the viewer. These angles are passed to the routine. Various precalculations are made for the trigonometric concerns of the *Map_Coordinates* function in order to make mapping calculations more efficient.

The *Init_Perspective* function

This routine sets the perspective flag so that the program knows whether to perform perspective projection in the *Map_Coordinates* routine. This routine also initializes the observer position coordinates (Mx, My, and Mz), as well as the distance from the screen parameter ds.

The *Map_Coordinates* function

This routine performs the basic transformation of points from a three-dimensional space (X, Y, Z) to a two-dimensional screen (Xp, Yp). Both orthographic and perspective projections may be specified. The origin of the three-dimensional space is located at the center of the display screen. The *Mx* and *My* offsets can be used to move the viewer relative to the screen. In other words, you can move the origin about the screen if perspective projection is chosen. You can make *Mz* less than *ds* (say *Mz* = 350 and *ds* = 500) in order to move closer to the origin if perspective projection is active.

Equations 3-1 and 3-2 represent the orthographic projection of three-space coordinates (X, Y, Z) to screen coordinates (Xp, Yp). Use Equation 3-3 for perspective calculation. Here the values of X and Y are divided by Z and modified by *ds* to create perspective. These equations are derived through matrix multiplications for translation and rotation about two axes. They are similar to the affine transformation routines, except that they are hard-coded for speed considerations.

$$x_t = m_x + x\cos\theta - y\sin\theta \qquad \text{(Equation 3-1)}$$

$$y_t = m_y + x\sin\theta\sin\phi + y\cos\theta\sin\phi + z\cos\phi \qquad \text{(Equation 3-2)}$$

$$z_t = m_z + x\sin\theta\cos\phi + y\cos\theta\cos\phi - z\sin\phi \qquad \text{(Equation 3-3)}$$

Figure 3-2 shows a three-dimensional letter projected onto a two-dimensional screen. The object that you are viewing falls with a *viewing volume* (a volume of space that you can "see" looking "through" your computer display). Basically, your two-dimensional screen is geometrically oriented with the three-dimensional space in which the object exists, thus projecting this object on to the screen.

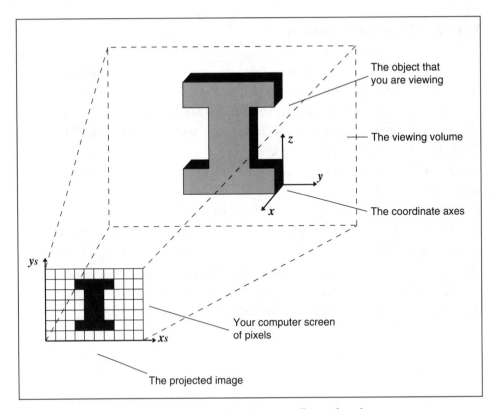

Figure 3-2. Projection of three-dimensional to two-dimensional

The *Cartesian_Plot_3D* function

This function plots a point described by rectangular or Cartesian coordinates (X, Y, Z). The function calls *Map_Coordinates* to project the point onto the screen and colors it with the appropriate color. Figure 3-3 shows a display of Cartesian coordinates.

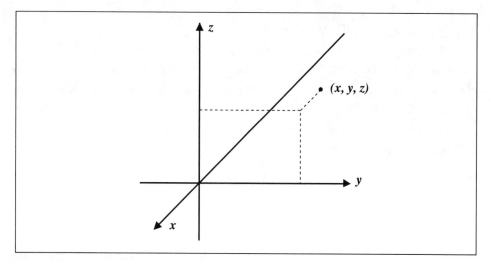

Figure 3-3. Cartesian plot

The *Cylindrical_Plot_3D* function

This function plots a point described by cylindrical coordinates (ρ, θ, z). Here, ρ is the radius of the cylinder and θ is the angle around the z-axis. Trigonometric relations transform the cylindrical coordinates into Cartesian coordinates. The function calls *Map_Coordinates* to project the point onto the screen and colors it the appropriate color. Figure 3-4 shows a display of cylindrical coordinates.

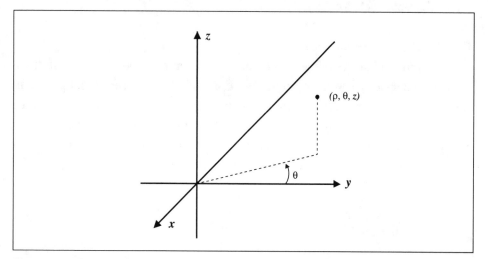

Figure 3-4. Cylindrical plot

The *Spherical_Plot_3D* function

This function plots a point described by spherical coordinates (r, θ, ϕ). Here r is the radius of the sphere, θ the angle around the z-axis from the x-axis in the xy-plane, and ϕ the angle off of the z-axis. Trigonometric relations transform the spherical coordinates into Cartesian coordinates. The function calls *Map_Coordinates* to project the point onto the screen and colors it the appropriate color. Figure 3-5 shows a display of spherical coordinates.

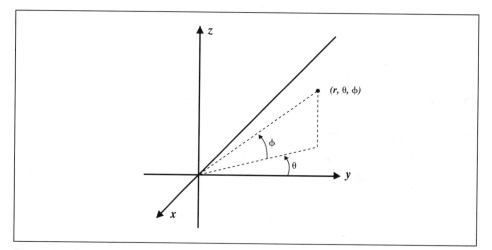

Figure 3-5. Spherical plot

The *Draw_Line_3D* function

This function draws a line of a certain color number from one point in three-dimensional space to another point. Two Cartesian three-dimensional points are passed to the routine in *TDA* type format and *Map_Coordinates* is called to project the points onto the two-dimensional display. A line is then drawn between the two projected screen coordinates. You can see the line-drawing process, first the projection and then the display, by examining Figure 3-6.

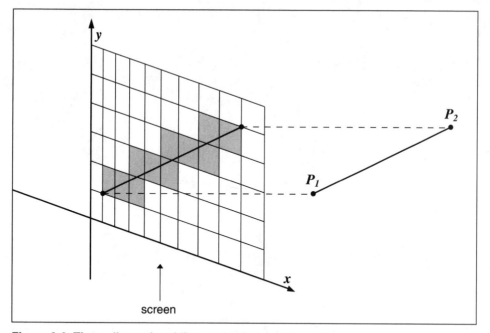

Figure 3-6. Three-dimensional line projection and drawing

In computer graphics, many objects are represented by *facets*. Facets are small polygons (usually triangular patches) that define the surface of an object. Sometimes you need to display such objects as *wire-frames* to represent the positions and orientations of the polygons that make up the object. Wire-frames of an object show the outlines of these three-dimensional facets. This three-dimensional line-drawing routine can be used to display such objects. You generate a wire-frame by drawing a three-dimensional line from one point of each facet to the next point and tracing out each polygonal facet of the object. Figure 3-7 shows an example of projecting a facet.

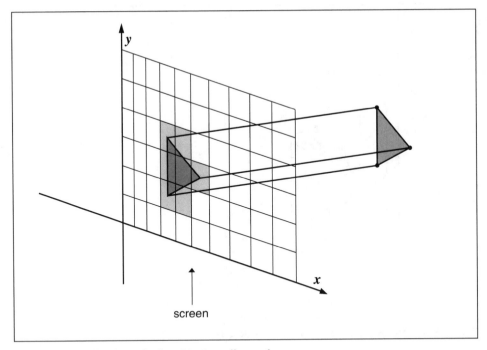

Figure 3-7. Projection of a facet to two dimensions

Pixel Routines

These routines put and get pixels (either singularly or in blocks). They handle the mapping of pixels specified by a color and the intensity to the appropriate color value for the seven-color palette created by *Init_Palette_2*.

The *Put_Pixel* function

This function is used to plot a pixel that is given a shade and an intensity. It begins by making sure that the given shade and intensity do not exceed the values stored in the constants *MaxCol* (7) and *MaxIntens* (35). If one does exceed its respective constant, the routine exits. Otherwise, the color is calculated and *Plot* is called to place the pixel onto the screen at the given x and y coordinates.

The *Get_Pixel* function

This function returns the value of a pixel stored at the given x and y coordinates. It performs the inverse operation from the *Plot* function (that is, it retrieves the color value directly from the graphics card's display), and accounts for any necessary page flipping. Note that the .BGI function *getpixel* is used actually to rend the pixel from the display device.

Setup of Coordinate Axes and Palette Routines

These are the routines that handle the display of the color palette and Cartesian axes on the screen. The x-axis is represented as a blue line, the y-axis is green, and the z-axis is cyan. White dots at the ends of the three lines indicate the most positive part of the lines. The palette display best shows the seven-color, 35-intensity palette created by the function *Init_Palette_2*.

The *Put_Axis_And_Palette* function

This function sets a flag to tell the programs whether you want the axis and palette to be displayed. This must be set before calling *Axis_And_Palette* (described later).

The *Display_Axis* function

This routine draws the three coordinate axes using the *Cartesian_Plot_3D* routine. The white points indicate the most positive parts of the axes.

The *Display_Palette* function

This routine displays in the form of colored squares running down the left side of the screen all the colors in the palette. Scaling factors for the size of the squares are first set up. Then four loops are initialized. The first is *Color*, ranging from 1 to *MaxCol*. The second is *Intensity*, ranging from 0 to *MaxInten*. These two loops determine the color of the square to be placed on the screen. The third loop is *X*, ranging from 0 to 4 times the scaling factor *sx*. The fourth is *Y* ranging from 0 to 4 times the scaling factor *sy*. These two loops determine the size of the square to be placed on the screen. Each pixel is placed on the screen by a call to *Put_Pixel*. This palette display routine shows the seven-color, 35-intensity palette created by the function *Init_Palette_2*.

The *Axis_And_Palette* function

This function tests to see if the *Draw_Axis_And_Palette* flag is set. If so, this function calls *Display_Axis* and *Display_Palette* to place the axis and palette on the screen. Since it uses these flags, you may include this in your program and simply set the flags appropriately to determine whether the axes and palette are actually drawn.

Using the Modules

Having examined both the mathematical and graphics interface modules, you are ready to learn how to use the modules in various graphics programs.

CHAPTER 4

Using the Modules

Previous chapters discussed standard C as a programming language and how the graphics libraries accompanying most C compilers do not meet the needs of three-dimensional graphics. As explained in Chapter 2 and Chapter 3, the mathematics and graphics modules were developed to help overcome these problems. This chapter examines how the modules create interesting graphics effects in some example programs. The first program in this chapter creates a two-dimensional fractal crystal growth. Subsequent routines create two-dimensional fractal coral and grass structures. A third dimension is then added with a simulated starfield fly-through and a three-dimensional particle-motion simulation.

The Crystal.C File

The algorithm used to create random fractal crystal growth is simple. You place a colored seed at the center pixel of the screen and then randomly throw pixel-sized paint at the screen. If you hit a pixel that is adjoining an existing painted pixel, the paint sticks. Otherwise, the paint washes away and disappears. This "paint throwing" process is simulated by randomly choosing a pixel near the crystal center, and then checking all of the pixels around this random point to see if they have already been drawn. If so, the new pixel is lighted; otherwise it is turned off and you proceed to the next proof.

When you examine the code in Listing 4-1, you will notice the use of the pseudo-random number generator. The *InitRand* function seeds the pseudo-random number generator with a number that acts as the basis for all future "random" numbers. With a given starting seed value, you are guaranteed to produce the exact same image. Therefore, remember your seed values for images you like. Note that *RandInt* is the integer version of the *Rand* function (found in the mathematics module).

```
/*
```

```
        Fractal "Crystal" Growth Generator
   Crystal.C = Monte-Carlo simulation of crystal growth
     Requires: BkDefs.H, BkGlobs.H, BkMath.H, BkMath.C,
                 BkGraph.H, BkGraph.C
  Copyright 1988,1992 Christopher D. Watkins and Stephen B. Coy
            (Translation to C by Addison Rose)
                  ALL RIGHTS RESERVED
```

A "crystal is grown by moving particles into a region containing a "seed" crystal. The particles move about in a random fashion, and if a particle touches the seed, it will stick. The resultant shapes are very similar to natural amorphous crystal growth. */

```c
#include <conio.h>
#include <math.h>
#include <stdlib.h>
#include <time.h>

#include "BkDefs.H"
#include "BkGlobs.H"
#include "BkMath.H"
#include "BkGraph.H"

#define  ScatterProbability    0.25

Palette_Register PalArray;

main() {
  short Success, Failure; int xval,
  yval, dx, dy, r, s; double Rad, Ph,
  PrtRad, TwoPi; unsigned char
  ScatProb;

  TwoPi = 2.0 * Pi;
  Rad = 5.0;

  Init_Graphics(1);

    Init_Palette(PalArray);
    Set_Palette(PalArray);

    CentreX = XRes / 2;
    CentreY = YRes / 2;
```

```
randomize();

// probability of scattering per interation
ScatProb = Round(1.0 / ScatterProbability);

// Put in the "seed"
Plot(CentreX, CentreY, 63);

while (!kbhit()) {

    // Pick a random angle to start at,
    // and put the point on a circle of Radius Rad
    Ph = random(32768) * TwoPi;
    xval = CentreX + Round(Rad * CosD(Ph));
    yval = CentreY + Round(Rad * SinD(Ph));

     // Pick a random direction
     dx = (random(32767) % 3) - 1;
     dy = (random(32767) % 3) - 1;

     Plot(xval, yval, 63);               // Plot the point

     Success = 0;
     Failure = 0;

     while (!Success && !Failure) {

       Plot(xval, yval, 0);              // Clear the point

       r = random(32768) % ScatProb;   // Has the particle scattered?

       if (r) {
         dx = (random(32767) % 3) - 1;  // pick a new direction
         dy = (random(32767) % 3) - 1;  // at random
       }

       xval = xval + dx;                 // Move the particle
       yval = yval + dy;

       Plot(xval, yval, 63);             // Plot the new point

       if ((Get_Pixel(xval+1, yval  ) != 0) ||  // Is the particle
           (Get_Pixel(xval+1, yval+1) != 0) ||  // touching any
           (Get_Pixel(xval, yval+1)   != 0) ||  // point that
           (Get_Pixel(xval-1, yval+1) != 0) ||  // is lit up?
```

```
(Get_Pixel(xval-1, yval )  != 0)  ||
(Get_Pixel(xval-1, yval-1) != 0)  ||
(Get_Pixel(xval, yval-1)   != 0)  ||
(Get_Pixel(xval+1, yval-1) != 0))
        Success = 1;

      // great speed can be achieved by setting up a 2-D array and
      // testing the points in the array, as opposed to Get_Pixel
      // from the screen

      // Is the particle out of bounds?

      if ( (xval < 0) || (xval > XRes) || (yval < 0) || (yval > YRes) )
        Failure = 1;

      // To speed things up, throw the particle out if it gets too
      // far away from the object

      else {
        PrtRad = IntSqrt(Sqr(xval - CentreX) + Sqr(yval - CentreY)); if
        (PrtRad > Rad + 15.0) Failure = 1;
      }

    }
    if (Failure) Plot(xval, yval, 0);          // Throw out the particle
    else {
      // Check to see If the radius is bigger than the object, and //
      adjust
      PrtRad = IntSqrt(Sqr(xval - CentreX) + Sqr(yval - CentreY));
      if (PrtRad > Rad - 8.0) Rad = PrtRad + 8.0;
      if (Rad > CentreX) Rad = CentreX;
      if (Rad > CentreY) Rad = CentreY;
    }

  }

  Exit_Graphics();
  return 0;
}
```

Listing 4-1. Crystal.C

This program uses the palette functions *Init_Palette* and *Set_Palette* to define the color palette of the display. Recall that the palette determines with what colors the pixel values (normally 0 - 255) are displayed. The variable *PalArray* is of type *Palette_Register* (an array of RGB elements that make up the 8-bit color palette).

The *Init_Graphics* and *Exit_Graphics* functions are both used in this program. Note that mode #0 is 320 x 200 x 256 color and that mode #4 is 1024 x 768 x 256 color. These two modes are the most commonly used by the software in this book because they are the fastest operating modes of the SVGA card.

Crystal.C makes extensive use of the *GetPixel()* function to determine whether the current pixel's neighbors are drawn.

The Plants.C File

This program, shown in Listing 4.2, provides a simple growth model of coral and grass. This model assumes there is an even source of light coming directly from above the ground. The model determines whether a potential plant growth is blocked from the sun by an existing growth. The program scans the column above the plant "pixel" to see if any other plant pixels have been set. If they have, then the potential growth does not occur, and further branching from this point does not occur. If light reaches the potential growth point, the plant grows toward the light by adding both a random vertical offset and a random horizontal offset (a two-dimensional branching effect). The random vertical growth (referred to as "reaching") pulls the growth toward the sky (light source). Growth starts by placing "seed" growths in the first row (the bottom of the screen) and applying the basic growth rule successive times. This type of algorithm is a form of cellular automata (linear and open).

```
/*
```

```
                     Plant Growth Simulation
         Plants.C = simulation of plant growth with light source above
              Requires: BkDefs.H, BkGlobs.H, BkMath.H, BkMath.C,
                            BkGraph.H, BkGraph.C
         Copyright 1988,1992 Christopher D. Watkins and Stephen B. Coy
                    (Translation to C by Addison Rose)
                         ALL RIGHTS RESERVED
```

```
*/
#include "stdio.h"
#include "dos.h"
#include "string.h"
```

PHOTOREALISM AND RAY TRACING IN C

```
#include "BkDefs.H"
#include "BkGlobs.H"
#include "BkMath.H"
#include "BkGraph.H"


int Polyps = 2;
int EqNo = 1;
int Color = 191;
int Delta1 = 1;
int Delta2 = 1;
int Delta3 = 1;

int MaxColumn = 1023;
int StartColumn = 511;
int StartRow = 750;

int Height[1024];
int Column;
int Row, MaxRow;
int Growing = 1;

Palette_Register PalArray;


main()
{
    InitRand(12.149);

    Init_Graphics(4);

    Init_Palette(PalArray);
    Set_Palette(PalArray);


    // initialize Height array for (Column = 0;
    Column <= MaxColumn; Column++)
      Height[Column] = -1;
    Height[StartColumn] = 0;

    switch (EqNo) {
      case 1 :
        for (Column = 2; Column <= Polyps; Column++)
          Height[RandInt(MaxColumn - 100) + 50] = 0; break;
      case 2 :
        for (Column = 35; Column <= (MaxColumn - 35); Column++)
```

```
          Height[Column] = 0; break;
      case 3 :
        for (Column = 35; Column <= (MaxColumn - 35); Column++) {
          Row = StartRow - Round(30 * SinD(Column / 100) ) + 30; Plot(Col-
          umn, Row, Color);
          Height[Column] = Row;
        }
        break;
      case 4 :
        for (Column = 15; Column <= (MaxColumn - 15); Column++)
          Height[Column] = Round(Column / 4); break;
    }

  while (Growing) {

    Column = RandInt(MaxColumn-2)+1;
    if ( (Height[Column-1] > -1) || (Height[Column+1] > -1) ) {

      // grow
      MaxRow = 0;

      if (Height[Column-1] > MaxRow)
        MaxRow = Height[Column-1] - RandInt(Delta1);

      if (Height[Column]  > MaxRow)
        MaxRow = Height[Column  ] - RandInt(Delta2);

      if (Height[Column+1] > MaxRow)
        MaxRow = Height[Column+1] - RandInt(Delta1);

      Height[Column] = MaxRow + Delta3;
      Row = StartRow - Height[Column];

      Plot(Column, Row, Color);
                                                    // halt if: top
      if ((Height[Column] == StartRow) ||           // of screen or
          (Column < 4) || (Column > MaxColumn-4) || // sides of
          kbhit() )                                 // screen or key
        Growing = 0;                                // pressed
    }
  }

  Exit_Graphics();
  return 0;
}
```

Listing 4-2. Plants.C

This program uses all of the same functions as Crystal.C. The *Init_Graphics* and *Exit_Graphics* routines, the *Init_Palette* and *Set_Palette* function, and the *InitRand* and *RandInt* functions are all used.

The Stars-3D.C Program

The Stars-3D.C program shown in Listing 4-3 creates the sensation of flying through a starfield. It accomplishes this by creating a one-dimensional array, where each element of the array holds the three-dimensional coordinate of a given star. All stars begin at a great distance from you. The flythrough effect is achieved by fixing the position of the viewer and moving all of the stars back at you at varying rates with perspective projection. The x and y coordinates of the stars remain fixed, while the z coordinate moves in the direction of the viewer at varying rates. Notice that as the stars get closer to you, they get brighter. When a star passes by you, its position is reset to a distance far in front of you, so that it can come back to you again as a new star. Also notice that the stars seem to speed up as they get closer to you. This effect is produced with the perspective projection calculations.

```
/*



              3-D Starfield Simulation
   Stars-3D.C. = 3-D simulation of flying through a starfield
        Requires: BkDefs.h BkGlobs.H, BkMath.H, BkMath.C,
                  BkGraph.H, BkGraph.C
   Copyright 1988,1992 Christopher D. Watkins and Stephen B. Coy
             (Translation to C by Larry Sharp)
                  ALL RIGHTS RESERVED



*/

#include <stdio.h>
#include <stdlib.h>
#include <dos.h>
#include <conio.h>
#include <math.h>
#include <string.h>

#include "BkDefs.H"
#include "BkGlobs.H"
```

```
#include "BkMath.H"
#include "BkGraph.H"


#define cblk 0
#define laststar 250
#define infinity -1000
#define windshield 400
#define minbright 24
#define maxbright 63
#define bitshifts 10
#define intscaling (1<<bitshifts)
#define brightness
Trunc((float)(maxbright-minbright)/(float)(windshield-
infinity)*(float)intscaling)
#define shiprange 35

typedef struct {
  int xpos;
  int ypos;
  int zpos;
  int zn;
  Byte rate;
  Byte hue;
} startype;

startype star[laststar+1]; Byte
color; Word i; Word starnum;
Palette_Register Pal_Array;

void ship(int x, int y, int z, Byte c) {
  Cartesian_Plot_3D(x, y, z, c);
  Cartesian_Plot_3D(x+1, y, z, c);
  Cartesian_Plot_3D(x-1, y, z, c);
  Cartesian_Plot_3D(x, y+1, z, c);
  Cartesian_Plot_3D(x, y-1, z, c);
  Cartesian_Plot_3D(x, y, z+1, c);
  Cartesian_Plot_3D(x, y, z-1, c);
}

void main()
{
  Init_Graphics(1);

  Init_Palette(Pal_Array);
  Set_Palette(Pal_Array);
```

```
Init_Perspective(true, 0, 0, 450, 500);
Init_Plotting(0, 90);

Put_Axis_And_Palette(false);
randomize();

for(i=0; i<=laststar; i++) {
  star[i].xpos=random(windshield<<1)-windshield;
  star[i].ypos=random(windshield<<1)-windshield;
  star[i].zpos=infinity;
  star[i].zn=star[i].zpos;
  star[i].rate=random(8)+5;
  star[i].hue=random(4)*64;
}
starnum=0;
do
{
  /*  Clear Old Star Position  */

  /*  note that if the star falls in the box
      (-shiprange,-shiprange,shiprange,shiprange) then it's a ship */

  if((star[starnum].xpos<-shiprange)||
     (star[starnum].ypos<-shiprange)||
     (star[starnum].xpos>shiprange) ||
     (star[starnum].ypos>shiprange))
    Cartesian_Plot_3D(star[starnum].xpos,
                      star[starnum].ypos,
                      star[starnum].zn, cblk);
  else
    ship(star[starnum].xpos, star[starnum].ypos, star[starnum].zn, cblk);

  if(star[starnum].zpos>windshield)
  {
    /* If Star is Past Windshield Then */
    /* Remove Star and Create Another  */

    star[starnum].xpos=random(windshield<<1)-windshield;
    star[starnum].ypos=random(windshield<<1)-windshield;
    star[starnum].zpos=infinity;
    star[starnum].rate=random(8)+5;
  }
  else
  {
    /* Else Update the Star Position */
    /*                 and Intensity */
```

```
      color=star[starnum].hue+minbright+(brightness*
      (star[starnum].zpos-infinity)))>>bitshifts;

      if((star[starnum].xpos<-shiprange)||
         (star[starnum].ypos<-shiprange)||
         (star[starnum].xpos>shiprange)||
         (star[starnum].ypos>shiprange))
         Cartesian_Plot_3D(star[starnum].xpos,
                           star[starnum].ypos,
                           star[starnum].zpos,color);
      else
         ship(star[starnum].xpos, star[starnum].ypos, star[starnum].zpos,
         color);

      star[starnum].zn=star[starnum].zpos;
      star[starnum].zpos=star[starnum].zpos + star[starnum].rate;
   }
   starnum=(starnum+1)%(laststar+1);
  }
  while(!kbhit());
  Exit_Graphics();
}
```

Listing 4-3. Stars-3D.C

All of the two-dimensional palette and initialization routines in this program are the same as in Crystal.C and Plants.C. However, this program adds some three-dimensional functions. The functions *Init_Plotting* and *Init_Perspective* allow for setup of the three-dimensional world. With *Init_Perspective* set to *True* for perspective projection, and the viewing position in three-dimensional space selected by *Init_Plotting*, *Cartesian_Plot3_D* allows you to project a three-dimensional point onto the two-dimensional screen with perspective. After each frame is drawn, the program checks to see if any of the stars have flown past the viewer position. If they have, they are moved back to their starting positions to produce a continuous motion effect. You can make several interesting enhancements to this program by reversing the motion, not erasing the old star positions for "warp" speed effects, changing the colors of the stars, etc.

The Three-Dimensional Orbit Simulation Sample Program

The 3D-3POrb.C program shown in Listing 4-4 simulates particle motion in three-dimensional space (in this case, three particles). The particles are given initial positions, velocities, and accelerations, and they are allowed to interact with one another through time. The basic procedure for simulating motion is to erase the current position of the particles, compute their new positions, and then redraw them. If the code that erases the old positions of the particles is removed (or commented out), the resulting display shows the trails (or paths) of the particles.

This program uses a simple physical model of particle motion and mutual interaction. Theoretically, a particle that is in motion continues to move in the same direction until a force is applied in some other direction. If, instead, the particle is moving along a circular path at a constant velocity, a changing velocity occurs toward the center of the circular path (a force is required to keep the particle moving in a circle). Changing velocity is referred to as *acceleration*, and this acceleration for circular motion is:

$$a = \frac{v^2}{r}$$

(Equation 4-1)

where a is acceleration, v is velocity, and r is the radius of the circular orbit. By Newton's second law of motion, force equals mass times acceleration. Therefore,

$$F = ma = \frac{mv^2}{r}$$

(Equation 4-2)

This force is called *centripetal force* and is the force acting toward the center of the circular path. This centripetal force keeps the particle orbiting about another particle. In effect, this force is the same as gravity. In the three-dimensional case, each object in the system is given a position (x_n, y_n, z_n) and a mass (m_n), where n indicates the number of the object. Object positions and the distances between them are measured in meters and the masses are measured in kilograms. The distance between the two objects is the length of the line that connects them. Using the (X,Y,Z) Cartesian coordinate system, the distances are

$$d_x = |x_2 - x_1|$$
$$d_y = |y_2 - y_1|$$
$$d_z = |z_2 - z_1|$$

(Equation 4-3)

The magnitude of the distance vector (d_x, d_y, d_z) is

$$d = \sqrt{d_x^2 + d_y^2 + d_z^2}$$
(Equation 4-4)

Now the gravitational force between the particles can be calculated using the Law of Universal Gravitation. This law states that the force caused by gravity, F_g, is directly proportional to the product of the masses $(m_1 * m_2)$ and inversely proportional to the distance (d) between them squared. The Gravitational Constant of Proportionality (g) has the value of 6.67E-11 (Nm/kg). The resulting equation is

$$F_g = g = \frac{m_1 m_2}{d^2}$$
(Equation 4-5)

This attractive force is along the direction of the line connecting the two objects. The force here is a vector quantity, having both magnitude and direction. Its components are F_x, F_y, and F_z.

Next consider a system of particles. Most orbiting patterns generated by the program here do not remain in equilibrium for a long period of time. Sooner or later, a particle picks up enough momentum to escape the orbiting pattern, or is pulled in by another mass.

Combining the equations for acceleration and gravitational force yields

$$a_{x1} = \frac{gm_2}{d^2} \times \frac{d_x}{d}$$

$$a_{y1} = \frac{gm_2}{d^2} \times \frac{d_y}{d}$$
(Equation 4-6)

$$a_{z1} = \frac{gm_2}{d^2} \times \frac{d_z}{d}$$

Since acceleration is the change in velocity with respect to the change in time, the following equations are obtained:

$$dv_x = a_x t$$
(Equation 4-7)
$$dv_y = a_y t$$
$$dv_z = a_z t$$

Given the initial velocity v_0, and traveling through time to time t, the new vector velocity is

$$v_x = v_{x0} + a_x t$$
$$v_y = v_{y0} + a_y t$$
$$v_z = v_{z0} + a_z t$$

(Equation 4-8)

Thus, the velocity at the end of the time interval is $v_0 + at$. You can approximate the average velocity throughout the time interval using the following equation:

$$v_{avg} = \frac{v_0 + v_0 + at}{2} = v_0 + at$$

(Equation 4-9)

Since the orbit simulator must show the positions of the particles as the time changes, you need a set of equations that relate position to time. Since the velocity is the rate of change of position with respect to time (over any time interval), the change in position is the average velocity multiplied by the time.

$$d_x = v_{x0} t + \frac{a_x t^2}{2}$$
$$d_y = v_{y0} t + \frac{a_y t^2}{2}$$
$$d_z = v_{z0} t + \frac{a_z t^2}{2}$$

(Equation 4-10)

Because you know the initial position (x_0, y_0, z_0), the position for any time is

$$x = x_0 + v_{x0} t + \frac{a_x t^2}{2}$$
$$y = y_0 + v_{y0} t + \frac{a_y t^2}{2}$$
$$z = z_0 + v_{z0} t + \frac{a_z t^2}{2}$$

(Equation 4-11)

With this mathematical background, you can understand the 3D-3POrb.C program shown in Listing 4-4. The preceding discussion centered on the dynamics of two particles in two-dimensional space. This program handles three particles in three-dimensional space. If you compare the discussion with the existing code, you find that there is only a slight difference in the exponent in the denominator for the calculation of *(d)*. You also discover that all possible combinations of one particle's effect on another particle are handled (that is, each particle interacts with every other particle).

```
/*

      3-D Three Particle Orbit Simulation
   3D-3POrb C = 3-D simulation of three orbiting particles
     Requires: BkDefs.H, BkGlobs.H, BkMath.H, BkMath.C,
               BkGraph.H, BkGraph.C
   Copyright 1988,1992 Christopher D. Watkins and Stephen B. Coy
               ALL RIGHTS RESERVED

   increase time step "dt" to greater than zero to increase speed */

#include "stdio.h"
#include "conio.h"
#include "math.h"

#include "BkDefs.H"
#include "BkGlobs.H"
#include "BkMath.H"
#include "BkGraph.H"


float X1, Y1, Z1, Vx1, Vy1, Vz1, Ax1, Ay1, Az1;
float X2, Y2, Z2, Vx2, Vy2, Vz2, Ax2, Ay2, Az2;
float X3, Y3, Z3, Vx3, Vy3, Vz3, Ax3, Ay3, Az3;
float D12, D23, D31, dt;
float Dx12, Dx23, Dx31;
float Dy12, Dy23, Dy31;
float Dz12, Dz23, Dz31;
float Tx12, Tx23, Tx31;
float Ty12, Ty23, Ty31;
float Tz12, Tz23, Tz31;
int Xp1, Yp1, Zp1, Xp2, Yp2, Zp2, Xp3, Yp3, Zp3;
int M1, M2, M3;
float s;
Palette_Register PalArray;
```

```
void main()
{
  Init_Graphics(4);

  Init_Palette_2(PalArray);
  Set_Palette(PalArray);

  Init_Perspective(false, 0, 0, 500, 500);
  Init_Plotting(190, 25);

  Put_Axis_And_Palette(true);
  Axis_And_Palette();


  M1=1;
  M2=6;
  M3=4;
  X1=-40.0;      Y1= 0.0;       Z1= 0.0;
  X2= 0.0;       Y2= 0.0;       Z2= 0.0;
  X3= 90.0;      Y3= 0.0;       Z3= 0.0;
  Vx1= 0.1010;   Vy1= 0.2500;   Vz1=-0.0240;
  Vx2= 0.0010;   Vy2= 0.0010;   Vz2=-0.0440;
  Vx3=-0.0200;   Vy3=-0.1010;   Vz3= 0.1240;
  dt=0.1;
  s=1.0;



  do
  {
// the next three lines of code remove the trails so that you see
// only the particles; comment these lines out to see particle trails

//    Cartesian_Plot_3D(X1*s, Y1*s, Z1*s, 0);
//    Cartesian_Plot_3D(X2*s, Y2*s, Z2*s, 0);
//    Cartesian_Plot_3D(X3*s, Y3*s, Z3*s, 0);

    X1+=Vx1*dt;
    Y1+=Vy1*dt;
    Z1+=Vz1*dt;

    X2+=Vx2*dt;
    Y2+=Vy2*dt;
    Z2+=Vz2*dt;

    X3+=Vx3*dt;
    Y3+=Vy3*dt;
```

```
Z3+=Vz3*dt;

    Cartesian_Plot_3D(X1*s, Y1*s, Z1*s, 143);
    Cartesian_Plot_3D(X2*s, Y2*s, Z2*s, 169);
    Cartesian_Plot_3D(X3*s, Y3*s, Z3*s, 205);

    Dx12=X1-X2;
    Dy12=Y1-Y2;
    Dz12=Z1-Z2;

    Dx23=X2-X3;
    Dy23=Y2-Y3;
    Dz23=Z2-Z3;

    Dx31=X3-X1;
    Dy31=Y3-Y1;
    Dz31=Z3-Z1;

    D12=sqrt(SqrFP(Dx12)+SqrFP(Dy12)+SqrFP(Dz12));
    D12=1.0/(D12*D12*D12);

    D23=sqrt(SqrFP(Dx23)+SqrFP(Dy23)+SqrFP(Dz23));
    D23=1.0/(D23*D23*D23);

    D31=sqrt(SqrFP(Dx31)+SqrFP(Dy31)+SqrFP(Dz31));
    D31=1.0/(D31*D31*D31);

    Tx31=Dx31*D31;
    Ty31=Dy31*D31;
    Tz31=Dz31*D31;

    Tx12=Dx12*D12;
    Ty12=Dy12*D12;
    Tz12=Dz12*D12;

    Tx23=Dx23*D23;
    Ty23=Dy23*D23;
    Tz23=Dz23*D23;

    Ax1=(M3*Tx31-M2*Tx12);
    Ay1=(M3*Ty31-M2*Ty12);
    Az1=(M3*Tz31-M2*Tz12);

    Ax2=(M1*Tx12-M3*Tx23);
    Ay2=(M1*Ty12-M3*Ty23);
    Az2=(M1*Tz12-M3*Tz23);
```

117

```
    Ax3=(M2*Tx23-M1*Tx31);
    Ay3=(M2*Ty23-M1*Ty31);
    Az3=(M2*Tz23-M1*Tz31);

    Vx1+=Ax1*dt;
    Vy1+=Ay1*dt;
    Vz1+=Az1*dt;

    Vx2+=Ax2*dt;
    Vy2+=Ay2*dt;
    Vz2+=Az2*dt;

    Vx3+=Ax3*dt;
    Vy3+=Ay3*dt;
    Vz3+=Az3*dt;
  }
  while(!(kbhit()));

  Exit_Graphics();
}
```

Listing 4-4. The 3D-3POrb.C Program

The program begins by establishing initial conditions (masses, positions, velocities, and accelerations) for all the particles. The time step is set to a constant. This
step can be any real number greater than 0 (moving forward in time). Particles can
move faster with a larger step, but the program will lose accuracy in position. A
loop is now entered that terminates by a keystroke. Within the loop, the particle
positions are converted to display coordinates, and points are plotted at each particle position. Next, the program computes the new position coordinates for each particle after a step in time. Once the new distances between each set of particles are
computed, the program uses them in the gravity equation to compute the effective
force on the particle. This force then generates the new accelerations and velocities. The program continuously loops, plotting positions and erasing old positions,
until a key is pressed. You may want to remove the erasures of the old positions so
that you can plot particle trails. Several sets of initial conditions are stored in the
program itself. Some of these data sets are "commented out," and to access them
you must "comment out" the active set and "uncomment out" the desired set. You
must recompile and link the program with each new set of initial conditions.

The Real Thing

Having explored some of the ways in which the graphics modules may be used, you are now ready for Part II of this book, where you meet Bob, an image-rendering star. All the modules discussed here are used extensively by Bob to create startlingly realistic imagery. Chapter 5 discusses the modules for vector and matrix manipulation. Subsequent chapters discuss the modules of the ray tracer and the theoretical basis of how this "magic" occurs.

Ray Tracing

CHAPTER 5

Ray Tracer Math Modules

Before examining the ray tracing program, you must first understand five code modules that comprise the foundation of Bob. These modules are Config.H, Defs.H, Proto.H, Extern.H, and Vector.C.

The Config.H module contains compiler-specific information, such as special definitions for the Watcom compiler. The module also contains information that is specific to Bob, for example, setting up such environmental constants as ray sampling counts for shooting multiple rays to light sources. Parser token counts and a random-number generator used by Bob are also included in Config.H. Listing 5-1 displays the code for the Config.H module.

```
/*
```

```
                        Bob-Ray Tracer
           Config.H = Configuration Specific Material
                     Copyright 1988-1992
            by Christopher D. Watkins & Stephen B. Coy
                     ALL RIGHTS RESERVED
```

```
*/

/* OS and compiler specific garbage */

#define index      strchr
#define rindex     strrchr

#ifdef __WATCOMC__

#define mktemp   tmpnam

#endif

/* Bob specific garbage */
```

```
#define   NSLABS         (3)
#define   BUNCHINGFACTOR (4)
#define   PQSIZE         (1000)

#define   L_SAMPLES      (8)        /* default # samples for spherical lights */
#define   MIN_LIGHT      (0.005)    /* min spotlight size */

#define   F_SAMPLES      (8)        /* default # samples for depth of field */

#define   MAXLEVEL       (20)       /* max recursion level, start at 0 */
#define   MINWEIGHT      (0.0001)   /* min weight for a ray to be considered */

#define   MAX_TOKEN      (80)       /* max token length */
#define   MAX_PARAMS     (10)       /* max number of parameters for file */

#define   NLAMBDA        (3)        /* not used anywhere */

/*************************************************************
 * If your compiler doesn't grok the void type, then define
 * NO_VOID here...
 *************************************************************/

#ifdef     NO_VOID
#define    void          char
#endif     /* NO_VOID */

/*************************************************************\
 *       random numbers anyone?  Returns a double 0.0 .. 1.0
\*************************************************************/

#define rnd()   (((double) rand())/RAND_MAX)
```

Listing 5-1. Config.H

The Defs.H module defines several macros, including many of the mathematical functions required by Bob. Here, all structures are type-defined, many flags are initialized, and routines such as *RayPoint* are also defined. Examine this module carefully as it will make understanding the rest of the material in this book much easier. Listing 5-2 contains the code for this module. Note that Defs.H includes Config.H as well.

```
/*

┌─────────────────────────────────────────────────────────────────┐
│                          Bob-Ray Tracer                           │
│                Defs.H = The center of all confusion               │
│                      Dependencies: Config.H                       │
│     Copyright 1988-1992 by Christopher D. Watkins and Stephen B. Coy │
│                        ALL RIGHTS RESERVED                        │
└─────────────────────────────────────────────────────────────────┘
*/


#include "config.h"

#ifdef     HUGE
#undef     HUGE
#endif

#define HUGE     (1.0e8)

/*
    generic helpful macros
*/

#define ABS(a)       (((a)<0)?(-(a)):(a))
#define FLOOR(a)     ((a)>0?(int)(a):-(int)(a))
#define CEILING(a)   ((a)==(int)(a)?(a):(a)>0?1+(int)(a):-(1+(int)(-a)))
#define ROUND(a)     ((a)>0?(int)((a)+0.5):-(int)(0.5-a))

#define MIN(a,b)     (((a)<(b))?(a):(b))
#define MAX(a,b)     (((a)>(b))?(a):(b))

/*
    typedefs for the world
*/

typedef double    Flt;
typedef Flt       Vec[3];
typedef Vec       Point;
typedef Vec       Color;
typedef Flt       Matrix[4][4];

/*─────────────────────────────────────*/

/* Some machines can't handle all the vector operations, so if we define
DUMB_CPP, we replace them with equivalent function calls */

#ifndef DUMB_CPP

#define MakeVector(x, y, z, v)        (v)[0]=(x),(v)[1]=(y),(v)[2]=(z)
```

125

```
#define VecNegate(a)        (a)[0]=(-(a)[0]);\
                            (a)[1]=(-(a)[1]);\
                            (a)[2]=(-(a)[2]);
#define VecDot(a,b)         ((a)[0]*(b)[0]+(a)[1]*(b)[1]+(a)[2]*(b)[2])
#define VecLen(a)           (sqrt(VecDot(a,a)))
#define VecCopy(a,b)        (b)[0]=(a)[0];(b)[1]=(a)[1];(b)[2]=(a)[2];
#define VecAdd(a,b,c)       (c)[0]=(a)[0]+(b)[0];\
                            (c)[1]=(a)[1]+(b)[1];\
                            (c)[2]=(a)[2]+(b)[2]
#define VecSub(a,b,c)       (c)[0]=(a)[0]-(b)[0];\
                            (c)[1]=(a)[1]-(b)[1];\
                            (c)[2]=(a)[2]-(b)[2]
#define VecComb(A,a,B,b,c)  (c)[0]=(A)*(a)[0]+(B)*(b)[0];\
                            (c)[1]=(A)*(a)[1]+(B)*(b)[1];\
                            (c)[2]=(A)*(a)[2]+(B)*(b)[2]
#define VecS(A,a,b)         (b)[0]=(A)*(a)[0];\
                            (b)[1]=(A)*(a)[1];\
                            (b)[2]=(A)*(a)[2]
#define VecAddS(A,a,b,c)    (c)[0]=(A)*(a)[0]+(b)[0];\
                            (c)[1]=(A)*(a)[1]+(b)[1];\
                            (c)[2]=(A)*(a)[2]+(b)[2]
#define VecMul(a,b,c)       (c)[0]=(a)[0]*(b)[0];\
                            (c)[1]=(a)[1]*(b)[1];\
                            (c)[2]=(a)[2]*(b)[2]
#define VecCross(a,b,c)     (c)[0]=(a)[1]*(b)[2]-(a)[2]*(b)[1];\
                            (c)[1]=(a)[2]*(b)[0]-(a)[0]*(b)[2];\
                            (c)[2]=(a)[0]*(b)[1]-(a)[1]*(b)[0]
#define VecZero(v)          (v)[0]=0.0;(v)[1]=0.0;v[2]=0.0
#define VecPrint(msg,v)     fprintf(stderr, "%s: %g %g %g\n", msg,\
                            (v)[0],(v)[1],(v)[2])

#endif /* not DUMB_CPP */

/*————————————————————*/

typedef struct Ray {
    Point P;
    Point D;
} Ray;

#define RayPoint(ray,t,point)    VecAddS(t,(ray)->D,(ray)->P,point)

/*
    texture map structure
*/

typedef struct t_texmap {
```

```
       Vec    position    /* upper left hand corner of image */
              normal,     /* same as projection direction */
              across,     /* across top of image to upper right */
              down;       /* down to lower left */
       Flt    scale;      /* defaults to 1.0, #units across full image */
       int    xres, yres; /* image size */
       unsigned char
         **red,
         **grn,
         **blu;
} Texmap;

/* surface structure */

typedef struct t_surface {
    Color   diff;                   /* diffuse */
    Texmap  *tm_diff;
    Color   spec;                   /* specular (reflected) */
    Texmap  *tm_spec;
    Color   amb;                    /* ambient */
    Texmap  *tm_amb;
    Flt     shine;                  /* specular spot exponent */
    Color   cshine;                 /* spec spot color */
    Color   trans;                  /* transparency */
    Texmap  *tm_trans;
    Flt     ior;                    /* index of refraction */
    Flt     fuzz;                   /* surface fuzz */
    int     flags;                  /* is this surface valid for shadow
caching */
    struct t_texture   *tex;        /* ptr for color texture */
    struct t_bump      *bump;       /* ptr for surface normal texture */
    Matrix  matrix;                 /* transformation matrix */
} Surface;

/* surface flags */

#define S_CACHE        (0x0001)
#define S_NO_ANTIALIAS (0x0002)
#define S_TRANSFORM    (0x0004)

#define S_TM_DIFF      (0x0008)
#define S_TM_SPEC      (0x0010)
#define S_TM_TRANS     (0x0020)
#define S_TM_AMB       (0x0040)
#define S_TM_MAPPING   (0x0078)  /* all bits for mapping */

typedef struct t_turbulence {
```

```
        int          term           /* # of terms in the series */
        Vec          trans,         /* pre-process numbers */
                     scale;
        Flt          amp;           /* post turbulence amplification */
} Turbulence;

typedef struct t_wave {
        Vec          center;
        Flt          wavelength,
                     amp,           /* should be about 0 to .6 */
                     damp,          /* damping per wavelength */
                     phase;         /* wavelength offset */
        struct       t_wave   *next /* next wave in line */
} Wave;


typedef struct t_texture {
        Flt          (*func)();     /* returns 0.0..1.0 */
        Flt          blur;          /* % blending between layers */
        Flt          fuzz;          /* white noise blending */
        Flt          r1, r2;        /* just because */
        int          terms;         /* for tex_noise() */
        Vec          trans,
                     scale;
        Surface      *surf[2];
        Turbulence   *turbulence;
        Wave         *waves;
} Texture;

typedef struct t_bump {
        Vec          trans,         /* apply to resulting normal */
                     scale;
        Turbulence   *turbulence;
        Wave         *waves;
} Bump;

typedef struct t_stack {
        void         *what;
        struct t_stack *prev;
} Stack;

typedef struct t_infile {
        char         *file_name;
        FILE         *fp;
        long         line;
        struct t_infile *next;
} Infile;
```

```
/*     light type constants */

#define L_DIRECTIONAL    (1)
#define L_POINT          (2)
#define L_SPHERICAL      (3)
#define L_SPOT           (4)


/*      light illumination constants */

#define L_INFINITE       (0)
#define L_R              (1)
#define L_R_SQUARED      (2)


/*      misc light flags */

#define L_NOSHADOWS      (1)
#define L_NOSPEC         (2)

typedef struct t_light {
    Vec       position;
    Vec       dir;
    Color     color;
    Flt       radius;         /* radius/spherical, max_angle/spotlight */
    Flt       min_angle,      /* angles for spot lights */
              max_angle;
    short     type;           /* what type is this? */
    short     illum;          /* how does the light fall off? */
    short     flag;           /* noshadows? nospec? */
    short     samples;        /* num samples for spherical light */
    struct    t_object *light_obj_cache[MAXLEVEL];
    struct    t_light  *next;  /* next light in list */
} Light;

typedef struct t_viewpoint {
    Vec    view_from;
    Vec    view_at;
    Vec    view_up;
    Flt    view_angle_x;
    Flt    view_angle_y;
    Flt    view_aspect;
} Viewpoint;

typedef struct t_camera {
    short    projection;
    Vec      lens_i,          /* vectors across lens */
             lens_j;
    Flt      aperture,        /* radius of lens */
```

```
            focal_length;    /* how far away are we focussed */
    short   samples;         /* num samples for non-pinhole camera */
} Camera;

/*
    Clipping
*/

#define C_PLANE      (0x01)
#define C_SPHERE     (0x02)
#define C_CONE       (0x04)
#define C_INSIDE     (0x10)

typedef struct t_clip {
    Vec     center,
            normal,
            apex, base;
    Flt     radius1, radius2, length;
    int     type;
    struct t_clip   *next;
} Clip;

typedef struct t_global_clip {
    Clip                    *clip;
    struct t_global_clip    *next;
} GlobalClip;


typedef struct t_object {
    unsigned short     o_type;
    Flt                o_dmin[NSLABS];
    Flt                o_dmax[NSLABS];
    struct t_objectprocs {
        int    (*intersect) ();
        void   (*normal) ();
    } * o_procs;
    Surface            *o_surf;
    void               *o_data;
    Clip               *clips;
    struct t_object *nex   /* next object in original list, sibling */
} Object;

typedef struct t_compositedata {
    unsigned long   size;
    Object          *children;
} CompositeData;
```

```
typedef struct t_objectprocs ObjectProcs;

typedef struct t_isect {
    Flt         isect_t;        /* distance to intersection */
    int         isect_enter;    /* entering? ie hit front? */
    Object      *isect_prim;    /* object we hit */
    Surface     *isect_surf;    /* surface def of hit object */
    Object      *isect_self;    /* pointer to self for queue elimination */
} Isect;

typedef struct t_pixel {
    unsigned char r, g, b, q;
} Pixel;

typedef struct t_transform {
    Matrix                  mat;
    struct t_transform      *next;
} Transform;

typedef unsigned char   Palette[256][3];

typedef struct t_background {
    Color   color;
    Vec     up;
    Palette pal;
} Background;

/* preprocessor macro structure */
typedef struct t_macro {
    char            *macro,     /* define'd word */
                    *text;      /* text to replace macro with */
    int             mlen,       /* length of macro */
                    tlen;       /* length of text */
    struct t_macro  *next;      /* stack link */
} Macro;

#ifndef PI
#define PI          (3.14159265358979323844)
#endif /* PI */

#define degtorad(x)     (((Flt)(x))*PI/180.0)

/* primitive types */

#define      T_COMPOSITE    (0)
#define      T_SPHERE       (1)
#define      T_POLY         (2)
```

```
#define         T_CONE          (3)
#define         T_RING          (4)
#define         T_TRI           (5)
#define         T_FUZZY         (6)

/* camera projections types */

#define         P_FLAT          (0)
#define         P_ORTHOGRAPHIC  (1)
#define         P_FISHEYE       (2)
#define         P_NO_PARALLAX   (3)

/* antialiasing mode */

#define         A_NONE          (0)
#define         A_CORNERS       (1)
#define         A_QUICK         (2)
#define         A_ADAPTIVE      (3)
```

Listing 5-2. Defs.H

The Proto.H module is nothing more than a list of prototypes for the functions found throughout Bob. Notice that comments are added before sets of externs to tell you the other code modules these prototypes are used for. Examine Proto.H in Listing 5-2 for an index to the major functions used in the ray tracer code. Note that Proto.H includes the file Pic.H.

```
/*
    ┌─────────────────────────────────────────────────────────┐
    │                     Bob-Ray Tracer                       │
    │          Proto.H = prototypes for functions              │
    │             Dependencies on: "Pic.H"                     │
    │                Copyright 1988-1992                       │
    │         Christopher D. Watkins & Stephen B. Coy          │
    │                ALL RIGHTS RESERVED                       │
    └─────────────────────────────────────────────────────────┘
*/

/* bound.c */
extern void     BuildBoundingSlabs (void);
extern void     FindAxis (Object *top, long count);
extern int      SortAndSplit (Object **handle, long count);

/* cone.c */
```

```
extern int     ConeIntersect (Object *obj , Ray *ray , Isect *hit);
extern void    ConeNormal (Object *obj , Isect *hit , Point P , Point N);
extern Object    *MakeCone (Vec basepoint , Flt baseradius ,
                            Vec apexpoint , Flt apexradius);


/* data.c */

/* error.c */
extern int     NullIntersect (void);
extern void    NullNormal (void);

/* file.c */
void           init_env(void);
FILE           *env_fopen(char *name, char *mode);

/* inter.c */
extern void    CheckAndEnqueue (Object *obj , Flt maxdist);
extern int     Intersect (Ray *ray , Isect *hit , Flt maxdist , Object
                          *self);

/* main.c */
extern int     main (int argc , char **argv);

/* memory.c */
extern void    *vmalloc(int size);

/* noise.c */
extern void    init_noise (void);
extern Flt     noise1 (Vec p);
extern void    noise3 (Vec p , Flt *v);
extern Flt     turb1 (Vec p , int lvl);
extern void    turb3 (Vec p , Vec v , int lvl);

/* parse.c */
extern int     yyparse (void);

/* pic.c */
#include "pic.h"
extern Pic     *PicOpen (char *filename , int x , int y);
extern void    PicWriteLine (Pic *pic , Pixel *buf);
extern void    PicClose (Pic *pic);

/* poly.c */
extern int     PolyIntersect (Object *obj , Ray *ray , Isect *hit);
extern void    PolyNormal (Object *obj , Isect *hit , Point P , Point N);
extern Object  *MakePoly (int npoints , Vec *points);
```

```
/* pqueue.c */
extern void    PriorityQueueNull (void);
extern int     PriorityQueueEmpty (void);
extern void    PriorityQueueInsert (Flt key , Object *obj);
extern void    PriorityQueueDelete (Flt *key , Object **obj);

/* preproc.c */
extern int     preproc (char *infile , char *outfile);
extern void    expand (char *src);
extern void    sub_macro (Macro *mptr , char *loc);
extern void    add_macro (char *txt);
extern void    remove_macro (char *str);
extern char    *brute (char *text , char *pat , int tlen , int plen);
extern void    clean_up (void);
extern int     vfgets (char *dst , int max_count , FILE *fp);
extern char    *get_next_token (char *text);
extern int     cpy_tok (char *dst , char *src);
extern int     is_tok (int c);

/* ring.c */
extern int     RingIntersect (Object *obj , Ray *ray , Isect *hit);
extern void    RingNormal (Object *obj , Isect *hit ,
                    Point P , Point N);
extern Object  *MakeRing (Vec pos , Vec norm ,
                    Flt min_rad , Flt max_rad);

/* screen.c */
extern void    Screen (Viewpoint *view , char *picfile , int xres ,
                    int yres);
extern void    ScrInit (Viewpoint *view , int xres , int yres ,
                    char *picfile);
extern void    Scan0 (void);
extern void    Scan1 (void);
extern void    Scan2 (void);
extern void    Scan3 (void);
extern void    Scan4 (void);
extern void    Adapt (int i , int j , Flt x , Flt y , Color color ,
                    int step);
extern void    Shoot (Flt x , Flt y , Color color);

/* shade.c */
extern void    Shade (int level , Flt weight , Vec P , Vec N , Vec I ,
                    Isect *hit , Color col , Flt ior);
extern void    reflect (Vec I , Vec N , Vec R, Flt dot);
extern int     refract (Flt eta, Vec I, Vec N, Vec T, Flt dot);

/* shadow.c */
```

```
extern int        Shadow (Ray *ray , Isect *hit , Flt tmax , Color color ,
                      int level , Light *lptr, int inside);
extern int        sShadow (Ray *ray , Isect *hit , Flt tmax , Color
                      color , int level , Light *lptr, int inside);

/* sphere.c */
extern int        SphereIntersect (Object *obj , Ray *ray , Isect *hit);
extern void       SphereNormal (Object *obj , Isect *hit , Point P ,
                      Point N);
extern Object     *MakeSphere (Vec pos , Flt radius , Flt fuzzy);

/* stats.c */
extern void       statistics (int line);
extern void       stat_tic(void);
extern void       init_tic(void);

/* texture.c */
extern Flt        tex_checker (Point P , Texture *tex);
extern Flt        tex_spherical (Point P , Texture *tex);
extern Flt        tex_noise (Point P , Texture *tex);
extern void       tex_fix (Surface *surf , Point P, Point OP);
extern void       map_fix (Surface *surf, Point P);
extern void       tex_project (Texmap *tm, Point OP, Flt *i, Flt *j);
extern void       tile (Texmap *tm, Flt *i, Flt *j);
extern void       get_map_entry (Texmap *tm, Flt i, Flt j, Color color);
extern void       tex_read_img (char *file, Texmap *tm);

/* tokens.c */

/* trace.c */
extern Flt      Trace (int level , Flt weight , Ray *ray , Color color ,
                      Flt ior , Object *self);
extern void       bkg (Vec dir, Color col);

/* tri.c */
extern int        TriIntersect (Object *obj , Ray *ray , Isect *hit);
extern void       TriNormal (Object *obj , Isect *hit , Point P , Point N);
extern Object     *MakeTri (Vec *point);
extern void       InvertMatrix (Vec in [3], Vec out [3]);
extern void       CheckTri (Vec *point);

/* vector.c */
extern Flt        VecNormalize (Vec vec);
extern void       identity (Matrix mat);
extern void       matrix_cat (Matrix m1 , Matrix m2 , Matrix dest);
extern void       trans_vector (Matrix mat , Vec in , Vec out);
extern void       trans_normal (Matrix mat , Vec in , Vec out);
```

135

```
extern void      matrix_inverse (Matrix in , Matrix out);

/* wave.c */
extern void      make_waves (Vec in, Vec out, Wave *head);

/* yystuff.c */
extern int       yyerror (char *str);
extern void      ReadSceneFile (char *real, char *temp);
extern void      ptrchk (void *ptr , char *str);
extern void      yypop_surf (void);
extern void      yystats(void);
extern void      yy_popfile(void);
extern void      yy_newfile(char *file);
extern void      trans_pop(void);

#undef P
```

Listing 5-3. Proto.H

The Extern.H module contained in Listing 5-4 consists of external definitions for all global variables found in Bob. Note that Extern.H includes the prototypes found in Proto.H, and also includes the standard library header files stdlib.H and stdio.H.

```
/*

              Bob-Ray Tracer
     Extern.H = external defs for all globals,
            also include prototypes
            Dependencies = Proto.H
            Copyright 1988-1992
     Christopher D. Watkins & Stephen B. Coy
            ALL RIGHTS RESERVED

*/


#include <stdlib.h>
#include <stdio.h>
#include "proto.h"


extern int           yylinecount;
extern Viewpoint     Eye;
```

```
extern Camera              camera;
extern int                 Xresolution;
extern int                 Yresolution;
extern int                 start_line, stop_line;
extern int                 bunching;

extern int                 antialias;
extern int                 jitter;
extern int                 adapt_dist;

extern Light               *light_head;
extern int                 nLights;
extern int                 no_shadows;
extern int                 caustics;
extern int                 exp_trans;
extern int                 fuzzy_ray;

extern Background          background;
extern Color               Ambient;
extern Color               HazeColor;
extern Flt                 HazeDensity;
extern Surface             *CurrentSurface;
extern Stack               *SurfTop;
extern Stack               *InfileTop;
extern Transform           *TransTop;
extern Clip                *ClipTop;
extern GlobalClip          *GlobalClipTop;
extern long                nPrims;
extern Flt                 rayeps;
extern char                *Progname;
extern char                Infilename[];
extern unsigned long       maxQueueSize;
extern unsigned long       totalQueues;
extern unsigned long       totalQueueResets;
extern int                 tickflag;
extern int                 resume;
extern int                 gr_mode;
extern unsigned long       nChecked;
extern unsigned long       nEnqueued;
extern unsigned long       nShadowCacheHits;

extern Flt                 minweight;
extern int                 maxlevel;
extern int                 deepest;
extern unsigned long       nRays;
extern unsigned long       nShadows;
extern unsigned long       nReflected;
```

```
extern unsigned long    nRefracted;
extern unsigned long    MemAllocated;

extern Vec              Slab[];
extern ObjectProcs      NullProcs;
extern Object           *Root;

extern char             _Copyright[];
extern char             _Program[];
extern char             _Version[];
extern char             _Date[];

extern FILE             *yyin;
extern int              cur_token;
extern char             cur_text[];
extern Flt              cur_value;
```

Listing 5-4. Extern.H

Listing 5-5 shows that the Vector.C module relies on Defs.H and Extern.H for its function.

```
/*
```

```
                        Bob-Ray Tracer
            Vector.C = Vector and Matrix functions for Bob
                    Dependencies = Defs.H, Extern.H
                        Copyright 1988-1992
                Christopher D. Watkins & Stephen B. Coy
                        ALL RIGHTS RESERVED
```

```
*/

#define SIZE    (4)

#include <stdio.h>
#include <math.h>
#include "defs.h"
#include "extern.h"

Flt    VecNormalize(vec)
    Vec    vec;
{
    Flt    len;
    /* len = (Flt)VecLen(vec); */
```

```
    len = VecDot(vec, vec);
    if(ABS(len)>rayeps) {
        len = sqrt(len);
        vec[0] /= len;
        vec[1] /= len;
        vec[2] /= len;
    } else {
        /* printf("%.4f %.4f %.4f == %.4f bummer\n", vec[0], vec[1
                vec[2], len); */
        len = 1.0;
        vec[0] = 1.0;
        vec[1] = 0.0;
        vec[2] = 0.0;
    }
    return(len);
}


void    identity(Matrix mat)
{
    int     i, j;

    for(i=0; i<4; i++)
        for(j=0; j<4; j++)
            if(i==j)
                mat[i][j] = 1.0;
            else
                mat[i][j] = 0.0;
}

void    matrix_cat(Matrix m1, Matrix m2, Matrix dest)
{
    Matrix  m3;
    int     i, j, k;

    for(i=0; i<4; i++) {
        for(j=0; j<4; j++) {
            m3[i][j] = 0;
            for(k=0; k<4; k++) {
                m3[i][j] += m1[i][k] * m2[k][j];
            }
        }
    }
    /* copy results to dest */
    for(i=0; i<4; i++) {
        for(j=0; j<4; j++) {
            dest[i][j] = m3[i][j];
```

```
        }
    }
}

void    trans_vector(Matrix mat, Vec in, Vec out)
{
    Flt     in4[4], out4[4];
    int     i, j;

    in4[0] = in[0];
    in4[1] = in[1];
    in4[2] = in[2];
    in4[3] = 1.0;

    for(i=0; i<4; i++) {
        out4[i] = 0.0;
        for(j=0; j<4; j++) {
            out4[i] += mat[j][i] * in4[j];
        }
    }
    out[0] = out4[0]/out4[3];
    out[1] = out4[1]/out4[3];
    out[2] = out4[2]/out4[3];
}       /* end of trans_vector */

void    trans_normal(Matrix mat, Vec in, Vec out)
{
    Vec     t1, t2;         /* tangent vectors */
    Vec     orig;           /* imaginary center */
    Flt     dot;

    VecNormalize(in);

    MakeVector(0.0, 0.0, 0.0, orig);

    /* create a vector not aligned with in */
    MakeVector(1.0, 0.0, 0.0, t1);
    dot = VecDot(t1, in);
    if(ABS(dot) > 0.8) {
        MakeVector(0.0, 1.0, 0.0, t1);
    }

    VecCross(in, t1, t2);   /* create t2 */
    VecCross(t2, in, t1);   /* create proper t1 */

    /* transform tangents */
```

```
    trans_vector(mat, t1, t1);
    trans_vector(mat, t2, t2);
    trans_vector(mat, orig, orig);

    VecSub(t1, orig, t1);
    VecSub(t2, orig, t2);

    VecCross(t1, t2, out);   /* recreate normal */

}       /* end of trans_vector */

/*
    matrix_inverse() — creates the inverse of a 4x4 matrix.
*/

void    matrix_inverse(Matrix m, Matrix n)
{
    Matrix  y;
    int     i, j, indx[4];
    double  d, col[4];

    matrix_copy(m, n);                    /* save original matrix */
    ludcmp(n, indx, &d);                  /* matrix lu decomposition */

    for (j = 0; j < SIZE; j++) {          /* matrix inversion */
        for (i = 0; i < SIZE; i++) {
            col[i] = 0.0;
        }
        col[j] = 1.0;
        lubksb(n, indx, col);
        for (i = 0;i < SIZE;i++) {
            y[i][j] = col[i];
        }
    }
    matrix_copy(y, n);
}

/******************************************************************
* lubksb()
* backward substitution
******************************************************************/

lubksb(a, indx, b)
    Matrix  a;              /* input matrix */
    int     *indx;          /* row permutation record */
    Flt     b[];            /* right hand vector (?) */
{
```

```
        int     i, j, ii=-1, ip;
        Flt     sum;

        for (i = 0;i < SIZE;i++) {
            ip = indx[i];
            sum = b[ip];
            b[ip] = b[i];
            if (ii>=0) {
                for (j = ii;j <= i-1;j++) {
                    sum -= a[i][j] * b[j];
                }
            }
            else if (sum != 0.0) {
                ii = i;
            }
            b[i] = sum;
        }
        for (i = SIZE-1;i >= 0;i-) {
            sum = b[i];
            for (j = i+1;j < SIZE;j++) {
                sum -= a[i][j] * b[j];
            }
            b[i] = sum/a[i][i];
        }
}


/******************************************************************
* ludcmp()
* LU decomposition.
******************************************************************/

ludcmp(a, indx, d)
    Matrix  a;                      /* input matrix. gets thrashed */
    int     *indx;                  /* row permutation record */
    Flt     *d;                     /* +/- 1.0 (even or odd # of row
                                       interchanges)*/
{
    Flt     vv[SIZE];               /* implicit scale for each row */
    Flt     big, dum, sum, tmp;
    int     i, imax, j, k;

    *d = 1.0;
    for (i = 0;i < SIZE;i++) {
        big = 0.0;
        for (j = 0;j < SIZE;j++) {
            if ((tmp = fabs(a[i][j])) > big) {
                big = tmp;
```

```
            }
        }
        if (big == 0.0) {
            printf("ludcmp(): singular matrix found...\n");
            exit(1);
        }
        vv[i] = 1.0/big;
    }
    for (j = 0;j < SIZE;j++) {
        for (i = 0;i < j;i++) {
            sum = a[i][j];
            for (k = 0;k < i;k++) {
                sum -= a[i][k] * a[k][j];
            }
            a[i][j] = sum;
        }
        big = 0.0;
        for (i = j;i < SIZE;i++) {
            sum = a[i][j];
            for (k = 0;k < j;k++) {
                sum -= a[i][k]*a[k][j];
            }
            a[i][j] = sum;
            if ((dum = vv[i] * fabs(sum)) >= big) {
                big = dum;
                imax = i;
            }
        }
        if (j != imax) {
            for (k = 0;k < SIZE;k++) {
                dum = a[imax][k];
                a[imax][k] = a[j][k];
                a[j][k] = dum;
            }
            *d = -(*d);
            vv[imax] = vv[j];
        }
        indx[j] = imax;
        if (a[j][j] == 0.0) {
            a[j][j] = 1.0e-20;        /* can be 0.0 also... */
        }
        if (j != SIZE-1) {
            dum = 1.0/a[j][j];
            for (i = j+1;i < SIZE;i++) {
                a[i][j] *= dum;
            }
        }
```

```
        }
    }

matrix_copy(m1, m2)
    Matrix  m1,                     /* source matrix */
        m2;                         /* destination matrix */
{
    int     i,j;

    for (i = 0;i < SIZE;i++) {
        for (j = 0;j < SIZE;j++) {
            m2[i][j] = m1[i][j];
        }
    }
}
#ifdef DUMB_CPP
/*
 * Some machines can't handle all the vector operations, so if we
 * define DUMB_CPP, we replace them with equivalent function calls...
 */

MakeVector(x, y, z, v)
    Flt     x, y, z;
    Vec     v;
{
    v[0] = x; v[1] = y; v[2] = z;
}

VecNegate(v)
    Vec     v;
{
    v[0] = -v[0];
    v[1] = -v[1];
    v[2] = -v[2];
}

Flt     VecDot(a, b)
    Vec a, b;
{
    return a[0] * b[0] + a[1] * b[1] + a[2] * b[2];
}

Flt     VecLen(a)
    Vec     a;
{
    return sqrt(VecDot(a, a));
}
```

```
VecCopy(a, b)
    Vec     a, b;
{
    b[0] = a[0];
    b[1] = a[1];
    b[2] = a[2];
}

VecAdd(a, b, c)
    Vec     a, b, c;
{
    c[0] = a[0] + b[0];
    c[1] = a[1] + b[1];
    c[2] = a[2] + b[2];
}

VecSub(a, b, c)
    Vec     a, b, c;
{
    c[0] = a[0] - b[0];
    c[1] = a[1] - b[1];
    c[2] = a[2] - b[2];
}

VecComb(A, a, B, b, c)
    Flt     A, B;
    Vec     a, b, c;
{
    c[0] = A * a[0] + B * b[0];
    c[1] = A * a[1] + B * b[1];
    c[2] = A * a[2] + B * b[2];
}

VecAddS(A, a, b, c)
    Flt     A;
    Vec     a, b, c;
{
    c[0] = A * a[0] + b[0];
    c[1] = A * a[1] + b[1];
    c[2] = A * a[2] + b[2];
}

VecCross(a, b, c)
    Vec     a, b, c;
{
    c[0] = a[1] * b[2] - a[2] * b[1];
```

```
    c[1] = a[2] * b[0] - a[0] * b[2];
    c[2] = a[0] * b[1] - a[1] * b[0];
}

#endif /* DUMB_CPP */
```

Listing 5-5. Vector.C

Note that many of the modules described throughout this text include Defs.H and Extern.H. Some of the functions found here are similar to functions found in the BkMath.C module described in Chapter 2. Basically, Vector.C is a modified subset of those BkMath.C functions that are required exclusively by the ray tracer. The following is a description of the functions found in Vector.C:

❖ *VecNormalize* is functionally the same as the function with the same name in BkGraph.C. This function normalizes the vector *vec* passed to it.

❖ *identity* creates an identity matrix out of a Matrix-typed variable.

❖ *matrix_cat* multiplies two Matrix-typed variables *m1* and *m2* and outputs a third called *dest*. This function is similar to the *Multiply3DMatrices* function in BkMath.C.

❖ *trans_vector* transforms a vector *in* to a vector *out* (similar to the *Transform* function using the affine transformations found in BkMath.C). Note that a matrix *mat* representing the transformation is passed to this routine.

❖ *trans_normal* transforms a normal vector.

❖ *matrix_inverse* computes the inverse of a four-by-four matrix *m* and outputs it as a new matrix *n*.

❖ *lubksb* is a backward substitution into a matrix.

❖ *ludcmp* is a decomposition function.

❖ *matrix_copy* copies the matrix *m1* into matrix *m2*. This function is the same as *MatCopy* in BkMath.C.

❖ *MakeVector* makes a vector from *x, y,* and *z* and calls it *v*. This function is the same as *Vec* in BkMath.C.

❖ *VecNegate* negates a vector *v* by changing the signs of the x, y, and z components of the vector. This function is the same as *VecNegate* in BkMath.C.

❖ *VecDot* returns the vector dot product of *a* and *b*. This function is the same as *VecDot* in BkMath.C.

❖ *VecLen* returns the length of the vector *a*. This function is the same as *VecLen* in BkMath.C.

❖ *VecCopy* copies vector *a* into vector *b*. This function is the same as *VecCopy* in BkMath.C.

❖ With the *VecAdd* function, vector *c* equals the addition of vectors *a* and *b*. This function is the same as *VecAdd* in BkMath.C.

❖ With the *VecSub* function, vector *c* equals vector *a* minus vector *b*. This function is the same as *VecSub* in BkMath.C.

❖ With the *VecComb* function, vector *c* equals the linear combination of vector *a* with floating-point *A* and vector *b* with floating-point *B*. This function is the same as *VecLinComb* in BkMath.C.

❖ With the *VecAddS* function, vector *c* equals floating-point *A* times each of the components of vector *a*, with the subsequent addition of vector *b*. This function is the same as *VecAddScalMult* in BkMath.C.

❖ With the *VecCross* function, vector *c* is equal to the cross product of vectors *a* and *b*. This function is the same as *VecCross* in BkMath.C.

With this understanding of some of the basic modules required by Bob, you are ready to examine ray tracing and the ray tracing program itself.

CHAPTER 6

Ray Tracing Theory

So far, you have learned about several mathematical tools that would be part of any reasonable graphics toolkit. You are now ready to learn about the production of life-like, entirely computer-generated, no-tricks-up-our-sleeves, graphics imagery. Your primary goal is to produce computer-generated imagery that can pass for photographs of real or imagined objects. Each of the many techniques available to render three-dimensional scenes has its own set of good and bad features. However, only the ray tracing method offers an approach that can truly simulate how a camera (or human eye) might distinguish a scene.

The object of ray tracing is to simulate how light propagates through an environment by tracing light rays through a scene to see which objects they interact with. This technique models the physical properties of light, matter, and the interaction between them. Since you are only concerned with the light rays that eventually reach your eye (or pass through the computer screen), you follow the light rays in reverse.

Rays are followed from the eye, through the "screen," and out into the scene. The rays are *traced* as they are reflected, refracted, diffracted, and focused according to the basic laws of optics. The mathematics used to produce this effect is both elegant and highly modular. Using the vector arithmetic already presented, the ray tracer can produce images of astonishing clarity and beauty.

The "classic" ray tracing algorithm is quite simple. You define the screen as an array of pixels and set up the screen in a viewing geometry as shown in Figure 6-1. For each screen pixel, you generate an initial ray starting at the eyepoint, passing through the screen, and out into some previously defined environment. The environment consists of three-dimensional objects, lights, and background models.

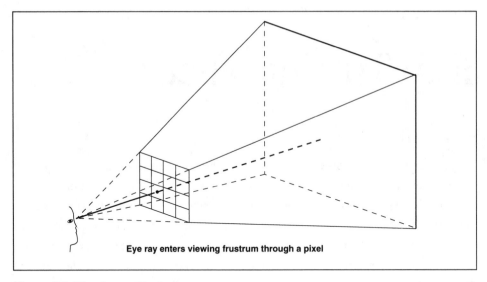

Eye ray enters viewing frustrum through a pixel

Figure 6-1. Viewing geometry

The ray tracing algorithm proceeds as follows:

1. Find the nearest object that the ray intersects (if any) and determine the point of intersection, as shown in Figure 6-2.

2. Calculate the *ambient* color of the object surface at the point of intersection based on the object's characteristics and the light sources.

3. Cast "shadow" rays from the point of intersection to each light source in the scene, as shown in Figure 6-3. These "shadow" rays generate the *diffuse* and *specular* lighting of the surface. The shadow rays also determine whether the point of intersection is shadowed from a light source by an obstructing object, either wholly or partially.

4. If the object surface is reflective, compute a new ray, starting at the intersection point and pointing in the "reflected" direction. Find the effective color of this ray by recursively calling this same procedure.

5. If the object surface is transparent, compute a new transmitted ray, again starting from the intersection point. Find the color of this ray and add it to the color of the other rays.

6. Add the object color to the color of the reflected and transmitted rays, and then return this as the color of the pixel.

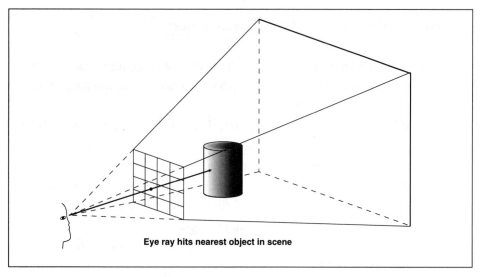

Eye ray hits nearest object in scene

Figure 6-2. Point of intersection

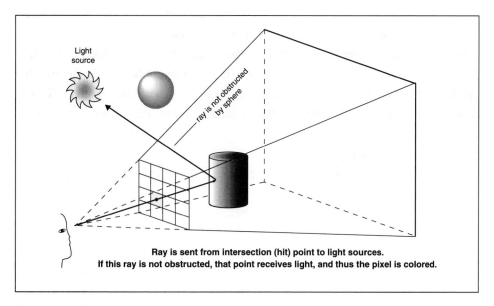

Ray is sent from intersection (hit) point to light sources.
If this ray is not obstructed, that point receives light, and thus the pixel is colored.

Figure 6-3. Shadow rays

This procedure has several interesting properties :

❖ It is inherently recursive, which makes the procedure ideally suited to C and other such languages. Each time a ray is cast, you repeat the procedure with the new ray.
❖ It is based on a mathematical model of how light interacts with objects. You can model how light is reflected and refracted through the scene in more accurate ways that direct projective methods cannot handle.
❖ It is very amenable to parallel processing (that is, having multiple CPUs work on different parts of the picture). Each pixel can be processed independently of the other pixels in the scene.
❖ While elegant, ray tracing computations can sap the resources of the most powerful CPU.

Although ray tracing satisfies the main goal of producing high-quality imagery, it also provides a method for testing our understanding of how light interacts with an environment. Many researchers have adapted their physical models of the interaction between light and matter to ray tracing programs to see if they produce images that look like the real thing. If so, then the researchers can be confident that the theoretical model is an accurate description of the processes that are taking place. This is especially true in modeling complex phenomena such as waves, clouds, and terrain.

Instant Ray Tracing

Listing 6-1 provides a pseudocode representation of the basic ray tracing algorithm.

```
main() {
  Ray *ray;
  long x, y;
  long pixel;
  Color color;
  Point screen_point;



  init_global_variables();  /* Basic initialization*/
  define_environment();     /* Where is everything? */
```

```
    do_precalculations();      /* Set up for rendering */

    for(y=0; y < yscreen; y++) {
      for(x=0; x < xscreen; x++) {

        /*
           Generate first ray from the eye to the position
           x, y on the screen
        */
        screen_point = make_vector_from_screen(x, y);
        ray = new_ray(screen_point, eyepoint);
        trace(ray, &color);
        pixel = color_composite(color);
        output[x, y] = pixel;


      }                          /* End of row */
    }                            /* End of image */

    write_image_to_output_file();
    exit(0);


}                                /* End of Main */

void
trace(ray, colorp)
Vector3D *ray;
Color *colorp;
{
  Isect *intersect;
  Color color, refl_color, trans_color;
  Ray   *shadow_ray, *refl_ray, *trans_ray;
  int   i;

  intersect = find_intersection(ray);
  if(intersect) {
    curobject = intersect->object;
                          /* We intersected an object,
                             so process it */

                          /* First color is the "intrinsic"
                             object color */

    color = curobject->ambient_color +
            (diffuse(curobject, intersection->point) * ambient_light);

    for(i = 0; i < numlights; i++) {
```

```
/*
    For each light, determine if it shadows the
    object, and if so, whether we are completely
    blocked, or only partially
*/

curlight = lights[i];
shadow_ray = new_ray(curlight->position,
                     intersect->position);
shade = shadow(shadow_ray);
color += (curlight->color * shade) *
         curobject->diffuse_color;
spec_color = compute_specular(intersect->point,
                              curlight);
color += spec_color;
free(shadow_ray);

} /* End of loop for all lights */

if(curobject->reflective) {
  /* Surface is reflective, so generate a new ray */
  refl_ray = compute_reflected(ray, curobject,
                               intersect->point,
                               intersect->normal);
  trace(refl_ray, &refl_color);
  color += refl_color * curobject->specular;
  free(refl_ray);
}

if(curobject->transparent) {
    /* Surface is, at least slightly, transparent */
    trans_ray = compute_transmitted(ray, curobject,
                                    intersect->point,
                                    intersect->normal);
trace(trans_ray, &trans_color);
color += trans_color * curobject->transparency;
free(trans_ray);
}

*colorp = color;

} else {  /* No intersections were found, so use
            background */
```

```
    get_background(ray, colorp);
   }


  return;
     /* All Finished, *colorp now contains our color */
  }
```

Listing 6-1. Ray tracing pseudocode

Each of the functions shown in Listing 6-1 is described here and in the next few chapters. This chapter addresses the overall structure. Note that the key function is *trace*, which takes an input ray and a color pointer (the returned color) as arguments. *Trace* is called recursively if the surface is reflective (mirror-like) or at least partially transparent (transmits light). The essence of the ray tracing approach is that you follow a light ray through the environment until each ray moves out of the environment into the background, or it strikes a light source. The process is inherently recursive, as rays are traced from one surface to another. The effective color of each ray is summed at the intersection point to find the color of the surface at that point.

The procedure uses several structures. The *Ray* structure consists of two three-dimensional vectors. The first vector represents the starting point of the ray and the second represents the direction the ray travels. This structure is then passed to the intersect routine to determine the nearest object (if any) that the ray intersects. If the *intersect* structure pointer is 0, then no objects are intersected. In this case, you simply find the background color and return. If the pointer is not 0, then an object was intersected by this ray. The *intersect* structure contains at least the following information:

Point ....(x, y, z) intersection point
Object ....Pointer to the intersected object
Normal ....Vector containing the surface normal at the point of intersection

The *object pointer* allows you to find the various object and surface attributes of the object. The surface attributes tell you whether the object is reflective, transparent, shiny (that is, it has a specular component), as well as other features that may be of interest.

Note that our theoretical procedure has several functions for computing the color at the point of intersection. Chapter 9 provides a complete description of the color model. For now, note that the color is an additive combination of the light hitting the object surface directly (diffuse and specular components) and the light received from other objects (reflections and transparency). The color is also modified by the effects of other objects in the scene creating shadows.

The *shadow* function takes a ray starting from the point of intersection and pointing at a given light source in the scene. The intensity of the light falling onto an object may be completely blocked by another object, partially blocked by a semi-transparent object (or multiple ones), or may be in the *shadow penumbra* (which is the shadow edge caused by diffraction of light around another object). Any and all of these cases can be handled at the cost of additional computation.

The *surface normal* (or *normal*) at a point on an object surface is a vector that defines the direction a surface faces, at a given point on the surface. A curved surface like a sphere has a different normal for each point on the surface. The normal is technically defined as a vector "perpendicular to the plane tangent to the surface at the point of intersection." It is also often referred to as the *gradient* of the surface. A planar object, like a square, has the same surface normal for the entire object since it lies entirely within a single plane. The surface normal for a sphere is a vector pointing from the origin of the sphere out through the intersection point. Determining the surface normal is more complicated for other shapes (see Chapter 8).

Once you have determined the normal, you use it extensively to determine not only the angle at which light rays bounce off the surface, but also to determine such things as whether the object is facing you or whether it can be seen at all. The vector dot product calculation provides an extremely effective computational tool for computer graphics.

Reflections on Light

The ray tracing algorithm takes into account not only the intrinsic color of an object, but also the effects of reflection and refraction. Figure 6-4 illustrates the reflection of one cylinder on another. You generate the reflected image by casting reflection rays from the surface of the first cylinder back out into the scene. Those rays that strike the second cylinder are assigned its colors. The reflected rays are then added into the original ray color of the first cylinder.

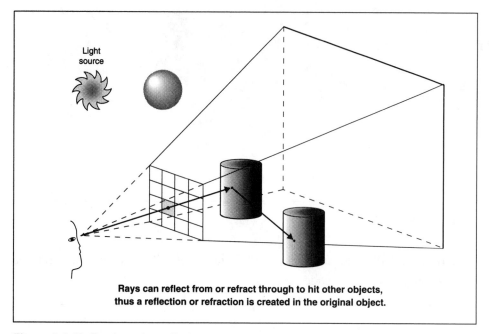

**Rays can reflect from or refract through to hit other objects,
thus a reflection or refraction is created in the original object.**

Figure 6-4. Reflection of a cylinder

Reflected rays are created whenever the intersected object surface has a nonzero *reflection coefficient,* the coefficient that represents the percentage of light reflected off the surface. For a mirror, this is usually about 100%. You generate the reflected ray by using the rule of optical reflection: the new ray has the same angle with respect to the surface normal as the incoming ray, but in the "outgoing" direction. This geometry is illustrated in Figure 6-5. The new ray has the intersection point as its starting point, and the new direction is computed by

```
REFL_DIR_ = RAY_DIR + 2*(RAY_DIR _dot_ NORMAL) * NORMAL        (Equation 6-1)
```

where NORMAL is the surface normal at the point of intersection and RAY_DIR is the direction vector of the incoming ray. As an example, consider how a mirror polygon reflects the images of several other objects in a scene. Figure 6-6 shows how a ray is traced from the polygon to the other objects in the scene. Again, note that because the *trace* procedure is defined recursively, you only need to compute

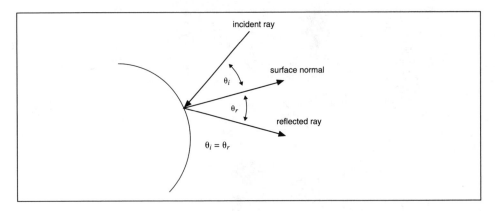

Figure 6-5. Reflection geometry

the reflected ray direction and call *trace* to find its color. This greatly simplifies the overall complexity of the code.

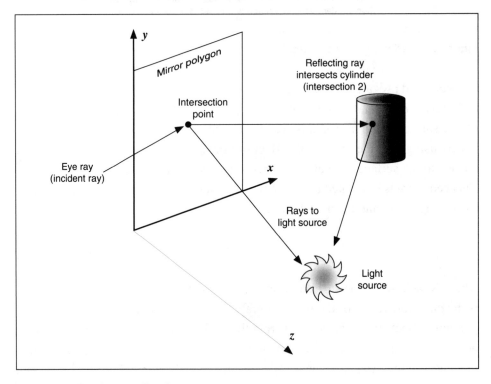

Figure 6-6. Tracing a reflection

Figure 6-7 shows a computational flow diagram of the reflection calculation, starting with a ray from the eye striking the mirror. A reflection ray is then computed, which is traced until it strikes another cylinder surface in the scene. The cylinder is reflective, and this reflection ray is also generated recursively. The process continues until all the rays either leave the scene, strike a light source, or hit non-reflective surfaces. Figure 6-8 shows the final computed image.

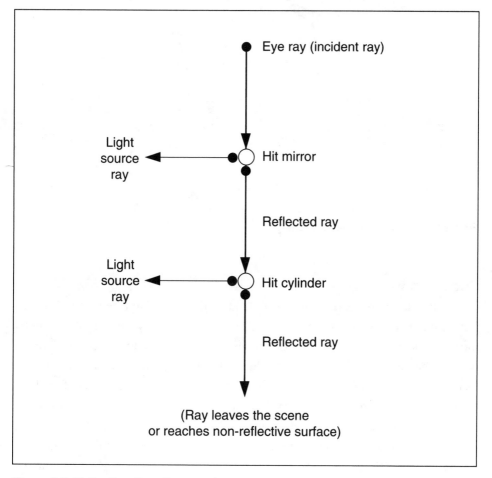

Figure 6-7. Reflection flow diagram

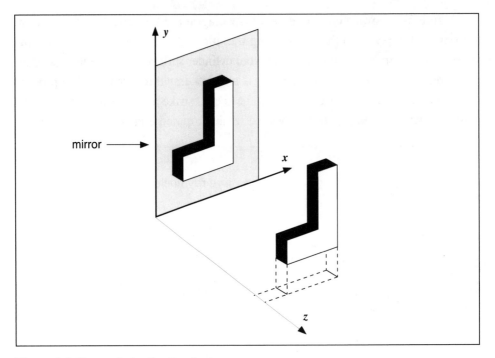

Figure 6-8. Computed reflection image

Focus on Refraction

In addition to reflection, we must also handle *refraction* (the transmission of light through a semitransparent surface). The transmitted ray calculation is slightly more complicated because refraction effects must be taken into account. Refraction occurs when light moves from one medium (usually air) into another medium (like water or glass). To model glass lenses, you must also consider the effect of the light emerging from the other side of the surface and back into the air (or even some other medium). To increase the computational burden even further, you must attenuate the ray's intensity is attenuated (reduced) by an amount based on the distance the ray travels through the medium before emerging on the other side. The calculation of the transmitted ray direction is a straightforward application of *Snell's Law* :

$$\sin(\theta_1)/\sin(\theta_r) = n_2/n_1 \qquad \text{(Equation 6-2)}$$

160

where θ_1 is the angle of the incoming ray with respect to the surface normal, θ_r is the angle of the transmitted ray, n_1 is the refractive index of incoming ray medium (normally 1.0 for air), and n_2 is the refractive index of the medium through which the transmitted ray passes. The geometry for this calculation is shown in Figure 6-9.

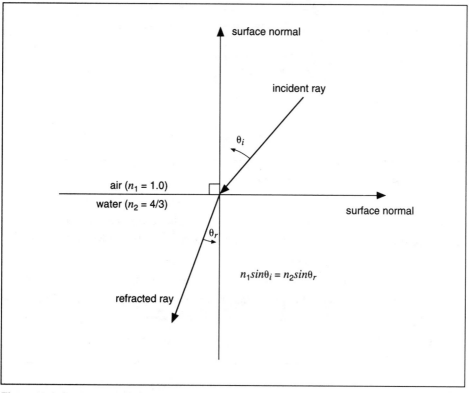

Figure 6-9. Refraction geometry

The transmitted ray is traced until it encounters the other side of the surface, or until it encounters another object. At the intersection point on the other side, a new ray is generated (again from Snell's Law), except that the angles are reversed (since the ray is emerging from the object material into the air). This technique allows for the modeling of sophisticated visual effects, such as the refraction of light by water shown in Figure 6-10. Notice that the position of the dowel below the waterline in this figure appears to shift, just as it does in the real world.

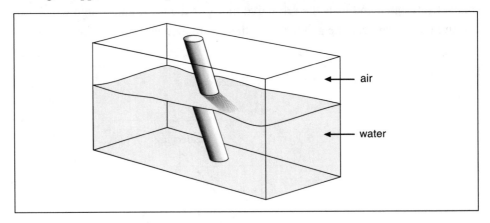

Figure 6-10. Refraction of light in water

Figure 6-11 illustrates how a ray is traced through a glass prism to strike a cylinder on the other side, and Figure 6-12 shows the computational breakdown of this process. The ray first strikes one side of the prism and then generates a refracted ray into the glass. This ray travels through to the other side of the prism and is refracted again as the ray leaves the glass to enter the air. This refracted ray then strikes the cylinder and returns its effective color. The ray intersecting the cylinder may also be reflected or refracted according to the properties of the cylinder.

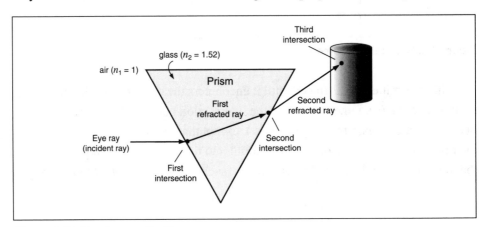

Figure 6-11. Tracing a reflection

Plate 1. Marble Columns and Clipped Surfaces forming a Crypt

Plate 2. Venus

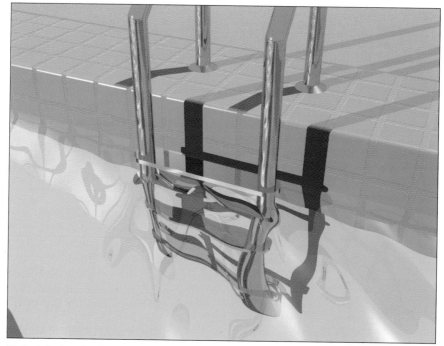

Plate 3. Swimming Pool Ladder

Plate 4. Example of Penumbra

Plate 5. Spider Turquoise Chess Board with Pieces and Glass of Red Wine

Plate 6. Pool Balls on Table with Cues

Plate 7. Earth, Moon, Andromeda Galaxy, and Dumbbell Nebula

Plate 8. Art Gallery

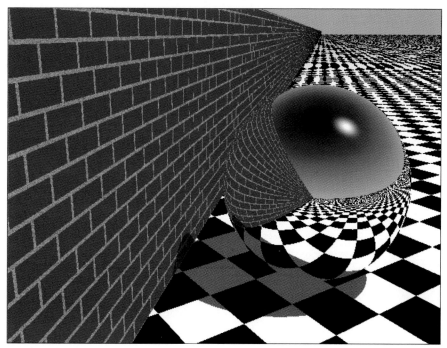

Plate 9. Anti-aliasing Turned Off

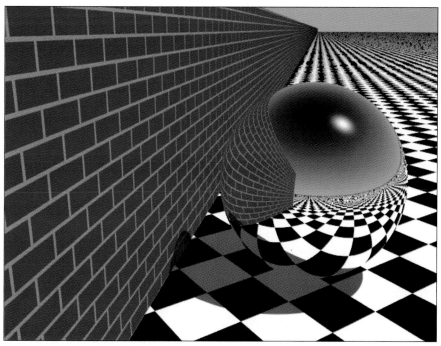

Plate 10. Anti-aliasing Turned On

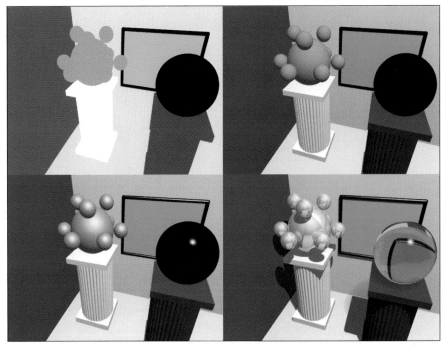

Plate 11. TL:Ambient TR: Diffuse Reflection BL: Specular Reflection BR: Recursive Ray Tracing

Plate 12. Added Bump Mapping, Texture Mapping, and Penumbra

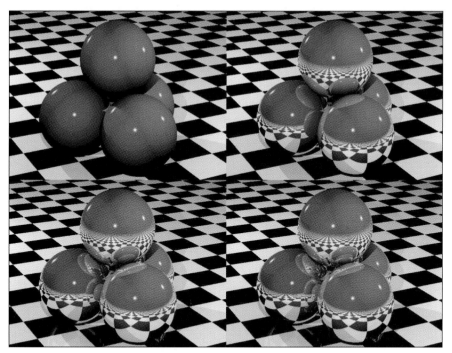

Plate 13. Illustration of Depth of Recursion

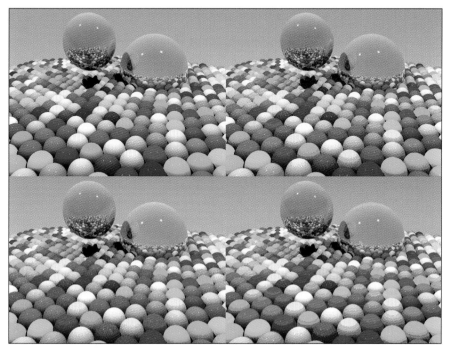

Plate 14. Dithering

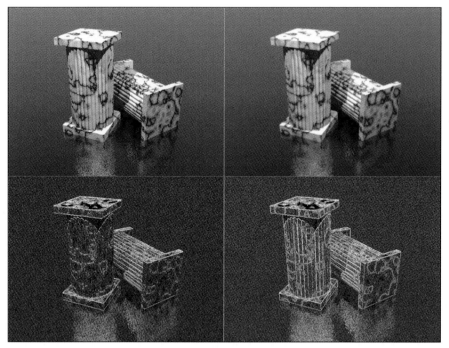

Plate 15. TL: No Filtering TR: Averaging BL: Horizontal BR: Laplacian Edge Detector

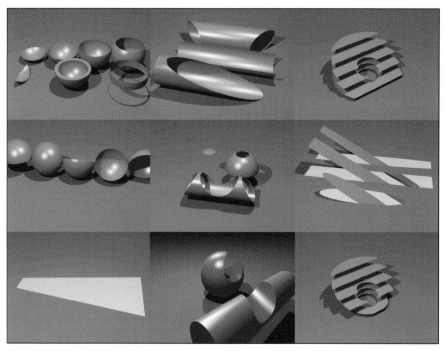

Plate 16. Clipped Objects

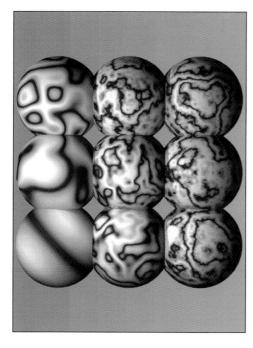

Plate 17. Varying Texture Amplitude on Spheres

Plate 18. Varying Texture Terms on Spheres

Plate 19. Looking Down into Checkered Box Through Fisheye

Plate 20. Example of Depth of Field

Plate 22. Blending of Procedural Textures

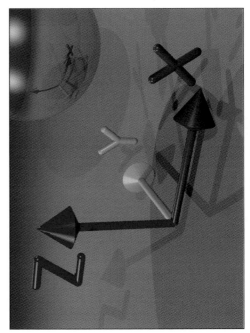

Plate 24. Three Dimensional Coordinate Axes

Plate 21. Shows Caustics for Transmissive Objects

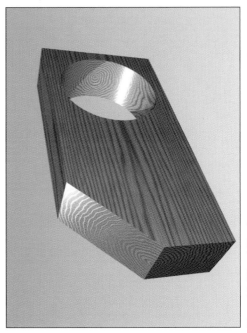

Plate 23. Wood Block

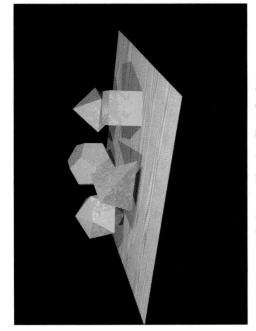

Plate 26. Platonic Solids on Wooden Floor Surface

Plate 28. Wooden Sphere in a Fractal Marble Wire Cage

Plate 25. Ice Cubes Floating in Water

Plate 27. Two Marble Columns

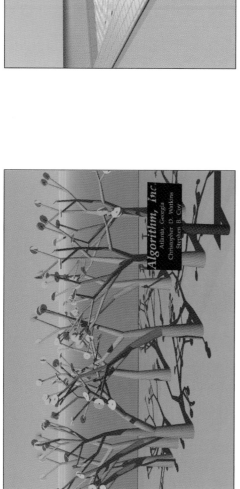

Plate 29. Rush's Lakeside Park at Dusk

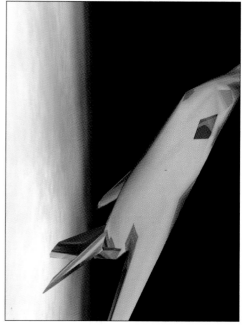

Plate 31. F117 Stealth in Turbulence Clouds and Haze

Plate 30. Swimming Pool with Waves, Diving Board, Ladder

Plate 32. Dice

Plate 34. Utah Teapot Floating in Wash Basin with Sphereflake

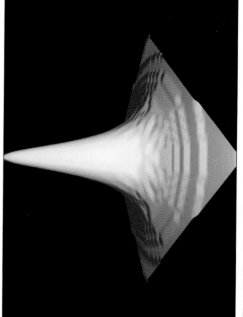

Plate 36. Ray-Traced Equation Plot

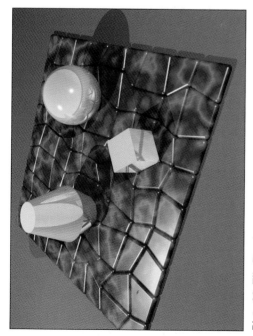

Plate 33. Tile Puzzle

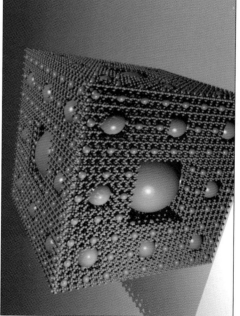

Plate 35. Fractal Object - Menger Sponge

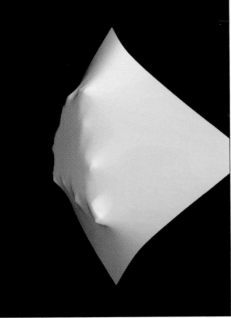

Plate 37. Water Generated from Summed Sinusoids

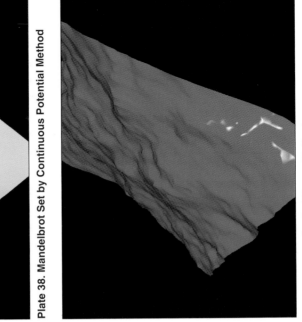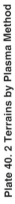

Plate 38. Mandelbrot Set by Continuous Potential Method

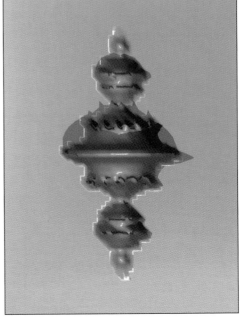

Plate 39. Quaternion—Solid of Revolution

Plate 40. 2 Terrains by Plasma Method

Plate 42. Models of Human Skull, Man's Face, Nefertiti's Face

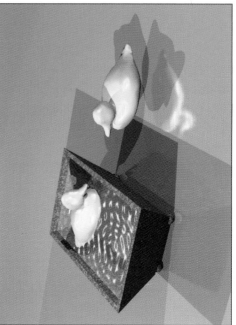

Plate 44. Ducks Swimming in a Basin

Plate 41. M&T Publishing, Inc. Logo

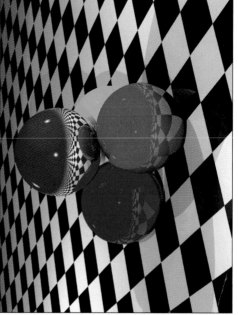

Plate 43. Stack of Spheres on a B&W Checkered Floor

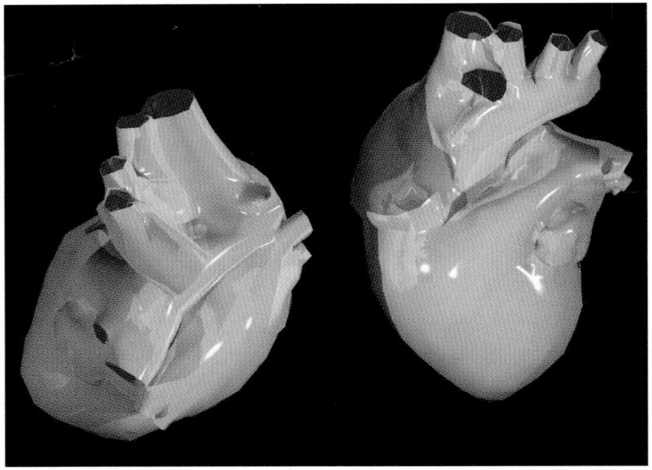

Plate 46. Surrealistic Drag Race

Plate 48. Bob Logo and Miscellaneous

Plate 45. Front and Side Views of the Human Heart

Plate 47. Shows Recursive Reflection

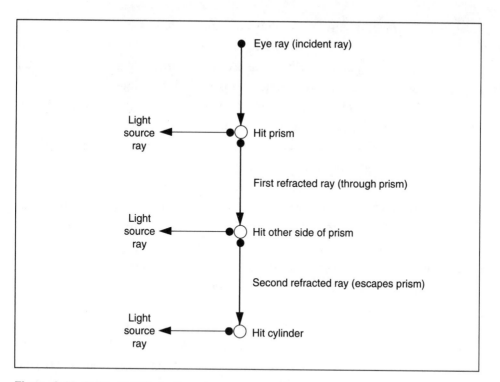

Figure 6-12. Refraction flow diagram

Because of the generality of this approach, you can put multiple prisms in the scene. Note also that the intensity of the refracted ray may be varied according to how far the ray travels through the glass. For even more sophisticated effects, you can simulate the way a prism breaks up light by assigning different refraction indices to the different colors (red, green, and blue). This would increase the computation time since now three rays (red, green, and blue) would be cast for each refracted ray.

Though the basic algorithm as discussed in this chapter is straightforward, many subtle implementation issues arise as you cast the algorithm into real code suitable for the PC environment.

Problems, Problems, Problems

Your primary goal is to produce visually appealing imagery that looks "real." Therefore, the topic of image quality becomes paramount in the production of the final imagery. Image quality covers a host of issues including:

❖ The elimination of aliasing artifacts (including the jagged edges, color stepping, and motion artifacts introduced during animation).

❖ Simulation of the effects of real camera lenses (that is, how a real camera would behave while photographing the scene). This includes the ability to set the focus, aperture, lens type, and other camera characteristics to photograph a simulated scene.

❖ The elimination of the unnaturally "clean" appearance of computer-generated objects. This is solved by the addition of surface texture to objects.

❖ The simulation of atmospheric effects such as haze, fog, smoke, and clouds for outdoor scenes.

❖ The realistic shadowing effects in which the shadows are not sharp-edged, but have visible penumbra as they do in real life.

All of these issues can be addressed in a variety of ways. However, the effects used to solve these problems are costly in terms of computer time because the addition of any of these effects can greatly increase the amount of time required to generate an image. For instance, a straightforward approach to anti-aliasing is simply to cast more than one ray per screen pixel (in other words, supersampling). You average the colors of these rays to get the output color of the pixel. An image that takes 15 minutes to generate with one ray per pixel will take 10 times longer to generate if we cast 10 rays per pixel. If you want to incorporate these additional computations to enhance image quality, you will be at least moderately concerned about efficiency.

Solutions, Solutions, Solutions

The remaining chapters in Part II of this book discuss the implementation of all the techniques presented thus far.

Chapter 7 discusses the basic implementation and data structures used by Bob. This chapter presents various anti-aliasing techniques from the simple to the complex, along with the trade-offs for each method. All of the anti-aliasing techniques involve casting more than one ray per screen pixel, so Chapter 7 introduces the concept of *distributed ray tracing* as a means of taking advantage of this to help compute other special effects. This concept involves choosing the rays to minimize aliasing artifacts, simulating the effects of camera lenses (such as depth of field), defining an aperture setting, and addressing motion blur effects.

Chapter 8 provides a detailed description of the computation of ray-object intersections. The basic algorithm does not really depend upon the types of objects you use, so long as you can derive the basic intersection properties (such as point, normal, color, and so on). This chapter provides a detailed description of the types of objects Bob supports and how the ray intersection is determined. It also describes the ideas behind *constructive solid geometry*, or *CSG*, to construct objects as collections of primitive shapes. Methods for *clipping* objects by other objects are discussed as well.

Chapter 8 also presents several methods for reducing the computational time even further by using more sophisticated object intersection tests. This chapter introduces the concept of *bounding objects* to allow you to decide quickly whether the ray intersects an entire group of objects. If it does not, then the work is completed for all of the objects in the group. Choosing which objects to group and how to group them becomes a major factor in the design of the ray tracing environment.

Chapter 9 provides a detailed description of the lighting model used by Bob. This includes the calculation of ambient, diffuse, specular, reflected, and refracted rays. In addition, this chapter discusses several methods of texturing object surfaces, including bump textures, image textures (putting a picture on a planar surface), and the latest in hot, hot, hot computer graphics techniques, solid (or volume) texturing. Chapter 9 also shows how to implement the shadow calculations, including how to model lights of finite size for casting shadows with penumbra.

Chapter 10 presents the source code for Bob and discusses how the various features from Chapter 9 are implemented. Chapter 11 is essentially the Bob owner's manual, providing the documentation for creating your own input files and databases for Bob. Chapter 11 refers to the theory presented in Chapters 7, 8, and 9, so be prepared to refer to those chapters for the mathematical descriptions of the various parameters.

Details, Please

Now that we have reviewed the basic theory behind ray tracing, let's move on to the actual implementation of Bob. From there, we can get into the fun stuff and create some pretty amazing pictures!

CHAPTER 7

The Ray Tracing Program

This chapter details the main algorithms for casting the initial rays from the eye through the screen and out into the scene. Most of this code is contained in the modules Screen.C and Trace.C (Listings 7-1 and 7-2).

These algorithms use four different types of projection geometries, each with its own unique features and uses. These algorithms also use various anti-aliasing methods to improve the overall image quality. All of these techniques involve the generation of more than one ray per screen pixel. Since processing of rays is the most computationally expensive part of the program, this chapter discusses ways to make processing more efficient. This chapter also examines how to simulate the effect of a camera lens and a nonzero aperture to generate depth-of-field effects. In addition, this chapter explores various methods for improving the overall efficiency of the Bob program by imposing various constraints on the calculations.

Projecting a Good Image

Chapter 6 described a viewing geometry in which you trace rays backward, starting at the viewer's eyepoint and moving out into the three-dimensional environment. The viewing screen consists of a rectangular region at a fixed distance from the eyepoint, usually 1.0 units in front of the eye (where units are arbitrary).

Note that the eyepoint is at the tip of a rectangular viewing pyramid, or *viewing frustrum*. The angle of frustrum is referred to as the *field of view*. The horizontal and vertical angles may be different, but usually the chosen aspect ratio of the view screen matches that of the display screen on which the picture is ultimately presented. The field-of-view angle has the effect of a telescopic lens. A small angle makes faraway objects appear large, but correspondingly limits the viewing region. Similarly, a large angle encompasses a larger area, but faraway objects project to smaller areas on the screen. New rays are generated using the standard *perspective projection* (referred to in the code as the *flat projection*). This projection is calculated as

```
Screen_Vector = (x/frustumWidth, y/frustumHeight, 0)
Screen_Ray = VecNorm(Center_Ray + Screen_Vector)
```

The *frustumWidth* and *frustumHeight* variables are the width and height of the screen in world coordinates (the coordinates of all of the other objects). The screen coordinate (x,y) is measured from the center of the screen. If the screen is (N x M) pixels, then x ranges from -N/2 to +N/2. Similarly, y ranges from -M/2 to +M/2. The *CenterRay* variable is the initial ray from the eyepoint to the center of the screen (x and y both 0).

These equations do not include the effects of roll. Roll is measured by defining two vectors, the *UP_Vector* (specifying the direction the top of the screen faces) and the *Left_Vector* (specifying where the left side of the screen faces). For an unrotated view, the *UP_Vector* is (0, 0, 1) and the *Left_Vector* is calculated from "up" and from the "to" and "from" points. *Screen_Vector* is the linear combination of these two values, weighted by the values (x/*frustumWidth*) for the *Left_Vector* and (y/*frustumHeight*) for the *Up_Vector*. Note also that the ray origin is always the eyepoint position.

The code for this calculation is shown in the *Shoot* procedure in the Screen.C program. To use other types of projections you must specify an algorithm for generating rays given an (x,y) screen position. The *Shoot* procedure provides several examples. The *orthographic projection* generates all rays perpendicular to the screen (that is, all light rays are parallel). To do this, simply make the ray origin use the same x and y values you computed for *Screen_Vector*. The z coordinate is 0 instead of 1. This projection has the effect of removing the perspective scaling for distance. Objects are a fixed size regardless of the distance from the viewpoint.

The *spherical projection* treats the screen as a section of a sphere rather than as a flat surface. Each pixel represents an equal angular area rather than an equal planar area. This type of projection produces results similar to the perspective projection for small angles. It can, however, produce full 360-degree panoramic views. Large angles exhibit angular distortion as compared to the perspective projection. To generate this projection, compute the ray direction using the following spherical coordinates :

```
Xdir = sin(2.0 * x / (xres-1))
Ydir = sin(2.0 * y / (yres-1))
Zdir = cos(2.0 * x / (xres-1)) * cos(2.0 * y / (yres-1))
```

where (*Xdir, Ydir, Zdir*) is the ray direction. Note that all the rays emanate from the eyepoint position.

A *fisheye (sphereical) projection* simulates a fisheye lens. You generate rays the same as for the perspective projection except that you exaggerate the direction as you scan pixels away from the center of the screen. This has the effect of "squashing" the view at the edges, just as a fisheye lens does. To do this, you scale the original *Screen_Vector* from the perspective projection by its length. The further away from the center you scan, the farther the ray is off-axis. This projection can create some interesting effects, especially in an animation sequence.

Figure 7-1 shows each of these projections. Several images of a box are presented as the box appears under each projection type. While some of these projections seem odd, they can be useful in visualizing certain aspects of a scene that are not always clear in a perspective projection.

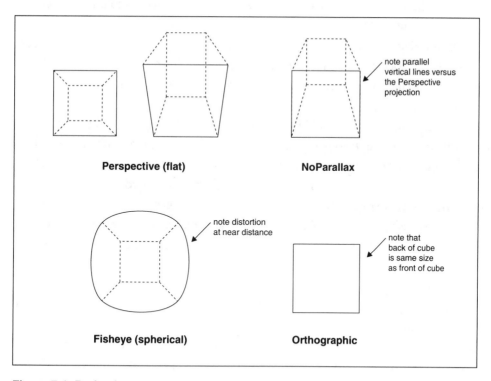

Figure 7-1. Projection types

Image Quality and Aliasing

The bane of computer graphics is the many aliasing problems, several of which were discussed in Chapter 6. *Aliasing* is defined in engineering as the erroneous appearance of low-frequency signals resulting from insufficient sampling of a high-frequency signal. The high-frequency signal then masquerades (or *aliases*) as a low-frequency signal in the sampled data. The most common form (though by no means the only one) in computer graphics is the "jaggies" or "stair-step" edges of scanned polygons. The problem results from the fact that the screen represents a finite sampling (the pixels) of an infinitely high spatial frequency signal (an edge or a texture pattern). When you create the rays for polygon types, you are sampling the scene. You can see how, in the absence of any other techniques, rays fractionally miss an object edge. This becomes most apparent with any kind of animated motion in which the aliasing problems become distracting along object edges. The problem also is evident when texture patterns are used. As the objects move into the distance, the pattern is sampled less and less frequently, which results in sampling errors.

Color Plate 9 shows some of the more common graphics aliasing artifacts. These artifacts are corrected in Plate 10. Plate 9 shows an image that depicts a situation typically arising in ray tracing. (These artifacts show up in other rendering packages, as well.)

Plate 9 illustrates the problems of sampling a high-contrast pattern as it moves off into the distance. Another common dilemma is the double problem that occurs when you sample a transparent sphere. Not only are the edges jagged, but the reflection introduces even more sampling artifacts in the magnified background image. Bump-mapped textured objects and texture maps (images mapped to an object surface) also cause problems. The nearer objects look reasonable because they are close enough to get reasonable sampling of the texture. However, the more distant object looks much worse since you sample the texture map much less frequently.

If the objects were rotating, the aliasing artifacts would appear even worse since the sampled points would vary from frame to frame in the animation. The basic problem with the ray tracing methodology as discussed thus far is that it is incorrect to think of a pixel representing just one ray into a scene. It is actually an area. You can visualize it by thinking of the four corners of a pixel as defining the base of a smaller viewing pyramid, just as the entire screen defines a viewing frustrum. You must know how the pixel's entire area of light behaves to integrate the results into the final color. Thus, you could handle the case where one portion of the projected pixel area hits an object edge, but another does not. However, this simply is not computationally practical (or necessary) on any machine. Instead, you can use various *anti-aliasing* techniques to help minimize the artifacts.

Anti-Aliasing to the Rescue

As you will see in the Screen.C code, the *Scan* function has several variations. Each function embodies a different anti-aliasing method with *Scan0* being the baseline method (that is, no anti-aliasing, just one ray through the center of each screen pixel). The successive versions of *Scan* are the implementations of the anti-aliasing methods described in the remainder of this chapter.

The primary method of combating the aliasing artifacts is *super-sampling* of rays (that is, casting several rays per pixel and averaging the results, as shown in Figure 7-2). Super-sampling is a natural approach to the problem. Visualize the screen as an area being sampled by the pixels of the display. The pixels, therefore, represent areas rather than points, and so it follows that you should sample them as well. The trick is deciding on the best way to do this.

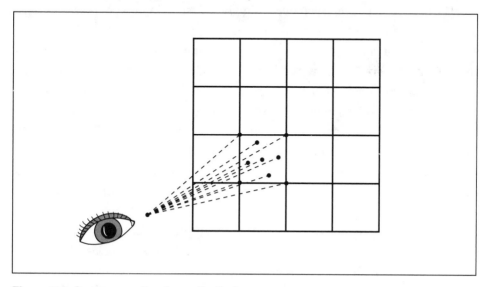

Figure 7-2. Super-sampling for anti-aliasing

As an implementation note, you may not want simply to average the rays together. Instead, add them together in a weighted manner, which represents the importance of each ray to the overall color. This type of operation is referred to as *filtering*. Usually, equal weights are used. However, in a more complicated anti-aliasing scheme, you may want to average in the rays for neighboring pixels, but assign them a lower weight in the average because they are farther away from the current pixel.

While super-sampling is a solution to these problems, the price you pay is that you must cast more rays. Casting rays is the most computationally intense part of the ray tracing program. It is well worth some effort to minimize the number of extra rays per pixel you must generate. With that in mind, consider casting a ray at each corner of the pixel and averaging the results. This method only requires one additional row and column of rays to be cast. As pixels are scanned, the previous row colors are saved and averaged into the next row. Note that this method is the same as computing an image one row and column larger than the original image, and averaging together every four pixels to produce an output image. While this method smooths out some of the edges, it also smooths out everything else and produces a "fuzzy" image.

Regular Sampling

The next anti-aliasing technique is simply to cast more rays per pixel by "stepping" in subpixel screen increments. For instance, each pixel may be divided into a four-by-four area in which a new ray is cast for each subpixel position. In this case, 16 rays per pixel are now cast instead of 1. Generally, the computational time is roughly proportional to the number of rays cast. An image that takes 5 minutes to generate now takes 80 minutes to compute. Bob provides the flexibility for you to experiment with the number of subsamples to see what produces the best results. This method handles almost all of the aliasing problems, but at a tremendous cost. It is not ideal because the sampling pattern is regularly spaced in the screen (that is, even steps in x and y and the same subpixel locations for all screen pixels).

Remember that aliasing problems result when a high-frequency signal is sampled at a sampling rate that is too low. With a regular sampling pattern, these high-frequency signals appear as low-frequency ones (or *beat frequencies*). One of the worst case tests of any anti-aliasing scheme is the checkerboard texture (alternating black and white) projected on a flat plane, as shown in Color Plate 9. As the pattern goes off into the horizon, the frequency of the checkerboard gets higher and higher because of the perspective (black and white squares appear closer). Eventually you encounter aliasing problems because the spacing is smaller than adjacent screen pixels. The regular sampling scheme creates new patterns in the image that look almost unrelated to the checkerboard spacing. It turns out that the human eye is sensitive to such sampling artifacts and such images become objectionable. Regular sampling, while simple to implement (especially in customized hardware), still produces some artifacts that can be addressed by other methods.

Given that some sort of super-sampling must be used to combat the aliasing artifacts, the trick now is to apply the super-sampling only to those pixels that intersect object edges or are in areas of high contrast (such as in a spotlight or a textured area). If half the final image is covered by the background or by a large smooth object, then half of the computation time has been wasted on regions that did not need it. Therefore, you must determine where to cast additional rays.

The principal method used by Bob to make this determination is called *adaptive super-sampling*. For the most part, adjacent screen pixels intersect the same objects, only at slightly different positions. Only the areas of high contrast exhibit noticeable aliasing problems. Therefore, you want to concentrate on these areas and not on large areas of smooth changes or on the background. You must detect edges or high-contrast transitions, such as in the checkerboard pattern.

This practice is called *adaptive anti-aliasing*. The ray tracer decides how many rays to cast by comparing colors of adjacent rays to see if they are within some user-defined threshold value (or alternatively, if they both intersect the background). Initially, you cast rays through the corners of each screen pixel. While this may seem as if you are casting many rays per pixel, you actually are casting only two, since every corner is shared by four screen pixels. You use the lower corners of the previous row as the upper corners of the row currently in process. Similarly, you use the right corner of the previous pixel as the left corner of the next pixel. Thus, for each screen pixel, you compute only the center ray and the lower-left corner.

The colors of the many rays are compared and, if they are all within the tolerance level, the values are averaged together and you move to the next screen pixel. If the colors are not within the tolerance level, the pixel is subdivided into four subpixels and you cast rays for each of these subpixels by using a recursive call to the *Adapt* procedure. The color difference in these rays is then checked. If it is still out of tolerance, you again subdivide the subpixel regions. This continues until all the rays are within the tolerance level, or until you reach a predefined maximum number of rays per pixel to cast. This method is implemented by the *Scan4* function in Screen.C.

Statistical Super-Sampling

Regular sampling patterns have their drawbacks. Because of these problems, you may want to shoot rays at random subpixel locations. This method (called *statistical super-sampling*) is appealing because the sampling errors no longer produce low-frequency beat patterns. The errors are now perceived as "noise" or a "dirty" surface. Usually, this kind of surface is less objectionable to the human eye than the regular patterns.

Statistical super-sampling is easy to implement by offsetting the regularly spaced subpixel locations by a random amount. For simplicity, the implementation uses uniformly distributed random offsets of 1/8 of a pixel. Both x and y are independently altered. These new subpixel positions are often referred to as *jittered*.

Other variations of this scheme are to abandon the regular pattern altogether and simply to cast rays at random positions throughout the pixel. This is desirable because it allows you to use fewer rays than with the regular sampling scheme. However, you must carefully distribute the rays evenly in the random-number generation. Without such precautions, you may have some pixels with rays bunched together rather than spread out across the pixel.

The Results

Color Plate 10 shows the results of applying the adaptive super-sampling technique to improve the images from Plate 9. Note that the images seem much more realistic and the texture artifacts now blend together nicely, just as you would expect in the real world. The image quality is only limited by the display resolution, and the amount of patience you have to perform computations. However, the images still do not quite represent how a camera would depict the scene because you have not yet modeled the interaction of light with the lens of a camera.

A Simple Camera Model

The standard ray tracing geometry shown in Figure 6-1 is a pin-hole camera model. The camera has no lens and the human eye is at a stationary point. The model unrealistically assumes that you have enough light to see everything at this point.

Real cameras use lenses to gather and focus light onto the film (as binoculars and telescopes use lenses to gather and focus light onto your eye). The lens, however, now introduces depth-of-field effects so that objects at the lens focal distance are in focus and those nearer or farther away are less in focus.

For the purposes of this discussion, assume that a lens is modeled with a given focal length. The camera aperture determines what light from the lens reaches the eye. The larger the aperture, the more out of focus objects that are not at the focal distance appear. As with the anti-aliasing schemes, the ideal situation would be to look at the projection of the entire aperture area through each screen pixel to determine the pixel's color.

Effectively, the viewing frustrum now is a mutated viewing cylinder with a circular aperture at the base instead of the single eyepoint. Because it is impractical to project the area, you instead generate sample rays through the aperture at random locations. This can be seen in the *Shoot* function in Screen.C. If the aperture size is nonzero, additional rays are generated whose starting positions are offset randomly from the aperture center in the plane of the aperture. This new ray points to the same point in the focal plane as the original, unaltered ray. Thus, you compute the location of the focal point of the original ray, and point the new ray at this same point. Each new ray now points in a slightly different direction and thus intersects a different object. The colors of aperture sample rays are averaged together to produce the net color of the ray.

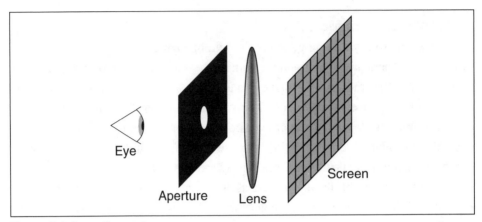

Figure 7-3. Lens Geometry

Plate 20 shows the effect of the nonzero aperture. Note the appearance of realistic focus effects. This technique imposes a high computation cost. Each ray has these new samples computed for it (since it is embedded in the *Shoot* function), so the total number of rays is *multiplied* by the number of aperture samples you compute. If you include the anti-aliasing methods, the total ray count gets quite high. Therefore, this additional effect should only be used when you are absolutely certain that everything else in the scene is correct and you want to produce quality pictures.

The *trace* Function

As described in Chapter 6, the *trace* function is the basic recursive function for computing the effective color of a ray. Because reflection and refraction effects are taken into account, it is inherently recursive. These effects are computed in the *shade* function in Shade.C. The reflected or refracted rays are computed by *shade* using the equations presented previously. You are certain to encounter situations where the recursion could continue forever (such as two mirrored objects facing one another). Similarly, you may want to limit artificially the levels of recursion in order to speed up the rendering process (such as when you want a quick view of the scene to see if the objects are correctly positioned).

The ray tracer accounts for this by setting a maximum recursion level. Each time a reflected or refracted ray is generated by *shade*, *trace* is called with the recursion level incremented by 1. If the recursion level is beyond the maximum, *trace* simply returns the color (0, 0, 0). Since colors are additive, (0, 0, 0) means no contribution. This feature provides explicit control over how many rays are generated. Color Plate 13 illustrates this by four views with the maximum levels set to 1, 2, 3, and 4, respectively. Note that as the recursion level increases, more effects (such as the object reflections) become evident. At level 1, there are no reflections. At level 2, first-order reflections become visible, but those reflections do not show up in the original mirrored object. They do appear at levels 3 and 4.

Another advantageous effect is reducing the transmitted and reflected ray intensities from the original ray intensity. The amount of reduction is a function of the material type that you define for the object. Except for perfect mirrors, however, the light intensity is reduced each time you generate new rays. Below a certain level, the ray will not make a significant contribution to the color. Therefore, you can set a minimum intensity level below which you ignore the ray. This provides a more physical means of limiting the recursion level rather than using an arbitrary cutoff. Typically, you use a cutoff level of 2% - 5%.

More Background

Up until now, the nebulous background has been an undefined entity. The *background* is the returned ray color whenever the ray does not intersect any objects or lights. The simplest case is to set a constant background color and return that color. However, while suitable for test images, this is not realistic. The next step up is to return a color dependent on the screen position or on the ray geometry.

Bob uses a simple gradient model that computes the dot product between the ray direction and an *UP_Vector* for the background. As with all normalized vectors, this value is the cosine of the angle between them. This value is then converted into an index with a range of 0 to 255. You use this index to produce a user-supplied background color look-up table. You use the fractional portion of the dot product value to interpolate between entries in the table. This technique provides a nice means of creating graded sky scenes where the sky may be light blue at the horizon and darker blue toward the zenith. The *UP_Vector* is normally just the vector (0, 0, 1), indicating the top of the sky. You may also create more interesting background color combinations, as shown in many of the plates.

Ultimately, you can make the background another image file, though that is not implemented in this ray tracer. The simplest mapping would be to have an image of the same resolution as the one you are generating. For a background pixel, simply return the corresponding screen pixel in the background image.

A much more general approach is to map some image onto an imaginary sphere surrounding the entire environment. This would use essentially the same texture-mapping calculations presented in Chapter 9. The ray direction can be dotted into a background *UP_Vector* and *LEFT_Vector* to find the horizontal and vertical angles representing your position. These angles can then be used for indexing into a two-dimensional array (just like the one-dimensional array for the graded skies). This technique is useful for putting new objects on scanned photographs. It is also a good way to animate characters on top of realistic backgrounds.

With the next chapter we move on to the computationally intense portion of the calculation, namely determining the intersection of rays and objects.

```
/*

    Screen.C = Contains the scan functions which determine
    what antialiasing is done and the function shoot() which
        handles the projection mode, depth of field, and
                actually calling the trace function
            Dependencies = defs.h, pic.h, extern.h
                    Copyright 1988-1992
            Christopher D. Watkins & Stephen B. Coy
                    ALL RIGHTS RESERVED

*/
#include <stdio.h>
#include <stdlib.h>
#include <math.h>
#include "defs.h"
#include "pic.h"
#include "extern.h"

static   Flt frustrumwidth,
         frustrumheight;
static   Point  viewvec, leftvec, looking_up, viewpoint;
static   Ray ray;              /* normal, untweaked ray */
static   int x_res, y_res;
static   Pic *pic;
```

```
void Screen(view, picfile, xres, yres)
    Viewpoint *view;
    char      *picfile;
    int        xres, yres;
{
    void ScrInit(),
        PicClose();

    ScrInit(view, xres, yres, picfile);

    switch(antialias) {
        case A_NONE:
            Scan0();
            break;
        case A_CORNERS:
            Scan1();
            break;
        case A_QUICK:
            Scan2();
            break;
        case A_ADAPTIVE:
            Scan3();
            break;
    }
    PicClose(pic);
}

void ScrInit(view, xres, yres, picfile)
    Viewpoint *view;
    int        xres, yres;
    char      *picfile;
{
    Pic       *PicOpen();

    /*
     * open the picture file...
     */

    pic = PicOpen(picfile, xres, yres);

    /*
     * determine the viewing frustrum
     */

    x_res = xres;
    y_res = yres;
```

```
    VecNormalize(view->view_up);
    VecSub(view->view_at, view->view_from, viewvec);
    VecNormalize(viewvec);
    VecCross(view->view_up, viewvec, leftvec);
    VecNormalize(leftvec);
    VecS((-1), leftvec, leftvec);   /* convert to right handed */

/* make view_up vector perpendicular to veiwvec and leftvec */

    if(camera.projection != P_NO_PARALLAX) {
        VecCross(leftvec, viewvec, view->view_up);
        VecNormalize(view->view_up);
    }
    VecCopy(view->view_up, looking_up);

    /* set up camera stuff */

    if(camera.aperture > 0.0) {    /* calc lens vectors */
        VecCopy(leftvec, camera.lens_i);
        VecCross(viewvec, camera.lens_i, camera.lens_j);
        VecNormalize(camera.lens_j);
        VecS(camera.aperture, camera.lens_i, camera.lens_i);
        VecS(camera.aperture, camera.lens_j, camera.lens_j);
    }

    VecCopy(view->view_from, ray.P);
    VecCopy(view->view_from, viewpoint);
    VecCopy(viewvec, ray.D);

    frustrumwidth  = tan(view->view_angle_x);
    frustrumheight = tan(view->view_angle_y);

}   /* end of ScrInit() */

/*
    Scan0 - Basic one ray per pixel, right through the center.
        Jitter value +- 0.5
*/

void    Scan0(void)
{
    Pixel       *buf;
    Color       color;            /* color of current traced ray */
    int         i, j;
    Flt         x, y;
    void        PicWriteLine(),
```

```
            Shoot();

    buf = (Pixel *)malloc(x_res * sizeof(Pixel));

    for(j=start_line; j<stop_line; j++) {
        for(i=0; i<x_res; i++) {
            if(jitter) {
                x = i + rand()/(Flt)RAND_MAX;
                y = j + rand()/(Flt)RAND_MAX;
            } else {
                x = i + 0.5;     /* hit center of pixel */
                y = j + 0.5;
            }

            Shoot(x, y, color);

            buf[i].r = (unsigned char) (255.0 * color[0]);
            buf[i].g = (unsigned char) (255.0 * color[1]);
            buf[i].b = (unsigned char) (255.0 * color[2]);
        }
        PicWriteLine(pic, buf);
        if(tickflag)
            statistics(j);
    }
    if(tickflag)
        fprintf(stderr, "\n");

    free(buf);
}   /* end of Scan0() */

/*
    Scan1 — Shoot a ray at each corner of the pixel and average
        the results.
        Jitter value +- 0.5
*/

void Scan1(void)
{
    Pixel   *buf, *oldbuf, *curbuf, *tmp;
    int     red, green, blue;
    Color   color;          /* color of current traced ray */
    int     i, j;
    Flt     x, y;
    void    PicWriteLine(),
            Shoot();
```

```
/*
 * allocate enough space for an entire row of pixels...
 * plus one more for the average...
 */

oldbuf = NULL;
curbuf = (Pixel *)malloc ((x_res+1) * sizeof (Pixel));
buf = (Pixel *)malloc ((x_res+1) * sizeof (Pixel));

for(j=start_line; j<stop_line; j++) {
    for(i=0; i<x_res+1; i++) {
        if(jitter) {
            x = i + rand()/(Flt)RAND_MAX;
            y = j + rand()/(Flt)RAND_MAX;
        } else {
            x = i + 0.5;     /* hit center of pixel */
            y = j + 0.5;
        }
        Shoot(x, y, color);

        curbuf[i].r = (unsigned char) (255.0 * color[0]);
        curbuf[i].g = (unsigned char) (255.0 * color[1]);
        curbuf[i].b = (unsigned char) (255.0 * color[2]);
    }
    if(oldbuf) {
        /* average the pixels, and write 'em out */
        for(i=0; i<x_res; i++) {
            red = ((int)curbuf[i].r + (int)curbuf[i+1].r
                + (int)oldbuf[i].r+ (int)oldbuf[i+1].r);
            green = ((int)curbuf[i].g + (int)curbuf[i+1].g
                + (int)oldbuf[i].g+ (int)oldbuf[i+1].g);
            blue = ((int)curbuf[i].b + (int)curbuf[i+1].b
                + (int)oldbuf[i].b+ (int)oldbuf[i+1].b);
            buf[i].r = (unsigned char) (red / 4);
            buf[i].g = (unsigned char) (green / 4);
            buf[i].b = (unsigned char) (blue / 4);
        }
        PicWriteLine(pic, buf);
        tmp = oldbuf;
        oldbuf = curbuf;
        curbuf = tmp;
    } else {
        oldbuf = curbuf;
        curbuf = (Pixel *) malloc ((x_res + 1) * sizeof (Pixel));
    }
```

```
        if(tickflag)
            statistics(j);
    }
    if(tickflag)
        fprintf(stderr, "\n");

    free(buf);
    free(curbuf);
}   /* end of Scan1() */


/*
    Scan2 - Undersampling, possible 18 to 1 speedup.
        No jitter option.
*/

void    Scan2(void)
{
    Pixel   *buf[7], *buff;
    int     *flags[7];
    Color   color;              /* color of current traced ray */
    int     x, y, xx, yy, i, j;
    void    PicWriteLine(),
        Shoot();
    int     comp(unsigned int, unsigned int);
    unsigned int    r, g, b;

    /* fill to next mod 6 scan line */
    if(start_line%6) {
        buff = (Pixel *)malloc(x_res * sizeof(Pixel));
        ptrchk(buff, "pixel buffer");

        /* calc stop line for single fill */
        yy = start_line + 6 - (start_line%6);
        for(j=start_line; j<yy; j++) {
            for(i=0; i<x_res; i++) {
                Shoot((Flt)i+0.5, (Flt)j+0.5, color);
                buff[i].r = (unsigned char) (255.0 * color[0]);
                buff[i].g = (unsigned char) (255.0 * color[1]);
                buff[i].b = (unsigned char) (255.0 * color[2]);
            }
            PicWriteLine(pic, buff);
            if(tickflag)
                statistics(j);
        }
        start_line = yy;
        free(buff);
```

```
    }

/* allocate pixel buffers */

for(i=0; i<7; i++) {
    buf[i] = (Pixel *)malloc((x_res+5) * sizeof(Pixel));
    ptrchk(buf[i], "sampling buffer");
    flags[i] = (int *)malloc((x_res+5) * sizeof(int));
    ptrchk(flags[i], "sampling flag buffer");
}

/* start actual sub-sampling */
for(i=0; i<x_res+5; i++) {   /* clear bottom row of flags */
    flags[6][i] = 0;
}
for(y=start_line; y<stop_line; y+=6) {

    /* copy bottom line to top */
    for(i=0; i<x_res+5; i++) {
        if(flags[0][i] = flags[6][i]) { /* only copy if valid */
            buf[0][i].r = buf[6][i].r;
            buf[0][i].g = buf[6][i].g;
            buf[0][i].b = buf[6][i].b;
        }
        /* clear rest of buf */
        for(j=1; j<7; j++) {
            flags[j][i] = 0;
        }
    }

    /* for(x=0; x<x_res+5; x+=6) { */
    for(x=0; x<x_res; x+=6) {
        /* shoot corners and middle */
        i = x; j = 0;
        if(!flags[j][i]) {
            flags[j][i] = 1;
            Shoot((Flt)i+0.5, (Flt)y+0.5, color);
            buf[j][i].r = (unsigned char)(255.0*color[0]);
            buf[j][i].g = (unsigned char)(255.0*color[1]);
            buf[j][i].b = (unsigned char)(255.0*color[2]);
        }

        i = x+6; j = 0;
        if(!flags[j][i]) {
            flags[j][i] = 1;
            Shoot((Flt)i+0.5, (Flt)y+0.5, color);
```

```
        buf[j][i].r = (unsigned char)(255.0*color[0]);
        buf[j][i].g = (unsigned char)(255.0*color[1]);
        buf[j][i].b = (unsigned char)(255.0*color[2]);
    }

    i = x; j = 6;
    if(!flags[j][i]) {
        flags[j][i] = 1;
        Shoot((Flt)i+0.5, (Flt)y+0.5+6, color);
        buf[j][i].r = (unsigned char)(255.0*color[0]);
        buf[j][i].g = (unsigned char)(255.0*color[1]);
        buf[j][i].b = (unsigned char)(255.0*color[2]);
    }

    i = x+6; j = 6;
    if(!flags[j][i]) {
        flags[j][i] = 1;
        Shoot((Flt)i+0.5, (Flt)y+0.5+6, color);
        buf[j][i].r = (unsigned char)(255.0*color[0]);
        buf[j][i].g = (unsigned char)(255.0*color[1]);
        buf[j][i].b = (unsigned char)(255.0*color[2]);
    }

    i = x+3; j = 3;            /* middle ray */
    if(!flags[j][i]) {
        flags[j][i] = 1;
        Shoot((Flt)i+0.5, (Flt)y+0.5+3, color);
        buf[j][i].r = (unsigned char)(255.0*color[0]);
        buf[j][i].g = (unsigned char)(255.0*color[1]);
        buf[j][i].b = (unsigned char)(255.0*color[2]);
    }

    /* the corners are shot, now fill in if needed */

    /* check upper left quad first */
    i = x+3; j = (y%6)+3;    /* middle ray */

    if(comp(buf[j][i].r, buf[j-3][i-3].r) &&
       comp(buf[j][i].g, buf[j-3][i-3].g) &&
       comp(buf[j][i].b, buf[j-3][i-3].b)) { /* close enough so
fill */
        if(!flags[j-1][i]) {
            buf[j-1][i].r = buf[j][i].r;
            buf[j-1][i].g = buf[j][i].g;
            buf[j-1][i].b = buf[j][i].b;
        }
```

```
if(!flags[j][i-1]) {
    buf[j][i-1].r = buf[j][i].r;
    buf[j][i-1].g = buf[j][i].g;
    buf[j][i-1].b = buf[j][i].b;
}
if(!flags[j-1][i-1]) {
    buf[j-1][i-1].r = buf[j][i].r;
    buf[j-1][i-1].g = buf[j][i].g;
    buf[j-1][i-1].b = buf[j][i].b;
}
if(!flags[j-2][i-2]) {
    buf[j-2][i-2].r = buf[j-3][i-3].r;
    buf[j-2][i-2].g = buf[j-3][i-3].g;
    buf[j-2][i-2].b = buf[j-3][i-3].b;
}
if(!flags[j-3][i-2]) {
    buf[j-3][i-2].r = buf[j-3][i-3].r;
    buf[j-3][i-2].g = buf[j-3][i-3].g;
    buf[j-3][i-2].b = buf[j-3][i-3].b;
}
if(!flags[j-2][i-3]) {
    buf[j-2][i-3].r = buf[j-3][i-3].r;
    buf[j-2][i-3].g = buf[j-3][i-3].g;
    buf[j-2][i-3].b = buf[j-3][i-3].b;
}
r = ((unsigned int)buf[j-3][i-3].r + (unsigned int)buf[j-
    3][i+3].r) >> 1;
g = ((unsigned int)buf[j-3][i-3].g + (unsigned int)buf[j-
    3][i+3].g) >> 1;
b = ((unsigned int)buf[j-3][i-3].b + (unsigned int)buf[j-
    3][i+3].b) >> 1;
r = buf[j-3][i-3].r;
g = buf[j-3][i-3].g;
b = buf[j-3][i-3].b;
if(!flags[j-3][i-1]) {
    buf[j-3][i-1].r = r;
    buf[j-3][i-1].g = g;
    buf[j-3][i-1].b = b;
}
if(!flags[j-2][i-1]) {
    buf[j-2][i-1].r = r;
    buf[j-2][i-1].g = g;
    buf[j-2][i-1].b = b;
}
if(!flags[j-3][i]) {
    buf[j-3][i].r = r;
```

```
buf[j-3][i].g = g;
buf[j-3][i].b = b;
                    }
                    if(!flags[j-2][i]) {
                        buf[j-2][i].r = r;
                        buf[j-2][i].g = g;
                        buf[j-2][i].b = b;
                    }
                    r = ((unsigned int)buf[j-3][i-3].r + (unsigned
                        int)buf[j+3][i-3].r) >> 1;
                    g = ((unsigned int)buf[j-3][i-3].g + (unsigned
                        int)buf[j+3][i-3].g) >> 1;
                    b = ((unsigned int)buf[j-3][i-3].b + (unsigned
                        int)buf[j+3][i-3].b) >> 1;
                    r = buf[j-3][i-3].r;
                    g = buf[j-3][i-3].g;
                    b = buf[j-3][i-3].b;
                    if(!flags[j-1][i-3]) {
                        buf[j-1][i-3].r = r;
                        buf[j-1][i-3].g = g;
                        buf[j-1][i-3].b = b;
                    }
                    if(!flags[j-1][i-2]) {
                        buf[j-1][i-2].r = r;
                        buf[j-1][i-2].g = g;
                        buf[j-1][i-2].b = b;
                    }
                    if(!flags[j][i-3]) {
                        buf[j][i-3].r = r;
                        buf[j][i-3].g = g;
                        buf[j][i-3].b = b;
                    }
                    if(!flags[j-1][i-2]) {
                        buf[j][i-2].r = r;
                        buf[j][i-2].g = g;
                        buf[j][i-2].b = b;
                    }
            } else {    /* else have to calc upper-left quad */
                for(i=x; i<x+4; i++) {
                    for(j=0; j<4; j++) {
                        if(!flags[j][i]) {
                            flags[j][i] = 1;
                            Shoot((Flt)i+0.5, (Flt)y+0.5+j, color);
                            buf[j][i].r = (unsigned char)(255.0*color[0]);
                            buf[j][i].g = (unsigned char)(255.0*color[1]);
                            buf[j][i].b = (unsigned char)(255.0*color[2]);
```

```
            }
        }
    }
}        /* end of upper-left quad */

/* check upper right quad */
i = x+3; j = (y%6)+3;    /* middle ray */

if(comp(buf[j][i].r, buf[j-3][i+3].r) &&
   comp(buf[j][i].g, buf[j-3][i+3].g) &&
   comp(buf[j][i].b, buf[j-3][i+3].b)) { /* close enough so
                                          fill */
    if(!flags[j][i+1]) {
        buf[j][i+1].r = buf[j][i].r;
        buf[j][i+1].g = buf[j][i].g;
        buf[j][i+1].b = buf[j][i].b;
    }
    if(!flags[j-1][i+1]) {
        buf[j-1][i+1].r = buf[j][i].r;
        buf[j-1][i+1].g = buf[j][i].g;
        buf[j-1][i+1].b = buf[j][i].b;
    }
    if(!flags[j-2][i+2]) {
        buf[j-2][i+2].r = buf[j-3][i+3].r;
        buf[j-2][i+2].g = buf[j-3][i+3].g;
        buf[j-2][i+2].b = buf[j-3][i+3].b;
    }
    if(!flags[j-3][i+2]) {
        buf[j-3][i+2].r = buf[j-3][i+3].r;
        buf[j-3][i+2].g = buf[j-3][i+3].g;
        buf[j-3][i+2].b = buf[j-3][i+3].b;
    }
    if(!flags[j-2][i+3]) {
        buf[j-2][i+3].r = buf[j-3][i+3].r;
        buf[j-2][i+3].g = buf[j-3][i+3].g;
        buf[j-2][i+3].b = buf[j-3][i+3].b;
    }
    r = ((unsigned int)buf[j-3][i-3].r + (unsigned int)buf[j-
        3][i+3].r) >> 1;
    g = ((unsigned int)buf[j-3][i-3].g + (unsigned int)buf[j-
        3][i+3].g) >> 1;
    b = ((unsigned int)buf[j-3][i-3].b + (unsigned int)buf[j-
        3][i+3].b) >> 1;
    r = buf[j-3][i+3].r;
    g = buf[j-3][i+3].g;
    b = buf[j-3][i+3].b;
```

```
    if(!flags[j-3][i+1]) {
        buf[j-3][i+1].r = r;
        buf[j-3][i+1].g = g;
        buf[j-3][i+1].b = b;
    }
    if(!flags[j-2][i+1]) {
        buf[j-2][i+1].r = r;
        buf[j-2][i+1].g = g;
        buf[j-2][i+1].b = b;
    }
    r = ((unsigned int)buf[j-3][i+3].r + (unsigned
        int)buf[j+3][i+3].r) >> 1;
    g = ((unsigned int)buf[j-3][i+3].g + (unsigned
        int)buf[j+3][i+3].g) >> 1;
    b = ((unsigned int)buf[j-3][i+3].b + (unsigned
        int)buf[j+3][i+3].b) >> 1;
    r = buf[j-3][i+3].r;
    g = buf[j-3][i+3].g;
    b = buf[j-3][i+3].b;
    if(!flags[j-1][i+3]) {
        buf[j-1][i+3].r = r;
        buf[j-1][i+3].g = g;
        buf[j-1][i+3].b = b;
    }
    if(!flags[j-1][i+2]) {
        buf[j-1][i+2].r = r;
        buf[j-1][i+2].g = g;
        buf[j-1][i+2].b = b;
    }
    if(!flags[j][i+3]) {
        buf[j][i+3].r = r;
        buf[j][i+3].g = g;
        buf[j][i+3].b = b;
    }
    if(!flags[j-1][i+2]) {
        buf[j][i+2].r = r;
        buf[j][i+2].g = g;
        buf[j][i+2].b = b;
    }
} else        /* else have to calc upper-right quad */
    for(i=x+3; i<x+7; i++) {
        for(j=0; j<4; j++) {
            if(!flags[j][i]) {
                flags[j][i] = 1;
                Shoot((Flt)i+0.5, (Flt)y+0.5+j, color);
                buf[j][i].r = (unsigned char)(255.0*color[0]);
```

```
                          buf[j][i].g = (unsigned char)(255.0*color[1]);
                          buf[j][i].b = (unsigned char)(255.0*color[2]);
                    }
              }
        }
}         /* end of upper-right quad */

/* handle lower left quad third */
i = x+3; j = (y%6)+3;    /* middle ray */

if(comp(buf[j][i].r, buf[j+3][i-3].r) &&
   comp(buf[j][i].g, buf[j+3][i-3].g) &&
   comp(buf[j][i].b, buf[j+3][i-3].b)) { /* close enough so
                                            fill */
    if(!flags[j+1][i]) {
        buf[j+1][i].r = buf[j][i].r;
        buf[j+1][i].g = buf[j][i].g;
        buf[j+1][i].b = buf[j][i].b;
    }
    if(!flags[j+1][i-1]) {
        buf[j+1][i-1].r = buf[j][i].r;
        buf[j+1][i-1].g = buf[j][i].g;
        buf[j+1][i-1].b = buf[j][i].b;
    }
    if(!flags[j+2][i-2]) {
        buf[j+2][i-2].r = buf[j+3][i-3].r;
        buf[j+2][i-2].g = buf[j+3][i-3].g;
        buf[j+2][i-2].b = buf[j+3][i-3].b;
    }
    if(!flags[j+3][i-2]) {
        buf[j+3][i-2].r = buf[j+3][i-3].r;
        buf[j+3][i-2].g = buf[j+3][i-3].g;
        buf[j+3][i-2].b = buf[j+3][i-3].b;
    }
    if(!flags[j+2][i-3]) {
        buf[j+2][i-3].r = buf[j+3][i-3].r;
        buf[j+2][i-3].g = buf[j+3][i-3].g;
        buf[j+2][i-3].b = buf[j+3][i-3].b;
    }
    r = ((unsigned int)buf[j+3][i-3].r + (unsigned
        int)buf[j+3][i+3].r) >> 1;
    g = ((unsigned int)buf[j+3][i-3].g + (unsigned
        int)buf[j+3][i+3].g) >> 1;
    b = ((unsigned int)buf[j+3][i-3].b + (unsigned
        int)buf[j+3][i+3].b) >> 1;
    r = buf[j+3][i-3].r;
```

```
    g = buf[j+3][i-3].g;
    b = buf[j+3][i-3].b;
    if(!flags[j+3][i-1]) {
        buf[j+3][i-1].r = r;
        buf[j+3][i-1].g = g;
        buf[j+3][i-1].b = b;
    }
    if(!flags[j+2][i-1]) {
        buf[j+2][i-1].r = r;
        buf[j+2][i-1].g = g;
        buf[j+2][i-1].b = b;
    }
    if(!flags[j+3][i]) {
        buf[j+3][i].r = r;
        buf[j+3][i].g = g;
        buf[j+3][i].b = b;
    }
    if(!flags[j+2][i]) {
        buf[j+2][i].r = r;
        buf[j+2][i].g = g;
        buf[j+2][i].b = b;
    }
    r = ((unsigned int)buf[j-3][i-3].r + (unsigned
        int)buf[j+3][i-3].r) >> 1;
    g = ((unsigned int)buf[j-3][i-3].g + (unsigned
        int)buf[j+3][i-3].g) >> 1;
    b = ((unsigned int)buf[j-3][i-3].b + (unsigned
        int)buf[j+3][i-3].b) >> 1;
    r = buf[j+3][i-3].r;
    g = buf[j+3][i-3].g;
    b = buf[j+3][i-3].b;
    if(!flags[j+1][i-3]) {
        buf[j+1][i-3].r = r;
        buf[j+1][i-3].g = g;
        buf[j+1][i-3].b = b;
    }
    if(!flags[j+1][i-2]) {
        buf[j+1][i-2].r = r;
        buf[j+1][i-2].g = g;
        buf[j+1][i-2].b = b;
    }
} else {      /* else have to calc lower-left quad */
    for(i=x; i<x+4; i++) {
        for(j=3; j<7; j++) {
            if(!flags[j][i]) {
                flags[j][i] = 1;
```

```
                    Shoot((Flt)i+0.5, (Flt)y+0.5+j, color);
                    buf[j][i].r = (unsigned char)(255.0*color[0]);
                    buf[j][i].g = (unsigned char)(255.0*color[1]);
                    buf[j][i].b = (unsigned char)(255.0*color[2]);
                }
            }
        }
    }       /* end of lower-left quad */

/* finally finish with lower right quad */
i = x+3; j = (y%6)+3;    /* middle ray */

if(comp(buf[j][i].r, buf[j+3][i+3].r) &&
   comp(buf[j][i].g, buf[j+3][i+3].g) &&
   comp(buf[j][i].b, buf[j+3][i+3].b)) { /* close enough so
                                               fill */
    if(!flags[j+1][i+1]) {
        buf[j+1][i+1].r = buf[j][i].r;
        buf[j+1][i+1].g = buf[j][i].g;
        buf[j+1][i+1].b = buf[j][i].b;
    }
    if(!flags[j+2][i+2]) {
        buf[j+2][i+2].r = buf[j+3][i+3].r;
        buf[j+2][i+2].g = buf[j+3][i+3].g;
        buf[j+2][i+2].b = buf[j+3][i+3].b;
    }
    if(!flags[j+3][i+2]) {
        buf[j+3][i+2].r = buf[j+3][i+3].r;
        buf[j+3][i+2].g = buf[j+3][i+3].g;
        buf[j+3][i+2].b = buf[j+3][i+3].b;
    }
    if(!flags[j+2][i-3]) {
        buf[j+2][i+3].r = buf[j+3][i+3].r;
        buf[j+2][i+3].g = buf[j+3][i+3].g;
        buf[j+2][i+3].b = buf[j+3][i+3].b;
    }
    r = ((unsigned int)buf[j+3][i-3].r + (unsigned
        int)buf[j+3][i+3].r) >> 1;
    g = ((unsigned int)buf[j+3][i-3].g + (unsigned
        int)buf[j+3][i+3].g) >> 1;
    b = ((unsigned int)buf[j+3][i-3].b + (unsigned
        int)buf[j+3][i+3].b) >> 1;
    r = buf[j+3][i+3].r;
    g = buf[j+3][i+3].g;
    b = buf[j+3][i+3].b;
    if(!flags[j+3][i+1]) {
```

```
            buf[j+3][i+1].r = r;
            buf[j+3][i+1].g = g;
            buf[j+3][i+1].b = b;
        }
        if(!flags[j+2][i+1]) {
            buf[j+2][i+1].r = r;
            buf[j+2][i+1].g = g;
            buf[j+2][i+1].b = b;
        }
        r = ((unsigned int)buf[j-3][i+3].r + (unsigned
            int)buf[j+3][i+3].r) >> 1;
        g = ((unsigned int)buf[j-3][i+3].g + (unsigned
            int)buf[j+3][i+3].g) >> 1;
        b = ((unsigned int)buf[j-3][i+3].b + (unsigned
            int)buf[j+3][i+3].b) >> 1;
        r = buf[j+3][i+3].r;
        g = buf[j+3][i+3].g;
        b = buf[j+3][i+3].b;
        if(!flags[j+1][i+3]) {
            buf[j+1][i+3].r = r;
            buf[j+1][i+3].g = g;
                            buf[j+1][i+3].b = b;
        }
        if(!flags[j+1][i+2]) {
            buf[j+1][i+2].r = r;
            buf[j+1][i+2].g = g;
            buf[j+1][i+2].b = b;
        }
    } else {    /* else have to calc lower-right quad */
        for(i=x+3; i<x+7; i++) {
            for(j=3; j<7; j++) {
                if(!flags[j][i]) {
                    flags[j][i] = 1;
                    Shoot((Flt)i+0.5, (Flt)y+0.5+j, color);
                    buf[j][i].r = (unsigned char)(255.0*color[0]);
                    buf[j][i].g = (unsigned char)(255.0*color[1]);
                    buf[j][i].b = (unsigned char)(255.0*color[2]);
                }
            }
        }
    }          /* end of lower-right quad */

}          /* end of x loop */

/* output scans */
for(j=0; j<6; j++) {
```

```
            PicWriteLine(pic, buf[j]);
        }
        if(tickflag)
            statistics(y+6);
    }       /* end of y loop (finally!) */
    if(tickflag)
        fprintf(stderr, "\n");
}       /* end of Scan2() */

/*
    comp - compares two numbers, returns 1 if close enough, 0 otherwise
*/

int comp(unsigned int a, unsigned int b)
{
    int diff;

    diff = a - b;
    if(diff > adapt_dist)
        return 0;
    else if(diff < -adapt_dist)
        return 0;
    else
        return 1;
}       /* end of comp() */

/*
    Scan3 — Adaptive supersampling with optional jitter.
        Jitter +- 0.125
*/

#define SIDE        (4)

#define RAW         (0)
#define COOKED      (1)
#define FUZZY       (2)

static unsigned char    win[SIDE+1][SIDE+1][4];     /* r,g,b,flag */
static unsigned char    *buff[4];

void    Scan3(void)
{
    Pixel   *buf;
    Color   color;          /* color of current traced ray */
    int     x, y, i, j;
    void    PicWriteLine(),
```

```
        Shoot();

buf = (Pixel *)malloc(x_res * sizeof(Pixel));
ptrchk(buf, "output buffer.");

for(x=0; x<4; x++) {
    buff[x] = (unsigned char *)malloc(SIDE*x_res+1);
    ptrchk(buff[x], "antialiasing buffer.");
}

for(i=0; i<SIDE+1; i++)    {           /* clear win flags */
    for(j=0; j<SIDE+1; j++) {
        win[i][j][3] = RAW;
    }
}
for(i=0; i<SIDE*x_res+1; i++) {        /* clear buff flags */
    buff[3][i] = RAW;
}

for(y=start_line; y<stop_line; y++) {

    /* clear left edge of win for starting a new row */
    for(j=0; j<SIDE+1; j++) {
        win[0][j][3] = RAW;
    }

    for(x=0; x<x_res; x++) {

        for(i=1; i<SIDE+1; i++) /* buff to top row of win */
        if(win[i][0][3] = buff[3][x*SIDE+i]) {    /* if cooked */
                win[i][0][0] = buff[0][x*SIDE+i];
                win[i][0][1] = buff[1][x*SIDE+i];
                win[i][0][2] = buff[2][x*SIDE+i];
            }

        for(i=1; i<SIDE+1; i++)    /* clear rest of win */
            for(j=1; j<SIDE+1; j++)
                win[i][j][3] = RAW;

        Adapt(0, 0, (Flt)x, (Flt)y, color, SIDE);

        buf[x].r = (unsigned char) (color[0]);
        buf[x].g = (unsigned char) (color[1]);
        buf[x].b = (unsigned char) (color[2]);

        for(i=0; i<SIDE+1; i++)    /* bottom row of win to buff */
```

```
                    if(buff[3][x*SIDE+i] = win[i][SIDE][3]) {     /* if cooked
*/
                        buff[0][x*SIDE+i] = win[i][SIDE][0];
                        buff[1][x*SIDE+i] = win[i][SIDE][1];
                        buff[2][x*SIDE+i] = win[i][SIDE][2];
                    }

            for(j=0; j<SIDE+1; j++)     {     /* right edge of win to left */
                if(win[0][j][3] = win[SIDE][j][3]) {    /* if cooked */
                    win[0][j][0] = win[SIDE][j][0];
                    win[0][j][1] = win[SIDE][j][1];
                    win[0][j][2] = win[SIDE][j][2];
                }
            }
        }
        PicWriteLine(pic, buf);
        if(tickflag)
            statistics(y);
    }
    if(tickflag)
        fprintf(stderr, "\n");

    free(buf);
    for(i=0; i<4; i++)
        if(buff[i])
            free(buff[i]);

}       /* end of Scan3() */

#define ARAND() (((rand()/(Flt)RAND_MAX)/4.0)-0.125)

void    Adapt(i, j, x, y, color, step)
    int     i, j;          /* where in win to put results */
    Flt     x, y;          /* upper left hand of pixel */
    Color   color;         /* return pixel color here in 0..255 range */
    int     step;          /* what level we're at */
{
    int     k, fuzzed;
    int     ave[3], c0[3], c1[3], c2[3], c3[3];

    if(win[i][j][3] == RAW) {
        if(jitter) {
            Shoot(x+(Flt)i/SIDE+ARAND(), y+(Flt)j/SIDE+ARAND(), color);
        } else {
            Shoot(x+(Flt)i/SIDE, y+(Flt)j/SIDE, color);
        }
```

```
        c0[0] = win[i][j][0] = (unsigned char) (255.0 * color[0]);
        c0[1] = win[i][j][1] = (unsigned char) (255.0 * color[1]);
        c0[2] = win[i][j][2] = (unsigned char) (255.0 * color[2]);
        if(fuzzy_ray) {
            win[i][j][3] = COOKED | FUZZY;
        } else {
            win[i][j][3] = COOKED;
        }
    } else {
        c0[0] = win[i][j][0];
        c0[1] = win[i][j][1];
        c0[2] = win[i][j][2];
    }

    if(win[i+step][j][3] == RAW) {
        if(jitter) {
            Shoot((Flt)x+(Flt)(i+step)/SIDE+ARAND(),
(Flt)y+(Flt)j/SIDE+ARAND(), color);
        } else {
            Shoot((Flt)x+(Flt)(i+step)/SIDE, (Flt)y+(Flt)j/SIDE, color);
        }

        c1[0] = win[i+step][j][0] = (unsigned char) (255.0 * color[0]);
        c1[1] = win[i+step][j][1] = (unsigned char) (255.0 * color[1]);
        c1[2] = win[i+step][j][2] = (unsigned char) (255.0 * color[2]);
        if(fuzzy_ray) {
            win[i+step][j][3] = COOKED | FUZZY;
        } else {
            win[i+step][j][3] = COOKED;
        }
    } else {
        c1[0] = win[i+step][j][0];
        c1[1] = win[i+step][j][1];
        c1[2] = win[i+step][j][2];
    }

    if(win[i][j+step][3] == RAW) {
        if(jitter) {
            Shoot((Flt)x+(Flt)i/SIDE+ARAND(),
            (Flt)y+(Flt)(j+step)/SIDE+ARAND(), color);
        } else {
            Shoot((Flt)x+(Flt)i/SIDE, (Flt)y+(Flt)(j+step)/SIDE, color);
        }

        c2[0] = win[i][j+step][0] = (unsigned char) (255.0 * color[0]);
        c2[1] = win[i][j+step][1] = (unsigned char) (255.0 * color[1]);
```

```
        c2[2] = win[i][j+step][2] = (unsigned char) (255.0 * color[2]);
        if(fuzzy_ray) {
            win[i][j+step][3] = COOKED | FUZZY;
        } else {
            win[i][j+step][3] = COOKED;
        }
    } else {
        c2[0] = win[i][j+step][0];
        c2[1] = win[i][j+step][1];
        c2[2] = win[i][j+step][2];
    }

    if(win[i+step][j+step][3] == RAW) {
        if(jitter) {
            Shoot((Flt)x+(Flt)(i+step)/SIDE+ARAND(),
                    (Flt)y+(Flt)(j+step)/SIDE+ARAND(), color);
        } else {
            Shoot((Flt)x+(Flt)(i+step)/SIDE, (Flt)y+(Flt)(j+step)/SIDE,
                    color);
        }

        c3[0] = win[i+step][j+step][0] = (unsigned char) (255.0 *
                    color[0]);
        c3[1] = win[i+step][j+step][1] = (unsigned char) (255.0 *
                    color[1]);
        c3[2] = win[i+step][j+step][2] = (unsigned char) (255.0 *
                    color[2]);
        if(fuzzy_ray) {
            win[i+step][j+step][3] = COOKED | FUZZY;
        } else {
            win[i+step][j+step][3] = COOKED;
        }
    } else {
        c3[0] = win[i+step][j+step][0];
        c3[1] = win[i+step][j+step][1];
        c3[2] = win[i+step][j+step][2];
    }

    for(k=0; k<3; k++) {
        ave[k] = c0[k] + c1[k] + c2[k] + c3[k];
        ave[k] /= 4;
    }

    fuzzed = win[i][j][3] &
        win[i+step][j][3] &
        win[i][j+step][3] &
```

```
        win[i+step][j+step][3] &
        FUZZY;

if(step==1 || fuzzed ||
    ABS(ave[0] - c0[0]) < adapt_dist &&
    ABS(ave[1] - c0[1]) < adapt_dist &&
    ABS(ave[2] - c0[2]) < adapt_dist &&
    ABS(ave[0] - c1[0]) < adapt_dist &&
    ABS(ave[1] - c1[1]) < adapt_dist &&
    ABS(ave[2] - c1[2]) < adapt_dist &&
    ABS(ave[0] - c2[0]) < adapt_dist &&
    ABS(ave[1] - c2[1]) < adapt_dist &&
    ABS(ave[2] - c2[2]) < adapt_dist &&
    ABS(ave[0] - c3[0]) < adapt_dist &&
    ABS(ave[1] - c3[1]) < adapt_dist &&
    ABS(ave[2] - c3[2]) < adapt_dist) {       /* close enough */
    color[0] = ave[0];
    color[1] = ave[1];
    color[2] = ave[2];

    return;
}

/* not close, so we have to subdivide */

step /= 2;
ave[0] = 0;
ave[1] = 0;
ave[2] = 0;

Adapt(i, j, (Flt)x, (Flt)y, color, step);
ave[0] += (unsigned char) (color[0]);
ave[1] += (unsigned char) (color[1]);
ave[2] += (unsigned char) (color[2]);

Adapt(i+step, j, (Flt)x, (Flt)y, color, step);
ave[0] += (unsigned char) (color[0]);
ave[1] += (unsigned char) (color[1]);
ave[2] += (unsigned char) (color[2]);

Adapt(i, j+step, (Flt)x, (Flt)y, color, step);
ave[0] += (unsigned char) (color[0]);
ave[1] += (unsigned char) (color[1]);
ave[2] += (unsigned char) (color[2]);
```

199

```
        Adapt(i+step, j+step, (Flt)x, (Flt)y, color, step);
        ave[0] += (unsigned char) (color[0]);
        ave[1] += (unsigned char) (color[1]);
        ave[2] += (unsigned char) (color[2]);

        color[0] = ave[0]>>2;
        color[1] = ave[1]>>2;
        color[2] = ave[2]>>2;
        return;
}    /* end of Adapt() */


void    Shoot(x, y, color)
    Flt        x, y;        /* where on screen to shoot */
    Color      color;       /* color to return from shot */
{
    Color      sum_color;   /* summed color for DOF effects */
    Flt        random;
    Ray        ray2;        /* ray tweaked for non-pinhole cameras */
    Vec        dir;
    int        sample;
    Flt        tx, ty, scale, P;

    switch(camera.projection) {
        case P_FLAT :
        case P_NO_PARALLAX:
            VecComb(-frustrumheight*(2.0*y/(Flt)y_res - 1.0),
                looking_up,
                frustrumwidth*(2.0*x/(Flt)x_res - 1.0),
                leftvec, dir);
            VecAdd(dir, viewvec, ray.D);
            VecNormalize(ray.D);
            break;
        case P_FISHEYE :
            tx = (x-x_res/2.0)/(Flt)x_res*Eye.view_angle_x*2.0;
            ty = -(y-y_res/2.0)/(Flt)y_res*Eye.view_angle_y*2.0;

            VecComb(sin(ty), looking_up, sin(tx), leftvec, dir);
            VecAddS(cos(tx)*cos(ty), viewvec, dir, ray.D);
            VecNormalize(ray.D);
            break;
        case P_ORTHOGRAPHIC :
            VecComb(-Eye.view_angle_y*(2.0*y/(Flt)y_res - 1.0),
                looking_up,
                Eye.view_angle_x*(2.0*x/(Flt)x_res - 1.0),
                leftvec, dir);
            VecAdd(dir, viewpoint, ray.P);
```

```
            break;
    }           /* end of projection switch */

    fuzzy_ray = 0;
    if(camera.aperture > 0.0) {
        MakeVector(0, 0, 0, sum_color);
        for(sample=0; sample<camera.samples; sample++) {
            dir[0] = ray.P[0] + ray.D[0]*camera.focal_length;
            dir[1] = ray.P[1] + ray.D[1]*camera.focal_length;
            dir[2] = ray.P[2] + ray.D[2]*camera.focal_length;
            VecCopy(ray.P, ray2.P);
            random = rnd();
            if(rnd() > 0.5) random = -random;
            VecAddS(random, camera.lens_i, ray2.P, ray2.P);
            random = rnd();
            if(rnd() > 0.5) random = -random;
            VecAddS(random, camera.lens_j, ray2.P, ray2.P);
            VecSub(dir, ray2.P, ray2.D);
            VecNormalize(ray2.D);

            Trace(0, 1.0, &ray2, color, 1.0, NULL);
            if (color[0] > 1.0) color[0] = 1.0;
            if (color[1] > 1.0) color[1] = 1.0;
            if (color[2] > 1.0) color[2] = 1.0;
            VecAdd(color, sum_color, sum_color);
        }
        VecS((1.0/(Flt)camera.samples), sum_color, color);
    } else {
        Trace(0, 1.0, &ray, color, 1.0, NULL);
        if (color[0] > 1.0) color[0] = 1.0;
        if (color[1] > 1.0) color[1] = 1.0;
        if (color[2] > 1.0) color[2] = 1.0;
    }
}    /* end of shoot */
```

Listing 7-1. Screen.C

```
/*
```

┌──┐
│   │
│   Trace.C = Where the rays are actually shot out into the world │
│   with grand hopes of hitting a primitive and adding color to the scene. │
│   Here we also deal with those poor rays whose lot in life │
│   is never to hit anything, proceeding out into never-never land. │
│   Dependencies = extern.h   │
│   Copyright 1988-1992   │
│   Christopher D. Watkins & Stephen B. Coy   │
│   ALL RIGHTS RESERVED   │
│   │
└──┘

```
        Trace returns the dist to the next hit.  This gives shade()
        a value to use for determining color attenuation for haze and
        transparent objects.
*/

#include <stdio.h>
#include <math.h>
#include "defs.h"
#include "extern.h"

Flt     Trace(level, weight, ray, color, ior, self)
    int     level;
    Flt     weight;
    Ray     *ray;
    Color   color;
    Flt     ior;            /* current material ior */
    Object  *self;
{
    Object     *prim;
    Vec     P, N;
    Isect      hit;

    if(level >= maxlevel) {
        color[0] = color[1] = color[2] = 0.0;
        return 0.0;
    } else if(level > deepest) {
        deepest = level;
    }

    nRays ++;

    if(Intersect(ray, &hit, HUGE, self)) {

        /* end of warning */
```

```
        prim = hit.isect_prim;
        RayPoint(ray, hit.isect_t, P);
        /* get normal vector of intersection */
        (*prim -> o_procs -> normal) (prim, &hit, P, N);

        Shade(level, weight, P, N, ray->D, &hit, color, ior);
        return hit.isect_t;
    } else {
        bkg(ray->D, color);

        return HUGE;
    }
}


void    bkg(Vec dir, Color col)
{
    Flt     dot, index;
    int     indx;

    if(background.color[0] < 0.0) {
        dot = -VecDot(dir, background.up);
        index = 127.0 * dot + 128.0;
        indx = index;
        index -= indx;
        col[0] = (1.0-index)*background.pal[indx][0]/256.0 +
                 index*background.pal[indx+1][0]/256.0;
        col[1] = (1.0-index)*background.pal[indx][1]/256.0 +
                 index*background.pal[indx+1][1]/256.0;
        col[2] = (1.0-index)*background.pal[indx][2]/256.0 +
                 index*background.pal[indx+1][2]/256.0;
    } else {
        VecCopy(background.color, col);
    }
}       /* end of bkg */
```

Listing 7-2. Trace.C

CHAPTER 8

Ray-Object Intersection Tests

The heart and soul of the ray tracing program is determining which object (or objects) a ray hits. Previous chapters described how the program reaches the point of casting rays into the scene. The *Intersect* function then magically returns information about the nearest object the ray intersects. The primary intersection information required by the program is:

❖ *Object*—A pointer to the object the ray intersects
❖ *Point*—The (x,y,z) coordinate where the ray intersects the object
❖ *Normal*—The surface normal (vector pointing away from the surface) at the point of intersection

With these three values, you can derive the color of the ray and determine whether to cast new rays for reflection or transmission. This chapter discusses the "classic" set of ray tracing for primitive object types (spheres, cones, rings, and polygonal objects). Chapter 12 and Chapter 13 discuss methods for generating images of more amorphous and elaborate objects (such as oceans and mountainous terrain).

No matter what type of scene you are generating, the basic intersection tests still must generate the primary information for each ray. Collections of the basic primitives make up complex objects. You can then move the collection of primitives as a single object. (A simple example is a model of a dumbbell consisting of a cylinder with a sphere on each end.) In addition, you can make even more complex shapes by *clipping* one object against another. (For instance, we can create a hemisphere by slicing a sphere with a plane.) Putting all of these techniques together provides the basis for *constructive solid geometry (CSG)*, which you use to create scenes of great detail and depth.

A scene of reasonable complexity may contain hundreds or even thousands of objects. Performing any kind of intersection test on this many objects for each pixel can quickly daunt even a supercomputer. Therefore, this chapter explores several methods for improving the efficiency of object searches through the use of bounding (or enclosing) volumes about groups of objects. This chapter also examines some of the areas of current research and schemes that other, more complex ray tracing programs use for environments that contain hundreds of thousands of objects.

The Definition of an Object

Up to this point, the definition of an object has been vague in order to present it in an "object-oriented" fashion. (In fact, computer graphics is an ideal paradigm for many of the concepts of object-oriented programming). For purposes of this chapter, an *object* defines a set of functions for determining how a ray intersects with it. The actual structure of the object is not needed by any other part of the main program. In fact, this book uses a C++ programming approach by providing both an intersection test function and a normal generating function as function pointers in the generic *Object* class defined in Defs.H. This provides a powerful means for adding new objects of any type to the basic set of primitives.

Parametric ray representation

A ray is described by two (x, y, z) triplets. The first triplet is the starting point of the ray. The second is a vector defining the ray direction. You can represent any point on the ray by introducing the parameter *t* and writing x, y, and z as functions of *t*, as shown here:

$$x = x_1 t + x_0 \qquad \text{(Equation 8-1)}$$

$$y = y_1 t + y_0 \qquad \text{(Equation 8-2)}$$

$$z = z_1 t + z_0 \qquad \text{(Equation 8-3)}$$

The coordinates (x_0, y_0, z_0) are the coordinates of the starting point of the ray and the coordinates (x_1, y_1, z_1) are the vector coordinates. Any point on the ray can be defined by a single number, namely t. All of the subsequent intersection calculations substitute this equation of a ray into the equation of the object primitive and solve for t (if a solution exists). If the value of t is a positive real number, then the ray intersects the object. If t is a negative or complex number, then the ray does not intersect the object. Note that t also measures the distance from the ray origin to the point of intersection. Finally, the point of intersection is found by substituting the value of t into these equations.

Sphere intersections

The surface of a sphere centered at the origin with radius r (see Figure 8-1) is defined by the following equation:

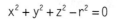

$$x^2 + y^2 + z^2 - r^2 = 0 \qquad\qquad\text{(Equation 8-4)}$$

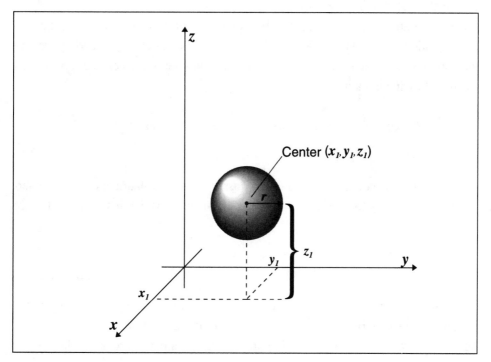

Figure 8-1. Sphere primitive object

If you substitute the parametric equations of the ray into this equation (using the same coordinate system with the origin at the center of the sphere), you obtain the following quadratic equation:

$$\left(x_1^2 + y_1^2 + z_1^2\right)t^2 + 2\left(x_0 x_1 + y_0 y_1 + z_0 z_1\right)t + \left(x_0^2 + y_0^2 + z_0^2\right) - 1 = 0$$

(Equation 8-5)

The roots of this equation (in the variable t) are the values of t for which the ray intersects the sphere. Solving with the quadratic formula provides the two roots of t. The smallest root represents the nearest intersection. Note that you must test the term $b^2 - 4ac$, which is the term you take the square root of for positive (real roots) or negative (complex roots) to see if the intersection occurs at all. This procedure is the same for a whole class of quadratic surfaces presented in the next section.

Quadratic surface intersections

A quadratic curve is one in which, like the previous sphere equation, the surface equation has terms of order 2 or less (that is, at most an x^2, y^2, and xy term in the equation). All such shapes are the cone and cylinder, which can be represented by the following equation:

$$ax^2 + 2bxy + 2cxz + 2dxw + ey^2 + 2fyz + 2gyw + hz^2 + 2izw + jw^2 = 0$$

(Equation 8-6)

Although this equation covers every possible kind of quadratic curve, it generally is not necessary to handle all of the cases. Instead, consider this simplified form:

$$Ax^2 + By^2 + Cz^2 + Ey = D$$

(Equation 8-7)

Using the same technique for substituting the parametric ray equations into the equation of the quadratic and then solving the resulting quadratic equation, you produce one of two equations, depending upon which parameters are defined. The first equation is

$$t^2\left(Ax_1^2 + By_1^2 + Cz_1^2\right) + 2t\left(Ax_0x_1 + By_0y_1 + Cz_0z_1\right) + \left(Ax_0^2 + Bx_0^2 + Cx_0^2 - D\right) = 0$$

(Equation 8-8)

The second possible equation is

$$t^2\left(Ax_1^2 + Cz_1^2\right) + 2t\left(Ax_0x_1 - Ey_1 + Cz_0z_1\right) + \left(Ax_0^2 - Ey_0 + Cz_0^2\right) = 0 \quad \text{(Equation 8-9)}$$

Note that the solutions to these equations must be real-valued in order for there to be an intersection. Complex-valued roots (those with a nonzero imaginary component) mean the ray does not intersect the object. You test the term whose square root is calculated to see whether it is positive or negative.

You can now create the basic quadratic primitives as specific cases of the previous general equation. The equation describing a cone of base diameter r and height h (not including a cap on the end) is

$$h^2x^2 - 2r^2y^2 + h^2z^2 = 0$$

(Equation 8-10)

See Figure 8-5 for a glance at the cone primitive.

Surface Normal Calculations

The procedure just discussed generates the point of intersection on the object surface. However, you also must generate the surface normal at that point. Chapter 6 described how to compute the *gradient* of the surface in order to compute the surface normal. The surface normal is the normalized value of the gradient. While this sounds complicated, it is quite easy for planar and quadratic surfaces. Calculating the surface normal involves the taking of partial derivatives with respect to the x, y, and z components of the surface equation. For the general equations discussed in the previous section, the gradient is either

$$\left(2t^2Ax_1 + 2tAx_0, 2t^2By_1 + 2tBy_0, 2t^2Cz_1 + 2tCz_0\right)$$

(Equation 8-11)

or

$$\left(2t^2Ax_1 + 2tAx_0, -E_1, 2tCz_1 + 2tCz_0\right)$$

(Equation 8-12)

At a point of intersection (x, y, z) on a sphere centered at the origin, the surface normal is a vector from the origin to the point of intersection. Similarly, the equations of a cone are substituted into this equation to find the gradient of the cone surface.

These are the quadratic primitives supported by Bob, but many others may be added as needed. A good example would be the addition of a torus primitive type. Most rendering programs, however, process objects defined as collections of polygons or planar shapes such as rings. Now the ray intersection calculation must solve two problems—where the ray intersects the plane in which the polygon lies and then determining whether the point of intersection actually lies inside the polygon boundaries.

Planar Object Intersections

Consider a simple case involving the intersection of a ray with a ring (see Figure 8-2). A ring has both an inner (possibly 0) and outer radius. This primitive is useful for generating circles because of the simplicity of the ray-intersection calculations, and is used as the ground plane for many of the scenes. To begin, you determine where the ray intersects the plane containing the ring. The equation for a plane is

$$ax + by + cz + d = 0$$

(Equation 8-13)

The intersection of the ray with the plane is obtained, as before, by substituting the parametric equations of the ray into the equation of the plane, resulting in the following equation:

$$t = \frac{a x_0 + b y_0 + c z_0 + d}{a x_1 + b y_1 + c z_1 + d}$$

(Equation 8-14)

This is the general equation, but you may choose a coordinate system centered at the middle of the plane, forcing the parameter D of the plane equation always to be 0. One nice feature of this form of the plane equation is that the vector (a, b, c) is the surface normal of the plane. Consequently, the denominator of the equation is the dot product of the normal to the plane and the ray direction. The numerator is the dot product of the normal to the plane with the difference between the origin of the plane coordinate system and the origin of the ray.

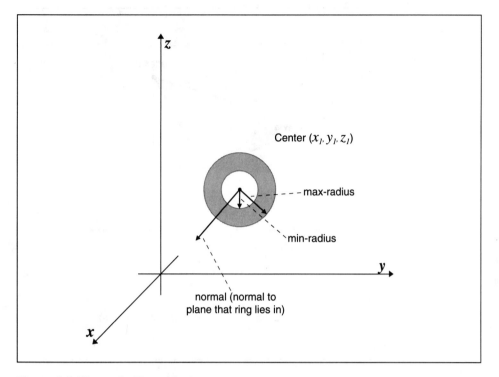

Figure 8-2. Ring primitive object

By substituting the value of *t,* you generate a vector from the plane coordinate origin to the point of intersection. To determine the length of this vector, use the square root of the dot product of the vector with itself. If this value falls between the values of the inner radius of the ring and the outer radius of the ring, the ray intersects the ring.

The procedure is similar for determining the intersection of the ray with a polygon (see Figure 8-3). However, you cannot use the distance of the intersection point from some central point as we did for the ring. Instead, use a result derived from the *Jordan curve theorem.* While this theorem is beyond the scope of this book, the method derived from this result is an elegant application of it.

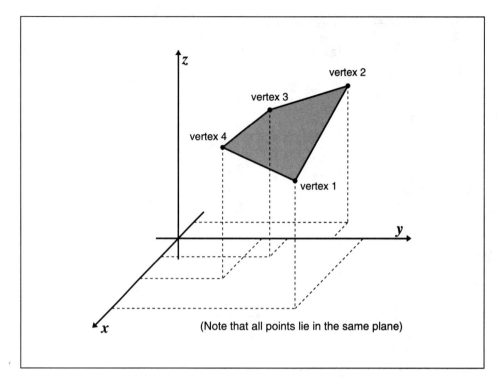

Figure 8-3. Polygon primitive object

The method begins by projecting a vector from the intersection point in any arbitrary projection of the plane. If the line has an odd number of intersections with the boundary of a closed object (such as a polygon), the intersection point is inside the object. Conversely, if there is an even number of intersections (including 0), the point is outside the object. To simplify the problem, the polygon vertices and intersection point are projected onto one of the three major coordinates axes (that is, you only use the (x, y), (x, z), or (y, z) coordinates). This reduces the problem to a two-dimensional scope and determines the same result. Use the polygon surface normal to choose which set to use. In general, if the surface normal is (x, y, z), you use the coordinates of the two smallest values. For example, if the surface normal is (0, 0, 1), then you use only the (x, y) coordinates.

The problem now is to pick an arbitrary direction, namely the direction (1,0), and to determine the intersection of this line with each edge of the polygon. The procedure is the same as for determining a ray intersection, except that you are now working in just two dimensions. You use linear equation solving to determine the point of intersection of the test line and polygon line, except in the case in which the polygon segment is parallel to the test line. Do not consider parallel edges. You then determine whether the intersection point is between the two vertices that define this edge. If so, count this as a single intersection point and continue processing.

This operation is implemented in the *Intersect* function in Poly.C (Listing 8-1, below). Note that since you are using the vector (1, 0) as the test line, you can perform some simple initial tests without constantly having to avoid the computation of the slope of the polygon edges. This helps make the computation more efficient.

Note that the quadratic surface ray-intersection tests generally are more efficient than the polygon tests. With the quadratic surfaces, you need only one test for intersection and one calculation of the intersection point. The intersection tests are more complicated and quite cumbersome for polygons with many sides or for complicated faceted objects. This is the exact opposite situation from more conventional rendering packages, in which quadratic surfaces are generally harder to render.

```
/*


          Polygon.C = The Polygon Primitive
  Copyright 1988, 1992 Christopher D. Watkins and Stephen B. Coy
              ALL RIGHTS RESERVED
          Dependencies = Defs.H, Extern.H


*/

#include <stdio.h>
#include <math.h>
#include "defs.h"
#include "extern.h"

typedef struct t_polydata {
    int     poly_npoints;
    Vec     * poly_point;
    Vec     poly_normal;
    Flt     poly_d;
```

```
    Flt    poly_p1, poly_p2;
} PolyData;

ObjectProcs PolyProcs = {
    PolyIntersect,
    PolyNormal,
};

int    PolyIntersect(obj, ray, hit)
    Object   *obj;
    Ray      *ray;
    Isect    *hit;
{
    Flt       n, d, t, m, b;
    Point     V;
    int       i, j, l;
    int       qi, qj;
    int       ri, rj;
    int       c1, c2;
    PolyData  *pd;

    pd = (PolyData *) obj->o_data;
    n = VecDot(ray->P, pd->poly_normal) + pd->poly_d;
    d = VecDot(ray->D, pd->poly_normal);

    /* check for ray in plane of polygon */

    if(ABS(d) < rayeps) {
        return 0;
    }

    t = -n/d;
    if(t < rayeps) {
        return 0;
    }

    RayPoint(ray,t,V);

    /* if clipping planes and doesn't pass, bail */
    if(obj->clips && !clip_check(obj->clips, V)) {
        return 0;
    }

    c1 = pd->poly_p1;
    c2 = pd->poly_p2;
```

```
l = 0;
for (i = 0; i < pd->poly_npoints; i++) {

    j = (i + 1) % pd->poly_npoints;

    qi = 0; qj = 0;
    ri = 0; rj = 0;

    if (pd->poly_point[i][c2] == pd->poly_point[j][c2])
        continue;          /*ignore horizontal lines */

    if (pd->poly_point[i][c2] < V[c2])
        qi = 1;
    if (pd->poly_point[j][c2] < V[c2])
        qj = 1;
    if (qi == qj)
        continue;

    if (pd->poly_point[i][c1] < V[c1])
        ri = 1;
    if (pd->poly_point[j][c1] < V[c1])
        rj = 1;

    if (ri & rj) {
        l++;
        continue;
    }

    if ((ri|rj) == 0)
        continue;

    /*
     * more difficult acceptance...
     */
    m = (pd->poly_point[j][c2] - pd->poly_point[i][c2]) /
        (pd->poly_point[j][c1] - pd->poly_point[i][c1]);

    b = (pd->poly_point[j][c2] - V[c2]) -
        m * (pd->poly_point[j][c1] - V[c1]);
    if ((-b/m) < rayeps)
        l++;
}

if ((l % 2) == 0)
    return 0;
```

```
    hit->isect_t = t;
    hit->isect_surf = obj->o_surf;
    hit->isect_prim = obj;
    hit->isect_self = obj;          /* polys are not self intersecting */

    return 1;
}

void    PolyNormal(obj, hit, P, N)
    Object    *obj;
    Isect     *hit;
    Point     P, N;
{
    PolyData * pd;
    pd = (PolyData *)obj->o_data;
    VecCopy(pd->poly_normal, N);
}

Object *MakePoly(npoints, points)
    int     npoints;
    Vec     *points;
{
    Object      *obj;
    PolyData    *pd;
    Vec         P1, P2;
    Flt         d, dmax, dmin;
    int         i, j;

    obj = (Object *) vmalloc (sizeof(Object));
    ptrchk(obj, "polygon object");
    obj->o_type = T_POLY;
    obj->o_procs = & PolyProcs;
    obj->o_surf = CurrentSurface;

    if(ClipTop) {
        obj->clips = ClipTop;
        ClipTop = GlobalClipTop->clip;
    } else {
        obj->clips = NULL;
    }

    pd = (PolyData *) vmalloc (sizeof(PolyData));
    ptrchk(pd, "polygon data");
    pd->poly_npoints = npoints;
    pd->poly_point = points;
```

```
/*
 * calculate the normal by giving various cross products...
 */

VecSub(pd->poly_point[0], pd->poly_point[1], P1);
VecSub(pd->poly_point[2], pd->poly_point[1], P2);

VecCross(P1, P2, pd->poly_normal);
VecNormalize(pd->poly_normal);

if (ABS(pd->poly_normal[0]) >= ABS(pd->poly_normal[1])
    && ABS(pd->poly_normal[0]) >= ABS(pd->poly_normal[2])) {
    pd->poly_p1 = 1;
    pd->poly_p2 = 2;
} else if (ABS(pd->poly_normal[1]) >= ABS(pd->poly_normal[0])
    && ABS(pd->poly_normal[1]) >= ABS(pd->poly_normal[2])) {
    pd->poly_p1 = 0;
    pd->poly_p2 = 2;
} else {
    pd->poly_p1 = 0;
    pd->poly_p2 = 1;
}

pd->poly_d = - VecDot(pd->poly_normal, pd->poly_point[0]);

obj->o_data = (void *) pd;

/*
 * now, calculate the values of
 * the dmin and dmax 'es for the globally defined slabs...
 */

for (i = 0; i < NSLABS; i ++) {
    dmin = HUGE;
    dmax = - HUGE;

    for (j = 0; j < pd->poly_npoints; j ++) {
        d = VecDot(Slab[i], pd->poly_point[j]);
        if (d < dmin) dmin = d;
        if (d > dmax) dmax = d;
    }
    obj->o_dmin[i] = dmin;
    obj->o_dmax[i] = dmax;
}

if(obj->clips) {
```

```
        bound_opt(obj);
    }

    return obj;
}
```

Listing 8-1. Poly.C

Triangular Patches

For planar objects such as polygons, this representation only allows one surface normal. Many complex objects are approximated as collections of polygonal patches, usually triangles or quadrilaterals. To produce the illusion of a smooth surface, you store separate surface normals at the vertices that generally will not lie in the plane of the polygon. This surface normal is computed as the average of the surface normals of each polygon patch that shares the single vertex. At any particular intersection point, you estimate the surface normal by interpolating the normals from the vertices to the point of intersection. This technique is referred to as *Phong shading*. The ray tracer implements this feature for triangular patches in the module Tri.C, below (Listing 8-2). The key point here is that you must not only determine whether the ray intersects the triangle, but also the interpolated surface normal based on the normals at the three vertices. Figure 8-4 shows the triangular patch primitive.

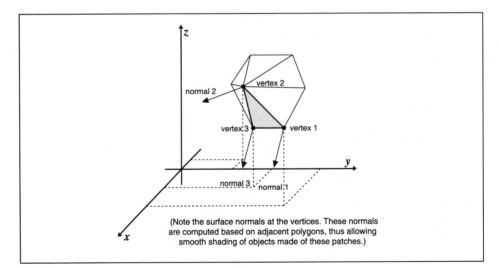

(Note the surface normals at the vertices. These normals are computed based on adjacent polygons, thus allowing smooth shading of objects made of these patches.)

Figure 8-4. Triangular patch primitive object

218

```
/*
```

```
┌─────────────────────────────────────────────────────────┐
│ ┌─────────────────────────────────────────────────────┐ │
│ │           Tri.C = The Triangular Patch Primitive      │ │
│ │   Copyright 1988, 1992 Christopher D. Watkins and Stephen B. Coy │ │
│ │                  ALL RIGHTS RESERVED                  │ │
│ │              Dependencies = Defs.H, Extern.H          │ │
│ └─────────────────────────────────────────────────────┘ │
└─────────────────────────────────────────────────────────┘
```

```
    TRIs are triangular patches with normals defined at the vertices.
    When an intersection is found, it interpolates the normal to the
    surface at that point.

    Algorithm is due to Jeff Arenburg.

    Basically, for each triangle we calculate an inverse transformation
    matrix, and use it to determine the point of intersection in the plane
    of the triangle relative to the "base point" of the triangle. We then
    figure its coordinates relative to that base point.  These base points
    are used to find the barycentric coordinates, and then in normal inter-
    polation...
*/

#include <stdio.h>
#include <math.h>
#include "defs.h"
#include "extern.h"

typedef struct t_patchdata {
    Vec     tri_P[3];
    Vec     tri_N[3];
    Vec     tri_bb[3];
    Vec     normal;         /* place to store normal */
} TriData;

ObjectProcs TriProcs = {
    TriIntersect,
    TriNormal,
};

int     TriIntersect(obj, ray, hit)
    Object  *obj;
    Ray     *ray;
    Isect   *hit;
{
    TriData     *td;
    Flt     n, d, dist;
    Flt     r, s, t;
```

```
Flt     a, b;
Vec     Q;

td = (TriData *) obj->o_data;

/*
 * The matrix td->tri_bb transforms vectors in the world
 * space into a space with the following properties.
 *
 * 1.  The sides of the triangle are coincident with the
 *     x and y axes, and have unit length.
 * 2.  The normal to the triangle is coincident with the
 *     z axis.
 *
 */

/*
 * d is the slope with respect to the z axis.  If d is zero, then
 * the ray is parallel to the plane of the polygon, and we count
 * it as a miss...
 */

d = VecDot(ray->D, td->tri_bb[2]);
if(ABS(d) < rayeps)
    return 0;

/*
 * Q is a vector from the eye to the triangle's "origin" vertex.
 * n is then set to be the distance of the transformed eyepoint
 * to the plane in the polygon.
 * Together, n and d allow you to find the distance to the
 * polygon, which is merely n / d.
 */

VecSub(td->tri_P[0], ray->P, Q);

n = VecDot(Q, td->tri_bb[2]);

dist = n / d;

if(dist < rayeps) {
    return 0;
}

/* calc intersect point, Q */
RayPoint(ray, dist, Q);
```

```
    /* if clipping and doesn't pass, bail */
    if(obj->clips && !clip_check(obj->clips, Q)) {
        return 0;
    }

    /*
     * Q is the point we hit.  Find its position relative to the
     * origin of the triangle.
     */

    VecSub(Q, td->tri_P[0], Q);

    a = VecDot(Q, td->tri_bb[0]);
    b = VecDot(Q, td->tri_bb[1]);

    if(a<0.0 || b<0.0 || a+b>1.0) {
        return 0;
    }

    r = 1.0 - a - b;
    s = a;
    t = b;

    hit->isect_t = dist;
    hit->isect_prim = obj;
    hit->isect_self = obj;
    hit->isect_surf = obj->o_surf;

    /* sum barycentric components to get real normal */

    VecZero(td->normal);
    VecAddS(r, td->tri_N[0], td->normal, td->normal);
    VecAddS(s, td->tri_N[1], td->normal, td->normal);
    VecAddS(t, td->tri_N[2], td->normal, td->normal);
    return 1;
}

void    TriNormal(obj, hit, P, N)
    Object    *obj;
    Isect    *hit;
    Point    P, N;
{
    TriData *td;

    td = (TriData *)obj->o_data;
```

```
    VecNormalize(td->normal);
    VecCopy(td->normal, N);
}

Object    *MakeTri(point)
    Vec    *point;
{
    Object    *o;
    TriData    *td;
    int    i, j;
    Flt    dmin, dmax, d;
    Vec    B[3];

    CheckTri(point);

    o = (Object *)vmalloc(sizeof(Object));
    ptrchk(o, "patch object");
    o->o_type = T_TRI;
    o->o_procs = &TriProcs;
    o->o_surf = CurrentSurface;

    td = (TriData *)vmalloc(sizeof(TriData));
    ptrchk(td, "patch data");

    if(ClipTop) {
        o->clips = ClipTop;
        ClipTop = GlobalClipTop->clip;
    } else {
        o->clips = NULL;
    }

    /*
     * copy in the points....
     */
    VecCopy(point[0], td->tri_P[0]);
    VecCopy(point[2], td->tri_P[1]);
    VecCopy(point[4], td->tri_P[2]);

    /*
     * and the normals, then normalize them...
     */
    VecCopy(point[1], td->tri_N[0]);
    VecCopy(point[3], td->tri_N[1]);
    VecCopy(point[5], td->tri_N[2]);
    VecNormalize(td->tri_N[0]);
    VecNormalize(td->tri_N[1]);
```

```
    VecNormalize(td->tri_N[2]);

    /*
     * construct the inverse of the matrix...
     * | P1 |
     * | P2 |
     * | N  |
     * and store it in td->tri_bb[]
     */

    VecSub(td->tri_P[1], td->tri_P[0], B[0]);
    VecSub(td->tri_P[2], td->tri_P[0], B[1]);
    VecCross(B[0], B[1], B[2]);
    VecNormalize(B[2]);

    InvertMatrix(B, td->tri_bb);

    for(i=0; i<NSLABS; i++) {
        dmin = HUGE;
        dmax = -HUGE;
        for(j=0; j<3; j++) {
            d = VecDot(Slab[i], td->tri_P[j]);
            if(d < dmin) dmin = d;
            if(d > dmax) dmax = d;
        }
        o->o_dmin[i] = dmin - rayeps;
        o->o_dmax[i] = dmax + rayeps;
    }

    o->o_data = (void *) td;

    return o;
}

void    InvertMatrix(in, out)
    Vec     in[3];
    Vec     out[3];
{
    int     i, j;
    Flt     det;

    out[0][0] = (in[1][1] * in[2][2] - in[1][2] * in[2][1]);
    out[1][0] = -(in[0][1] * in[2][2] - in[0][2] * in[2][1]);
    out[2][0] = (in[0][1] * in[1][2] - in[0][2] * in[1][1]);
```

```
    out[0][1] = -(in[1][0] * in[2][2] - in[1][2] * in[2][0]);
    out[1][1] = (in[0][0] * in[2][2] - in[0][2] * in[2][0]);
    out[2][1] = -(in[0][0] * in[1][2] - in[0][2] * in[1][0]);

    out[0][2] = (in[1][0] * in[2][1] - in[1][1] * in[2][0]);
    out[1][2] = -(in[0][0] * in[2][1] - in[0][1] * in[2][0]);
    out[2][2] = (in[0][0] * in[1][1] - in[0][1] * in[1][0]);

    det =
    in[0][0] * in[1][1] * in[2][2] +
    in[0][1] * in[1][2] * in[2][0] +
    in[0][2] * in[1][0] * in[2][1] -
    in[0][2] * in[1][1] * in[2][0] -
    in[0][0] * in[1][2] * in[2][1] -
    in[0][1] * in[1][0] * in[2][2];

    det = 1 / det;

    for (i = 0; i < 3; i ++) {
        for (j = 0; j < 3; j++) {
            out[i][j] *= det;
        }
    }
}

/*
    CheckTri() - make sure that all the vertex normals are on the
        same side of the patch.
*/

void    CheckTri(Vec *point)
{
    Vec     N, A, B;
    int     i;
    Flt     dot;

    /* calc surface normal as cross of edge vectors */

    VecSub(point[0], point[2], A);
    VecSub(point[0], point[4], B);
    VecCross(A, B, N);

    /* compare with each normal and flip if needed to same side */

    for(i=0; i<3; i++) {
        dot = VecDot(N, point[i*2+1]);
```

```
        if(dot <= 0.0) {
            VecNegate(point[i*2+1]);
        }
    }
}
```

Listing 8-2. Tri.C

The results of using triangular patches are shown in many of the color plates. Plate 5 shows chess pieces that are modeled by triangular patches. The ice cubes in Plate 25 are modeled as patches. Plates 44 through 46 use patches to make up complex shapes like ducks, the human heart, and cars.

Constructing Complex Objects

The primitives discussed thus far are useful, but are primarily used to build up more complex object models. Chapter 11 discusses hierarchical models that may be built as collections of primitives, and these models may themselves be used as primitives in other models. You can use affine transformations to scale, rotate, and translate any of these objects so that they may be moved as a single entity. However, simply positioning objects together is often insufficient because the primitive set described so far is too small. The types of objects you can create can be greatly expanded through the use of a technique known as *object clipping*.

The simplest example of object clipping is to slice an object with a plane (Figure 8-5 shows how a clipping plane is used to create a half-ring). For example, a hemispherical bowl may be created by slicing a sphere with a plane through the center. You can render the part of the sphere surface on one side of the plane and not the other. A clipping plane is specified by an origin point through which the plane passes and a surface normal. The ray tracer first checks to see if a ray intersects the object without the clipping plane. If so, it then checks to see on which side of the clipping plane the intersection point lies. For a plane, you construct the vector from the plane origin point to the point of intersection. If the dot product between this vector and the plane surface normal is positive, then the intersection is on the "unclipped" side of the plane. If it is not positive, the intersection is clipped out, and the ray tracer proceeds as if no intersection occurred.

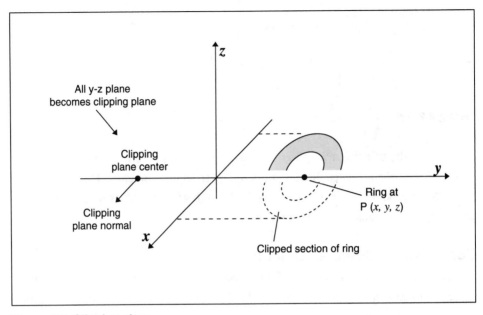

Figure 8-5. Clipping plane

You can also use other shapes for clipping. The ray tracer allows spheres and cones to be used as clipping surfaces. They may be used inclusively (only points inside the clipping surface are shown) or exclusively (only points outside the clipping surface are shown). For the sphere, compute the distance from the intersection point to the clipping sphere origin. If this distance is less than the sphere radius, the intersection is allowed (or ignored, depending on whether it is an inclusive or exclusive clip). Similarly, you determine whether the point is inside or outside of the cone. The Clip.C module (Listing 8-3) demonstrates the implementation of this. An example in which clipping is used to produce an object with a stripe is shown in Color Plate 6, where the stripes on pool balls are created using this clipping technique.

```
/*
```

```
*/

#include <stdio.h>
#include <math.h>
#include "defs.h"
#include "extern.h"

/*
    clip_check() - check a point against a list of clips.
        Returns 1 if passes, 0 if fails.
*/

clip_check(Clip *head, Vec P)
{
    Vec     V;
    Flt     dist;

    while(head) {
        VecSub(P, head->center, V);
        if(head->type & C_PLANE) {
            if(VecDot(V, head->normal) < 0.0)
                return 0;
        } else if(head->type & C_SPHERE) {
            dist = V[0]*V[0] + V[1]*V[1] + V[2]*V[2];
            if(head->type & C_INSIDE) {
                if(dist > head->radius1) {
                    return 0;
                }
            } else if(dist < head->radius1) {    /* must be outside sphere */
                return 0;
            }
        } else if(head->type & C_CONE) {
            Vec     ap;
            Flt     ap_dot, percent, radius, dist;

            VecSub(P, head->apex, ap);
            ap_dot = VecDot(ap, head->normal);
```

```
                if(ap_dot<0.0 || ap_dot>head->length) {
                    if(head->type & C_INSIDE) {
                        return 0;
                    }
                } else {            /* on "inside" of ends */
                    percent = ap_dot/head->length;
                    radius = percent*head->radius2 + (1.0-percent)*
                            head->radius1;
                    radius = radius * radius;
                    VecAddS(ap_dot, head->normal, head->apex, ap);
                    dist = (ap[0]-P[0]) * (ap[0]-P[0]) +
                            (ap[1]-P[1]) * (ap[1]-P[1]) +
                            (ap[2]-P[2]) * (ap[2]-P[2]);
                    if(head->type & C_INSIDE) {
                        if(dist>radius) {
                            return 0;
                        }
                    } else {
                        if(dist<radius) {
                            return 0;
                        }
                    }
                }          /* if inside of ends */

            } else {
                fprintf(stderr, "\nInternal error.  Unknown clip type %04x.\n",
                                                    head->type);
                last_call(1);
            }

            head = head->next;        /* move on down */
        }

    return 1;
}       /* end of clip_check() */
/*
    bound_opt — optimize the bounding box of an object which has
        one or more clips.  Only works for planes and inside
        spheres.
*/

bound_opt(Object *obj)
{
    Clip            *cl;
    int             i, i1, i2;
    Flt             intersect,
            b1, b2,         /* values of box corner */
```

```
        c1, c2,     /* values of clip center for "other" axes */
        d1, d2;     /* values of clip normal for "other" axes */

cl = obj->clips;
while(cl) {
    if((cl->type&C_SPHERE) && (cl->type&C_INSIDE)) {
        Flt     radius;

        radius = sqrt(cl->radius1);
        for(i=0; i<3; i++) {     /* for each axis */
            if(obj->o_dmax[i]  > cl->center[i]+radius) {
                obj->o_dmax[i] = cl->center[i]+radius;
            }
            if(obj->o_dmin[i]  > cl->center[i]-radius) {
                obj->o_dmin[i] = cl->center[i]-radius;
            }
        }
    } if((cl->type&C_CONE) && (cl->type&C_INSIDE)) {
        for(i=0; i<3; i++) {     /* for each axis */
            if(cl->apex[i] > cl->base[i]) {
                if(obj->o_dmax[i] > cl->apex[i]+cl->radius1) {
                    obj->o_dmax[i] = cl->apex[i]+cl->radius1;
                }
                if(obj->o_dmin[i] > cl->base[i]-cl->radius2) {
                    obj->o_dmin[i] = cl->base[i]-cl->radius2;
                }
            } else {
                if(obj->o_dmax[i] > cl->base[i]+cl->radius2) {
                    obj->o_dmax[i] = cl->base[i]+cl->radius2;
                }
                if(obj->o_dmin[i] > cl->apex[i]-cl->radius1) {
                    obj->o_dmin[i] = cl->apex[i]-cl->radius1;
                }
            }
        }
    } else if(cl->type & C_PLANE) {
        for(i=0; i<3; i++) {               /* for each axis */
            i1 = (i+1)%3;
            i2 = (i+2)%3;
            if(cl->normal[i] == 0.0) {      /* clip perpendicular to
                                              axis, nothing happens */
                continue;
            }

            /* get clip center values */
            c1 = cl->center[i1];
            c2 = cl->center[i2];
```

```
      d2 = cl->normal[i2];

      /* get b's */
      b1 = (d1 > 0.0) ? obj->o_dmax[i1] : obj->o_dmin[i1];
      b2 = (d2 > 0.0) ? obj->o_dmax[i2] : obj->o_dmin[i2];

      intersect = cl->center[i];
      intersect += (c1-b1)*d1/cl->normal[i];
      intersect += (c2-b2)*d2/cl->normal[i];

      if(cl->normal[i] > 0.0) {        /* shrink min */
        if(obj->o_dmin[i] < intersect) {
          obj->o_dmin[i] = intersect;
        }
      } else {                          /* shrink max */
        if(obj->o_dmax[i] > intersect) {
          obj->o_dmax[i] = intersect;
        }
      }
    }        /* end of i loop for each axis */
  }        /* end of if clipping plane */

  cl = cl->next;
  }        /* end of while loop */
}        /* end of bound_opt() */
```

Listing 8-3. Clip.C

Note that to create elaborate effects, you can use multiple clipping surfaces in virtually any combination. For example, you create a cube with rounded corners by enclosing the cube with an inclusive clipping sphere. You can also use clipping objects around lights as well as objects in a scene. Thus, you can create a spotlight effect by enclosing a light source in a clipping cone. Only rays intersecting the light through the cone are counted. Color Plate 1 shows an elaborate use of clipping to create the complex ceiling of a room. See Figure 8-5 for a look at a clipping plane used to create a half-ring.

230

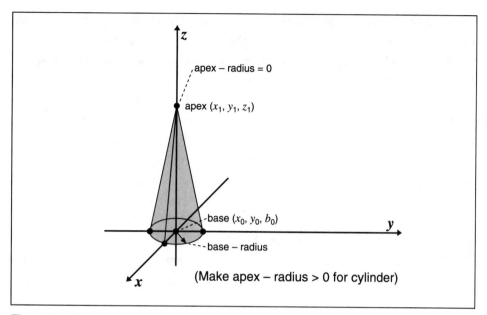

z

apex − radius = 0

apex (x_1, y_1, z_1)

base (x_0, y_0, b_0)

base − radius

y

(Make apex − radius > 0 for cylinder)

x

Figure 8-6. Cone primitive object

Constructive Solid Geometry

The term *constructive solid geometry* (*CSG*) refers to the process of creating complex objects by using unions, intersections, and other logical operations to combine primitive elements. If your object is representable by such a combination, then CSG can result in an efficient representation with a minimum amount of storage. For instance, a dumbbell modeled as a cylinder with two spheres on the end only requires the storage of three primitives. Any reasonably faceted representation of this would require hundreds of polygons to represent the same thing. However, the opposite is true with other types of models, usually because they are not composed of smooth or continuous surfaces.

Bob allows you to combine objects by using affine transformations to position them relative to one another. You use clipping surfaces for object intersections. For instance, to render just the intersection of two spheres, you can place clipping planes to bound the intersection so that only portions of the spheres in the intersection are drawn. This approach to modeling requires some creativity and practice to produce the best combination of objects for a particular scene. However, it can produce a very compact representation that can be rendered quite efficiently.

For a given ray, you must determine the nearest object the ray intersects (other than the one from which the ray started). This means you must search the entire list of objects to find the nearest one, (in other words, the one whose intersection yields the minimum value of the parameter t along the ray).

If you take the straightforward approach of simply casting rays and testing every object in the object list for each ray, you quickly saturate the computing requirements of even the simplest scenes. For example, a list of 10 requires no less than (10 + #lights*5 + reflected + refracted) intersection calculations per ray. If the ray is reflected, then even more rays are cast. With anti-aliasing enabled, the number of rays per screen pixel increases dramatically. You could easily perform 100 intersection tests per screen pixel. With a screen resolution of 320 x 240, this corresponds to 7,680,000 intersection tests. For 100 objects, this increases to more than 75 million intersection tests. Even on the fastest computers, this takes a long time and is not efficient. Over the years, people have developed many techniques for improving the efficiency.

Bounding volumes

Complex objects are comprised of collections of more primitive objects. Given this object definition, you can construct a *bounding volume* that completely contains the object it encloses. If a ray does not intersect this bounding volume, it does not intersect any of the objects in the bounding volume and those objects can be removed from further consideration for this ray. The algorithm implemented in the ray tracer is primarily based on one published by Kay and Kajiya in the SIGGRAPH proceedings on bounding methods from 1986.

The hierarchical database is defined as a simple list of objects to be drawn, where each object may be a primitive or comprised of other objects. It would be better to turn this list into a hierarchical tree in which each node has a bounding volume for all of the child nodes beneath it. Ideally, you want the tree to be relatively balanced (an equal number of objects on each side), though this seldom will be accomplished exactly. Furthermore, you want to group objects that are "close" to one another to help minimize the bounding volume sizes.

There are many ways of constructing such a tree from a list of objects, and some are better than others on certain types of scenes. Once the hierarchical tree is generated, you compute the bounding volume of a node since its bounding volume is derived from the bounding volumes of the nodes beneath it. Once again, you use a recursive process to accomplish this task. The next step is to decide what kind of bounding volume to use.

The simplest type of bounding volume is that of the *bounding box* (see Figure 8-7). You find the minimum and maximum extent of the object in the x, y, and z axes, and then consider any affine transformations that may be applied to the object. This minimum and maximum now defines the bounding box. Although this practice has the virtue of being simple to compute, it is not a good bound for many objects, especially when they lie at a 45-degree angle with respect to the axes. A long thin box rotated and pitched at 45 degrees, for instance, will have its bounding box increased dramatically.

The bounding box test described so far still requires that you determine whether a given ray intersects the box.

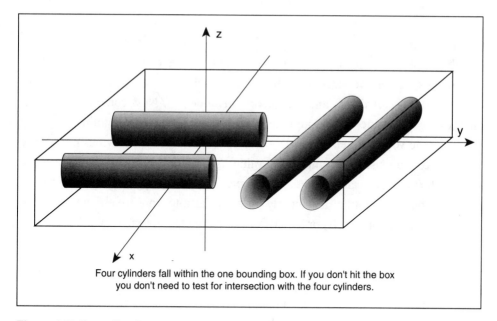

Four cylinders fall within the one bounding box. If you don't hit the box
you don't need to test for intersection with the four cylinders.

Figure 8-7. Bounding boxes and object grouping

Bounding planes

You can generalize the bounding box by defining bounding plane pairs, referred to as *Slabs* in the modules. Examine Figure 8-7 again. Each slab is defined by a normalized vector that indicates which direction the slab faces. Think of a ray starting from the eyepoint, pointing in the direction of the slab toward an object. You must find the extent (minimum and maximum) of the object along this vector. For instance, the bounding box could be defined by the vectors (1, 0, 0), (0, 1, 0), and (0, 0, 1). As with the ray casting, you use the parametric form of the ray to find the values for the minimum (when the entire object is in front of the plane perpendicular to this ray) and maximum (when the entire object is behind the plane). These values are referred to as *dmin* and *dmax*. You use more slabs to produce tighter volumes (less wasted space) about the objects.

The default settings of the ray tracer generate bounding boxes. Note that this calculation is done only once for the entire database tree. The precomputed values of *dmin* and *dmax* are then used to simplify the ray-volume intersection tests required by all the rays.

To determine if a ray intersects the bounding volume, compute the values of the parameter t for the two sides of each slab. For each slab, the minimum value of t (closest side) is called t_{near} and the maximum value t_{far}. Now compare the maximum of the t_{near} values (tmax) and the minimum of the t_{far} values (tmin). If the ray intersects the volume, then t_{max} is less than t_{min}. Otherwise, the ray has missed the volume. So, you must now compute the values of t for each slab. However, this is the same as the ray-plane calculation described previously for polygonal objects. The following is the computation in a slightly different form to improve efficiency, where $d(i)$ is actually either *dmin*[i] or *dmax*[i] as precomputed for each object:

```
t=(d(i)-VecCot(slab[i],ray.P)/VecDot(slab[i],ray.D))
```
(Equation 8-15)

The dot product calculations need only be computed once for each ray. Furthermore, the divide can be turned into a multiply during this step. Thus, the overall computation of t becomes much more efficient.

The Hierarchical Tree

You can further increase your ray tracing efficiency by storing the database as a hierarchical tree. While there are many algorithms for constructing such a tree, the *median cut* approach is one of the most popular. The algorithm for the median cut performs recursively for each node, starting at the original linked list of objects. Basically, all objects are sorted along one of the slab directions by using the *dmin* and *dmax* values already computed. The object list is then divided according to the median value (half on either side). Each sublist is recursively subdivided, but the axis about which to divide the objects is redetermined. The axis to subdivide is determined according to which one has the largest variation in the minimum and maximum values along the slab directions. The recursion stops whenever you have less than the *bunching* primitives (where *bunching* is a *#defined* constant) left in the current subtree. The *SortAndSplit* function in the Bound.C module (Listing 8-4) shows this process. Note that the tree structure need only be built once per scene, not per ray.

As the hierarchical tree is built, the bounding volume for each node is generated. If the element is a primitive object, that primitive's already computed bounding volume is used. Otherwise, the node's bounding volume is generated as the boundary of all of the child nodes.

```
/*
```

```
         Bound.C = generate bounding slabs and tree structure
     Copyright 1988, 1992 Christopher D. Watkins and Stephen B. Coy
                        ALL RIGHTS RESERVED
                   Dependencies - defs.h, extern.h
```

```
*/
```

```
#include <stdio.h>
#include <stdlib.h>
#include "defs.h"
#include "extern.h"

static long     total;          /* # objects in main list */
static Flt      Median;         /* 2*median value along axis */
static int      Axis;           /* axis to split along */

/*
```

```
 * This function attempts to use median cut
 * to generate tighter bounding volumes than the old
 * code...
 */

void BuildBoundingSlabs(void)
{
    total = nPrims;
    while(SortAndSplit(&Root, total))
        ;                       /* this line intentionally left blank */
    if(tickflag) {
        printf("\n\tAfter adding bounding volumes, %ld prims.\n", nPrims);
        printf("\tExtent of scene\n");
        printf("\tX   %g - %g\n", Root->o_dmin[0], Root->o_dmax[0]);
        printf("\tY   %g - %g\n", Root->o_dmin[1], Root->o_dmax[1]);
        printf("\tZ   %g - %g\n", Root->o_dmin[2], Root->o_dmax[2]);
    }
}


void    FindAxis(Object *top, long count)
{
    Flt    mins[NSLABS];
    Flt    maxs[NSLABS];
    int    i, j , which;
    Flt    d = -HUGE, e, x, y, z;
    long   cnt;

    cnt = count;
    for(i=0; i<NSLABS; i++) {        /* zero out min/max */
        mins[i] = HUGE;
        maxs[i] = -HUGE;
    }
    x = y = z = 0.0;

    while(count-) {
        if(top == NULL) {
            fprintf(stderr, "NULL top in FindAxis, count = %ld\n", count);
            last_call(1);
        }
        for(j=0; j<NSLABS; j++) {
#ifdef OLD_CODE
            if(top->o_dmin[j] < mins[j])
                mins[j] = top->o_dmin[j];
            if(top->o_dmax[j] > maxs[j])
                maxs[j] = top->o_dmax[j];
#else
            e = top->o_dmin[j] + top->o_dmax[j];
```

```
                if(e < mins[j])
                    mins[j] = e;
                if(e > maxs[j])
                    maxs[j] = e;
#endif
        }
        x += top->o_dmin[0] + top->o_dmax[0];
        y += top->o_dmin[1] + top->o_dmax[1];
        z += top->o_dmin[2] + top->o_dmax[2];
        top = top->next;
    }

    for(i=0; i<NSLABS; i++) {
        e = maxs[i] - mins[i];
        if(e>d) {
            d = e;
            which = i;
        }
    }

    Axis = which;
    switch(Axis) {
        case 0 : Median = x/cnt; break;
        case 1 : Median = y/cnt; break;
        case 2 : Median = z/cnt; break;
    }

/*      printf("count = %lu axis = %lu median = %.4f\n", cnt, Axis,
            Median);   */
}



int     SortAndSplit(Object **top_handle, long count)
{
    Object  *top, *hi, *lo, *cur, *tmp, *hi_end, *lo_end;
    long    lo_cnt, hi_cnt, i, j;
    Flt     dmin, dmax;

    if(count <= 0)
        return 0;

    top = *top_handle;
    if(count > bunching) {           /* need to split */
        FindAxis(top, count);
        hi_cnt = 0;
        lo_cnt = 0;
        cur = *top_handle;
```

```
hi = (Object *)NULL;
lo = (Object *)NULL;
for(i=0; i<count; i++) {
    if(Median > (cur->o_dmin[Axis] + cur->o_dmax[Axis])) {
        lo_cnt++;
        tmp = cur;
        cur = cur->next;
        tmp->next = lo;
        if(lo == NULL) {
            lo_end = tmp;
        }
        lo = tmp;
    } else {
        hi_cnt++;
        tmp = cur;
        cur = cur->next;
        tmp->next = hi;
        if(hi == NULL) {
            hi_end = tmp;
        }
        hi = tmp;
    }
}        /* end of i loop */

/*
    Fix if either list is length 0 by arbitrarily
    splitting into two.  Should never happen with
    new FindAxis code.
*/

if(lo_cnt == 0) {
    lo_end = hi;
    for(i=0; i<count/2; i++) {
        tmp = hi;
        hi = hi->next;
        tmp->next = lo;
        lo = tmp;
        hi_cnt-;
        lo_cnt++;
    }
} else if(hi_cnt == 0) {
    hi_end = lo;
    for(i=0; i<count/2; i++) {
        tmp = lo;
        lo = lo->next;
        tmp->next = hi;
```

```
            hi = tmp;
            lo_cnt-;
            hi_cnt++;
        }
    }

    /* insert sublists into main list */

    *top_handle = hi;
    hi_end->next = lo;
    lo_end->next = cur;
    SortAndSplit(&hi_end->next, lo_cnt);
    SortAndSplit(top_handle, hi_cnt);

    return 1;
} else if(count > 1) {              /* create a composite only if more than
                                       one object */
    Object          *cp;
    CompositeData   *cd;

    cp = (Object *)vmalloc(sizeof(Object));
    ptrchk(cp, "composite object");

    cp->o_type = T_COMPOSITE;
    cp->o_procs = &NullProcs;        /* die if you call any  */
    cp->o_surf = NULL;               /* no surface...        */
    cd = (CompositeData *)vmalloc(sizeof(CompositeData));
    ptrchk(cd, "composite data");
    cd->size = count;
    total = total-count+1;

    /*
        Replace the objects in the main list with the
        new composite object.  The objects being removed
        are added to the new objects children list.
    */

    cd->children = top;
    *top_handle = cp;

    i = count;
    while(-i) {                /* make top point to last child object */
        top = top->next;
    }
    cp->next = top->next;   /* connect new comp object to remainder of
                                list */
```

```
    top->next = NULL;        /* last child's next pointer */

    /* calc bounding slabs for new composite object */

    for(i=0; i<NSLABS; i++) {        /* for each slab */
        dmin = HUGE;
        dmax = -HUGE;
        top = cd->children;          /* point to first child */
        for(j=0; j<count; j++) {
            if(top->o_dmin[i] < dmin)
                dmin = top->o_dmin[i];
            if(top->o_dmax[i] > dmax)
                dmax = top->o_dmax[i];
            top = top->next;
        }
        cp->o_dmin[i] = dmin;
        cp->o_dmax[i] = dmax;
    }
    cp->o_data = (void *) cd;
    ++nPrims;
    yystats();

    return 0;
    }
    return 0;        /* only happens with list of length 1 */
}        /* end of SortAndSplit() */
```

Listing 8-4. Bound.C

Searching Those Objects

Given a ray, you traverse the tree to search for the nearest object the ray intersects (minimum value of the parameter t). Start at the top node and test the ray against the bounding volume of that node. If the ray misses the bounding volume, no further processing of that node is required. If not, then continue testing the children of this node. This algorithm proceeds recursively through the tree, searching for the nearest object at each node level.

This kind of search can also be improved with a technique used in paging algorithms. This technique, called a *priority queue*, is shown in the module Pqueue.C. In this case, the value you use for sorting is the minimum intersection value t generated when you perform the ray-volume intersection calculation.

The search begins from the top node of the tree. The top node is added to the priority queue to start things off. The algorithm then proceeds by testing each node on the queue until the queue is empty. If a ray intersects the bounding volume of a node, then all of the children of that node are tested and, if intersected by the ray, added to the queue. If the node is a primitive object, then the ray-object intersection test is performed and the value of t is determined. If this is less than the current minimum, then this primitive becomes the nearest object until another one supersedes it.

Note that a node can be rejected if the value of t for the bounding volume of that node is greater than the current *tmin* value. Thus, the queue automatically sorts the object list dynamically. Whenever an object is added to the queue, the *Insert* function inserts it into the proper order. Thus, the nodes are always tested from near to far. The Inter.C module shows how this algorithm is implemented. The *CheckAndEnqueue* procedure checks to see if the bounding volume is intersected by the ray, and if so, adds it to the priority queue.

Listing 8-5 (Pqueue.C) and Listing 8-6 (Inter.C) follow.

```
/ *
```

```
        PQueue.C = priority queue
  Copyright 1988, 1992 Christopher D. Watkins and Stephen B. Coy
                  ALL RIGHTS RESERVED
            Dependencies - defs.h, extern.h
```

```
* /
```

```
#include <stdio.h>
#include <math.h>
#include "defs.h"
#include "extern.h"

typedef struct t_qelem {
  Flt      q_key;
  Object   *q_obj;
} Qelem;

static int    Qsize;
```

```
Qelem     Q[PQSIZE];

void     PriorityQueueNull(void)
{
    Qsize = 0;
    totalQueueResets ++;
}

int      PriorityQueueEmpty(void)
{
    return (Qsize == 0);
}

void     PriorityQueueInsert(
        Flt key,
        Object *obj)
{
    register    i;
    Qelem          tmp;

    totalQueues++;
     Qsize++;
    if(Qsize > maxQueueSize)
        maxQueueSize = Qsize;
    if(Qsize >= PQSIZE) {
        fprintf(stderr, "Exhausted priority queue space, dying...\n");
        last_call(1);
    }
    Q[Qsize].q_key = key;
    Q[Qsize].q_obj = obj;

    i = Qsize;
    while(i>1 && Q[i].q_key<Q[i/2].q_key) {
        tmp = Q[i];
        Q[i] = Q[i/2];
        Q[i/2] = tmp;
        i = i / 2;
    }
}

void     PriorityQueueDelete(
        Flt *key,
        Object **obj)
{
    Qelem     tmp;
    int      i, j;
```

```
if(Qsize == 0) {
    printf("Priority queue is empty, dying...\n");
    last_call(1);
}

*key = Q[1].q_key;
*obj = Q[1].q_obj;

Q[1] = Q[Qsize];
Qsize-;

i = 1;

while(2*i <= Qsize) {

    if(2*i == Qsize) {
        j = 2*i;
    } else if (Q[2*i].q_key < Q[2*i+1].q_key) {
        j = 2*i;
    } else {
        j = 2*i + 1;
    }

    if (Q[i].q_key > Q[j].q_key) {
        tmp = Q[i];
        Q[i] = Q[j];
        Q[j] = tmp;
        i = j;
    } else {
        break;
    }
}
}
```

Listing 8-5. Pqueue.C

```
/*
```

```
┌──────────────────────────────────────────────────────────────┐
│  Inter.C = routines that shuffle through the tree of bounding objects │
│              and try to find the nearest intersection           │
│     Copyright 1988, 1992 Christopher D. Watkins and Stephen B. Coy │
│                      ALL RIGHTS RESERVED                        │
│                  Dependencies - defs.h, extern.h               │
└──────────────────────────────────────────────────────────────┘
```

```
_*/
```

```c
#include <stdio.h>
#include <math.h>
#include <assert.h>
#include "defs.h"
#include "extern.h"

/*
 * intersect.c
 * Much nicer now, uses the nifty priority queue search
 * as suggested by Kajiya...
 */

Flt     num[NSLABS];
Flt     den[NSLABS];

/*********************************************************************
 * CheckAndEnqueue(obj, maxdist)
 * Check the current ray (as paramaterized with the num and den
 * arrays above) against the bounding volume of obj.
 * If we intersect the bounding volume, then insert it into the
 * priority queue.
 *
 * Note: should be broken into two separate procedures...
 *********************************************************************/

void    CheckAndEnqueue(obj, maxdist)
    Object     *obj;
    Flt     maxdist;
{
    register     i;

    Flt     tmin, tmax;
    Flt     dmin = -HUGE;
    Flt     dmax = maxdist;

    nChecked++;
```

```
    for(i=0; i<NSLABS; i++) {

        if(den[i] == 0.0)
            continue;

        /* enters the slab here...    */
        tmin = (obj->o_dmin[i] - num[i]) / den[i];
        /* and exits here...          */
        tmax = (obj->o_dmax[i] - num[i]) / den[i];

        /* but we may have to swap...    */
        if(tmin < tmax) {
            /* if exited closer than we thought, update    */
            if(tmax < dmax)
                dmax = tmax;
            /* if entered farther than we thought, update    */
            if(tmin > dmin)
                dmin = tmin;
        } else {
            /* if exited closer than we thought, update    */
            if(tmin < dmax)
                dmax = tmin;
            /* if entered farther than we thought, update    */
            if(tmax > dmin)
                dmin = tmax;
        }

        if(dmin>dmax || dmax<rayeps)
            return;
    }
    PriorityQueueInsert(dmin, obj);
    nEnqueued++;
}

/*********************************************************************
 * Intersect(ray, hit, maxdist, self)
 *
 * Returns true if we hit something in the root model closer than
 * maxdist.
 * Returns the closest hit in the "hit" buffer.

   Self is a pointer to the last object hit.  If self is NULL then
   the ray either originated at the eye or the last object may be
   self-intersecting ie spheres and cones.  This can be used to
   eliminate doing an intersection test with the last object.
 *********************************************************************/
```

```
Intersect(ray, hit, maxdist, self)
    Ray     *ray;
    Isect   *hit;
    Flt     maxdist;
    Object  *self;
{
    Isect           nhit;
    int             i;
    Flt             min_dist = maxdist;
    Object          *cobj, *child;
    Object          *pobj = NULL;
    CompositeData   *cdp;
    Flt             key;

  /* If the object is simple, then return the hit that it gives you */

    if(Root->o_type != T_COMPOSITE)
        return (Root->o_procs->intersect) (Root, ray, hit);

    for(i=0; i<3; i++) {
        num[i] = ray->P[i];
        den[i] = ray->D[i];
    }

    /* start with an empty priority queue */
    PriorityQueueNull();

    CheckAndEnqueue(Root, maxdist);

    for (;;) {

        if(PriorityQueueEmpty())
            break;

        PriorityQueueDelete(&key, &cobj);

        if(key > min_dist) {

            /*
             * we have already found a primitive
             * that was closer, we need look no further...
             */
            break;

        } else if(cobj->o_type == T_COMPOSITE) {
            /*
```

```
         * if it is in the queue, it got hit.
         * check each of its children to see if their
         * bounding volumes get hit.
         * if so, then push them into the priority
         * queue...
         */

        cdp = (CompositeData *) cobj->o_data;
        child = cdp->children;

        while(child) {
            if(self != child) {
                CheckAndEnqueue(child, maxdist);
            }
            child = child->next;
        }

    } else {

        /*
         * we have a primitive
         * intersect with the primitive, and possibly
         * update the nearest hit if it is indeed closer
         * than the one we currently have...
         */

        if((cobj->o_procs->intersect) (cobj, ray, &nhit)) {
            if(nhit.isect_t < min_dist) {
                pobj = cobj;
                *hit = nhit;
                min_dist = nhit.isect_t;
            }
        }
    }
}

if (pobj)
    return 1;
else
    return 0;
}
```

Listing 8-6. Inter.C

Other Algorithms

There are many other types of algorithms for storing objects, for constructing the database tree, and for searching the object list to determine ray-object intersections. The most interesting new data type being used today is that of *voxels*. A voxel is the three-dimensional equivalent of a pixel. You describe any object by dividing it up into small digitized cubes, with a unique set of cube values that describe the opacity, color, reflectivity, and so on for that particular voxel.

Rays are cast into the volume using the three-dimensional version of scan conversion. This provides tremendous flexibility when producing arbitrary images of amorphous objects such as clouds and the human anatomy. However, it comes at a cost. The amount of data storage is much larger than for the methods described in this chapter. As computer storage becomes cheaper and compression algorithms are improved, these conditions can be alleviated to the point of practicality.

Chapter 9 discusses the intersection information used to compute the object color based on the lighting, object shadowing, and texture of the object surface.

CHAPTER 9

Seeing the Light

The intersection calculation from Chapter 8 provides three basic pieces of information: a pointer to the object, the (x, y, z) coordinates of the intersection point, and the surface normal vector. From this information, you can derive the color of the ray caused by the intersection with the object surface. By adding this color to any other rays generated for reflection and refraction, you produce the total ray color. This chapter develops a model that takes into account the use of multiple lights, shadowing, atmospheric effects, and texturing to achieve realistic images.

A Shady Model

A shading model is implemented in the module Shade.C found on the accompanying disk. The computer graphics model of shading is based on a simplified physical model. This model is "simplified" because a complete physical model cannot be computed in a finite amount of time. The lighting models in Shade.C generally have been "fudged" to create a desired effect. However, the assumptions and approximations in Shade.C do produce acceptable results. All the color terms described in this section are additive. This means that you compute each color individually and sum the terms to produce the net color of the ray. This model takes advantage of the fact that light energy is linear. In other words, you compute the effects for each light in the scene individually and add the results together.

To understand this model, you must first understand some minor terminology and definitions. The *incident ray* is the ray you are currently processing. The surface normal, N, is the normal at the point of intersection. The reflection vectors for both the incident ray and the rays to the light sources are generated exactly as described in Chapter 6 by using the laws of optical reflection. The following variables are used:

K_d ....diffuse coefficient

K_s ....specular (reflective) coefficient

K_t...................transmitted coefficient

K_a ....ambient coefficient
K_h ....specular highlight
N_s ....specular exponent
N ....surface normal at intersection point
V ....vector of incident ray
R ....vector for reflected ray
E ....vector from the eyepoint to the intersection point
L_n ....vector toward nth light source
H_n ....reflected L_n vector (the direction light reflects directly off the surface)
I ....illumination (the desired color)
I_a ....ambient illumination
I_r ....illumination of reflected ray
I_t ....illumination of transmitted ray
I_n ....illumination of nth light source

To determine the total illumination value, *I*, sum the components as follows:

$$I = ambient + diffuse + specular + transmitted + specular\ highlights$$

Note that in the following sections, you use only a single light source by computing I_n. The I_n are then summed over all light sources to produce the total illumination, *I*.

Background color (K_a)

The simplest lighting component is the background or *ambient* lighting. Ambient light emanates from all around the environment, points in all directions, and is uniformly distributed throughout the scene. *Ambient light* assumes the same properties as the light intensity assigned to rays not intersecting any objects or lights in the scene (unless you are using a background image described in Chapter 7). A daylight scene has a much brighter ambient component than a nighttime scene. An object may have its own ambient lighting component, such as self-luminous objects like glowing spheres, street lights, fireflies, and so on. The upper-left image of Color Plate 11 shows the effect of ambient illumination.

Diffuse color (K_d)

The *diffuse color* of an object is essentially the color of the object under white light. A red ball is red because it reflects the red component of light on the surface and absorbs the others. If you shine a light on a red ball, the light is not reflected the way a mirror would reflect it (in only one direction) but rather is reflected in all directions. The part of the surface facing the light receives the most intensity per unit area, while the parts facing away receive no light at all (see Figure 9-1). Therefore, you see those areas facing the light source (surface normal points in the direction of the light source) as the brightest, independent of viewing direction since a diffuse surface scatters light equally in all directions. Because of this directional independence, the diffuse intensity is a function of the angle between the surface normal and the light direction, or equivalently, a function of the dot product of the two:

```
Kd = -VecDot(N, Ln);
```
(Equation 9-1)

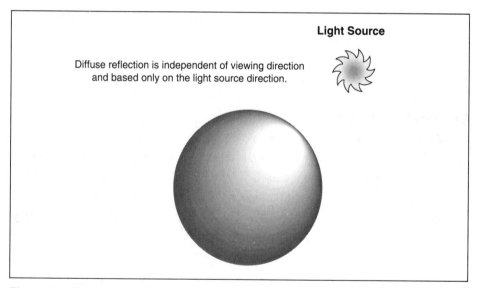

Figure 9-1. Diffuse reflection

The *Lambertian* diffuse reflectance model states that the light intensity is directly proportional to this dot product. If *Diffuse* is less than or equal to 0, it is treated as 0. These values correspond to the portions of the surface facing away from the light and are thus automatically shadowed from the light source. In the absence of shadows and texture, you simply multiply the intrinsic diffuse color of the object by *Diffuse* to get the net diffuse intensity at this point.

But if you shine a green light on a blue ball, you must take the diffuse color vector and multiply each component (red, green, and blue) by the corresponding light color components. A red light typically has color (1, 0, 0). Note that the diffuse color would be 0 if the ball were purely blue or green.

In addition to scaling based on the angle, Bob also provides the option of reducing the light intensity as a function of distance from the intersection. Physically, light intensity falls off as 1/distance^2. However, because of the approximations you make concerning the diffuse and ambient light in the environment, you can obtain a better looking result by using 1/distance scaling (see Figure 9-5). This kind of intensity scaling works for light sources such as light bulbs, but is not needed for daylight scenes. The sun intensity does not change appreciably over the distances of your average scene (unless you are viewing the scene from a great distance). When the scaling is in effect, you effectively can change the strength of the lightbulbs you use in the scene by adjusting this intensity fall-off distance.

The upper-right image in Color Plate 11 shows the effects of adding in the diffuse component. Note that you can now tell which way the light is pointing.

A speculative addition (K$_h$)

Many surfaces have mirror-like qualities. Metal and plastic surfaces at least partially reflect the light source directly. This is referred to as a *specular* effect (see Figure 9-2). An image of the light source itself is reflected off the surface. In order for this reflected light to reach your eye, you must be positioned in such a way that the light source reflects in the direction of your eye. This is exactly the same as the reflected ray calculation discussed in Chapter 6. The angle between the eyepoint vector and the surface normal must be "close" to the angle between the light vector and surface normal. Unless the surface is a perfect mirror, the light always is diffused slightly and forms a reflective spot on the surface. This spot, known as the *specular highlight*, is the color of the light source because, after all, it is a distorted reflection of the light source.

The vector H_n is the direction the light would be reflected if the surface were a perfect mirror. As with the diffuse coefficient, the perceived intensity is a function of the angle between the vector (H_n) and the eyepoint vector (E). Unlike the diffuse component, you must be facing in the proper direction to perceive the spot.

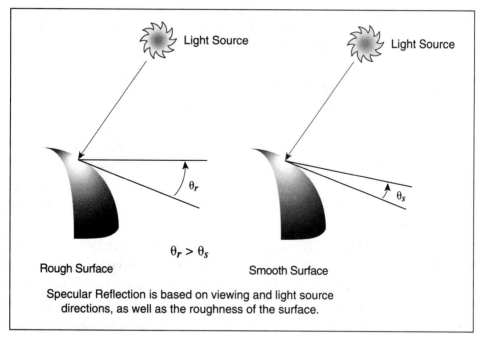

Figure 9-2. Specular reflection

Note that if you are viewing a shiny flat surface, the image of a light source reflected on the surface moves as you do. The model used in Bob (and by virtually every other rendering program) is the Phong model. The standard equation for computing the specular highlight is:

$$K_h = (-VecDot(H, E)) ** N_s;$$ (Equation 9-2)

Note that by introducing the exponent N_s, you can control the apparent spot size. The larger N_s is, the tighter the spot size. This is not a particularly physical model, but rather one that you can easily control to produce realistic specular highlights. The lower-left image of Plate 11 shows the addition of specular highlights.

The computation of diffuse and specular highlights is performed for each light source. The effect of shadowing will be discussed shortly. The net effect is that you generate a scale factor that is either 0 (light is blocked), 1 (light is totally unblocked), or between 0 and 1 (intersection point is in shadow penumbra, meaning you can partially see the light). The color is then scaled by the shadow coefficient and added to the ambient lighting terms to produce the total light contribution caused strictly by the surface. You still must examine the reflected or transmittal rays to account for the light coming from other surfaces.

Reflection and (K_s) refraction (K_t)

The coefficients K_s and K_t determine how much light is reflected and transmitted. If K_s is 0, the surface is diffuse and you have no reflected rays. Similarly, if K_t is 0, the surface is completely opaque. If either of these is nonzero, new rays are cast and their respective colors are found by the recursive call of the *trace* function. The reflected ray color is weighted by K_s and the refracted (transmitted) ray is weighted by K_t. All contributions are then summed over all light sources and the total color (I) is returned as the color of the ray.

K_s and K_t are actually RGB (red-green-blue) vectors since you may want to weigh the colors differently. This allows for the simulation of colored glass in which certain colors are transmitted and others reflected. For instance, blue glass might have K_t of (.1,.1,.7). The lower-right image of Plate 11 shows the addition of reflection rays. The upper-left image of Plate 11 shows the effects of including refracted rays.

Texture, Texture, Texture

One of the problems with ray traced images is that objects appear unnaturally clean and smooth. Almost all surfaces in the real world are textured. To achieve a realistic appearance, you must add texture surfaces using various patterns, images, and random variations. The goal here is not only to add just about any kind of texture to an object, but also to allow for random textures that can be easily parameterized.

The idea of *texture mapping* (or the mapping of an image onto another surface) is conceptually simple. When a point on the surface needs to be rendered, the color for that point is determined by transforming the three-dimensional intersection point to a two-dimensional point in the texture map image. The color of the texture map at that point is input to the shading model to determine the color of the surface at the intersection point. Using this technique, you can render relatively simple geometric models with a great amount of apparent complexity.

While texture mapping is a powerful technique, it does have its limitations. The most obvious limitation is mapping a two-dimensional image onto a three-dimensional object without excessively distorting the texture-mapped image. Flat surfaces are no problem, but surfaces with complex shapes can be difficult to map. Even for a relatively simple surface such as a sphere, the texture map must be distorted to get it to fit onto the three-dimensional surface. For spheres, this results in the compression of the texture at the poles.

Peachey [1985] and Perlin [1985] simultaneously developed the idea of *solid texturing* to solve this problem. The underlying principle of solid texturing is to create a three-dimensional texture map from which the textured object appears to be carved. This texture map either may be defined explicitly as a three-dimensional array of values (which consumes huge amounts of memory) or be defined by a procedural function. The procedural function takes an (x,y,z) point and returns the surface characteristics at that point. Perlin introduced the *noise( )* function to generate many of his procedural textures. To this day, the images he produced for his SIG-GRAPH paper in 1985 are considered some of the best in computer graphics.

Bob's implementation of procedural solid texturing expands on the ideas introduced by Perlin and Peachey while attempting to provide a coherent user interface to the definition of the textures. Currently, most implementations of solid texturing only allow a few predefined textures to be used. In order to get new textures, you must have access to the source code and possess the skills to code the desired function and its interfaces. Bob uses a few basic functions to provide extensive control over the parameters passed to these functions. By combining these functions and controlling their inputs, you can create a broad range of surface textures without having exceptional programming skills.

These same functions can be used in another texturing technique known as *bump mapping*. With bump mapping, the surface normal is perturbed to endow the surface with a bumpy or wavy appearance.

Bump mapping was originally championed by the guru of computer graphics, Jim Blinn, while he was studying the problem of modeling wrinkled surfaces. On a finely wrinkled surface like an orange, your perception of the wrinkles is not caused by the folds themselves, but rather by how the light bounces off the surface created by the folds. The surface normal is highly variable, even though the surface itself is relatively smooth. Thus, Blinn reasoned that you need not model the folds, but instead you simply vary the surface normal vector in a random fashion across the surface. When this normal is used by lighting calculations, the variations cause the surface to appear rough and uneven when, in fact, it is still perfectly smooth.

Map that Image

Bob only allows mapping of images onto planar surfaces. The solid texturing and bump mapping approaches are used for the nonplanar primitives.

The basic operation is to convert the three-dimensional intersection point for an index into the texture map. Since the two-dimensional value normally is floating point, you interpolate adjacent pixel values in the texture map to get the texture value you want for the intersection point. By default, this texture value is used as the diffuse color at this point, but you can also use it to modulate any of the other attributes (most notably the transparency K_t).

To map a texture map onto a planar surface, you first define an origin point where the upper-right corner of the image is to be located on the object. Then you define two other vectors. The *across vector* defines the horizontal direction of the image and the *down vector* defines the vertical direction of the image. These should be at right angles to one another and lie in the plane of the surface onto which you are mapping. Finally, you use a scale parameter to scale the image size. The *Ximage*, *Yimage* texture coordinates are then:

```
dotx = VecDot(P - ORIGIN(image), ACROSS)
doty = VecDot(P - ORIGIN(image), DOWN)
Ximage = Xres * dotx / scale
Yimage = Yres * doty / scale
```
(Equation 9-3)

where P is the intersection point, ORIGIN(*image*) is the origin point of the image, and *Xres* and *Yres* are the horizontal and vertical pixel resolutions of the image. Note that as scale increases, the image is magnified.

Bob also allows for the case in which the image does not lie in the same plane as the polygon to which it is being mapped. In this case, the vector P - ORIGIN(*image*) is first projected onto the image plane. This technique also allows the image to be mapped onto a curved surface, with the resulting distortions described previously.

Several plates show examples of image mapping, including the image in Color Plate 12.

Solid Texturing

Solid texturing is primarily concerned with defining functions of space over all of x, y, and z. Bob evaluates this function at the point of intersection and uses this value to modulate the diffuse coefficient, the transmissivity, the reflection coefficient, or any of the other attributes you choose. This discussion centers on modulating the diffuse coefficient, but keep in mind that it can be applied to the other attributes as well.

You must now find a suitable class of functions that simulate real world textures like marble or clouds. In general, Bob's solid texturing works as follows. You define two surfaces and a texture function. The intersection point is passed to the texture function, which returns a weighting factor. This factor, in the range 0.0 to 1.0, is then used to blend together the two surfaces. The details of the texture functions and this blending are described later in this chapter.

One of a class of *noise* functions may be used to add turbulence to the texture by modifying the intersection point prior to passing it to the *texture* function. Note that while it is convenient to talk about the surface coefficients as if they are a single number, they are generally an RGB (red-green-blue) triple. When calculating the illumination of an intersection point, the shading equation is used for each of the elements of the RGB triple to produce an RGB color value for output.

The discussion of solid textures must first address how random noise is used to create textures. You can then derive generalized solid texturing algorithms. Bob provides the facility for combining the methods together to create a near infinite number of texturing possibilities. Listing 9-1 shows the code listing for Texture.C, the textures module.

```
/*

  ┌─────────────────────────────────────────────────────────────┐
  │                    Bob - Ray Tracer                           │
  │           Texture.C = Procedural textures                     │
  │           and image texture mapping functions.               │
  │  Copyright 1988, 1992 Christopher D. Watkins and Stephen B. Coy│
  │                  ALL RIGHTS RESERVED                          │
  │            Dependencies : defs.h, extern.h                    │
  └─────────────────────────────────────────────────────────────┘

  calling sequence for all functions is

  float = tex_func(P, *Texture);
```

The return value is a number between 0.0 and 1.0 which determines
the relative weights of the composite surface.
*/

```c
#include <stdlib.h>
#include <stdio.h>
#include <math.h>
#include "defs.h"
#include "extern.h"

/*
    Check — create a checkerboard, strange
*/

Flt     tex_checker(P, tex)
    Point   P;
    Texture     *tex;
{
    register int    i;
    int         p[3];
    Vec         point;
    Flt         blur;

    blur = HUGE;

    for(i=0; i<3; i++) {
        if(tex->scale[i]==0) {
            p[i] = 0;
        } else {
            point[i] = (P[i] + tex->trans[i])/tex->scale[i];
            p[i] = floor(point[i]);
            point[i] -= p[i];
            if(point[i]>.5)
                point[i] = 1.0 - point[i];
            blur = MIN(point[i], blur);
        }
    }

    blur *= 2.0;
    if(blur >= tex->blur)
        blur = 0.0;
    else
        blur = (1.0 - blur/tex->blur)/2.0;

    if((p[0]+p[1]+p[2]) & 0x01) {
        return 1.0-blur;
    } else {
        return blur;
    }
```

```
}

/*
    spherical
*/

Flt     tex_spherical(P, tex)
    Point   P;
    Texture *tex;
{
    int     i;
    Flt     r, dist;
    Vec     p;

    r = tex->r1 + tex->r2;
    dist = 0.0;
    for(i=0; i<3; i++) {
        if(tex->scale[i]==0) {
            p[i] = 0;
        } else {
            p[i] = (P[i] - tex->trans[i])/tex->scale[i];
        }
        dist += p[i]*p[i];
    }
    dist = sqrt(dist);                  /* what a bummer! */
    dist += tex->r1/2;                  /* center first color */
    dist = fmod(dist, r);

    if(dist < tex->r1) {                /* still in the r1 range */
        dist = dist/tex->r1;
        if(dist > 0.5) {
            dist = 1.0 - dist;          /* fold if needed */
        }
        if(dist >= tex->blur/2.0) {     /* we're in the flat */
            return 1.0;
        } else {
            return 0.5 + dist/tex->blur;
        }
    } else {                    /* into the r2 range */
        dist = (dist - tex->r1)/tex->r2;
        if(dist > 0.5) {
            dist = 1.0 - dist;          /* fold if needed */
        }
        if(dist >= tex->blur/2.0) {     /* we're in the flat */
            return 0.0;
        } else {
            return 0.5 - dist/tex->blur;
        }
    }
```

```
}                                          /* end of spherical */

/*
    noise - BANG, SPLAT, POW!!!
*/

Flt      tex_noise(P, tex)
    Point   P;
    Texture *tex;
{
    int     i;
    Flt     result;
    Vec     p;

    for(i=0; i<3; i++) {
        if(tex->scale[i]==0) {
            p[i] = 0;
        } else {
            p[i] = (P[i] - tex->trans[i])/tex->scale[i];
        }
    }

    result = turb1(p, tex->terms);

    return result;

}        /* end of tex_noise() */

/*
    tex_fix() — figure out which surface to use as point P
*/

void     tex_fix(surf, P, OP)
    Surface *surf;
    Point   P, OP;  /* translated and original point */
{
    register int    i;
    Flt             w0, w1;
    Surface         *surf0, *surf1;
    Texture         *texture;
    Point           tmp, p_in, p_out;

    texture = surf->tex;
    surf0 = texture->surf[0];
    surf1 = texture->surf[1];

    if(texture==NULL) {
        return;
        fprintf(stderr, "Fooey, null pointer for texture structure.\n");
        last_call(1);
```

```
}
if(surf0==NULL) {
    return;
    fprintf(stderr, "Fooey, null pointer for surf0 structure.\n");
    last_call(1);
}
if(surf1==NULL) {
    return;
    fprintf(stderr, "Fooey, null pointer for surf1 structure.\n");
    last_call(1);
}

VecCopy(P, tmp);                    /* save point */

if(texture->turbulence) {           /* tweak P if turbulent */
    VecCopy(P, p_in);
    for(i=0; i<3; i++) {
        p_in[i] *= texture->turbulence->scale[i];
    }
    turb3(p_in, p_out, texture->turbulence->terms);
    VecAddS(texture->turbulence->amp, p_out, P, P);
}

if(surf0->tex)                      /* recurse down left branch */
    tex_fix(surf0, P, OP);
if(surf1->tex)                      /* recurse down right branch */
    tex_fix(surf1, P, OP);

w0 = (texture->func)(P, texture);
w0 = ABS(w0);
if(w0 < 0.0) {
    w0 = 0.0;
} else if(w0 > 1.0) {
    w0 = 1.0;
}
w1 = 1.0 - w0;

/* handle any image mapping */
if(surf0->flags & S_TM_MAPPING) {
    map_fix(surf0, OP);
}
if(surf1->flags & S_TM_MAPPING) {
    map_fix(surf1, OP);
}

for(i=0; i<3; i++) {
    surf->diff[i] = w0 * surf0->diff[i] +
            w1 * surf1->diff[i];
    surf->spec[i] = w0 * surf0->spec[i] +
```

```
                    w1 * surf1->spec[i];
            surf->trans[i] = w0 * surf0->trans[i] +
                    w1 * surf1->trans[i];
            surf->amb[i] = w0 * surf0->amb[i] +
                    w1 * surf1->amb[i];
            surf->cshine[i] = w0 * surf0->cshine[i] +
                    w1 * surf1->cshine[i];
    }
    surf->ior = w0 * surf0->ior +
            w1 * surf1->ior;
    surf->fuzz = w0 * surf0->fuzz +
            w1 * surf1->fuzz;
    surf->shine = w0 * surf0->shine +
            w1 * surf1->shine;

    /* both cache and no_antialias flags must be set for
        textured surface to have them */

    if(surf0->flags & surf1->flags & S_CACHE) {
        surf->flags |= S_CACHE;
    } else {
        surf->flags &= ~S_CACHE;
    }
    if(surf0->flags & surf1->flags & S_NO_ANTIALIAS) {
        surf->flags |= S_NO_ANTIALIAS;
    } else {
        surf->flags &= ~S_NO_ANTIALIAS;
    }

    VecCopy(tmp, P);           /* restore point */

}       /* end of tex_fix() */


/*
    map_fix() — fill in the surface structure element(s) based
        on the point of intersection and the texture map.
*/

void    map_fix(Surface *surf, Point P)
{
    Flt     x, y;              /* image intersection */

    if(surf->flags & S_TM_DIFF) {   /* we've got a diffuse map */
        tex_project(surf->tm_diff, P, &x, &y);
        tile(surf->tm_diff, &x, &y);
        get_map_entry(surf->tm_diff, x, y, surf->diff);
    }
    if(surf->flags & S_TM_SPEC) {   /* we've got a specular map */
        tex_project(surf->tm_spec, P, &x, &y);
```

```
            tile(surf->tm_spec, &x, &y);
            get_map_entry(surf->tm_spec, x, y, surf->spec);
      }
      if(surf->flags & S_TM_TRANS) {    /* we've got a transparent map */
            tex_project(surf->tm_trans, P, &x, &y);
            tile(surf->tm_trans, &x, &y);
            get_map_entry(surf->tm_trans, x, y, surf->trans);
      }
      if(surf->flags & S_TM_AMB) {       /* we've got an ambient map */
            tex_project(surf->tm_amb, P, &x, &y);
            tile(surf->tm_amb, &x, &y);
            get_map_entry(surf->tm_amb, x, y, surf->amb);
      }
}       /* end of map_fix() */


/*
    tex_project() - For the texture defined by surf->tm_???
        project the point P onto the image plane and return
        the indices for the image
*/

void    tex_project(Texmap *tm, Point P, Flt *x, Flt *y)
{
    Point   PP,     /* point projected onto plane of image */
            V;
    Flt     dot;

    /* project intersection point onto image plane */
    VecSub(P, tm->position, V);
    dot = VecDot(tm->normal, V);
    VecAddS(-dot, tm->normal, P, PP);

    /* calc offsets in across and down directions */
    VecSub(PP, tm->position, V);
    dot = VecDot(tm->across, V);
    *x = dot / tm->scale;
    dot = VecDot(tm->down, V);
    *y = dot * (double)tm->yres/tm->xres / tm->scale;
    *y = dot / tm->scale;

}       /* end of tex_project() */


/*
    tile() - Take the raw indices and based on the tile pattern return
        the indices that are within the image bounds.
*/

void    tile(Texmap *tm, Flt *x, Flt *y)
{
```

```
        *x = fmod(*x, 1.0);
        if(*x < 0.0) {
            *x += 1.0;
        }
        *y = fmod(*y, (double)tm->yres/(double)tm->xres);
        if(*y < 0.0) {
            *y += (double)tm->yres/(double)tm->xres;
        }
}          /* end of tile() */

/*
    get_map_entry() — Given a texture structure and the indices
        into the map this function fills in the color at that
        point.  Note that indices are actually backwards.
*/

void    get_map_entry(Texmap *tm, Flt x, Flt y, Color color)
{
    Flt     r, g, b;
    int     i, j, map_index;

    /* get integer indices */
    i = x * (tm->xres);
    j = y * (tm->xres);

    color[0] = tm->red[j][i]/255.0;
    color[1] = tm->grn[j][i]/255.0;
    color[2] = tm->blu[j][i]/255.0;

}          /* end of get_map_entry() */

/*
    tex_read_img() — Read a .img file into a texture map structure
*/

void    tex_read_img(char *file, Texmap *tm)
{
    FILE    *fp;
    int     w, h,             /* width and height */
            i, j,
            cnt, red, grn, blu;

    fp = env_fopen(file, "rb");
    if(!fp) {
        fprintf(stderr, "Error opening file %s for texture mapping.\n",
                file);
        last_call(1);
    }
```

```
/* get width and height from header */
w = fgetc(fp)<<8;
w += fgetc(fp);
h = fgetc(fp)<<8;
h += fgetc(fp);

/* waste other stuff */
fgetc(fp); fgetc(fp);
fgetc(fp); fgetc(fp);
fgetc(fp); fgetc(fp);

/* allocate memory for image in RAM */

tm->red = (unsigned char **)vmalloc(sizeof(unsigned char *) * h);
ptrchk(tm->red, "image texture map");
for(j=0; j<h; j++) {
    tm->red[j] = (unsigned char *)vmalloc(sizeof(unsigned char) * w);
    ptrchk(tm->red[j], "image texture map");
}
tm->grn = (unsigned char **)vmalloc(sizeof(unsigned char *) * h);
ptrchk(tm->grn, "image texture map");
for(j=0; j<h; j++) {
    tm->grn[j] = (unsigned char *)vmalloc(sizeof(unsigned char) * w);
    ptrchk(tm->grn[j], "image texture map");
}
tm->blu = (unsigned char **)vmalloc(sizeof(unsigned char *) * h);
ptrchk(tm->blu, "image texture map");
for(j=0; j<h; j++) {
    tm->blu[j] = (unsigned char *)vmalloc(sizeof(unsigned char) * w);
    ptrchk(tm->blu[j], "image texture map");
}

/* read in the image */
for(j=0; j<h; j++) {
    i = 0;
    while(i < w) {
        cnt = fgetc(fp) & 0xff;
        blu = fgetc(fp) & 0xff;
        grn = fgetc(fp) & 0xff;
        red = fgetc(fp) & 0xff;
        while(cnt) {
            tm->red[j][i] = red;
            tm->grn[j][i] = grn;
            tm->blu[j][i] = blu;
            i++;
            cnt-;
        }
    }
}        /* end of loop for each scan line */
```

```
      fclose(fp);

      tm->xres = w;
      tm->yres = h;
}         /* end of tex_read_img() */
```

Listing 9-1. Texture.C

Noise and Turbulence

Many of Bob's textures rely on the *noise()* function in the Noise.C module shown in Listing 9-2 to provide a semi-random, natural feel to them. The *noise()* function provides repeatable random numbers which are invariant under rotation and translation and which have a narrow limit in frequency. The transformational invariance is required to allow textured models to be moved in space while keeping their surface textures constant. For example, as a chair with a wood texture is moved, its grain pattern should not shift and change as a result of the movement. The narrow frequency band requirement is beneficial since, given a noise curve of a known frequency, it is fairly easy to create a curve of any desired frequency characteristics by scaling and summing the simpler curve. A narrow frequency range means that the function does not vary too much and does not vary too little, but changes just the right amount over space. The *noise()* function is also a continuous function over space.

```
/*
```

```
                      Bob - Ray Tracer
                   Noise.C = noise functions
        Copyright 1988, 1992 Christopher D. Watkins and Stephen B. Coy
                      ALL RIGHTS RESERVED
                   Dependencies : defs.h, extern.h
```

```
*/
```

```
#include <stdio.h>
#include <stdlib.h>
#include <math.h>
#include "defs.h"
#include "extern.h"
```

```
#define NOISE_SEED (666)

#define NUMPTS   512
#define P1       173
#define P2       263
#define P3       337
#define phi      0.6180339

static Flt pts[NUMPTS];

/*
    init_noise() - generate noise points +- 0.5
*/

void    init_noise()
{
    int    i;

    srand(NOISE_SEED);
    for(i=0; i<NUMPTS; i++) {
        pts[i] = rand()/(Flt)RAND_MAX - 0.5;
    }
}

#define HASH(a,b,c)     (a+b+c & NUMPTS-1)

Flt     noise1(p)
    Vec    p;
{
    int    xi, yi, zi, xa, xb, ya, yb, za, zb;
    Flt    xf, yf, zf;
    Flt    p000, p100, p010, p110;
    Flt    p001, p101, p011, p111;

    xf = p[0];
    yf = p[1];
    zf = p[2];

    xi = floor(xf);
    xa = floor(P1*(xi*phi - floor(xi*phi)));
    xb = floor(P1*((xi+1)*phi - floor((xi+1)*phi)));

    yi = floor(yf);
    ya = floor(P2*(yi*phi - floor(yi*phi)));
    yb = floor(P2*((yi+1)*phi - floor((yi+1)*phi)));

    zi = floor(zf);
    za = floor(P3*(zi*phi - floor(zi*phi)));
    zb = floor(P3*((zi+1)*phi - floor((zi+1)*phi)));
```

```
    p000 = pts[HASH(xa, ya, za)];
    p001 = pts[HASH(xa, ya, zb)];
    p010 = pts[HASH(xa, yb, za)];
    p100 = pts[HASH(xb, ya, za)];
    p011 = pts[HASH(xa, yb, zb)];
    p110 = pts[HASH(xb, yb, za)];
    p101 = pts[HASH(xb, ya, zb)];
    p111 = pts[HASH(xb, yb, zb)];

    xf = xf - xi;
    yf = yf - yi;
    zf = zf - zi;

    /* Since we're just doing linear interpolation between the points
       we need to "bend" the line a bit to fake a spline interpolation.
       This looks almost as good as the spline interpolation but
       is much faster. */

    if(xf > 0.5) {
        xf = 1.0 - xf;
        xf = 2.0 * xf * xf;
        xf = 1.0 - xf;
    } else {
        xf = 2.0 * xf * xf;
    }
    if(yf > 0.5) {
        yf = 1.0 - yf;
        yf = 2.0 * yf * yf;
        yf = 1.0 - yf;
    } else {
        yf = 2.0 * yf * yf;
    }
    if(zf > 0.5) {
        zf = 1.0 - zf;
        zf = 2.0 * zf * zf;
        zf = 1.0 - zf;
    } else {
        zf = 2.0 * zf * zf;
    }

    return  p000 * (1-xf) * (1-yf) * (1-zf) +
        p001 * (1-xf) * (1-yf) * zf      +
        p010 * (1-xf) * yf     * (1-zf) +
        p100 * xf      * (1-yf) * (1-zf) +
        p011 * (1-xf) * yf      * zf     +
        p110 * xf      * yf     * (1-zf) +
        p101 * xf      * (1-yf) * zf     +
        p111 * xf      * yf     * zf;
}
```

```
void    noise3(p, v)
    Vec     p;
    Flt     *v;
{
    Vec     tmp;

    v[0] = noise1(p);
    tmp[0] = p[1]+P1;
    tmp[1] = p[0]+P2;
    tmp[2] = p[2]+P3;
    v[1] = noise1(tmp);
    tmp[0] += P2;
    tmp[1] += P3;
    tmp[2] += P1;
    v[2] = noise1(tmp);
}

void    DNoise(p, v)
    Vec     p;          /* point to tweak */
    Flt     *v;         /* return vector */
{
    Vec     tmp;
    Flt     center;

    center = noise1(p);
    tmp[0] = p[0] + 0.1;
    tmp[1] = p[1];
    tmp[2] = p[2];
    v[0] = (noise1(tmp) - center) * 10.0;
    tmp[0] = p[0];
    tmp[1] += 0.1;
    v[1] = (noise1(tmp) - center) * 10.0;
    tmp[1] = p[1];
    tmp[2] += 0.1;
    v[2] = (noise1(tmp) - center) * 10.0;
}       /* end of DNoise() */


Flt     turb1(p, lvl)
    Vec     p;          /* input point, gets thrashed */
    int     lvl;        /* max number of levels */
{
    Flt     result = 0.0;
    int     i;

    for(i=0; i<lvl; i++) {
        result += noise1(p)/(Flt)(1<<i);
        VecS(2.0, p, p);
    }
```

```
    return result;
}
void    turb3(p, v, lvl)
    Vec     p,      /* input point, gets thrashed */
            v;      /* return vector */
    int     lvl;    /* max number of levels */
{
    Vec     c;
    int     i;

    MakeVector(0, 0, 0, v);
    for(i=0; i<lvl; i++) {
        noise3(p, c);
        /* DNoise(p, c); */
        VecS(1.0/(Flt)(1<<i), c, c);
        VecAdd(c, v, v);
        VecS(2.0, p, p);
    }
}
```

Listing 9-2. Noise.C

noise() takes a three-dimensional vector as input and returns a single number in the range 0.0 to 1.0 (see Figure 9-3). Given the same input, *noise()* always returns the same result. Inputs that are close to each other produce results that are also close to each other (meeting the narrow frequency range requirement). Inputs that are far from each other (far relative to the frequency range) result in values that have no relation to each other. Given these constraints, many possible implementations of *noise()* can be implemented.

Bob's implementation follows the one suggested by Perlin with a few changes that make it simpler and less computationally expensive. The idea is to set up an integer lattice where each integral point has a random value associated with it. If the input point coincides with a lattice point, then the value at that point is returned. If the input falls between the lattice points, the result is interpolated from the neighboring points. Creating an array with all possible integer lattice points is out of the question, so a small one-dimensional array is created.

In Bob's case this array contains 512 elements. Bob uses a hash function to map the input vectors to a single index. Perlin suggests a cubic spline for the result interpolation, since using a linear interpolation, causes creases (apparent edges) in the resulting texture.

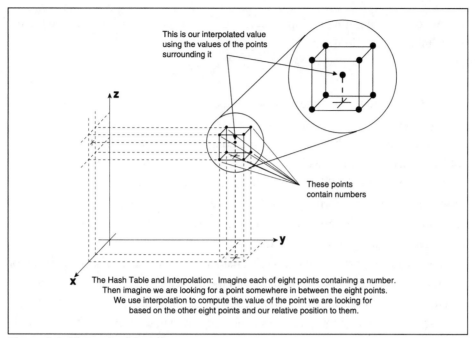

The Hash Table and Interpolation: Imagine each of eight points containing a number.
Then imagine we are looking for a point somewhere in between the eight points.
We use interpolation to compute the value of the point we are looking for
based on the other eight points and our relative position to them.

Figure 9-3. The *noise()* function

Since one of Bob's design goals is to run well on PC-class CPUs, the speed of
the linear interpolation has been chosen over the better results of the spline interpolation. To compensate for the creases, results are "pushed" away from the lattice
points. This has the effect of making their slope 0 at these points and providing
approximately the same results as the spline interpolation without the added overhead. The "pushing" is done by squaring and re-scaling the results. This adds some
extra cost to the evaluation of the noise function. However, the cost is still significantly less than doing the spline interpolation and the resulting images have similar quality. The fact that the *noise()* function is being used to create semi-random,
turbulent textures helps hide any loss in quality.

Three other functions associated with *noise()* are *noise3()*, *turb()*, and *turb3()*.
noise3() is the three-dimensional analog of noise and thus produces a vector of three
sampled noise values. The implementation of *noise3()* in Bob consists of three calls
to *noise()*, each with the original input vector offset in a different direction. This
provides enough noncorrelation between the three calls, while allowing for the
repeatability required for texturing. *turb()* and *turb3()* are functions that emulate *1/f*

fractal noise by summing multiple octaves of *noise()* and *noise3()*. The formula for the turbulence functions is:

```
turb(P, n) == sum(noise(P*2i)/2i) for i = 1 to n
```

where *P* is the input point and *n* is the number of octaves.

turb3() is the same except that *noise3()* is called and the result is a vector rather than a real number. While the preceding equation is simple, what it is doing may not be immediately obvious. During each iteration, the input point is scaled by a factor of 2. Effectively, this samples the random function represented by *noise()* at a lower sampling rate (hence, the resulting function appears to be at a higher frequency). At the same time, the return value from *noise()* is divided by a factor of 2, in effect, dividing its amplitude in half.

The turbulence procedure is directly analogous to using midpoint subdivision for the creation of fractal surfaces. In fact, with the proper scaling, *turb()* can be used to provide the altitude for fractal terrain generation. For terrain generation the "pushing" used to smooth the results can be safely dispensed with, providing faster results. Color Plate 31 shows an example of clouds generated with the *turb()* function.

This method also has some other advantages over the midpoint subdivision scheme. With the midpoint subdivision algorithm, you must keep all the points in the grid in memory at once. If you use the *turb()* function, however, points may be evaluated randomly. Since the points may be evaluated randomly, you do not need to determine a subdivision level beforehand. You use a sample per pixel to ensure that the cost for rendering the terrain is directly proportional to the number of pixels in the image.

The number of iterations that you use depends on the desired effect. For a fully fractal appearance, the number of iterations must be sufficient to raise the frequency of the resulting noise above that of the sampling of the output. In other words, you do not need to go beyond the point where the details you are adding appear smaller than half the pixel size you are rendering.

This limit, called the *Nyquist limit*, results from the fact that images generated by ray tracing are discretely sampled. Pixel size determines the upper limit of the frequency that can be accurately displayed. By sampling at a higher rate than can be displayed (that is, generating more iterations than needed), you add some low-amplitude noise to the image. The result does not change noticeably, except in the increased execution time. Sometimes you'll want to cut the iteration process shorter to produce a texture whose frequency components do not appear to be fractal in nature.

Solid Texture Patterns

Remember, solid textures are based on the three-dimensional coordinate of the point on the surface of the object being rendered in the current pixel. The basis for Bob's implementation of solid texturing is a *surface definition tree*. This tree is a binary tree in which each leaf is a nontextured surface defined by you. The nonleaf nodes contain your texture definitions but no surface coefficients. You calculate surface coefficients for the nonleaf nodes as a weighted average of the coefficients of their children. You determine the weighting between the two children by the texture function defined in the parent node. You determine the coefficients at the root of the tree by performing a depth-first evaluation of the tree. The shading function uses these coefficients to determine the appearance of the surface at the intersection point. The depth-first evaluation of the tree is done in the procedure *tex_fix( )* found in Texture.C.

Bob supports two basic approaches for determining the weighting between child nodes using texture functions. The simplest case is to input the intersection point to the *turb( )* function and use the resulting single real value as the weight. You use this weight, w, to control the blending of the two child surfaces using linear interpolation. For example, the diffuse coefficient of the surface, K_d, at the intersection point, p, is calculated by

```
w = turb(P, octaves);
diffnew = w * diffsurf1 + (1.0 - w) * diffsurf2;
```

where *octaves* is the number of terms in the series as specified by you in the input file. Using simple black-and-white surfaces for the input results in a granite-like texture. By scaling the input coordinates nonuniformly (that is, stretching them along an axis), you can give the graininess of the resulting texture a directional bias. This procedure is especially effective in a wood texture to provide the appearance of fibers within each of the grain layers (see Plate 23 and Plate 26).

Bob also supports two geometrically-based texture patterns: *checker* and *spherical*. These functions take as input the intersection point and output the weight. They also have some user-defined parameters that control blurring at the edges and scaling. The basic checker function is as follows:

```
w = (Pi + Pj + Pk) mod 2
```

where P_i is the integer part of P_x, P_j is the integer part of P_y, and P_k is the integer part of P_z.

The weight (w) is then either 0 or 1, specifying which surface is active at that intersection point (P). The resulting image then displays a surface that appears to be carved out of a three-dimensional checkerboard. You control the relative size of the checks by scaling P prior to passing it to the checker function. Bob assumes that a scale factor of 0 along an axis is equivalent to not changing w based on that axis. For example, if P is scaled to 0 in both the x and y axes, then the resulting function is equivalent to

```
w = Pk mod 2.
```

The resulting texture looks like slabs of material alternating along the z axis. These alternating slabs are a good base from which to create marble textures. We can also have the checker function return a weight somewhere between 0 and 1 based on how close the intersection point (P) is to the edge between materials. Bob allows you to specify a blend value between 0 and 1. Set at 0, the resulting checker has sharp, well-defined edges. Set at 1, the checker colors are fully blended across the transition region to provide a blurry-looking checker pattern.

In addition to scaling the point P before passing it to the checker function for evaluation, you can also apply turbulence to it. By combining scaling, blending, and turbulence with the checker function, you can create a wide variety of surface combinations. Plate 22 is a great example of this in generating the marble texture.

Advantages of rendering a checkerboard with this method include speed and ease of modeling. Using texturing, the entire top of the checkerboard can be modeled as a single polygon. Without texturing, a series of 64 polygons must be defined and rendered. The extra cost of the checker function is so small that it is easily paid back in time saved performing intersection tests. Plates 17 and 18 show the application of texture to a sphere.

Spherical Textures

The spherical pattern is only slightly more complicated. You create this pattern with concentric spherical shells of alternating surfaces. Bob allows each surface to have its own thickness (or radius), thus allowing thick and thin layers to alternate.

Like the checker pattern, the spherical pattern may also be scaled. In this case, the result is layered ellipsoids rather than spheres. If you set one of the scaling axes to 0, concentric cylinders result.

This feature is especially useful for creating realistic wood textures. With two scaling axes set to 0, the result is alternating slabs of material much like the checker pattern produces. However, since each surface has a radius associated with it, the alternating slabs may have differing thicknesses. You can use this effect to good advantage with some textures. Blending and turbulence are also fully supported while using spherical patterns.

Plate 23 shows an example of the wood texture applied to a block. Note that because this texture is created from a solid texture, you can slice the block in an animation sequence and the two freshly cut ends will have the appropriate matching textures, just like a real piece of wood. Using these techniques, you can produce checkerboards that combine red and mirrored checks. You can achieve more subtle patterns by modulating just the specular exponent of the surfaces, N_s. One goal kept in mind during the development of Bob was the ability to use textured surfaces as the input for further texturing.

Making Waves

In addition to using random noise to perturb textures, Bob also supports the use of sine waves. Within the texture media these waves act like compression waves, alternately pushing and pulling the point passed to the texture function along a line from the point of intersection to the source of the wave. Waves are defined by a source, wavelength, amplitude, phase, and damping factor.

The source specifies the point from which the wave emanates, and the wavelength defines the distance between wave peaks. The amplitude determines how far the point is pushed by the wave. The phase is a number in the range 0..1 that determines the phase of the wave at the source point (is the wave up, down, 0, or somewhere in between). This is useful for animation purposes. The phase can be incremented on a frame-by-frame basis to provide the illusion of moving waves. The damping factor determines the fall-off (an exponential measurement) that the wave's amplitude distance experiences. A default value of 1.0 results in no fall-off, while a value of 0.8 results in an 80% decrease in wave amplitude for each wavelength distance from the intersection point in from the wave source. A surface may be affected by more than one wave source. You sum the offsets generated by the waves to produce the total offset for the intersection point. Waves are implemented as follows:

P ....Point of intersection

P'...New point to be fed to one of the geometric functions

O_n ....Offset generated by wave n

S_n...Source of wave n

len_n ....Wavelength of wave n

amp_n ....Amplitude of wave n

amp'_n ....Amplitude of wave n adjusted for damping fall-off

$phase_n$....................................Phase of wave n

$damp_n$ ....Damping factor for wave n

$dist_n$ ....Distance in wavelengths wave n has traveled

$On = P - S_n$ ....Calculate vector from source to intersection point

$dist_n = |O_n| / len_n + phase_n$......Calculate distance in wavelengths

$amp'_n = amp_n * damp_n dist_n$ ....Calculate adjusted amplitude with exponential damping

$O_n = amp'_n * O_n / |O_n|$ ....Multiply adjusted amplitude by normalized vector from source to intersection point to get offset

$P' = \_waves O_n$ ....Sum offsets

Waves seem to have limited use in generating interesting solid textures, and they are primarily used in procedural bump mapping, described in the next section. Listing 9-3 shows the Wave.C module

```
/*
```

```
                        Bob - Ray Tracer
            Wave.C = Totally New Wave Functions - Dude
     Copyright 1988, 1992 Christopher D. Watkins and Stephen B. Coy
                       ALL RIGHTS RESERVED
                  Dependencies = Defs.H, Extern.H
```

```
*/
```

```c
#include <stdio.h>
#include <math.h>
#include "defs.h"
#include "extern.h"

void    make_waves(P, R, waves)
    Vec     P,        /* the point in question */
            R;        /* where to put the result */
    Wave    *waves;   /* top of the linked list */
{
    Vec     diff;              /* diff between point and source */
    Flt     dist;              /* dist from point to source of wave */
    Flt     amp;               /* current height of wave */

    MakeVector(0, 0, 0, R);    /* just to be sure */
    while(waves) {
        VecSub(P, waves->center, diff);
        dist = VecNormalize(diff);
        dist /= waves->wavelength;       /* where in cycle are we? */
        dist += waves->phase;            /* add on offset */

        if(waves->damp < 1.0) {          /* account for damping */
            amp = waves->amp * pow(waves->damp, dist);
        } else {
            amp = waves->amp;            /* no damping */
        }

        amp *= cos(dist * PI*2.0);

        VecAddS(amp, diff, R, R);

        waves = waves->next;
    }           /* end of while loop */
}           /* end of make_waves() */
```

Listing 9-3. Wave.C

Bump Mapping

You can implement the noise and wave functions used during procedural solid texturing to provide procedural bump mapping (see Figure 9-4). You use the results from the functions to perturb the surface normal (N) based on the point of intersection. This perturbed normal is the one that you use in the shading calculations. Since the surface's brightness, highlights, reflection, and refraction are all dependent on the surface normal, a small change is all that's needed to effect a large difference in the resulting image.

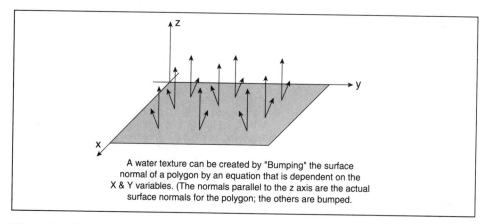

A water texture can be created by "Bumping" the surface
normal of a polygon by an equation that is dependent on the
X & Y variables. (The normals parallel to the z axis are the actual
surface normals for the polygon; the others are bumped.

Figure 9-4. Bump textures

Note that in this case, you are modifying a normalized (length 1.0) vector rather than a point. Thus, you want to keep the amplitude of the bumping to less than 1 because values larger than 1 risk inverting the normal relative to the surface's original normal. Since this is a physical impossibility, there is no intuitively "correct" way to deal with this problem. A simple solution is to flip the bumped normal back to the proper side of the surface. Another, rarer possibility is that the resulting bumped normal has length 0. Once again, there is no "correct" solution, but a simple fix is to use the original surface normal in this case.

Color Plates 25 and 30 demonstrate the effects of applying procedural bump mapping using the wave functions to surfaces. Note in Plate 30 that even though the water appears to have a wavy surface, its intersection with the edge of the pool is perfectly smooth. While this defect is undesirable, the cost of rendering the water's surface as thousands of triangular patches instead of a single primitive makes the defect much more tolerable. Also note that the cost of evaluating the wave function at each intersection point is fairly high, especially if you have more than one set of waves to evaluate.

The Atmosphere

Outdoor scene realism is greatly enhanced by the addition of atmospheric effects such as fog and haze. These are created when the atmosphere scatters light over a distance. The simplest model of such scattering is that of exponential decay, which assumes a uniform scattering medium. The ray color is blended with a background haze color using the following equation:

```
Alpha = exp(-distance/Haze_Distance)
Color = Alpha*ray_color + (1-Alpha)*Haze_Color          (Equation 9-4)
```

where *Haze_Distance* is the visibility distance, *distance* is length of the vector *E*, and *Haze_Color* normally is the background color.

As objects get farther away, they slowly merge into the haze (see Figure 9-5). You achieve a fog effect by evaluating Alpha as a function of the intersection point position as well as the distance. For example, you can produce a layered fog effect by setting Alpha equal to 1.0 if the point is above the top of the fog layer. Otherwise, you evaluate this equation when the point drops below the fog height.

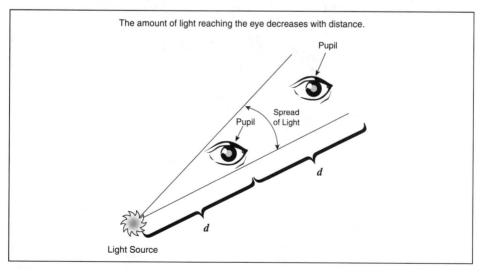

Figure 9-5. Distance fall-off of intensity

Shadows

As described in Chapter 6, you evaluate shadows by casting rays from the intersection point toward each of the light sources. If the ray intersects any opaque objects in between, the light is not visible and no further processing is needed (see Figure 9-6). If the ray intersects a transparent object, the light intensity is reduced by the transmissivity of the intervening object. If the ray reaches the light (or equivalently, goes out of the scene), the light is visible and its full intensity is used (and scaled for distance).

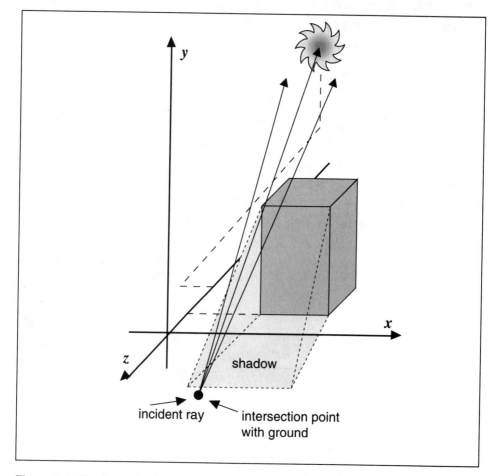

Figure 9-6. Shadow effects

Point light sources only require a single shadow ray to be cast from the intersection point. For finite extent light sources (such as the spherical light sources in Bob), you must cast multiple shadow rays in order to approximate the effect of the finite size. The ratio of shadow rays that hit the light to the total number of rays determines how far the point is in the shadow. In either case, you use the shadowing coefficient to scale the light intensity in the calculations. You scale down both the diffuse and specular components proportional to the shadow coefficient. Color Plate 4 shows an example of the effects of soft shadowing.

On to the Code

As you can see, the lighting model is elaborate and takes some time to learn how to use effectively. You should create your own sample images to see how changing the various texture and lighting parameters affect the look of a scene. Chapter 10 examines the code to see where all the features in this and Chapter 8 are implemented.

The Ray Tracer Code

Previous chapters discussed both the theoretical basis for Bob and some of the implementation-specific features and considerations of Bob's design. This chapter examines the code and shows how the individual modules fit together to implement Bob's features and functionality. The basic program flow of Bob is as follows:

- ❖ Read in a scene previously defined in a .B file by using either Ed (Chapter 14) or manual entry.
- ❖ Process all macro definitions and include directives in the file to make a single (temporary) input file.
- ❖ Parse the ASCII command file. Create the internal data structures representing the scene definition. Set all rendering options as internal flags.
- ❖ Render the scene using whatever options (anti-aliasing, recursion depth, shadow casting, and so forth) are set.
- ❖ Write the finished scene to the output .IMG file.
- ❖ Continue processing successive frames in an (optional) animation sequence.
- ❖ Convert .IMG file into a .TGA 24-bit color file using the IMG2TGA conversion utility and display with *View* (Chapter 16) or convert to .GIF format using IMG2GIF (Chapter 15) and display with *VPic* or the *GIFView* viewing utility.

Chapter 11 provides a user's guide to the syntax of the input files for Bob. The modules of Bob are shown in Table 10-1.

Table 10-1. File modules in Bob

Utility Functions

Defs.H ....Graphics module header file

Vector.C ....Basic vector and matrix manipulation routines

Parser Modules

Preproc.C ....Preprocessor routines for macros and include files

Parse.C ....Parses tokens into data structures

Tokens.C..................Converts ASCII strings into symbolic tokens

Yystuff.C ....General parse utility routines

Tokens.H..................Defines all of the token macros

Primitive Definitions

Tri.C ....Phong-shaded triangle primitive definitions

Sphere.C.................Sphere primitive

Cone.C.....................Cone and cylinder primitive

Ring.C ....Annular planar ring primitive

Poly.C ....Planar polygon primitive

Main Program

Main.C......................Main program

Version.C ....Prints current version on the screen

File.C.........................File-handling and I/O routines

Pic.C ....Run-length encoding routines used to process the .IMG output files

Data.C ....Initializes all of the globals in Extern.H Error.C error-processing routines

Memory.C ....Special memory-allocation routines

Stats.C ....Run-time statistic calculations

Defs.H ....Definition of all the main data structures

Pic.H ....Definition of .IMG file structures

Proto.H ....Function prototypes for all common functions

Config.H ....Configuration-specific global information

Extern.H ....Definition of all global variables

Main Ray Tracing Modules

Screen.C..................Loops through each output pixel, generating initial rays

Trace.C ....Main ray tracing routine

Inter.C ....Determines nearest ray-object intersection

Bound.C...................Builds object bounding boxes

Clip.C ....Routines for processing clipping surfaces; determines if an intersection is outside clipped area

Pqueue.C ....Priority queue processing routines

Lighting Calculations
Shade.C ....Computes ray color based on object, surface normal, reflections, and refractions
Shadow.C ....Computes shadowing effects from each light source

Texture Mapping
Texture.C ....Main texturing routines including image mapping and bump mapping
Noise.C ....Perlin noise function definitions
Wave.C ....Compute wave(s) value at a given point

---

Part and Parser

In order to make the definition of scenes more user-friendly, Bob recognizes a language, similar to C in syntax, that a user enters into an ASCII scene-definition file. This language is referred to as the EDL (Environment Definition Language) throughout the rest of the book. The exact syntax is defined in Chapter 11.

Parsing refers to the process of having a program convert phrases in the language into internal structures that it can then understand during the actual rendering process. Basically, Bob converts ASCII descriptions into data elements of C structures. For instance, a sphere is defined by the statement:

```
sphere {
radius 10.0;
position 0, 0, 0;
color white;
};
```

The parser's job is to read this statement from the ASCII file, and then create the appropriate sphere structure with its elements set to the specified values. The EDL language utilizes a C-type syntax in order to maximize the correspondence between the source code and data files. The definitions of objects in the .B files look like the structure definitions in the .H files.

This type of file parsing has been handled for years in the UNIX environment using such utilities as YACC (Yet Another Compiler Compiler) and BISON (a variation of YACC). These utilities provide a means of defining the language syntax, and then automatically generate C code to parse the language you have defined.

Because it is impractical to include these utilities with Bob's source code, the ray tracing program in this book has its own parser shown in the Parse.C module.

Note that all the functions begin with a name of the form *yy_<function name>*, in deference to their YACC origins.

The parser has the following three basic tasks:

❖ Preprocessing the input file by expanding all macro definitions and reading all included files.

❖ Converting each of the symbolic names (like *sphere*) into *tokens* that are recognizable by the parser.

❖ Creating the various object definitions (like sphere, rings, cones, and so forth).

Preprocessing

The preprocesser is contained in the file Preproc.C and adds the ability to use macros and include files. Macros work the same as they do for the C preprocessor except that macros are not allowed to have arguments.

The preprocessor reads through the main input file, looks for (and stores) any macro definitions it encounters, and processes any *#include* directives. To simplify the program, an intermediate file, YYZ.B, is created that is essentially a fully expanded (all macro substitutions made and all include files processed) version of the input file. While scanning the input file, the preprocessor substitutes the macro definition for any macros it encounters. Similarly, any included files are read in and inserted into the intermediate file.

When you examine this file, you note that all the macros have been expanded, comments removed, and excess white space (spaces, carriage returns, tabs, and so forth) removed. The preprocessor also inserts the additional commands *bb_newfile* and *bb_popfile* that allow the parser to keep track of which included file and line number within that file generated each line. By always returning back to the original files, the error reporting is more useful.

A Token Parser

Once the preprocessing pass is complete, the intermediate file is scanned to generate *tokens*. A token may be a keyword, a number, or braces. The main parsing function, *yyparse()*, processes the file by retrieving each successive token and calls the appropriate action with a large *switch* statement. The *get_token()* function gets the next token from the input file. It reads the intermediate file one character at a time, building the token and determining what type of token it is. The Tokens.C module shows the token processing and includes some additional comments about the ability to understand abbreviations versus overall parsing speed.

When you examine Parse.C, note that for each token you have a corresponding function named *yy_<token name>()* that parses the definition for that token. The general structure of these functions is as follows:

```
yy_token()
{
     Get the left brace at the beginning of this section.
     Allocate and initialize any needed structures.
     Set all default values for this structure.

     While the next token is not the right brace
     finishing this section

     Handle the current token.

     Do any needed clean up calculations and check to see
     that all required information was specified.

     All done, return.
}
```

Note that *get_token()* returns an enumerated value corresponding to whatever token it happens to be. The program extensively uses *switch* statements to process the token. You can add the new keyword definitions to Tokens.H and the recognition of the new keywords in Tokens.C. All the parsing routines are in Parse.C and the token processing routine in Tokens.C. As types are added, the code gets larger, and the recompile times increase. You can break the code into separate modules by putting your new token parsing modules into a separate file to reduce the compile times.

Primitive Files

To make Bob easily upgradable in order to follow an object-oriented development path, all of the code specific to a primitive is kept in a single file. This simplifies the task of adding a new primitive. Because Bob uses function pointers in the object definition to perform the intersection and surface normal calculations, the single file further simplifies operations. The rest of the code need not know the details of the primitive structure or how the intersection and normal calculation tests are performed.

Each primitive file contains three functions specific to that primitive. This discussion centers on Sphere.C, but all of the modules are set up identically. Sphere.C contains the *MakeSphere()*, *SphereIntersect()*, and *SphereNormal()* functions.

The *MakeSphere()* function creates the sphere-specific primitive data structure, *SphereData*, from the data fetched by the parser. The function *yy_sphere()* in Parse.C grabs the center and radius of the sphere and calls *MakeSphere()* to create an appropriate *Object* structure. The *SphereData()* structure is filled in with the information passed to *MakeSphere()*. The *Object*'s boundaries are then calculated based on the sphere size. The *bound_opt()* function from Clip.C is then called to see if any of the (optional) clipping surfaces reduce the overall bounding box about the sphere. A pointer to the completed *Object* structure is then returned to the *yy_sphere()* function. This new object is then added to the total linked list of objects defining the scene being created by the parser.

The *SphereIntersect()* function is called to determine if a ray intersects the sphere surface. (Chapter 8 presented the mathematics of the test.) If any intersections occur, the function returns the two values *t1* and *t2* corresponding to the distances along the ray where the intersections take place (one entering and one leaving the surface). A negative intersection point corresponds to an intersection behind the origin of the ray and can be ignored. The positive intersection points are passed to *clip_check()* to see if they are visible or if they've been clipped out, as described in Chapter 8. If they pass the clip test, the nearest point is returned as the intersection.

The *SphereNormal()* function is called to determine the surface normal at an intersection point on the sphere. This is used in the subsequent lighting, reflection, and refraction calculations.

Note that every object also has surface attributes such as the diffuse color, ambient color, reflectivity, and so forth. The surface attributes are kept in a separate surface structure. Bob uses a *CurrentSurface* pointer to retain the definition of the last surface processed by the parser. Each time a new primitive object is created, the *CurrentSurface* pointer is assigned to that object's surface pointer. In this way, surface attributes are independent of the primitive type and each primitive parse routine does not also have to know about surface attributes.

Scanning the Screen

Remember that any ray tracer scans the screen (usually in raster order) by generating a ray from the eyepoint through the screen and out into the scene. The generation of these initial rays is handled by the scan functions (*scan1()*, *scan2()*, and so on) in the module Screen.C. The *screen()* function is called by the main program and performs the basic raster scanning. It begins by calling *ScrnInit()* and then calls one of the scan routines based on which anti-aliasing options you choose.

The *ScrnInit()* function has the sole purpose of setting up the vectors needed by *Shoot()* that define the viewing frustrum in three-dimensional space. Recall that you define this viewing direction by using the vector *viewvec* (which points in the direction you are looking), the *up* vector (which defines which way is up), and the field of view angle. The *up* vector lines up with the vertical axis of the screen.

A "left" vector aligned with the horizontal axis is the cross product of the *viewvec* and *up* vector and consequently is perpendicular to both. Generally, you do not require the *up* vector to be perpendicular to *viewvec*. You can generate one, though, by taking the cross product of *viewvec* and the newly created *left* vector. You now have three orthogonal vectors defining a right-handed three-dimensional coordinate system. If you use the *up* vector directly (normally (0, 0, 1)), you generate a *parallax projection*, in which all vertical lines stay vertical on the screen, regardless of how the view is pitched up or down. This option is useful in some applications such as architectural renderings.

All of the scan functions call the *Shoot()* function as needed for each pixel or subpixel. The ray origin is always the eyepoint (except when processing a finite aperture for depth-of-field effects) and the ray direction is determined according to the type of projection shown in Chapter 6. The *Shoot()* function takes an x,y location in pixel coordinates on the screen as input and generates the initial ray. If the jitter option (essentially, randomizing the subpixel location where the ray is shot through the pixel) is enabled, then the *scan()* function adds a random offset to the coordinate it passes to *Shoot()*. Note that the amount of jitter is based on the particular *scan()* function. If you have no anti-aliasing active, the jitter option offsets the ray position ± half a pixel. In some of the subpixel anti-aliasing modes, this offset will be less (usually corresponding to ± one-half of a subpixel position). Once an entire scanline is completed, the *PicWriteLine()* function is called to write it to the output .IMG file.

Trace

Trace.C contains the two functions *trace()* and *bkg()*. The *trace()* function first makes sure that you have not exceeded the maximum recursion level, *max_level*. If you have, *trace()* returns black as the resulting color. Since ray colors are additive, black is the same as no color at all. If you have not exceeded the maximum allowable recursion level, then *trace()* calls the function *Intersect()* to find the nearest object with which the ray intersects.

Intersect() does all of the work and *trace()* simply provides the framework for recursively calling *Intersect()*. If *Intersect()* returns a positive value, then the ray hit something. If not, then *bkg()* is called to get the background color based on the direction the ray was going when it left the known universe. This may be either a constant color or an interpolated color based on the pitch angle of the ray for the graded sky effect, as described in Chapter 9. If the ray hit an object, *Intersect()* returns an *Intersect* data structure that contains the intersection point, the surface normal at that point, and a pointer to the object that was struck. The *shade()* function in Shade.C is called to determine the color of the ray. The *shade()* function, in turn, calls *trace()* if reflected, refracted, or shadow rays need to be traced. The entire process then repeats.

Intersection

The Inter.C module contains the basic intersection calculation algorithm, as described in Chapter 8. The Pqueue.C module is the implementation of the priority queue, which keeps the nearest struck object at the head of the queue. The priority queue routines are generic in that they order the queue according to the parameter *q_key* and retain a pointer to the objects being sorted as *q_obj*. The *q_key* is the distance along the particular ray being traced. However, the same routines can be used for ordering other types of data. This is a good example of a C implementation of a C++ type container class.

The Inter.C module contains the following functions:

❖ *Intersect()*—The main entry point to the whole group of functions, *Intersect()* is passed a ray and returns a pointer to the primitive the ray hits, or NULL if nothing is hit.

❖ *CheckAndEnqueue( )*—This compares the ray against the object's bounding box to see if it hits the bounding box and if it is closer than the current value of *min_dist*. If both conditions are met, then *PriorityQueueInsert( )* is called to add the object to the queue.

The Pqueue.C module contains the following functions:

❖ *PriorityQueueNull( )*—Clears the queue
❖ *PriorityQueueEmpty( )*—Returns true if the queue is empty
❖ *PriorityQueueInsert( )*—Inserts an object into the queue
❖ *PriorityQueueDelete( )*—Deletes an object from the queue

Strictly speaking, the implementation of the priority queue is not really a "queue" in the pure sense of the word. As objects are placed into the queue, the insert function tries to put them into the queue in a somewhat sorted order with the closest ones going to the top of the queue. The "sorting" is an attempt at balancing good results and fast execution. Each time a new object is inserted, Bob tests it against the object in the middle of the queue. If it is closer, the objects are swapped. Bob continues this test until the current object is farther away than the object halfway to the head of queue. This provides a sorting time on the order of log(n) time, and always puts the nearest current object at the head of the list. Notice also that the queue is a fixed size array. While this is an easy way to implement the queue, it does lead to an arbitrary limit on the ray tracer.

Planes that Bound

The Bound.C module contains the two basic functions that build the bounding box hierarchy: *FindAxis( )* and *SortAndSplit( )*. The *FindAxis( )* function uses a modified median-cut algorithm in that it looks for the axis with greatest variation rather than just choosing a new axis to split arbitrarily. The parser produces a linked list of objects that must be put into a heirarchical tree, as described in Chapter 8.

The *SortAndSplit( )* function implements the basic algorithm. This function is passed a pointer to the top of the current list of objects and a count of the number of objects in the current list. If the count is greater than the bunching level (the maximum number of objects allowed in a single leaf), the list is split along the coordinate axis returned by *FindAxis()*. The split is by which side of the median value computed by *FindAxis()* the bounding box of the object resides. The *SortAndSplit()* function is then called for the two newly created lists. If the count is greater than 1 but less than the bunching level, the objects are grouped together as a single *composite object*. The bounding box for this object is then computed as the bounding box for all the individual objects. This new composite object is added as a finished node of the tree. The composite object is then effectively treated as a single primitive for subsequent processing.

The pseudocode for the *SortAndSplit()* function is as follows:

```
SortAndSplit(Object *top, long count) {
    if count > bunching              // need to split
    Call FindAxis() to figure out which axis we need to split the
    object across. Split the list of objects into two lists at the
    median point determined by FindAxis(). Recursively call Sor-
    tAndSplit() on each of the new lists.

return 1    // ie not done yet
    else if count > 1
    Allocate a new composite object. Replace the objects in the
    current list with the composite object while adding the objects
    to the child list of the composite.
    From the children, calculate the bounding box for the compos-
    ite.

return 0    // we're done
    else
return 0    // there was only one
            // object in the list


}
```

Made in the Shade

Once the nearest intersection point has been found, the color of the ray is determined by using a call to the *Shade()* function in the Shade.C module. The basic lighting algorithm and its subsequent myriad options are described in Chapter 9.

The Shadow.C module defines the *Shadow()* function, which computes the shadow effects from each of the light sources. It handles *extended* light sources as well as the point light sources. In order to help speed up the shadow computations, an *object cache* keeps track of the last object that a shadow ray hit for a given recursion level. A separate cache exists for each light source since if an intervening object exists, it will be the same for many shadow rays.

The *Shadow()* function also provides a crude model of *caustic* effects. The term "caustic" refers to the light patterns caused by either reflection or refraction of light on a curved surface. Examples of caustics include the light focused by a magnifying glass and the changing patterns of light on the bottom of a swimming pool as the sunlight refracts through the surface of the water. These effects can be extremely complex to compute, so Bob uses an approximation of the effect.

Usually, the amount of shadowing is a function of the transparency of the intervening objects and the distance to the light source. Bob's approximation to caustics is to modulate the transparency based on the angle the shadow ray leaves the transparent surface, similar to the computation of the specular intensity. While a simple approximation, it does produce the desired effect.

The Texture.C, Noise.C, and Wave.C modules provide all the routines for image mapping, bump mapping, and solid texture discussed in Chapter 9. Note that Bob can modulate not only the basic diffuse color, but other attributes as well. These can provide some interesting effects if you vary them.

One of the potential problems with using surface fuzz or bump mapping is the possibility of creating a surface normal that points in the wrong direction (that is, in the opposite direction from the actual surface). The problem is that the visibility algorithm uses the surface normal direction to determine if the surface is facing away from the ray. If so, then the surface can be ignored. Bob "tweaks" the normal and folds it back so that it points back toward the ray origin and upward relative to the unmodified surface. The reason for the folding is to provide a continuous look to the bump-mapped surface rather than showing discontinuities.

The Path to *BOB*

As Bob was developed, it become obvious that files could become quite cluttered on the disk. To help alleviate this problem, Bob allows the use of an environment variable called *BOB* to define the working set of paths Bob should search for files. The File.C module contains the *init_env()* function, which gets the information associated with the environment variable *BOB* and defines an array, *paths*, and possible paths.

The second half of the work is done by the function *env_fopen()*. This function takes the same parameters and has the same return values as the *fopen()* function, except that it tries all the paths defined in the *paths* array as possible locations for the files. In other words, *env_fopen()* prefixes the passed file name with the path names and tries *fopen()*. If *fopen()* fails, then *env_fopen()* tries the next path until the file is successfully opened. You may want to create a batch file that defines *BOB* or put the definition in your AUTOEXEC.BAT for each project on which you are working.

Memory Problems

Because Bob can use a considerable amount of memory, the basic memory allocation and deallocation functions have been enhanced. In most cases, the *malloc()* function has been replaced by the *vmalloc()* function found in the Memory.C module. Since *vmalloc()* grabs 32K at a time from the system, you use less overhead. This makes it quite easy to keep track of how much memory is being allocated as the primitives are parsed and the bounding tree is built. This in turn allows *BOB* to know when an out-of-memory condition is about to occur and react accordingly.

Making the Scene

Chapter 11 provides a detailed description of the EDL language for creating an input .B file for Bob. It also shows how to run Bob and generate the .IMG output image file.

How to Use the Ray Tracer

Chapter 10 reviewed the individual code modules of the ray tracer and discussed how these modules function together to produce the finished images. This chapter describes how to create the necessary input files that define the environment to be rendered by Bob. This chapter describes each of the possible options and provides working examples. This chapter is intended as a reference guide to all the available commands.

The disk accompanying this book contains the source code, an executable version of Bob, some sample input files, and tools for processing the image for VGA display after it has been generated. The Bob.EXE file has been compiled to run on any MS-DOS-based system with an 80386 processor or better, a math coprocessor, and at least 2 MB of system memory. If you have a much more capable machine (such as a fast 386 or 486 with extra memory) you should compile Bob using the Watcom Compiler and DOS extender to take advantage of the extra horsepower.

You may want to print out the example Bob input files (those files with a .B extension) that appear on the enclosed disk. These printouts may prove helpful.

Running over Bob

Specifying a complex environment is analogous to designing a movie set. You must specify where all the lights are positioned, what kind of lights to use, what background to use, what the actors (scene objects in this case) should do, what costumes they wear (color and texturing of objects), and assorted other elements that define the total environment. Unlike a stage director, you must specify all these with mathematical precision for the computer. To ease this problem, an *Environment Description Language* (EDL) enables you to specify these effects using English-like phrases. In addition, this ray tracer can put the descriptions in modular form through the use of include files and macros, exactly as is done in the C language. In fact, you will notice that C language syntax is prevalent throughout EDL. (EDL is a self-consistent language for specifying or controlling a process.)

Bob uses a two-stage process to read in the input file with the preprocessor and the EDL parser. This process functions in much the same way as the C compiler. The preprocessor reads through the main input file, looks for and reads in all included files to create a single "file" to be passed to the parser and expands all macro definitions. This expanded file is then interpreted by the parser to determine the internal environment description needed by the program.

Once the environment is specified, you use Bob to render the scene and create an output image file for viewing on the display. The steps in generating an image with Bob are

1. Create an input file (Input.B) with your favorite text editor. The example file Axis.B on the disk is a good reference.

2. Run Bob by entering the following command at the DOS prompt:

   ```
   BOB Axis
   ```

3. Wait until done. This can take from a few minutes to a couple of days, depending on the complexity of the image and the speed of your machine. Axis.B will not take too long.

4. Convert the result, Axis.IMG, into a .GIF file by typing at the DOS command line:

   ```
   IMG2GIF -m -d Axis
   ```

   where the -m flag tells IMG2GIF to use median cut to determine the palette. The -d flag turns on Floyd-Steinberg dithering. Chapter 15 discusses these topics in more detail.

5. View the image. If you are using shareware *VPic*, use the command:

   ```
   VPic Axis.GIF
   ```

   If you are using Bob's viewer, use the command:

   ```
   GIFView Axis.GIF
   ```

Scene description files in Bob use the file extension .B and the output image files use the .IMG file extension. The Bob preprocessor supports included files using the C syntax for *include*. Included files may have any extension. The syntax for including a file into your input file is

```
#include "filename"
```

Even though you may use any file-naming convention, the following file extensions are used throughout the examples:

.B ....Required main scene description file input to Bob
.IMG.............24-bit RGB image file output by Bob
.MAP...........Palette file for IMG2GIF or background mapping
.BC ....Include file with color definitions (see Color.BC)
.BO ....Include file with object definition
.BS ....Include file with surface definitions

The .IMG files produced by Bob are full 24-bit (8-bits for each of red, green, and blue) color images. They also use a *run-length-encoding* compression technique to reduce their size. Chapter 15 and Chapter 16 discuss the details of the image format. Since 24-bit graphics cards are relatively rare on PCs, the enclosed disk includes a tool (IMG2GIF.EXE) to convert the .IMG files into standard .GIF files that can be displayed by using the shareware programs *VPic* or *CShow*. Also included are versions of both 8-bit and 24-bit conversion (IMG2GIF) and display (Disp) programs. These are discussed in Chapters 15 and 16.

To make Bob easy to use, the *BOB* environment variable is recognized and used to search for any files Bob tries to open. To set the variable, put the following line in your AUTOEXEC.BAT file:

```
set bob=c:\bob
```

You can now put input files that you use often into this directory and they will be found no matter which directory you run Bob from. Potential candidates for this include Color.BC, .MAP files, and any models that you build. Multiple paths are also supported by using this command:

```
set bob=c:\bob\colors;c:\bob\models;d:\foo\bar
```

When trying to open a file, Bob first looks in the current directory and then through the directories in the path list if the file is not found.

Commander Bob

Bob supports a number of command-line flags. These flags allow you to control the operation of the program without changing the input file. The following command-line flags are currently supported:

-s ....Run in silent mode (no statistics display)

-r.................Resume

-i x y.............Set image size to x by y pixels

-n.................No shadows (same as studio flag)

-d #..............Set maximum recursion depth value

-a mode ....Set anti-alias mode (valid modes are "none", "quick", "corners", and "adaptive"; you only have to give the first letter of the mode)

-p.................Do not use the preprocessor

-b #..............The bunching factor

The -r option is particularly useful for images that take a long time to complete. Bob can pick up where it left off if you interrupt the program with CTRL-C or CTRL-BREAK. Once either of these key sequences is struck, Bob completes the current scan line (which may still take several minutes), save its state, and then exits to DOS. The image computation may then be resumed later by using the -r option on the command line. Note that this only works if the statistics display is enabled (the default).

Statistics

While it is running, Bob displays seemingly random numbers that are related to the image-generation progress. When Bob is first invoked, it displays the current version number and the copyright notice. It then displays the filename of each of the input files (main input file and included files) as the preprocessor scans them. Next, Bob displays a running total of lights and primitives (spheres, cylinders, polygons, and so forth) as the parser reads the preprocessed input file.

Once the file is completely read in, the automatic bounding box code is called. As it generates bounding boxes, the primitives count correspondingly increases. Once the bounding box generation is completed, Bob displays the scene extent (in other words, the minimum and maximum values for each of the x-, y-, and z-axes that the primitives cover). Once the extent is displayed, Bob begins the actual rendering process. Bob also tracks memory usage and displays this information on the statistics screen while parsing the input file.

When the image is completed, the screen is cleared and a full display of image statistics appears.

The first line of this display shows the resolution (in pixels) of the output image. The next line shows the current line being processed by Bob. Normally, the line number increments by 1 for each line processed, but in "quick" mode, the line number increments by 6.

The next four lines contain information about the number of rays cast. *Eye rays* are the rays cast directly from the viewpoint out into the scene. *Reflected rays* are those generated when a ray hits a reflective surface (such as a mirror) and is reflected out into the scene again. *Refracted rays* are those generated when a ray intersects a transparent surface. Note that for surfaces such as glass, both a reflected and refracted ray are generated. The total ray count is shown as the sum of all three types of rays. If there are no reflective or transparent surfaces in your scenes, the corresponding ray count remains 0.

The next set of statistics concerns shadow rays. *Shadow rays* are the rays shot from the point of intersection toward each light in order to determine if there are any other primitives in the scene blocking the light (casting a shadow). Bob uses a technique known as a *shadow cache* to speed up this process (described in Chapter 9 and Chapter 10). The "cache hits" statistic increments each time a cached object was found to cast a shadow, so no additional processing (additional shadow rays) is needed. The "cache percentage" is the ratio of the number of "cache hits" to the number of shadow rays. The closer this percentage is to 100%, the more efficient is the cache in preventing unnecessary computation.

The next number is the average number of rays cast per pixel. This number provides an indication of how hard the ray tracer is working to generate the image. With no anti-aliasing, reflection, or refraction, this number is 1.0 (only one eye ray per pixel). The adaptive anti-aliasing feature can push this as high as 16, depending on the object sizes and complexity. Reflected and refracted rays also add to this total. If you use the quick mode, this number may go as low as .066 (1/16). A value less than 1.0 indicates that the ray tracer is filling in values for some pixels rather than actually casting a ray. This is generally unacceptable for any high-quality renderings. This number is most useful in determining how long an image will take to generate. As you experiment with the various options of anti-aliasing, ray depth, number of reflections, number of lights, and so on, you will gain a feel for how long your machine will take to generate an image. Generally, the compute time will be proportional to the number of rays cast per pixel and the image resolution.

The next set of statistics relates to the use of the bounding box generation. As described in Chapter 9, the automatic bounding box generator creates a tree-like hierarchy of bounding boxes against which each ray is tested. If the ray intersects a bounding box, the objects inside the bounding box (either other bounding boxes or primitives) are put into a priority queue for further intersection testing. The ray is then tested against the elements in the queue until all primitives have been processed.

The "bounds checked" number shows the number of bounding box intersection tests. The "queue inserts" number shows how many objects passed the bounding box check and were put into the priority queue. The "queue resets" number displays the total number of times the priority queue was reset. The priority queue is reset once for each ray, once for each shadow ray, and each time a shadow cache hit occurs. Thus,

Queue Resets = Total Rays + Shadow Rays + Cache Hits

The "max queue size" number shows the maximum number of objects in the priority queue at any one time during the rendering. These statistics taken together provide a feel for the complexity of the scene being rendered. Generally, the more objects, and, particularly, the more reflective or refractive objects in the scene, the larger these numbers will be.

The last statistic, the "max recursion depth", represents the maximum recursion level the ray tracer used while rendering the image. This generally will be a function of the number of reflective and refractive surfaces in the scene. It is presented as a pair of numbers separated by a /, showing the actual recursion level and the maximum allowed level. If your actual number is equal to the maximum level, the scene is likely more complex (more reflections) than could be handled by that maximum setting.

These statistics are updated as the program is running. They are often useful if you set some parameter too high. They can be used to find problems when things run too quickly (like no rays are being cast or objects are not visible) and your image comes out all black.

Input File (.B) Format

This section is your reference guide for the syntax of the .B input files. First, consider a few rules of thumb :

❖ Bob is case-sensitive. Therefore, Object, object, and ObJeCt are all treated as different names.

❖ Bob is right-handed. A right-handed coordinate system is used to define the location of objects in space. You can remember what this means if you look at your right hand. With your palm out, your fingers point along the positive x-axis. The heel of your hand is the origin. Curl your fingers in to make a fist. Your fingers curl toward the positive y-axis in a counterclockwise movement. Extend your thumb upwards. Your thumb now points along the positive z-axis. (See Figure 11-1.). All coordinates are specified as (x,y,z) triplets in this coordinate system. Note that you must consider this when
making polygon facets for objects because the order of the vertices determines the direction the facet faces using the "right-hand" rule.

❖ Bob likes his colors specified as RGB triplets (red, green, blue), where each component ranges from 0.0 to 1.0. However, you can substitute words for colors by using the Color.BC file, which should be included at the top your input file. A predefined series of macros substitutes color triplets for corresponding words. You may add your own colors or make other .BC files. Whenever an RGB triplet is required, you may simply use one of the color words.

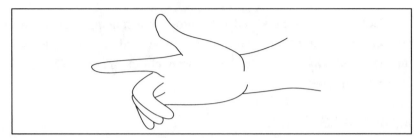

Figure 11-1. The "Right-hand" rule.

❖ Comments may be inserted anywhere in the input file by using the basic C/C++ commenting convention. Multiline comments start with /* and end with */. Anything between the comment delimiters is ignored. Single line comments start with // and end at the end of the line. For example,

```
/*      This is a comment
which spans multiple lines   */

//      This is a single line comment
```

As with any type of programming, you should use comments liberally since notes in your input files help remind you or anyone else reading the file what the input is trying to do. Comments also can be used to block out part of the input file while you are setting it up. This helps speed up test renderings.

Input File Layout

A typical input file has the following structure :

```
<Initialization>              For example, #include COLOR.BC
<Studio Definition>           Defines the environment
<Lights>                      One or more lighting definitions
<Surface 1>                   Definition of surface characteristics
<Object 1>

    .

    .

<Surface n>
<Object n>
```

The *initialization* includes general definitions that are used by all objects (such as in Colors.BC). The *Studio* definition describes the output image size, anti-aliasing, and viewpoint position. The *Lights* definition defines each light in the scene (its color, size, and intensity). *Surface* definitions establish the surface characteristics (such as color, reflectivity, refractive index, and texturing). *Object* definitions define the geometry of the objects (location in space, orientation, and so forth). The surface characteristics of an object are taken from the last *Surface* definition in the file. This makes it easy to apply the same surface characteristics to multiple objects.

Bob uses a C/C++ syntax style for specifying all the elements of the environment. In particular, the major environment controls are treated as structures; they appear in the input file in the following format:

```
<structure keyword> {
        <another structure> {
                keyword <arg1> <arg2> ...
                .
                .
        }
}
```

Within a structure, various keywords define the structure elements, just as members of a structure do in C/C++. Structures may be nested and keywords may appear sequentially on the same line or on separate lines. To avoid confusion, you should put each separate keyword on a separate line. Most elements of a structure have default values that are used if the corresponding keyword is not specified.

Preprocessor

Bob uses a two-pass process to read the input file. The first pass uses a preprocessor to process macro definitions (do macro substitution) and read in include files. During this implementation, Bob uses the input file to create a temporary file, YYZ.B. This file is the result of performing all macro substitutions and including the specified *#include* files. In this respect, Bob is similar to the C compiler preprocessor. You can delete YYZ.B after processing is completed, but sometimes it is useful for examining what exactly the parser sees (such as when the wrong file was included).

Macros

The preprocessor's macro capability is similar to that of the C compiler. The major difference is that Bob's macros do not allow for arguments and C macros do. Therefore, Bob uses a simple *string substitution processor*. You are associating a name with another string. When the preprocessor sees the name in the input file, it substitutes the appropriate string and continues. A simple example of this is the color definitions in the file Color.BC. In Color.BC, the colors white and blue are defined as follows:

```
#define blue    (0 0 1)
#define white   (1 1 1)
```

Once defined, you can then use the word "white" wherever you normally would have to type (1 1 1). Note that the parentheses ensure the string is treated as a group. This is generally good practice for macros in Bob just as it is in C/C++. For example, a blue surface with a white highlight may be specified as follows:

```
surface {
        diffuse blue
        shine 20 white
}
```

Macro names must start with a letter and may contain letters, numbers, and the underscore character (_). As with the general naming conventions, macro names are case-sensitive. A macro may be undefined by using the *#undef* keyword, as in the following statement:

```
#undef blue
```

This feature is useful if you have an include file defining a macro at the top that might be the same macro as in another file. If you *#undef* the macro at the end of your include file, it does not conflict with any definition outside of the include file. Generally, this is only used in advanced applications with many include files created by separate individuals.

If you define the same macro more than once, the old values are put onto a stack and the newest one is always used. If you then undefine the macro, only the newest one is deleted and the next newest definition is then active. In order to define a macro that is longer than one line, use the backslash (\) as a continuation character.

```
#define BLUE_PLASTIC            \

surface {                       \
          diffuse blue          \
          shine 20 white        \
}
```

Note the last line in this example does not have an ending backslash. Once the macro is defined, you can then just use the name BLUE_PLASTIC in the input file wherever you would normally type in the whole surface declaration.

Include directive

The *#include* preprocessor directive allows you to include other files into your input file. Look at the sample input files and notice that among the first lines in the file is a line such as:

```
#include Color.BC
```

This causes the parser to read in the Color.BC file to define a standard set of colors (macros) for later use in the input file. The *#include* command is also useful for including objects into your scene. This capability is most useful when you create separate object definitions that can then be placed in any position and multiple times by using the *Transformation* command.

The EDL Parser

Once the preprocessor has created the YYZ.B file, Bob "parses" (interprets) the amalgamated scene description. Remember, the scene description consists of a number of structures whose members define the environment. Each of these structures and their corresponding keywords are described in this section.

The *studio* structure

The *studio* structure in the scene file defines all those things that are neither lights, objects, nor object clips. This includes the resolution of the final image, the location of the camera (viewpoint), the direction the camera is pointing, the background color, and various rendering options. Most of the options provide default values that may be overridden.

The basic *studio* definition looks like this:

```
studio {
        from x y z
        at x y z
        up x y z
        angle ang
        resolution i j
        start line
        stop line
        aspect asp
        projection mode

        ambient acolor
        background bcolor
        haze density

        antialias mode
        threshold dist
        jitter

        aperture size
        focal_length dist
        samples n

        no_shadows
        no_exp_trans
        caustics

        depth max_depth
}
```

studio parameters

The descriptions in this section define the function and default value for each *studio* parameter. Note that this section assumes you have read Chapter 6 through Chapter 10. Refer to those chapters for the mathematical description of the functions these parameters control. This section is primarily intended as a reference guide so that you may interpret the sample .B files and create your own.

from is the location of the camera. This parameter has no default.

at is where in the scene the camera is pointed. Technically, this is where a ray from the viewpoint (*from*) through the center of the screen would intersect. This parameter has no default.

up is a vector defining the camera orientation, or *roll angle*. Usually you want the camera pointing up, so a value of (0 0 1) is used. This can be adjusted to roll the image around the axis of the camera. The default is (0 0 1).

angle is the field-of-view angle given in degrees. This controls whether you are using a wide-angle lens (close to 180 degrees), a telephoto lens (< 10 degrees) or a normal lens (something in between). This parameter has no default.

resolution is the size of the image in pixels, *i* pixels across and *j* pixels down. This may be overridden from the command line using the -i switch. This parameter has no default.

start and *stop* allow you to specify the beginning and ending line numbers to process. This is useful for testing new input files and isolating bugs. If you are networked, you might consider using this to split up an image for rendering on multiple computers. After the sections are completed, you can use the Paste.EXE program to glue them together. You will encounter problems using *start* with the resume (-r) flag. Avoid the combination. This parameter has no default.

aspect is the aspect ratio of the screen. This is the ratio of width to height of the screen for which you are rendering your images. The NEC 3D monitor has an aspect ratio of about 4/3 and the Amiga 1084 has an aspect ratio of about 1.2. To determine the proper aspect ratio for your screen, measure the width and height of a screen image and then divide the width by the height. Determining the correct aspect ratio of your screen ensures that circles look like circles instead of ovals. Remember, aspect ratio should be the width/height ratio of the displayed image regardless of the image resolution. Together with the resolution, these values are used to determine the aspect ratio of the pixels. This parameter has no default.

projection controls how the three-dimensional world is mapped onto the two-dimensional screen. The "spherical" projection produces an effect somewhat like a fish-eye lens. In a spherical projection, each pixel represents a constant angular area rather than constant screen area. The "spherical" mode allows for fields of view greater than 180 degrees. (You can even use a 360-degree field of view to make a complete panorama.)

The "orthographic" projection mode produces an image in which all the eye rays are parallel to each other (that is, no perspective divide is applied). The effect is that objects have the same size on the screen regardless of their distances from the viewer. For this mode the *angle* (field-of-view) parameter has no meaning and is replaced with a *width* parameter. The *width* parameter defines the screen width in the world coordinate system. The "parallax" projection mode produces a two-point projection instead of a three-point projection like the "flat" mode. In the "parallax" mode, all vertical lines stay vertical on the screen. This mode was implemented specifically for architectural renderings, but is sometimes useful in other contexts. Note that "vertical" is defined by the direction of the up vector. The default value for "projection" is "flat".

ambient is the color of the background light. In the real world, a general level of background light is caused by the scattering of light from all the diffuse surfaces (such as the walls, floors, and so on). This light generally is coming from all directions and so suffuses the scene. Most ray tracers (including Bob) cannot handle this diffuse interreflection (or rather, it would be far too computationally expensive to generate).

To emulate diffuse interreflection, Bob allows you to set an *ambient* light value. This acts like a light shining in every direction at once and does not cast any shadows. For an inside scene, values of about (.2 .2 .2) work well. Outside scenes look a bit more realistic with a higher *ambient* value. Most ray traced images have the *ambient* value set to (0 0 0) or black. This produces the sharpest contrasts and gives the image a super-real effect. The default value for ambient is (0 0 0).

background is the color returned if no objects are intersected while tracing a ray. Popular choices are black and sky-blue. If haze is defined, *background* is the color of the haze. Alternatively you can use

```
background { palette.map up x y z  }
```

This produces a graduated background using the colors in the Palette.MAP file. The file can have any name but must have the .MAP extension. The file is the same format as the IMG2GIF palette files described in Chapter 15 and Chapter 16. The first color in the file is the color that appears in the direction of the up vector. If no up vector is specified, then the up vector from the *studio* structure is used. The default for *background* is black.

haze is the density of the fog or haze in the scene. The *haze* value affects the color of the ray according to the equations described in Chapter 6. Haze increases the computation time but can provide an enhanced sense of perceived depth to a scene, especially an outdoor one. The default for *haze* is 0, which results in no haze effect.

antialias determines whether anti-aliasing is performed and what type is used.

Chapter 6 discusses various anti-aliasing algorithms. This option can be overridden from the command line using the -a switch. The valid modes are:

"none"—Shoot one ray per pixel, right through the pixel center. As the name implies, no anti-aliasing is performed, but the image is computed much more quickly than without. This is the default.

"quick"—This does a subsampling approximation of the image. In areas of even color (that is, small color variation), the ray tracer skips pixels to find one where the color is changing. This is the fastest mode, but the results are not useful for much more than test images. On a blank image, this should be about 15 times faster than the "none" mode. In general, the speed increases about 3-5 times. This is a great mode for performing test renderings.

"corners"—Shoot a ray at each corner of each pixel and average the results. Since the corners are shared by adjoining pixels, this means only one ray per pixel is computed. The results are almost as quick as "none," but usually have a better look. This is effectively the same as taking the image from the "none" mode and averaging every four pixels together. You can view this by applying a low-pass box filter to the image.

"adaptive"—Shoot rays at the corners of the pixel. If the colors of all four rays are within a certain threshold of each other, the program moves to the next pixel. If the colors differ by more than the threshold value, the pixel is subdivided into four subpixels and recursively sampled again. The corners of the subpixels are compared against the threshold and, if they are still too far apart, they are subdivided once more. The result is that in areas of constant or smoothly changing intensity only one ray per pixel is shot. At edges or other sharp color transitions, as many as 25 rays per pixel may be averaged to determine the color of the pixel. This method produces reasonable results with a small amount of computational overhead. Bob does not currently implement this technique, but may in a future version.

threshold is the value used by the adaptive mode of anti-aliasing. Valid values range from 0 to 255. This parameter is also used by the "quick" mode. In general, lower values produce better results but take more time. The default *threshold* is 16.

jitter is a flag that tells the system to offset the location of the ray on the screen a small random amount for each pixel. For example, instead of the ray being shot through the center of the pixel, it is shot slightly offset from the center, a different amount for each pixel. This has the effect of making some sampling artifacts less objectionable to the eye. In particular, the sampling of the checkerboard texture on a distance object appears much smoother with *jitter* than with normal anti-aliasing.

aperture is an optional parameter that allows the ray tracer to model a more realistic camera. Combined with the *focal_length* parameter, this effectively defines a camera lens that allows you to focus objects in the scene. With an aperture greater than 0, objects at the focal-length distance appear in sharp focus while objects nearer or farther from the viewpoint are blurred. The larger *aperture* is, the more exaggerated the blurring. Using a nonzero *aperture* greatly increases the amount of time needed to generate an image because Bob uses the technique of distributed ray tracing to model the effects of a camera with a nonzero *aperture*. This significantly increases the number of rays necessary to calculate the color of a pixel. The default is to shoot eight rays instead of one ray whenever *aperture* is greater than 0. This value can be controlled with the "samples" parameter below. The default value is 0, which models a pinhole camera.

focal_length determines the distance from the camera to the focal plane where objects are rendered in focus. This option is used in conjunction with the *aperture* option. Objects that are a distance equal to the focal length away from the camera are in sharp focus. The default for the *focal_length* is the distance between the *from* and *at* points that determine the viewpoint and the viewing direction.

samples controls the number of rays shot when a nonzero *aperture* is used. The default is 8.

no_shadows causes all shadow calculations to be turned off. The speed increase gained by turning off shadows is especially useful when performing test images of a new scene. This option can be invoked from the command line by using the -n switch.

no_exp_trans is the flag that turns off the exponential attenuation of the rays as they pass through transparent objects. Rays intersecting a transparent surface gener-

ate a refracted ray that travels through the surface. A real surface (such as glass) atten-
uates the intensity of the ray as it travels through the surface. The amount of attenuation is a function of the distance the ray travels through the material, and so depends
on the thickness of the surface and on the angle of the ray with respect to the surface.
The steeper the angle of the ray with respect to the surface, the more material the ray
passes through before exiting on the other side. The amount of attenuation is related
exponentially to the amount of material through which the ray travels.

Note that this is exactly the same effect as *haze*, where you compute the distance the ray travels through the atmosphere and color the ray according to a mix
of the background color and the unattenuated ray color. In this case, the color of the
material is mixed into the ray color. This effect, however, can cause problems with
a single-sided piece of glass (such as a sphere with a glass surface). For a single-
sided surface (no corresponding piece on the other side), Bob assumes the material thickness to be the entire distance from the surface to the nearest light source.
Since this is unrealistic, you can simply turn off the attenuation computation altogether with this flag. The ray color is then attenuated by a fixed amount (you still
want it partially colored by the material) independent of the distance the ray travels. This tint control also affects shadow rays.

caustics is an experimental flag that turns on Bob's faked caustics. Caustics are
those patterns produced as light passes through a transparent object. These patterns
are generated by internal reflections within the material (light reflecting inside the
material from the two sides) and are too complex to compute in a finite amount of
time on a PC. The code provided here is an experiment to simulate the effect. The
effect is fairly subtle, but does seem to make some images look better.

depth enables you to limit the maximum recursion level to which rays are traced.
Each time a ray is cast, you determine the intersection with other objects. If the
object has a reflective or refractive surface, new rays are cast from the intersection
point. The *depth* parameter controls how far you pursue this calculation. A depth
of 1 forces only eye rays to be traced. A depth of 2 traces first level reflections and
refractions. Setting the depth to 1 or 2 is an excellent way to reduce the computation time and quickly preview images to see that the geometry is correct. This parameter may be overridden on the command line using the -d option. The maximum
allowed value is 20, which is also the default.

Lights

Remember that the background ambient light essentially comes from everywhere in the scene. The background color is assigned to rays that leave the scene, or those that do not intersect any objects or lights.

The four types of lights are *point, directional, spherical,* and *spot.* A *point light* is a light source occupying a single point in space. It has a position, color, and attributes that determine how much the light intensity varies with distance from the light. A surface is illuminated by a point light source if it is not in shadow and is not facing away from the light source. A *directional light* behaves like a point light source infinitely far away with no reduction in intensity based on distance. A surface is illuminated by a directional light source if the surface is not in shadow and the surface is facing the light.

A *spherical source* actually has a physical radius to it and can provide shadows with penumbra (soft edges). To compute this effect, however, requires considerably more processing because multiple shadow rays must be cast toward the light to determine how much light is actually shining on the surface. *Spot lights* produce a cone of light whose intensity falls off depending on the angle of the ray with respect to the cone of light. These are ideal for highlighting certain areas of your model. You can create a similar effect by putting a point light inside a cone object. In most cases, however, spot lights require fewer shadow rays be cast, making them more efficient.

The definition for a *point light* source is as follows:

```
light {
  type point
  falloff f              // defaults to 0
  position x y z
  color r g b
}
```

The intensity of the light varies according to the equation:

```
I = I₀ / (distᶠ);
```

where I_0 is the base intensity of the light and *dist* is the distance from the light source to the surface point for which you are computing the color.

Physically, light intensity varies as $1/(\text{dist}^2)$ ($f = 2$). This parameter is variable for two reasons. First, $f = 0$ allows for generation of the image where the light intensity does not change at all with distance. This is useful for making sure that no spurious lighting effects are introduced. Second, Bob (like most ray tracing programs) does not accurately model the diffuse interreflection of light between objects (note that this would require an astronomical number of rays to compute since the light diffusely reflects off every surface in the scene).

Effectively, this means you have more ambient light in a scene than just the light falling on the surface directly from the light source. Other light emanates from everywhere else as well. You simulate this effect by making the intensity not fall off quite as rapidly (such as setting $f = 1$). In any case, this is a useful parameter to vary to see how it affects the overall scene appearance.

The definition for a *directional light* source is as follows:

```
light {
  type directional
  color r g b
  direction dx dy dz
}
```

The direction also may be specified by a *from* and *at* pair, as shown here:

```
light {
  type directional
  color r g b
  from x y z
  at x y z
}
```

The direction vector indicates the direction the light travels. Directional lights are assumed to be infinitely far away (such as the sun or moon). Therefore, you have no variation in intensity as a function of distance. Note that the keyword *direction* provides the same effect as saying the light is *from* (0 0 0) and *at* the direction you want it to face. A surface must be facing the light (in other words, the surface normal at the point of the surface being evaluated must point in the opposite direction of the light) for the light to make a color contribution.

The definition for a *spherical light* source is as follows:

```
light {
  type spherical
  position x y z
  radius r
  color r g b
  falloff f
  samples n
}
```

Shadows cast from spherical lights produce penumbra. Normally, when a ray hits a surface, a shadow ray is shot toward each light. If the shadow ray hits any surface on the way to the light, that light is blocked and the surface is in the shadow of the blocking object. With spherical light sources, multiple shadow rays are shot. Each one is shot to a random point within the radius of the light. If the light is half-blocked by an object, approximately half the shadow rays are blocked and half will pass through to the light. You use the ratio of blocked to unblocked shadow rays to determine the strength of the shadow.

As you might expect, processing the additional shadow rays adds considerable time to the rendering. Spherical lights sometimes are referred to as *extended light sources*. Although they are not implemented here, you can extend the code to include light sources of different shapes (such as cylinders to model fluorescent bulbs). This would require even more shadow rays and is not implemented by Bob. The number of shadow rays shot each time is controlled by the *studio* parameter *samples*. The default value for this is 16.

The definition for a spot-light source is as follows:

```
light {
  type spot
  position x y z
  direction dx dy dz
  min_angle angle1
  max_angle angle2
  color r g b
  falloff f
}
```

As with the directional light, the *direction* parameter may be replaced with the *at x y z* statement to specify the direction light is facing. The *direction* defines the long axis of a cone whose apex is the light source. *min_angle* and *max_angle* define the shape of the cone of light produced by the spot light. As with the other type of light source, you compute the angle between the direction vector (central cone axis

314

for spots) and the vector from the light source to the surface point under consideration. If this angle is less than *min_angle*, the surface is fully illuminated by the light and behaves like a point light. If the angle is between *min_angle* and *max_angle*, the light intensity falls off according to the following equation:

```
I = I0 * (angle - min_angle) / (max_angle - min_angle);
```

Note that this intensity change is in addition to any intensity fall-off caused by the distance of the surface from the light source. If the angle is greater than *max_angle*, the surface point is not illuminated by the light. For example, if you want a cone of light 30 degrees wide with sharp edges, you define *min_angle* and *max_angle* to be 30. To get the same size light, but one that fades out at the edges, you define *max_angle* to be 30 and *min_angle* to be 0.

Two other parameters that may be specified for each light source are *no_shadows* and *no_spec*. The *no_shadows* parameter indicates that no shadow computations should be performed for this light. The *no_spec* parameter turns off the computation of specular (surface highlighting) effects for this light. These are useful for providing more realistic effects, such as using a directional light source to simulate ambient lighting. A low-intensity setting of (.2, .2, .2) produces subtle shading effects that look more realistic than the constant color added by ambient background color.

Note that even if a light is within the viewing scene, it does not appear as an object. Since this is sometimes desired, you can make it visible by using a sphere to wrap a transparent shell around the light. For example,

```
//      Define a point light at 2 3 4 that shows up in the scene
//      as a light with radius 1.

light {
  center 2 3 4
  type point
  color white
}

//      glass shell

surface {
  ambient white       // same color as the light
  transparent white   // totally transparent
}
```

```
sphere {
  center 2 3 4
  radius 1
}
```

Since the surface is fully transparent, it does not affect the light intensity. The sphere is still treated as an object, whose color is the color of the light. It will thus be added to the scene as appropriate.

Surfaces

The *surface* structure enables you to define the surface characteristics of the objects you are rendering (including such attributes as color, reflectivity, and texture). When you define a surface in the input file, it is applied to all the primitives following it until a new surface is defined. This allows you to enter multiple objects without having to repeat the surface characteristics. It also provides a simple way to apply different surfaces to the same object. A simple *surface* structure is as follows:

```
surface {
  diffuse r g b          // defaults to 0 0 0 (black)
  ambient r g b          // defaults to 0 0 0
  specular r g b         // defaults to 0 0 0
  shine pow              // defaults to 0
  transparent r g b      // defaults to 0 0 0
  ior num                // defaults to 1.0
  fuzz magnitude         // defaults to 0.0
  no_antialias           // turn off antialiasing
}
```

You use each of these components to determine the color of rays intersecting the surface of an object. Chapter 6 provides the complete mathematical description of how the color is computed from these parameters.

The *diffuse* color is the color of the object as seen when illuminated by a full white light. This is what you would normally think of as the color of the object in the absence of fancy lighting effects. A value of (0 0 0) signifies a black object while a value of (1 1 1) indicates white. The contribution of this component depends on the intensity of light falling on the surface at any given point.

The *ambient* term, sometimes also referred to as the "self-luminous component," is the color of the object in the absence of any lights, or in total darkness. The *specular* component specifies the reflectivity of the surface, for each of the red, green, and blue components. A value of (1 1 1) produces a mirror-like reflection.

The *shine* parameter determines how large the specular spot (the image of the light reflected in the surface) appears on a surface. Low values such as (1 - 10) produce large, soft-edged specular highlights while high values of 1000 or more produce a small, sharp spot. Normally, the brightness and color of the spot is directly proportional to the *specular* component.

Sometimes you may want a blue object with *specular* highlights without having to perform the extra work involved with tracing reflected rays. Therefore, Bob allows this second form for defining *specular* spots:

```
shine pow r g b
```

In this case, you use the specified color instead of the *specular* component of the surface. In other words, the surface does not reflect other objects in the scene, but rather shows *specular* highlights.

The *transparent* parameter defines the surface transparency, again for each of the red, green, and blue components. A value of (1 1 1) produces a glass-like surface, since all colors are passed through equally. A value of (1 0 0) produces a surface like red glass, since it only allows red light to pass through. A surface with a *transparent* component of (.9 .9 .9) appears partially transparent with the amount of light passed through based on the thickness of the object (that is, where the new ray exits the object).

The index of refraction, *ior*, determines how much the ray is bent as it passes into the transparent surface. This is the angle of the new ray with respect to the angle that the original ray entered the surface. In reality, this is related to the relative densities between the surface and the atmosphere. Values of about 1.1 to 1.3 work well to simulate the effect of glass. The *ior* of diamond is 2.6.

fuzz adds random variations to the surface normal of the object when its color is determined. Since the *diffuse* color of the object is affected by the angle the light hits the surface, this randomization produces a coarse texture pattern on the object. Applied to mirrored or transparent surfaces this produces an effect much like frosted glass. Generally, small values of *fuzz*, .01 to .3, seem to work best.

The *no_antialias* flag disables the adaptive anti-aliasing calculation for that surface. In general, this feature is not desirable except in a few special cases. The original reason for this parameter was that fuzzy surfaces can cause the adaptive anti-alias option to shoot many rays and slow down the image generation considerably.

317

(*fuzz* causes the colors of adjacent areas to vary more than normal, and thus forces the adaptive anti-aliasing to shoot more rays). By adding the *no_antialias* flag to the surface definition, you still get the benefits of the adaptive anti-aliasing along the edges of the objects, but you avoid the slowdown that can be caused by any large, fuzzy surfaces. Note, however, that this also changes the appearance of the surface compared to leaving the anti-aliasing enabled. The surface appears more grainy because less averaging is performed. Try cutting the amount of *fuzz* in half when using this flag to preserve the amount of color variation in the surface.

Keywords used in Bob that may be abbreviated are *surf*, *diff*, *amb*, *spec*, and *trans*. Here are some example surfaces :

```
//      simple red surface
surface {
  diff 1 0 0
}

//      self-luminous blue
surface {
  ambient 0 0 1
}

//      mirror with specular highlights
surface {
  spec 1 1 1
  shine 100
}

//      glass with some reflection
surface {
  spec .3 .3 .3
  shine 30
  trans .7 .7 .7
  ior 1.2
}
```

As a general rule of thumb, the sum

```
ambient + diffuse + specular + transparent
```

should be less than or equal to (1 1 1). This will ensure that the contributions of all light sources produce unity on the surface.

Bump mapping

Remember that one problem with ray traced images is that they often look too clean. The surrealistic look is enhanced by the fact that all the objects are unnaturally pristine and smooth.

Bump mapping is a means of giving a surface some texture by simulating the effect of bumps or ripples in the surface. Because it is impractical to distort the surface with numerous little features, you simulate the effect by modulating (varying according to some function) the surface normal across the surface. Since the surface normal is what affects the color, reflection, and refraction effects, you attain virtually the same visual effect as if you had drawn many little surfaces. This technique allows a simple surface to appear very complicated. Bump definitions are included inside the simple surface definitions, as in the following:

```
surface {
  diffuse red
  bump {
      . . .
  }
}
```

A sample wave bump map looks like this:

```
bump {
  wave {
      center 1 2 3
      wavelength 2.0
      amplitude 0.2
      damping 0.9  // defaults to 1.0
      phase 0.0    // defaults to 0.0
  }
}
```

The wave bump map creates the effect of a wave emanating from some point in the scene, such as on the surface of a pool. The surface normal is varied according to the equation

```
N = N₀ + amplitude * (1.0 - (wavelength/dist * damping)) *
sin(2 * Pi * ((P - center)/wavelength + phase))
```

where N_0 is the surface normal at the point P you are evaluating and *dist* is the distance from P to the point center (that is, the length of P - *center*). Note that this expression is evaluated for each of the x,y,z components of the normal. The *center* parameter defines the source of the wave and *wavelength* defines the crest-to-crest distance of the wave. The *amplitude* parameter defines the maximum amount that the surface normal is bumped. Values under 1 are definitely best. The *damping* parameter defines how much the amplitude falls with distance. In this example, the *amplitude* decreases by 10% for each *wavelength* of distance from the source. The *phase* is a number between 0 and 1 that defines a starting offset for the phase of the wave (in other words, the places where the wave peaks and troughs are located).

When the *phase* parameter is smoothly varied from frame to frame in an animation sequence, the wave appears to move out from the center point. You can define multiple waves within the bump structure. You can create a realistic rippled surface by defining three or four wave sources at various locations with differing *wavelengths* and *amplitudes*.

Another form of bump mapping is known as *turbulence*. The definition of *turbulence* in the surface structure is as follows:

```
bump {
  turbulence {
       scale 1 1 1
       offset 0 0 0
       amplitude .5
       terms 4
  }
}
```

turbulence produces fractal-like patterns on the surface. The *turbulence* function starts by taking the location of the ray intersection and returning a random number in the range ± *amplitude*. The *scale* and *offset* factors are applied to the xyz location before the *turbulence* function is called. The *terms* parameter allows you to build a fractal-like surface. When *terms* is greater than 1, the turbulence function is repeatedly called (*terms* times) and the total is accumulated. Each successive *term* in the sum has its scaling doubled and the *amplitude* halved. This produces the varying levels of self-similarity associated with fractals. The sample file Bob.B uses this feature and a nonsymmetric scaling (different scaling in x,y,z) to produce the "spun-chrome" look on the large sphere.

Turbulence and wave definitions may be included with each other inside a bump definition.

320

Textured surfaces

Bob also allows the use of solid texturing to enhance the realism of the rendered surfaces. Textured surfaces are really just two surfaces with a definition of where on the object and how the two surfaces are blended together. The surfaces can be "layered" in one of three patterns: checker, spherical, or noise.

The checker pattern produces a three-dimensional checker. The size of the blocks is controlled by the scale factor. If one of the scale parameters is 0, the pattern is assumed not to change along that axis. An example would be a simple checkerboard pattern with checkers 2 units on a side colored black and white. This pattern is defined to extend infinitely along the z-axis, as shown here:

```
surface {
  texture {
      pattern checker
      scale 2 2 0
      offset 0 0 0 // default
      fuzz 0       // default
      blend 0      // default
      surface { diff black }
      surface { diff white }
  }
}
```

A scale of (2 0 0) creates a pattern that changes every 2 units in the x direction, but is continuous in the y and z directions. This is equivalent to 2-unit thick slabs of material stacked along the x-axis.

The spherical pattern produces concentric layers of alternating surfaces. When one of the scale parameters is 0, concentric cylinders are formed with the axis of the cylinders along the zeroed axis. This is useful for wood textures. The spherical pattern also requires two radius definitions for the layers. The first radius is used for the first surface, and the second radius is used for the second surface. The following is an example of the spherical pattern.

```
surface {
  texture {
      pattern spherical
      scale 2 2 0
      radius 1
      radius 2
      surface { diff black }
```

```
        surface { diff white }
    }
  }
```

The *noise* pattern uses the output of the *noise* function directly to pick between the two surfaces. This is useful for producing textures such as granite. By using unequal scaling values in the x, y, and z directions, you can get a streaked-looking surface. You can use tan and brown surfaces to produce a fine wood-grain look. The following is an example of the use of the noise pattern.

```
surface {
  texture {
      pattern noise
      terms 4
      scale x y z
      surface { diff white }
      surface { diff black }
  }
}
```

You can use the *fuzz* and *blend* parameters to soften the edges between two surfaces. Their values range from 0 to 1. The *blend* parameter produces a smooth transition between the surfaces. The value of the *blend* parameter determines the width of this transition area. The *fuzz* parameter adds noise to the point being checked in proportion to its value. This produces a coarse, speckled transition between the surfaces.

You can also use the *turbulence* function to texture surfaces. By varying the parameters the effect can be made to range from a slight perturbance in the pattern, to a marble look, to excessive turbulence.

Primitives

Primitives are the basic drawing elements for Bob. Chapter 6 describes each of these in detail. This section provides the syntax for creating each of the primitive types.

Sphere

The sphere is the simplest of the primitives supported by Bob and generally the fastest to perform an intersection test. The format for a sphere is

```
sphere {
  center x y z
```

```
        radius r
    }
```

where *x y z* is the location in space for the center of the sphere and *r* is the sphere's radius. As an example, consider two glass spheres, one of which is hollow and one of which is solid. The hollow surface has a thickness of .1 by defining two spheres, one inside the other, as shown here:

```
//      glass surface

surface {
trans 1 1 1
shine 200 1 1 1
ior 1.2
}

//      solid globe

sphere {
center 1 0 0
radius .9
}

//      hollow globe

sphere {
center -1 0 0
radius .9
}       // outer surface
sphere { center -1 0 0
radius .8
}       // inner surface
```

As an interesting experiment, Bob includes a fuzzy spheres option. These spheres appear fuzzy because they have no fixed radius. To define a fuzzy sphere, define a normal sphere and add a *fuzz* parameter. This defines how variable the radius will be. Each time the ray tracer performs an intersection test with the fuzzy sphere, the radius to test against is randomly chosen to lie between the radius and radius + fuzz, as shown here:

```
//      fuzzy sphere with radius between 0.5 and 2
sphere {
  center 0 1 2
  radius .5
  fuzz 1.5
}
```

Ring

The ring primitive may also be described as a washer or disk. The definition for a ring consists of a location, a surface normal, and a minimum and maximum radius. The minimum radius may be 0, which produces a solid disk without a center hole. Because the intersection for the ring is faster than for a polygon, the ring is a good choice to use as a ground plane underneath the objects you are ray tracing. The format for the ring definition is

```
ring {
  center x y z
  normal a b c
  min_radius r0
  max_radius r1
}
```

The surface normal a b c need not be normalized, but it must be nonzero. The surface normal determines the direction the ring is oriented. In other words, it is the direction through the center of the hole. If you simply want a disk without a center hole, the min/max radius definitions may be replaced with a single radius definition as shown here:

```
ring {
  center x y z
  normal a b c
  radius r
}
```

Polygon

Polygons may have any number of vertices greater than three. The vertices must all lie within the same plane, or else the results are strange. The order of the vertices may be either clockwise or counterclockwise. However, the direction the polygon is facing (the surface normal) is determined by the right-hand rule, so define the vertices in counterclockwise order, as shown here:

```
polygon {
  points 4
  vertex  1  1 0
  vertex  1 -1 0
  vertex -1 -1 0
  vertex -1  1 0
}
```

This produces a square polygon 2 units on a side, centered at the origin, with a surface normal equal to (0 0 1).

Triangular patch

The triangular patch is useful for building objects with complex shapes that you want to appear smooth. The patch is defined by three vertices, just as in a polygon patch, except now you also provide explicit surface normals at all three vertices. The surface normal at any point along the patch is a weighted average of the normals at the three corners. Thus, the color varies smoothly across the surface. Manually creating such patches is not useful, but having a computer-generated set of patches can produce pleasing results.

```
patch {
  vertex 1 0 0 normal .1 0 1
  vertex 0 1 1 normal 0 .1 1
  vertex 0 0 .5 normal -.1 -.1 1
}
```

Cone

Bob implements truncated cones. They have a radius both at the base and at the apex. They are, however, open-ended, which means that they do not have caps on either end. When the radii are equal, the cone magically becomes a cylinder. To get a pointed cone, enter 0 for one of the radii, as shown here:

```
cone {
  base 1 1 1 base_radius 4
  apex 0 0 5 apex_radius 1
}
```

Rings are useful for capping the ends of cones. Even for a cone at an odd angle, the position and normal of the ring can be easily calculated. To cap the apex end of the cone, the ring's center is equal to the apex, the ring's radius is equal to the *apex_radius*, and the ring's normal is equal to the vector

```
apex - base
```

Using this example, the definition for a ring to cap the apex end of the cone is as follows:

```
ring {
  center 0 0 5
  radius 1
  normal -1 -1 4
}
```

Transformations

Bob's transformation commands enable you to move, scale, and orient objects. Transformation commands apply to all the primitives and follow them until they are "popped" from the transformation stack. As described in Chapter 4, the net transformation for an object is matrix multiplication of all of the transformations currently on the transformation stack. The format for a transformation command is as follows:

```
transform {
  scale    s
  rotate   x y z
  translate        dx dy dz
}
```

scale changes the size of the objects and may also be defined as a vector to create objects that are scaled differently in each axis. Unfortunately, this does not work with all primitives. Only polygons and patches can be scaled nonuniformally. The *rotate* command rotates the object a given number of degrees around each axis. The *translate* command moves the object.

Any of these may be left out (they default to 0) or used more than once. They can also be used in any order and are applied to the objects in the order that they are given. It is important that you use the correct order. An object that is rotated 90 degrees around the z-axis and translated 10 units along the x-axis ends up at (10 0 0) with a 90-degree twist. If the operations are applied in the other order, the object ends up at (0 10 0). Sometimes it helps to play around with real objects and work through some of the transformations first.

Remember that all rotations are done around the axes, not necessarily around the center of the object. Keep this in mind when building new objects. Put (0 0 0) at the "natural" center of rotation for the object. This helps greatly when building scenes with the objects. For example, the natural "center" for a car model would be at ground level in the center of the car. This allows the car to be positioned easily.

To remove the last transformation from the transform stack, use the *transform_pop* command. Often you need to nest transform commands in order to build a model of a complicated multipart object that can be moved as a unit. For example, you may want to create a tank model with a turret that you can rotate. Assume that the body of your tank model is in the file Tank.BO and the turret is in Turret.BO. To place the tank in your scene, your input file looks like this:

```
#define TURRET_ANGLE     (30)     // rotation for turret

transform { translate x y z }   // move whole tank

#include tank.BO// include body geometry
transform { rotate 0 0 TURRET_ANGLE }
#include turret.BO       // include turret geometry

transform_pop           // clean up transform stack
transform_pop
```

With this technique, you can build and position complicated models with relative ease.

Image Textures

You may want to incorporate actual graphically scanned or video digitized images in your rendered images. Perhaps you want to incorporate a previously rendered image into your newly rendered image. Textured images enable you to accomplish these tasks. You use a .IMG file for the diffuse, transparent, specular, or ambient component(s) of a surface. In doing so, you color a planar surface with the image, thus making it appear to be that image. The syntax is as follows:

```
surf {
    diff {
        image foo.img
        position x y z //image upper left hand corner
        across  x y z //vector pointing across top of image
                      //from upper left to upper right corners
        normal  x y z //surface normal for the image
        scale        n//size the image
    }
}
```

The default scale, 1.0, means that the top edge of the image measures 1 unit across. For a 640 x 480 image, that means the image is 1.0 x 0.75 units in size. Images are tiled in a regular, repeating pattern. This is great for producing objects such as brick walls, roadways, and sidewalks.

Transformations of surfaces with image maps should work fine except when you use nonuniform scaling in your transform statement. Do not do that. The image is not "wrapped" around the objects affected, but rather it is projected straight along the normal vector for the given object. Color Plate 8 shows an art gallery with texture mapped wall hangings. The texture maps are projected straight along the normal vectors of the walls, thus mapping the images to the walls as though they were hanging on the walls.

Clipping

You can clip primitives to produce more complicated shapes. A primitive may be clipped by the following three types of clips: a plane, sphere, or cone. The clipping surface cuts through part of the primitive, thus cutting away a piece of the primitive. For example, a sphere can be clipped against a plane to produce a hemisphere, or a cone can be used to clip a hole through another cone. Clips are defined within a primitive's definition. You may have more than one clip per primitive. Any transformations of the primitive are also applied to the clips.

A clip is processed in a reasonably straightforward manner. If a ray intersects a primitive, it is then checked against any clips for that primitive. For a plane clip, you check to see on what side of the clip plane the intersection occurs. If it occurs on the clipped side, the surface is not visible and the ray is processed as if the intersection never occurred. Similarly, if the intersection point occurs inside a sphere or cone clip, the point is considered invisible and processing continues as if the primitive were not intersected.

A clipping plane is defined by a point and a normal, as shown here:

```
clip {
      center x y z
      normal x y z
}
```

The part of the primitive on the side the normal is facing is considered visible, while the other side is considered clipped out. For example, if you want to get a hemisphere of radius 1 centered at the origin, it would look like this:

```
sphere {
    center 0 0 0 radius 1
    clip {
  center 0 0 0 normal 0 0 1
    }
}
```

Note that the clip's normal is pointing upward. This gives you the top half of the sphere. If you change the normal to (0 0 -1), you get the bottom half.

Clipping spheres are defined as follows:

```
clip {
    center x y z
    radius r
    inside or outside
}
```

With a clipping sphere or cone, you can choose to keep either the part of the primitive inside of the sphere or the part of the primitive outside of the sphere.

Clipping cones look like this:

```
clip {
    apex x y z       apex_radius r
    base x y z       base_radius r
    inside or outside
}
```

Just as with the cone primitive, a cylinder can be created by using a single radius value.

Occasionally, you may want to apply the same clips to a group of primitives. To do this, you define global clips by using the *global_clip* keyword, as shown here:

```
global_clip {
    clip { ... }
    clip { ... }
    clip { ... }
}
```

The *clip_pop* keyword causes the previous setting of global clips to be popped off the stack, much like the *transform_pop* keyword does for transformations.

On with the Show

The following chapters examine how to create procedural database generators to provide much more complicated objects, as well as a three-dimensional modeling tool that allows you to construct three-dimensional objects.

PART III

Production of Object Databases for the Ray Tracer

CHAPTER 12

Procedural Object Databases

The next three chapters present methods for creating complex object databases. The programs presented in these chapters all generate .BO files for Bob that ultimately break down an object into the primitives Bob supports, (spheres, cones, rings, and so forth). If you can express a methodology for generating the object, you can write a program to actually generate the scene file.

This chapter shows several example programs that generate a complex object from a mathematical description or procedure. An object defined this way is called a *procedural object*. For example, you can define a brick wall by literally building it brick by brick. This program would have a basic brick object and then compute where all the bricks are positioned. As each brick is computed, the appropriate position information is written out to a .B file for Bob.

The most common examples of procedural objects are based on *fractals*, a concept first popularized by Benoît Mandelbrot. However, a procedural object can be a much more general type of object than just fractal. Any object that can be described by some procedure (usually recursive in nature) can be created by a program and rendered by Bob. The examples presented here generate such objects as fractal trees, SphereFlakes, Menger Sponges, tile puzzles, and a hex-sphere pattern. Keep in mind, though, that these examples are just the beginning. A wide range of objects can be generated with procedural methods.

Growing Trees

The first example is based on concepts of Aono and Kunii and their work on geometric model trees. In this example, you create a tree trunk and branches that are modeled from spheres and cylinders. Figure 12-1 shows how the fractal tree-growing algorithm works. Notice that spheres fill the ends of cylinders, and that

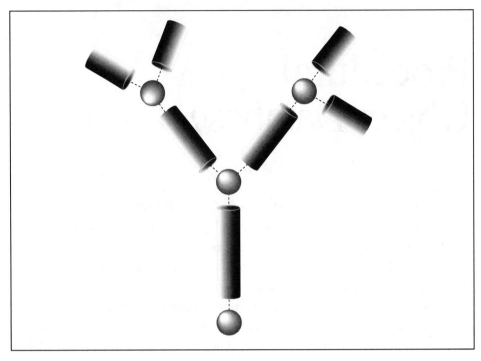

Figure 12-1. Fractal tree

multiple cylinders are connected to the same sphere to produce the tree limbs and branches.

The algorithm for generating the tree uses a recursive process that creates two new branches from the end of the current branch. Each of these new branches is smaller and shorter (with some random variation) than the original branch. You track the recursion level (which corresponds to the branching level) against a maximum recursion level set before the program begins. Once the program has reached this maximum recursion level, the tree routine creates 2-disk leaves, and then exits rather than creating new branches. Note that during each call, the branch is written out to the file Trees.BO, which defines the tree for Bob. Note also that in order to write the .BO file, we will use DOS pipes. To do this, after you have completed the program, type:

```
Trees > Trees.BO
```

so that the program's output is piped to the file.

Listing 12-1 shows the program Trees.C. Once you run Trees.C, you have a tree database. Bob can now accept your tree and generate a view. Use the Lakeside.B file to test your tree. The tree algorithm can be fun to play with. Many additions are possible, including (but not limited to) changing the branch angles, varying the number of new branches generated, varying the width and height of the branches, and so forth.

```
/*
```

```
              Recursive 3-D Tree Generator
      Trees.C = recursive trees from spheres and cylinders
   Copyright 1988,1992 Christopher D. Watkins and Stephen B. Coy
                    ALL RIGHTS RESERVED
```

```
/*

      trees — Generates strange looking recursive trees. Unless
              you have lots of disk space and time you shouldn't go much
              beyond level 8 or so.

      NUM_BRANCHES — Controls how many new branches are created at each
                     joint.
      START_RADIUS — The starting trunk radius.
      RADIUS_SCALE — Scale factor by which the branch radius is reduced at
                     each level.
      START_LENGTH — Starting branch segment length.
      LENGTH_SCALE — Scale factor by which the branch segment length is
                     adjusted at each level. Does not need to be less than
                     one.
      MAX_ANGLE —    The maximum angle a branch will bend from its parent.
      LEAF_RADIUS —  Size of the leaves. Way ugly things, too.

*/
#include <stdio.h>
#include <stdlib.h>
#include <math.h>

#define DEFAULT_MAX_LEVEL      (5)
#define NUM_BRANCHES           (2)
#define START_RADIUS           (6.0)
#define RADIUS_SCALE           (0.6)
#define START_LENGTH           (30.0)
#define LENGTH_SCALE           (0.9)
#define MAX_ANGLE              (60)
#define LEAF_RADIUS            (3.0)
```

```
#define LEAF_SURF      (0)
#define BRANCH_SURF    (1)

int     start_level = DEFAULT_MAX_LEVEL;

main(int ac, char **av)
{
    if(ac == 2) {
    start_level = atoi(av[1]);
    }

    /* output sphere at base */
    surface(BRANCH_SURF);
    printf("sphere { center 0 0 0 radius %g }\n", START_RADIUS);

    /* build a tree */
    tree(START_LENGTH, START_RADIUS, start_level);

}   /* end of main() */

tree(double length, double radius, int level)
{
    int branch; double new_length, new_radius, new_level;

    if(level == 0) {
        surface(LEAF_SURF);
        printf("ring { center 0 0 0 normal %d %d %d radius %g }\n",
                rnd(360), rnd(360), rnd(360), LEAF_RADIUS);
        return;
    }

    new_length = length * LENGTH_SCALE;
    new_radius = radius *   RADIUS_SCALE;
    new_level = level - 1;

    surface(BRANCH_SURF);

    /* rotate current branch */
    if(level != start_level) {
        printf("transform { rotate %d %d %d }\n",
                rnd(MAX_ANGLE)-rnd(MAX_ANGLE),
                rnd(MAX_ANGLE)-rnd(MAX_ANGLE),
                rnd(MAX_ANGLE)-rnd(MAX_ANGLE));
    }

    /* output current segment */
    printf("cone { base 0 0 0 apex 0 0 %g base_radius %g apex_radius
            %g }\n",
        length, radius, new_radius);
```

```
    printf("sphere { center 0 0 %g radius %g }\n", length,
          new_radius);

    /* move coordinate system to tip */
    printf("transform { translate 0 0 %g }\n", length);

    /* build branches */
    for(branch=0; branch<NUM_BRANCHES; branch++) {
          tree(new_length, new_radius, new_level);
    }

    /* pop coordinate system move */
    printf("transform_pop\n");

    /* pop rotation */
    if(level != start_level) {
          printf("transform_pop\n");
    }

}    /* end of tree */

int rnd(int i)
{
    return (int)(((double)rand()/(double)RAND_MAX) * i);
}

surface(int surf)
{
    static int      prev_surf = (-1);

    if(surf == prev_surf) {
          return;
    }

    if(surf == LEAF_SURF) {
          printf("surface { diffuse green }\n");
    } else {
          printf("surface { diffuse medium_tan }\n");
    }
}      /* end of surface() */
```

Listing 12-1. Trees.C

Donuts and Tori

This program generates a model of a torus as a collection of triangular patches, spheres, or facets. A *torus* is a mathematically precise donut. It is a cylinder of radius R wrapped around the donut center. The main axis of the cylinder lies along a circle of radius ρ in the XY plane. For convenience, two angles (θ and ϕ) define the torus. θ represents the angle moving around the center of the donut. In this case, however, ϕ is the angle with respect to the center of the cylinder that intersects a line at angle θ from the center of the donut. You compute the (x, y, z) point on the torus for a given θ and ϕ using the following equations :

$$x = (\rho + R \times \cos(\phi)) \times \cos(\theta)$$
$$y = (\rho + R \times \cos(\phi)) \times \sin(\phi)$$
$$z = R \times \sin(\phi)$$

With these equations, the Torus.C program uses a double nested loop to increment θ and ϕ by the step size you specify. Note that both θ and ϕ run from 0 to 360 degrees. Within the loop, two triangular patches are made from the four points defined by (θ, ϕ), (θ + dθ, ϕ), (θ, ϕ + dϕ), and (θ+ dθ, ϕ + dϕ). Since you want a smooth surface, the surface normal is computed at all four points on the torus and then stored with each triangular patch. As with the primitives, the surface normal is computed as the gradient (partial derivatives) at the points of interest.

Listing 12-2 shows the Torus.C program. While this program produces a suitable model, it is far less efficient than actually adding the torus to Bob as a primitive, as described in Chapter 8. In addition, this method limits the resolution of the torus. The Torus.C program produces a finite number of patches, and so the torus always will have some sharp edges if you get close enough to it. As with the trees, you will compile the Torus program and then use DOS pipes as follows:

```
Torus 3 2 16 16 patches > t16_16p.BO
```

You can see your creation using the Tor2.B file.

```
/*
```

```
*/
#include <stdio.h>
#include <stdlib.h>
```

```
#include <math.h>

#define PI        (3.1415927)

#define SPHERES (0)
#define SMOOTH (1)
#define FACETS (2)

main(int ac, char **av)
{
    int       mode;
    int       seg1, seg2, i, j;
    double    lr, sr, t0, t1, p0, p1, dt, dp;
    double    st0, st1, ct0, ct1, sp0, sp1, cp0, cp1;
    double    x0, x1, y0, y1;

    if(ac != 6) {
            usage(av[0]);
    }

    lr = atof(av[1]);
    sr = atof(av[2]);
    seg1 = atoi(av[3]);
    seg2 =  atoi(av[4]);
    if(strcmp(av[5], "spheres") == 0) {
            mode = SPHERES;
    } else if(strcmp(av[5], "facets") == 0) {
            mode = FACETS;
    } else if(strcmp(av[5], "patches") == 0) {
            mode = SMOOTH;
    } else {
        fprintf(stderr, "Error, unkown mode type %s\n", av[5]);
        fprintf(stderr, "Mode must be either spheres, patches or
                facets.\n");
        exit(1);
    }

    dt = 2.0 * PI / seg1;
    dp = 2.0 * PI / seg2;
    for(i=0; i<seg1; i++) {
            t0 = i * dt;
            t1 = ((i+1)%seg1) * dt;
            st0 = sin(t0); ct0 = cos(t0);
            st1 = sin(t1); ct1 = cos(t1);

        if(mode == SPHERES) {
            printf("sphere { center %g %g %g radius %g }\n", st0*lr,
                    ct0*lr, 0.0, sr);
            printf("cone { apex %g %g %g base %g %g %g radius %g }\n",
```

```
                    st0*lr, ct0*lr, 0.0, st1*lr, ct1*lr, 0.0, sr);
    } else {
        for(j=0; j<seg2; j++) {
            p0 = j * dp;
            p1 = ((j+1)%seg2) * dp;
            sp0 = sin(p0); cp0 = cos(p0);
            sp1 = sin(p1); cp1 = cos(p1);
            x0 = lr * ct0;
            y0 = lr * st0;
            x1 = lr * ct1;
            y1 = lr * st1;

            if(mode == SMOOTH) {
                printf("patch {\n");
                printf("\tvertex %g %g %g normal %g %g %g\n",
                        x0+sr*cp0*ct0, y0+sr*cp0*st0, sr*sp0,
                        x0+sr*cp0*ct0-x0, y0+sr*cp0*st0-y0,
                        sr*sp0);
                printf("\tvertex %g %g %g normal %g %g %g\n",
                        x0+sr*cp1*ct0,  y0+sr*cp1*st0, sr*sp1,
                        x0+sr*cp1*ct0-x0, y0+sr*cp1*st0-y0,
                        sr*sp1);
                printf("\tvertex %g %g %g normal %g %g %g\n",
                        x1+sr*cp0*ct1, y1+sr*cp0*st1, sr*sp0,
                        x1+sr*cp0*ct1-x1, y1+sr*cp0*st1-y1,
                        sr*sp0);
                printf("}\n");
                printf("patch {\n");
                printf("\tvertex %g %g %g normal %g %g %g\n",
                        x0+sr*cp1*ct0, y0+sr*cp1*st0, sr*sp1,
                        x0+sr*cp1*ct0-x0, y0+sr*cp1*st0-y0,
                        sr*sp1);
                printf("\tvertex %g %g %g normal %g %g %g\n",
                        x1+sr*cp1*ct1, y1+sr*cp1*st1, sr*sp1,
                        x1+sr*cp 1*ct1-x1, y1+sr*cp1*st1-y1,
                        sr*sp1);
                printf("\tvertex %g %g %g normal %g %g %g\n",
                        x1+sr*cp0*ct1, y1+sr*cp0*st1, sr*sp0,
                        x1+sr*cp0*ct1-x1, y1+sr*cp0*st1-y1,
                        sr*sp0);
                printf("}\n");
            } else {
                printf("polygon { points 3\n");
                printf("\tvertex %g %g %g\n", x0+sr*cp0*ct0,
                        y0+sr*cp0*st0, sr*sp0);
                printf("\tvertex %g %g %g\n", x0+sr*cp1*ct0,
                        y0+sr*cp1*st0, sr*sp1);
                printf("\tvertex %g %g %g\n", x1+sr*cp0*ct1,
                        y1+sr*cp0*st1, sr*sp0);
```

```
                printf("}\n");
                printf("polygon { points 3\n");
                printf("\tvertex %g %g %g\n", x0+sr*cp1*ct0,
                       y0+sr*cp1*st0, sr*sp1);
                printf("\tvertex %g %g %g\n", x1+sr*cp1*ct1,
                       y1+sr*cp1*st1, sr*sp1);
                printf("\tvertex %g %g %g\n", x1+sr*cp0*ct1,
                       y1+sr*cp0*st1, sr*sp0);
                printf("}\n");
            }
        } /* end j loop around minor radius */
    } /* end if mode spheres */
  } /* end i loop around outside */
} /* end of main() */

usage(char *prog) {
    fprintf(stderr, "Usage:    %s major_radius minor_radius segs1
            segs2  mode\n", prog);
    fprintf(stderr, "    where segs1 is # of segments around major
            radius\n");
    fprintf(stderr, "    and segs2 is # of segments around minor
            radius.\n");
    fprintf(stderr, "    (of course segs2 is ignored when mode ==
            spheres\n");
    fprintf(stderr, "    mode can be spheres, patches or facets.\n");

    exit(1);
} /* end of usage() */
```

Listing 12-2.Torus.C

A Puzzling Object

The next example is a tile puzzle shown in Color Plate 33. The algorithm used to generate this object is simple. First, create a grid of points in the XY plane. Leave all the edge points of the grid lying in the plane, but they may be displaced along the edge to produce uneven edge spacing. Now displace all of the points inside of the grid, making sure that the displacements all lie within the same plane as the tile puzzle. This process is shown in Figure 12-2.

The tile puzzle is formed with spheres and cylinders. You use spheres around all the displaced grid points and connect the points using cylinders. Note the polygon on top of the spheres. The points of the polygon have the same x and y coordinates as the sphere center, but the z coordinates have been offset by the radius of the sphere to place the polygon on top of the sphere.

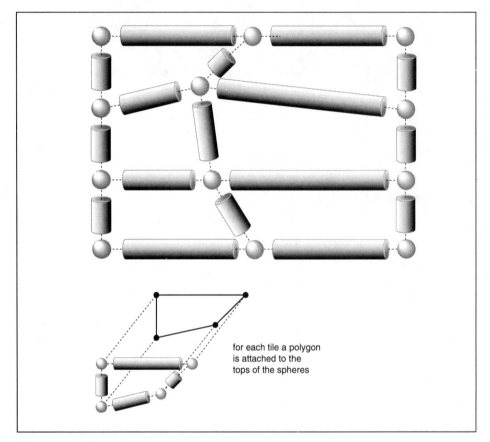

for each tile a polygon
is attached to the
tops of the spheres

Figure 12-2. Tile puzzle

As with the other examples, the TilePuzl.C program (Listing 12-3) generates
an object file called Tiles.BO when the DOS pipe function is used as follows:

```
Tilepuzl > Tiles.BO
```

```
/*
```

```
                    Tile Puzzle Generator
          TilePuzl.C = generates rounded-edged tiles
   Copyright 1988,1992 Christopher D. Watkins and Stephen B. Coy
                    ALL RIGHTS RESERVED
```

```
*/
```

```
#include <stdio.h>
#include <stdlib.h>
#include <math.h>

#define RADIUS (0.1)
#define EDGE   (10)
#define TWEEK  (0.3)

double  grid[EDGE][EDGE][2];

main()
{
    int i, j, k;
    double rnd();

    /* init grid */
    for(i=0; i<EDGE; i++) {
        for(j=0; j<EDGE; j++) {
            grid[i][j][0] = i;
            grid[i][j][1] = j;
        }
    }

    /* tweak inner grid points if needed */
    if(TWEEK > 0.0) {
        for(i=1; i<EDGE-1; i++) {
            for(j=1; j<EDGE-1; j++) {
                if(rand() & 0x0100)
                    grid[i][j][0] += rnd()*TWEEK;
                else
                    grid[i][j][0] -= rnd()*TWEEK;
                if(rand() & 0x0400)
                    grid[i][j][1] += rnd()*TWEEK;
                else
                    grid[i][j][1] -= rnd()*TWEEK;
            }
        }
    }

    /* output tiles */
    for(i=0; i<EDGE-1; i++) {
        for(j=0; j<EDGE-1; j++) {
            /* top surface */
            printf("polygon { points 4\n"); printf("\tvertex %.3f %.3f %.3f\n",
                    grid[i][j][0]+RADIUS, grid[i][j][1]+RADIUS, RADIUS);
            printf("\tvertex %.3f %.3f %.3f\n", grid[i][j+1][0]+RADIUS,
                    grid[i][j+1][1]-RADIUS, RADIUS);
            printf("\tvertex %.3f %.3f %.3f\n", grid[i+1][j+1][0]-
```

```
                    RADIUS, grid[i+1][j+1][1]-RADIUS, RADIUS);
           printf("\tvertex %.3f %.3f %.3f\n", grid[i+1][j][0]-
                    RADIUS, grid[i+1][j][1]+RADIUS, RADIUS);
           printf("}\n");
           /* spheres */
           printf("sphere { center %.3f %.3f 0 radius %.3f }\n",
                    grid[i][j][0]+RADIUS, grid[i][j][1]+RADIUS,
                    RADIUS);
           printf("sphere { center %.3f %.3f 0 radius %.3f }\n",
                    grid[i][j+1][0]+RADIUS, grid[i][j+1][1]-RADIUS,
                    RADIUS);
           printf("sphere { center %.3f %.3f 0 radius %.3f }\n",
                    grid[i+1][j+1][0]-RADIUS, grid[i+1][j+1][1]-RADIUS,
                    RADIUS);
           printf("sphere { center %.3f %.3f 0 radius %.3f }\n",
                    grid[i+1][j][0]-RADIUS, grid[i+1][j][1]+RADIUS,
                    RADIUS );
           /* cylinders */
           printf("cone { apex %.3f %.3f 0 base %.3f %.3f 0 radius
                    %.3f }\n", grid[i][j][0]+RADIUS,
                    grid[i][j][1]+RADIUS, grid[i+1][j][0]-RADIUS,
                    grid[i+1][j][1]+RADIUS, RADIUS);
           printf("cone { apex %.3f %.3f 0 base %.3f %.3f 0 radius
                    %.3f }\n", grid[i][j][0]+RADIUS,
                    grid[i][j][1]+RADIU S, grid[i][j+1][0]+RADIUS,
                    grid[i][j+1][1]-RADIUS, RADIUS);
           printf("cone { apex %.3f %.3f 0 base %.3f %.3f 0 radius
                    %.3f }\n", grid[i+1][j+1][0]-RADIUS,
                    grid[i+1][j+1][ 1]-RADIUS, grid[i+1][j][0]-RADIUS,
                    grid[i+1][j][1]+RADIUS, RADIUS);
           printf("cone { apex %.3f %.3f 0 base %.3f %.3f 0 radius
                    %.3f }\n", grid[i+1][j+1][0]-RADIUS,
                    grid[i+1][j+1][ 1]-RADIUS, grid[i][j+1][0]+RADIUS,
                    grid[i][j+1][1]-RADIUS, RADIUS);
      }
  }

}      /* end of main() */

double rnd()
{
return (double)rand()/RAND_MAX;
}
```

Listing 12-3. TilePuzl.C

Light and Flaky Spheres

Color Plate 34 contains an example of the Sphereflake, as named by Eric Haines. You generate the Sphereflake by recursively budding spheres from the sides of larger spheres. This is similar to the Trees.C program in that new spheres are generated as siblings of parent spheres. The recursion proceeds until the maximum recursion level is reached, the same as for the trees. A few levels of recursion can yield a quite complex object.

Listing 12-4 shows the SphrFlak.C program. SphrFlak.C creates the file SphFlk3.BO when the DOS pipe is used as follows:

```
Sphrflak > SphFlk3.BO.
```

This Object is used in the scene Basin1.BO.

```
/*

    ┌─────────────────────────────────────────────────────────────────┐
    │                          Sphere Flake                             │
    │       SphrFlak.C = generates a sphereflake from spheres           │
    │   Copyright 1988,1992 Christopher D. Watkins and Stephen B. Coy   │
    │                       ALL RIGHTS RESERVED                         │
    └─────────────────────────────────────────────────────────────────┘

    flake - Create a sphereflake-like object.  Inspired by
            Eric Haines' work.

    Note: This is kind of sloppy since it generates spheres which are
          internal to other spheres. Don't worry about it too much though.
          Also be aware that the number of spheres this
          generates goes up pretty fast as you increase the
          recursion level.

          # spheres = sum of i=0,level-1 of 12**i

          level   # spheres
          1           1      12**0
          2          13      12**0 + 12**1
          3         157      12**0 + 12**1 + 12**2
          4        1885      12**0 + 12**1 + 12**2 + 12**3
          5       22621      12**0 + 12**1 + 12**2 + 12**3 + 12**4
*/

#include <stdio.h> #include <stdlib.h> #include <math.h>
```

```
#define MAX      (3)
#define RADIUS (1.0)
#define RADIUS_SCALE    (3.0)

main(int ac, char **av)
{
    int      max_level = MAX;

    if(ac == 2) {
        max_level = atoi(av[1]);
    }

    flake(RADIUS, max_level);
}   /* end of main() */

flake(double radius, int level)
{
    double new_radius;
    int i;

    new_radius = radius / RADIUS_SCALE;

    /* output current sphere */
    printf("sphere { center 0 0 0 radius %g }\n", radius);

    if(level <= 1) {
        return;
    }

    —level;

    /* output 12 sub-spheres */

    /* do 6 around equator first */
    for(i=0; i<6; i++) {
        printf("transform { translate 0 %g 0 rotate 0 0 %d }\n",
                radius+new_radius, i*60);
        flake(new_radius, level);
        printf("transform_pop\n");
    }

    /* now top 3 */
    for(i=0; i<3; i++) {
        printf("transform { translate 0 %g 0 rotate 54.7356 0 %d }\n",
                radius+new_radius, 30 + i*120);
        flake(new_radius, level);
        printf("transform_pop\n");
    }
```

```
    /* now bottom 3 */
    for(i=0; i<3; i++) {
        printf("transform { translate 0 %g 0 rotate -54.7356 0 %d }\n",
                radius+new_radius, 90 + i*120);
        flake(new_radius, level);
        printf("transform_pop\n");
    }

}       /* end of flake */
```

Listing 12-4. SphrFlak.C

A Very Absorbent Sponge

Color Plate 35 shows another fractal (recursive) object, a Menger Sponge. This is an object that appears in Mandelbrot's book, *The Fractal Geometry of Nature*. The sponge is constructed out of many spheres. (You must be careful with this one or you will get a truly ludicrous number of spheres.) In the sponge, the spheres are the same size (small) with their positions computed by recursive subdivision of some base shape (such as a cube or tetrahedron). This database takes a while to ray trace, but the effect is interesting. The program Sponge.C generates the output file Sponge.BO when using the DOS pipe

```
    Sponge > Sponge.BO
```

You can see your creation by rendering the scene Sponge.B.

```
/*

    ┌─────────────────────────────────────────────────────────┐
    │                                                           │
    │                     Menger Sponge                         │
    │         Sponge.C = recursive Menger Sponge generator      │
    │   Copyright 1988,1992 Christopher D. Watkins and Stephen B. Coy │
    │                  ALL RIGHTS RESERVED                      │
    │                                                           │
    └─────────────────────────────────────────────────────────┘

*/

#include <stdio.h>
#include <stdlib.h>

#define MAX_LEVEL       (3)

int     max_level = MAX_LEVEL;
```

```
main(int ac, char **av)
{
    int     foo(double, double, double, double, int);

    if(ac == 2)
        max_level = atoi(av[1]);

    foo(0.0, 0.0, 0.0, 1.0, 0);
}

foo(x, y, z, rad, level)
    double x, y, z, rad;
    int level;
{
    double offset;
    int i, j, k;

    /* spit out current level */
    printf("sphere { center %.4f %.4f %.4f radius %.4f }\n", x, y, z,
        rad);

    level++;
    if(level > max_level)
        return;

    offset = rad * 2.0;
    rad /= 3.0;
    for(i=-1; i<2; i++) {
        for(j=-1; j<2; j++) {
            for(k=-1; k<2; k++) {
                if(i || j || k) {
                    foo(x+i*offset, y+j*offset, z+k*offset, rad, level);
                }
            }
        }
    }
}
```

Listing 12-5. Sponge.C

A Hex on You

The Hexer.C program places spheres onto a planar surface in a hexagonal pattern, creating a solid floor of spheres. The Hexer.C program appears in Listing 12-6, with the resulting object shown on the cover of this book. Hexer.C creates the object file Hex.BO when using the DOS pipe:

```
Hexer>Hexgrid2.BO
```

The scene file HEX2.B is used to see the Hexgrid2.BO object.

```c
/*

    ┌─────────────────────────────────────────────────────────────┐
    │                        Hex Generator                          │
    │  Hexer.C = generates a surface of hexagonal patterns of spheres│
    │  Copyright 1988,1992 Christopher D. Watkins and Stephen B. Coy │
    │                     ALL RIGHTS RESERVED                        │
    └─────────────────────────────────────────────────────────────┘

*/

#include <stdio.h>
#include <stdlib.h>
#include <math.h>

#define NUM_EDGE          (16)

main()
{
    int               i, j;
    double            sqrt3, x, y;

    sqrt3 = sqrt(3.0);

    for(i=0; i<NUM_EDGE; i++) {
        y = sqrt3 * i;
        for(j=0; j<NUM_EDGE+NUM_EDGE-i-1; j++) {
            x = j*2 - (NUM_EDGE-1)*2 + i;
            printf("surf { diff %.3f %.3f %.3f shine 1000 1 1 1 }\n",
            (double)rand()/RAND_MAX, (double)rand()/RAND_MAX,
            (double)rand()/RAND_MAX);
            printf("sphere { center %.4f %.4f 0 radius 1 }\n", x, y); if(i
            != 0) {
                printf("surf { diff %.3f %.3f %.3f shine 1000 1 1 1 }\n",
                (double)rand()/RAND_MAX, (double)rand()/RA ND_MAX, (dou-
                ble)rand()/RAND_MAX);
                printf("sphere { center %.4f %.4f 0 radius 1 }\n", x, -y);
            }
        }
        x -= 1.0;
    }
}
```

Listing 12-6. Hexer.C

Even More Complicated Databases

So far, discussions have centered on objects that are basically defined by recursive procedures. None of these techniques is quite suitable for generating an image of something more complex, like terrain with random hills, lakes, and forests. Chapter 13 discusses how to use a z-buffered technique to create reasonable terrain models. Chapter 14 introduces Ed, the database generator. Ed enables you not only to create a scene, but also to interactively edit the scene, change object position, orientation, and scale.

CHAPTER 13

Z-Buffer Data

Chapter 12 introduced procedural object database generation. This chapter examines another type of procedural object database, referred to as *z-buffer** databases. In a z-buffer database, you use a rectangular array to store the z-coordinates of a surface. The array represents regularly spaced sample points in x and y. This is essentially the same as an image, except instead of storing a color value, you store a z-coordinate at each point in the image.

Figure 13-1 shows a simple grid of nine points, three sample points in the x-axis, three in the y-axis. Notice that the center point of the grid is offset slightly in the positive z direction. You can use this grid to model a surface by creating triangles between all the adjacent grid points. Note that you cannot use polygons because you generally cannot guarantee that any four adjacent points lie in a plane.

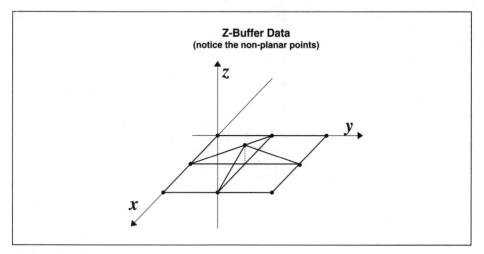

Figure 13-1. Simple grid

*We use the term *z-buffer* loosely. The term usually refers to the rendering algorithm. Perhaps the term *heightfield* would be more appropriate

The programs presented in this chapter all generate an appropriate rectangular array of data and then break the array into appropriate triangular patches that can be written into a .BO file for Bob. The z-buffer representation of a surface is a means of digitizing an arbitrary surface. For complex surfaces such as terrain, this is the only reasonable means of representing the surface. In addition to generating the triangular patches from this data, you must also estimate the surface normals at the triangle corners. You accomplish this by using a surface gradient.

Wire-Frame Contour of z-Buffer Data

The first program enables you to view z-buffer data as a collection of triangles. Figure 13-2 shows such a wire-frame image of the data from Figure 13-1. The term "wire-frame" refers to the fact that you simply draw the edges of the triangles, rather than fill them in as Bob does. This provides a much faster means of previewing the data before rendering it.

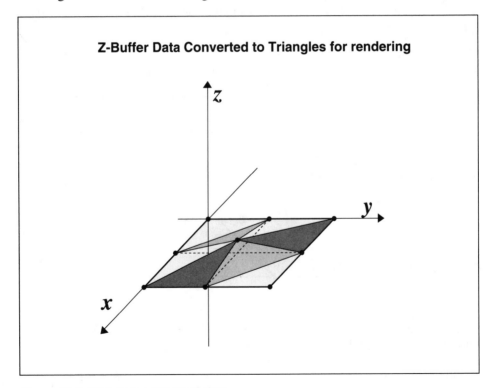

Figure 13-2. Wire-frame image of data

The data is converted into the triangular patches that Bob renders. The triangularization of the z-buffer data takes a group of four points and connects the edges and one set of opposite corners.

Ray Tracing z-Buffer Databases

As an additional aid to z-buffer object generation, you also have the BkZbuf.C module shown in Listing 13-2. This module does the actual conversion of the z-buffer data into sets of triangular patches. The BkZbuf.C module performs one basic function: to generate the triangular patch coordinates for Smooth.EXE to compute the approximate surface normal at each patch vertex. The first function is easy. The program simply scans through the array, two adjacent rows at a time. Each set of four points is broken into two triangular patches. The slightly more difficult problem is estimating the surface normal.

```
/*
```

```
            BkZBuf.H = z-Buffer module header
   Copyright 1988,1992 Christopher D. Watkins and Stephen B. Coy
                  ALL RIGHTS RESERVED
```

```
*/

#define MaxRes 160

extern int Height[MaxRes+1][MaxRes+1];
extern int Scaling;
extern int MaxHeight;
extern int Res;

extern void HeightBufferScalingFactor();

extern FILE *TextDiskFile; extern Name ObjectFile;

extern void ClearHeightBuffer();

extern void SaveHeightBuffer(Name FileName);
```

```
extern void GetObjectFile();

extern void GetObjectColor(int C);

extern int Write_RAW_Data;
```

Listing 13-1. BkZbuf.H

```
/*
```

```
                        BkZBuf.C = z-Buffer module
        Copyright 1988,1992 Christopher D. Watkins and Stephen B. Coy
                        ALL RIGHTS RESERVED
```

```
*/
```

```
#include "stdlib.h"
#include "stdio.h"
#include "dos.h"
#include "conio.h"
#include "ctype.h"
#include "math.h"
#include "malloc.h"
#include "string.h"

#include "BkDefs.H"
#include "BkMath.H"
#include "BkGraph.H"
#include "BkZBuf.H"
```

```
/*
```

```
                    Declare Constants and Variables
```

```
HeightBufferScalingFactor - scales height for integer manipulation
*/
```

```
int Height[MaxRes+1][MaxRes+1];
int Scaling;
int MaxHeight;
int Res;
```

```
void HeightBufferScalingFactor()
{
Scaling=32767/MaxHeight;
}

/*
```

```
┌─────────────────────────────────────────────────────────┐
│  ┌───────────────────────────────────────────────────┐  │
│  │         Clear, Load, and Save Height Buffer Data    │  │
│  └───────────────────────────────────────────────────┘  │
└─────────────────────────────────────────────────────────┘
```

```
    ClearHeightBuffer - clears all heights to zero
    SaveHeightBuffer  - saves height buffer
    LoadHeightBuffer  - loads height buffer
    GetObjectFile     - get filename
    GetObjectColor    - text representation of color
*/

FILE *TextDiskFile;
Name ObjectFile;

void ClearHeightBuffer()
{
   int i, j;

   for(i=0; i<=MaxRes; i++)
   {
      for(j=0; j<=MaxRes; j++)
       Height[i][j]=0;
   }
}

void SaveHeightBuffer(Name FileName)
{
   int i, j;

   if (Write_RAW_Data == 1)
     strcat(FileName, ".RAW");
   else
     strcat(FileName, ".BO");
   TextDiskFile=fopen(FileName, "w+b");
   if(ferror(TextDiskFile))
   {
```

```
            Exit_Graphics();
            printf("Can't open file!\n");
            getch();
            exit(1);
        }
    for(i=0; i<Res; i++)
    {
        for(j=0; j<Res; j++)
        {
            if (Write_RAW_Data == 1)
            {
                fprintf(TextDiskFile,  "%5.3f  %5.3f  %5.3f\n\r", (float)i,
                                        (float)j, (float)Height[i][j] /
                                        (float)Scaling);
                fprintf(TextDiskFile,  "%5.3f  %5.3f  %5.3f\n\r", (float)i+1,
                                        (float)j, (float)Height[i+1][j] /
                                        (float)Scaling);
                fprintf(TextDiskFile,  "%5.3f  %5.3f  %5.3f\n\r", (float)i,
                                        (float)j+1, (float)Height[i][j+1] /
                                        (float)Scaling);
                fprintf(TextDiskFile,  "%5.3f  %5.3f  %5.3f\n\r", (float)i+1,
                                        (float)j, (float)Height[i+1][j] /
                                        (float)Scaling);
                fprintf(TextDiskFile,  "%5.3f  %5.3f  %5.3f\n\r", (float)i+1,
                                        (float)j+1, (float)Height[i+1][j+1] /
                                        (float)Scaling);
                fprintf(TextDiskFile,  "%5.3f  %5.3f  %5.3f\n\r", (float)i,
                                        (float)j+1, (float)Height[i][j+1] /
                                        (float)Scaling);
            }
            else
            {
                fprintf(TextDiskFile, "polygon {\npoints 3\n\r\t vertex %5.3f
                                        %5.3f %5.3f\n\r", (float)i, (float)j,
                                        (float)Height[i][j] / (f loat)Scaling);
                fprintf(TextDiskFile, " \t vertex %5.3f %5.3f %5.3f\n\r",
                                        (float)i+1, (float)j,
                                        (float)Height[i+1][j] / (float)Scaling);
                fprintf(TextDiskFile, "\t vertex %5.3f %5.3f %5.3f\n\r}\n\r",
                                        (float)i, (float)j+1,
                                        (float)Height[i][j+1] / (float)Scaling);
                fprintf(TextDiskFile, "polygon {\npoints 3\n\r\t vertex %5.3f
                                        %5.3f %5.3f\n\r", (float)i+1, (float)j,
                                        (float)Height[i+1][j] / (float)Scaling);
                fprintf(TextDiskFile, " \t vertex %5.3f %5.3f %5.3f\n\r",
                                        (float)i+1, (float)j+1,
                                        (float)Height[i+1][j+1] / (float)Scaling);
```

```
                fprintf(TextDiskFile, "\t vertex %5.3f %5.3f %5.3f\n\r}\n\r",
                                      (float)i, (float)j+1,
                                      (float)Height[i][j+1] / (float)Scaling);


            }
        }
    }
    fclose(TextDiskFile);
}

void GetObjectFile()
{
    int i;
    Byte x, y;

    printf("\nEnter File Name -> ");
    x=wherex();
    y=wherey();
    gets(ObjectFile);
    if(!(strcmp(ObjectFile, "")))
    {
        strcpy(ObjectFile, "MOUNTAIN");
        gotoxy(x, y);
        puts(ObjectFile);
    }
    puts("");
    for(i=0; i<strlen(ObjectFile); i++)
     ObjectFile[i]=toupper(ObjectFile[i]);
}

void GetObjectColor(int C)
{
    switch(C)
    {
        case 0 : puts("Black"); break;
        case 1 : puts("Blue"); break;
        case 2 : puts("Green"); break;
        case 3 : puts("Cyan"); break;
        case 4 : puts("Red"); break;
        case 5 : puts("Magenta"); break;
        case 6 : puts("Brown/Yellow"); break;
        case 7 : puts("Grey"); break;
    }
}
```

Listing 13-2. BkZbuf.C

Referring back to Figure 13-1, you can estimate the surface normal at a given point by looking at the height variations of the surrounding eight points. The basic idea is to perform a least-squares fit of a plane (the plane that comes closest to all nine points). The surface normal for this plane is your estimated surface normal at this point of the surface. The estimated surface normal is

```
Xnorm = ((Z11 - Z31) + (Z12 - Z32) + (Z13 - Z33) ) / 3.0
Ynorm = ((Z11 - Z13) + (Z21 - Z23) + (Z31 - Z33) ) / 3.0
Znorm = Cell_Size
```

where Zij refers to the Z value at location (i,j) in the array relative to the current point, Z11 is the upper-left corner, and Z33 is the lower-right corner element. The Cell_Size is the spacing between adjacent cells in the units of Z. If your terrain model had height specified in feet, Cell_Size would represent how far apart in feet the adjacent points in the grid were. The vector must be normalized to produce a unit-length surface normal. Note that the actual surface normal calculation will occur in a post-processing, using the Smooth.EXE program described later.

Programs to Generate z-Buffer Databases

The simplest type of z-buffer database is when the z-values are the result of some two-dimensional mathematical function. The z values are computed by evaluating the function at each of the sample points. The PlotEqn.C program shown in Listing 13-3 generates just such a z-buffer database.

```
/*
```

```
                          Equation Plotter
                 PlotEqn.C = plots equations surprise
       Copyright 1988,1992 Christopher D. Watkins and Stephen B. Coy
           Requires : BkDefs.H, BkGlobs.H, BkMath.H, BkMath.C,
                           BkGraph.H, BkGraph.C
                          ALL RIGHTS RESERVED
```

```
*/
```

```
#include "stdio.h"
#include "stdlib.h"
#include "dos.h"
#include "conio.h"
```

```
#include "math.h"
#include "string.h"

#include "BkDefs.H"
#include "BkGlobs.H"

#include "BkMath.H"
#include "BkGraph.H"
#include "BkZBuf.H"


/*
```

```
┌─────────────────────────────────────────────────────────────┐
│  ┌──────────────────────────────────────────────────────┐   │
│  │                    Equations                          │   │
│  └──────────────────────────────────────────────────────┘   │
└─────────────────────────────────────────────────────────────┘
```

```
*/


#define Span 5

char ObjF[]="PLOTEQN1";

float zf(float x, float y)
{
  float c;

  c=SqrFP(x)+SqrFP(y);
  return(75.0/(c+1.0));
}


/*
#define Span 5

char ObjF[]="PLOTEQN2";

float zf(float x, float y)
{
  return(6.0*(cos(x*y)+1.0));
}
*/
```

```
/*
#define Span 5

char ObjF[]="PLOTEQN3";

float zf(float x, float y)
{
  float c;

  c=SqrFP(x)+SqrFP(y);
  return(20.0*(sin(sqrt(c))+1.0));
}
*/

/*
#define Span 2.75

char ObjF[]="PLOTEQN4";

float zf(float x, float y)
{
  float c;

  c=SqrFP(x)+SqrFP(y);
  return(10.0*(1.0+sqrt(c)+sin(SqrFP(c)*0.1)+sin(x*y)));
}
*/

/**********************************************************************/

void CreateEquationPlotHeightBuffer(float Xlft, float Xrgt,
                                    float Ybot, float Ytop)
{
  int ix, iy, iz;
  float x, y;
  float dx, dy;

  MaxHeight=MaxRes*100;
  HeightBufferScalingFactor();
  dx=(Xrgt-Xlft)/(Res-1);
  dy=(Ytop-Ybot)/(Res-1);
  for(ix=0; ix<Res; ix++)
  {
    x=Xlft+ix*dx;
    for(iy=0; iy<Res; iy++)
```

```
    {
      y=Ybot+iy*dy;
      iz=Round(zf(x, y));
      if(iz<0)
      {
        Exit_Graphics();
        printf("Adjust the equation : z value less than zero\n");
        delay(2000);
        exit(1);
      }
      Height[ix][iy]=iz;
      Cartesian_Plot_3D(ix-Res/2, iy-Res/2, iz, (iz*MaxCol)%255);
    }
  }
}


/*
┌────────────────────────────────────────────────────────────┐
│                                                              │
│                        Main Program                          │
│                                                              │
└────────────────────────────────────────────────────────────┘

*/

void main()
{
  clrscr();
  printf("Creating Equation Plot Height Buffer\n\n");
  ClearHeightBuffer();
  Res=50;
  Write_RAW_Data = 1;
  Init_Perspective(false, 0, 0, 500, 500);
  Init_Plotting(240, 18);
  Init_Graphics(0);
  CreatEquationPlotHeightBuffer(-Span, Span, -Span, Span);
  strcpy(ObjectFile, ObjF);
  SaveHeightBuffer(ObjectFile);
  Exit_Graphics();
}
```

Listing 13-3. The PlotEqn.C program

The beginning of the program contains a list of values for the parameter *ObjF*, (the name of the object file), for the parameters *Span*, *Contour*, and *Offset* for the four different equations (depending on appropriate editing of this source file). In addition, the function *zf* (which determines the value of z as a function of x and y for the particular case) is listed for each. For each run of the program, all these sets of values except one are commented out.

The program begins by setting up the Height buffer and 3-D environment to watch your object being constructed. Then *CreateEquationPlotHeightBuffer* is called, passing to it the parameters for the left and right x boundaries (which are set to *–Span* and *Span*), the bottom and top y boundaries (which are set to *–Span* and *Span*), the number of facets in the horizontal direction (which is set to *Contour*), and the number of facets in the vertical direction (which is set to *Contour*).

The limits *Xlft*, *Ytop*, *Xrgt*, and *Ybot* (which were passed to this function as *Span* and *Contour*) are then used to compute *dx* and *dy* stepping factors.

Then the *CreateEquationPlotHeightBuffer* function begins its looping by setting X to a function of *ix* and Y to a function of *iy*. It then continues with a pair of nested "for" loops that are iterated until every value of X and Y is treated, thus covering all facets of the displayed object. At each iteration, for each of the four vertices of the facet, the value of z is computed and then stored in the Height buffer.

This program generates an output object file called PlotEqn1.RAW to PlotEqn4.RAW, depending on which one you computed. You can display this file by rendering the appropriate PlotEqn1.B to PlotEqn4.B file. Color Plate 36 shows a sample result.

You can extend this concept to use more complex functions. The Ocean.C program shown in Listing 13-4 generates waves by summing together multiple sinusoids with different amplitudes, phases, and frequencies. As with PlotEqn.C, you can change the types of waves, number of terms, and so forth by editing the source file and recompiling. This is similar to the wave texture discussed in Chapter 9. The Ocean.C program creates the output file Ocean.BO. Color Plate 37 shows an example of the result.

```
/*
```

```
                    Ocean from Summed Sinusoids
      Ocean.C = generates an ocean (pretty powerful software - Eh?)
      Copyright 1988,1992 Christopher D. Watkins and Stephen B. Coy
           Requires : BkDefs.H, BkGlobs.H, BkMath.H, BkMath.C,
                           BkGraph.H, BkGraph.C
                         ALL RIGHTS RESERVED
```

```
*/
```

```c
#include "stdio.h"
#include "stdlib.h"
#include "dos.h"
#include "conio.h"
#include "math.h"
#include "string.h"

#include "BkDefs.H"
#include "BkGlobs.H"

#include "BkMath.H"
#include "BkGraph.H"
#include "BkZBuf.H"
```

```
/*
```

```
                              the Ocean
```

```
*/
```

```c
#define Span 5

char ObjF[]="OCEAN";

float zf(float x, float y)
{
  float f1, f2, f3, f4;
  float Ampl, Dampen, Dampen2;
  float OceanWavePhase = 20.0;
  float OceanWaveAmpl = 10.0;
```

```
        /* sum four sinusoids for ocean height value at a given point */

            f1=sin(Radians(21.50*x+60.70*y+OceanWavePhase));
            f2=sin(Radians(11.25*x+11.50*y+OceanWavePhase));
            f3=sin(Radians(42.50*x+20.80*y+OceanWavePhase));
            f4=sin(Radians(10.75*x+42.00*y+OceanWavePhase));

            Ampl=OceanWaveAmpl*(f1+f2+f3+f4)*0.25 + 10.0;

            return(Ampl);
}


/* ******************************************************************/

void CreatOceanHeightBuffer(float Xlft, float Xrgt,
                            float Ybot, float Ytop)
{
  int ix, iy, iz;
  float x, y;
  float dx, dy;

  MaxHeight=MaxRes*200;
  HeightBufferScalingFactor();
  dx=(Xrgt-Xlft)/Res;
  dy=(Ytop-Ybot)/Res;
  for(ix=0; ix<=Res; ix++)
  {
    x=Xlft+ix*dx;
    for(iy=0; iy<=Res; iy++)
    {
      y=Ybot+iy*dy;
      iz=Round(zf(x, y));
      if(iz<0)
      {
        Exit_Graphics();
        printf("Adjust the equation : z value less than zero\n");
        delay(2000);
        exit(1);
      }
      Height[ix][iy]=iz;
      Cartesian_Plot_3D(ix-Res/2, iy-Res/2, iz, (iz*MaxCol)%255);
    }
  }
}
```

```
/*

┌─────────────────────────────────────────────────────────────┐
│ ┌─────────────────────────────────────────────────────────┐ │
│ │                     Main Program                        │ │
│ └─────────────────────────────────────────────────────────┘ │
└─────────────────────────────────────────────────────────────┘

*/

void main()
{
clrscr();
  printf("Creating Ocean Height Buffer\n\n");
  ClearHeightBuffer();
  Res=60;
  Write_RAW_Data = 1;
  Init_Perspective(false, 0, 0, 500, 500);
  Init_Plotting(240, 45);
  Init_Graphics(0);
  CreatOceanHeightBuffer(-Span, Span, -Span, Span);
  strcpy(ObjectFile, ObjF);
  SaveHeightBuffer(ObjectFile);
  Exit_Graphics();
}
```

Listing 13-4. Ocean.C

Fractal Programs to Generate z-Buffer Databases

Consider a z-buffer based on the Mandelbrot set. The Mandelbrot set is defined by iterating the following equation:

$$z_n = z_{n-1}^2 + c \qquad \text{(Equation 13-1)}$$

For each point in the grid, assign the complex variable c using the x coordinate for the real part, and the y coordinate for the imaginary part of the complex number. The function is then iterated until the magnitude of z exceeds a specified maximum value or until you have performed a maximum number of iterations. Then you take the logarithm of the magnitude to get the final height value. The logarithm helps make a relatively smooth data set. The CPM-MSET.C program shown in List-

ing 13-5 generates the objects CPMMSET1.RAW and CPMMSET2.RAW. Color
Plate 38 shows the result.

```
/*
```

```
                    3-D Mandelbrot Set Generator
        CPM-MSET.C = generates Mandelbrot Set Terrain by the
                      Continuous Potential method
       Copyright 1988,1992 Christopher D. Watkins and Stephen B. Coy
           Requires : BkDefs.H, BkGlobs.H, BkMath.H, BkMath.C,
                         BkGraph.H, BkGraph.C
                         ALL RIGHTS RESERVED
```

```
*/
```

```
#include "stdio.h"
#include "stdlib.h"
#include "dos.h"
#include "conio.h"
#include "math.h"
#include "string.h"

#include "BkDefs.H"
#include "BkGlobs.H"

#include "BkMath.H"
#include "BkGraph.H"
#include "BkZBuf.H"

/*
    125 iterations maximum
*/

#define XMin    -2.50
#define XMax     1.35
#define YMin    -1.80
#define YMax     1.80
#define Iter 32 #define Scal 32767

char ObjF[]="CPMMSET1";
```

```
/*
#define XMin    -0.19
#define XMax    -0.13
#define YMin     1.01
#define YMax     1.06
#define Iter     125
#define Scal     3276700

char ObjF[]="CPMMSET2";
*/

float MSetPot(float cx, float cy, int MaxIter, int *Iters)
{
  float x, y;
  float x2, y2;
  float temp;

  x=cx;
  x2=SqrFP(x);
  y=cy;
  y2=SqrFP(y);
  *Iters=0;
  while((*Iters<MaxIter) && (x2+y2<20000.0))
  {
    temp=cx+x2-y2;
    y=cy+2*x*y; y2=SqrFP(y);
    x=temp;
    x2=SqrFP(x);
    ++*Iters;
  }
  if(*Iters<MaxIter)
    return(0.5*log10(x2+y2)/pow(2, *Iters));
  else
    return(0.0);
}

void MSetCPM(int nx, int ny, int MaxIter, float Xmin, float Xmax,
             float Ymin, float Ymax)
{
  int ix, iy;
  int Iters;
  float cx, cy;
  float dx, dy;
```

```
    dx=(Xmax-Xmin)/nx;
    dy=(Ymax-Ymin)/ny;
    for(iy=0; iy<=ny; iy++)
    {
      cy=Ymin+iy*dy;
      for(ix=0; ix<=nx; ix++)
      {
        cx=Xmin+ix*dx;
        Height[ix][iy]=Round(MSetPot(cx, cy, MaxIter, &Iters)*Scal);
        Put_Pixel(ix, iy, (Iters/7), (Iters%35));
      }
    }
}

void InverseHeightBuffer()
{
  int i, j;
  int Max;

  Max=0;
  for(i=0; i<=MaxRes; i++)
  {
    for(j=0; j<=MaxRes; j++)
    {
      if(Height[i][j]>Max)
        Max=Height[i][j];
    }
  }
  for(i=0; i<=MaxRes; i++)
  {
    for(j=0; j<=MaxRes; j++)
    {
      Height[i][j]=Max-Height[i][j];
    }
  }
}

/*
```

```
┌─────────────────────────────────────────────────────────────┐
│                                                               │
│                        Main Program                          │
│                                                               │
└─────────────────────────────────────────────────────────────┘
```

```
*/

void main()
{
```

```
clrscr();
Res=60;
MaxHeight=35;
HeightBufferScalingFactor();
Write_RAW_Data = 1;
Init_Graphics(0);
ClearHeightBuffer();
MSetCPM(Res, Res, Iter, XMin, XMax, YMin, YMax);
InverseHeightBuffer();
strcpy(ObjectFile, ObjF);
SaveHeightBuffer(ObjectFile);
Exit_Graphics();
}
```

Listing 13-5. The CPM-MSET.C program

Three-Dimensional Mandelbrot Sets

The CPM-MSET.C program shown in Listing 13-5 creates the database for a three-dimensional Mandelbrot set. The program begins with two sets of constants, for creating two different Mandelbrot set databases. One is commented out. If you want to run this one, remove the comment indicators (/* and */) from around the second set of constants and put them around the first set of constants instead.

The main program clears the screen, sets up some initial parameters, and then calls *InitGraphics* to enter the graphics mode. The program then calls *ClearHeightBuffer* to zero out the height array. Next, the program enters two nested "for" loops to iterate for every point on the two-dimensional display. For each iteration of the inner loop, a "while" loop is run which iterates for the Mandelbrot equation as many times as specified by *Iter*, or until the square of the *xy* vector becomes greater than 20,000.

Instead of directly plotting a color that is a function of the number of iterations, the program uses the exiting values of x^2 and y^2 to compute the value of *MSetPot*. In the same sense that the potential of an electric field is calculated, this value is the continuous potential of the point with respect to the set. It can also be scaled and used as a height for a three-dimensional display. The program computes this height for the appropriate member of the height array. For reference as to how the plot is proceeding, the program also plots a point to the screen in the appropriate color for a two-dimensional display.

The continuous potential method yields a potential that is smallest at the boundary of the Mandelbrot set, and that gets larger and larger as the distance of the point from the set boundary increases. This produces a three-dimensional display in which the set itself is down in a hole, with sides that slope sharply down to it.

The display is more interesting if the set is a plateau on top of a mountain, with the sides sloping upward. To achieve this effect, the program calls the *Inverse-HeightBuffer* function after the nested loops are complete. This function first determines the maximum height that is stored in the buffer, and then subtracts every member of the height array from it to create a new value for the member. As a result, the Mandelbrot set itself is at the maximum height and the points that previously were highest are now at zero.

The program then calls *SaveHeightBuffer*, which stores the height array in a database file. Color Plate 38 shows a scene generated with the Mandelbrot set program and the z-buffering technique.

Three-Dimensional Julia Sets

The CPM-JSET.C program shown in Listing 13-6 creates the database for a three-dimensional Julia set. The program begins with two sets of constants that you use to create two different Julia set databases. Again, one is commented out. If you want to run this one, remove the comment designators from around the second set of constants and put them around the first set of constants. The program is similar to that for the Mandelbrot set, except that the variables used in the iterated equation are different.

```
/*

    3-D Julia Set Generator
CPM-JSET.C = generates Julia Set Terrain by Continuous Potential
 Copyright 1988,1992 Christopher D. Watkins and Stephen B. Coy
        Requires : BkDefs.H, BkGlobs.H, BkMath.H,
             BkMath.C, BkGraph.H, BkGraph.C
              ALL RIGHTS RESERVED

*/

/*
```

The Continuous Potential Method for the Julia Set

```
    c  =  p   +   q  i        ACP = attractive cycle period

        p           q
       ___         ___
      0.31        0.04       -
     -0.11        0.6557     -   JSet  ACP=3  before decay into Cantor set
     -0.194       0.6557     -   after decay into Cantor set
     -0.12        0.74       -
      0.0         1.0        -   lightning dendrite
     -0.74543     0.11301    -   seahorse valley c-value
     -1.25        0.0        -   parabolic case  c>1.25 ACP=2, c<1.25

        ACP=4
     -0.481762   -0.531657   -
     -0.39054    -0.58679    -
     -0.15652    -1.03225    -   dendrite with beads (secondary MSet)
      0.11031    -0.67037    -   Fatou dust
      0.27334     0.00742    -   parabolic case  small c  ACP=20

      125 iterations maximum
*/

#include "stdio.h"
#include "stdlib.h"
#include "dos.h"
#include "conio.h"
#include "math.h"
#include "string.h"
#include "mem.h"

#include "BkDefs.H"
#include "BkGlobs.H"

#include "BkMath.H"
#include "BkGraph.H"
#include "BkZBuf.H"

#define cp      -0.12
#define cq       0.74
#define XMin    -1.4
#define XMax     1.4
#define YMin    -1.4
#define YMax     1.4
```

```
#define Iter      32
#define Scal      32767

char ObjF[]="CPMJSET1";

/*
#define cp        0.31
#define cq        0.04
#define XMin      -1.4
#define XMax      1.4
#define YMin      -1.4
#define YMax      1.4
#define Iter      32
#define Scal      32767

char ObjF[]="CPMJSET2";
*/

int Iters;

float JSetPot(float p, float q, float cx, float cy, int MaxIter)
{
  float x, y;
  float x2, y2;
  float temp;

  x=cx;
  x2=SqrFP(x);
  y=cy;
  y2=SqrFP(y);
  Iters=0;
  while((Iters<MaxIter) && (x2+y2<20000.0))
  {
    temp=p+x2-y2;
    y=q+2*x*y;
    y2=SqrFP(y);
    x=temp;
    x2=SqrFP(x);
    ++Iters;
  }
  if(Iters<MaxIter)
    return(0.5*log10(x2+y2)/pow(2, Iters));
  else
    return(0.0);
}

void JSetCPM(int nx, int ny, int MaxIter,
             float p, float q,
             float Xmin, float Xmax,
```

```
                float Ymin, float Ymax)
{
  int ix, iy;
  float cx, cy;
  float dx, dy;
  int z;

  dx=(Xmax-Xmin)/nx;
  dy=(Ymax-Ymin)/ny;
  for(ix=0; ix<=(nx/2); ix++)
  {
    cx=Xmin+ix*dx;
    for(iy=0; iy<=ny; iy++)
    {
      cy=Ymin+iy*dy;
      z=Round(JSetPot(p, q, cx, cy, MaxIter)*Scal);
      Height[ix][iy]=z;
      Height[Res-ix][Res-iy]=z;
      Put_Pixel(ix, 199-iy, Iters/7, Iters%35);
      Put_Pixel((Res-ix), 199-(Res-iy), Iters/7, Iters%35);
    }
  }
}

void InverseHeightBuffer()
{
  int i, j;
  int Max;

  Max=0;
  for(i=0; i<=MaxRes; i++)
  {
    for(j=0; j<=MaxRes; j++)
    {
      if(Height[i][j]>Max)
        Max=Height[i][j];
    }
  }
  for(i=0; i<=MaxRes; i++)
  {
    for(j=0; j<=MaxRes; j++)
    {
      Height[i][j]=Max-Height[i][j];
    }
  }
}
```

```
/*

    ┌────────────────────────────────────────────────────────┐
    │                                                          │
    │                      Main Program                        │
    │                                                          │
    └────────────────────────────────────────────────────────┘

*/

void main()
{
  clrscr();
  Res=60;
  MaxHeight=35;
  HeightBufferScalingFactor();
  Write_RAW_Data = 1;
  Init_Graphics(0);
  ClearHeightBuffer();
  JSetCPM(Res, Res, Iter, cp, cq, XMin, XMax, YMin, YMax);
  InverseHeightBuffer();
  strcpy(ObjectFile, ObjF);
  SaveHeightBuffer(ObjectFile);
  Exit_Graphics();
}
```

Listing 13-6. The CPM-JSET.C program

The main program clears the screen, sets up some initial parameters, and then calls *InitGraphics* to enter the graphics mode. The program then calls *ClearHeight-Buffer* to zero out the height array. Next, the program enters two nested "for" loops to iterate for every point on the two-dimensional display. For each iteration of the inner loop, a "while" loop is run which iterates for the Julia set equation as many times as specified by *Iter,* or until the square of the xy vector becomes greater than 20,000.

Instead of directly plotting a color that is a function of the number of iterations, the program uses the exiting values of x^2 and y^2 to compute the value of *MSetPot*. In the same sense that the potential of an electric field is calculated, this value is the continuous potential of the point with respect to the set. It can also be scaled and used as a height for a three-dimensional display. The program computes this height for the appropriate member of the height array. For reference as to how the plot is proceeding, it also plots a point to the screen in the appropriate color for a two-dimensional display .

374

The continuous potential method shown in Listing 13-6 yields a potential that is smallest at the boundary of the Julia set, and that gets larger and larger as the distance of the point from the set boundary increases. This produces a three-dimensional display in which the set itself is down in a hole, with sides that slope sharply down to it.

The display is more interesting if the set is a plateau on top of a mountain, with the sides sloping upward. To achieve this effect, the program calls the *Inverse-HeightBuffer* function after the nested loops are complete. This function is a duplicate of the same function described above for the Mandelbrot set. The program then calls *SaveHeightBuffer,* which stores the height array in a database file. Recall that for the Julia set, the value c is held constant and you generate different starting values of z using the x and y coordinates as above. This program generates the objects CPMJSET1.RAW and CPMJSET2.RAW.

If you have a four-dimensional object, you can make it three-dimensional by taking a slice out of it (holding one of the dimensions fixed, for instance).

Fractals Using Quaternions

A *quaternion* is similar to a three-dimensional vector, except that it has a strange characteristic: multiplication of quaternions does not follow the commutative law. For most types of numbers,

$$a \times b = b \times a \qquad \text{(Equation 13-2)}$$

In other words, the order in which the numbers are multiplied does not matter. You get the same result no matter which order is used. This is known as the commutative law. This law does not hold true for quaternions. In fact, if a and b are quaternions, then the following is true:

$$ab = -(ba) \qquad \text{(Equation 13-3)}$$

You define a quaternion as consisting of a scalar q_0, and a three-dimensional vector having components q_1, q_2, and q_3, directed along the mutually orthogonal axes identified by the unit vectors i, j, and k. These vectors follow the rules for vector cross products in a right-hand coordinate system.

$$
\begin{aligned}
ij &= k & ji &= -k \\
jk &= i & kj &= -i \\
ki &= j & ik &= -j
\end{aligned}
$$
(Equation 13-4)

and

$$ijk = i^2 = j^2 = k^2 = -1$$
(Equation 13-5)

You can write the quaternion as

$$Q = q_0 + iq_1 + jq_2 + kq_3$$
(Equation 13-6)

or alternatively as

$$Q = q_0 + \underline{q}$$
(Equation 13-7)

The underlining means that the variable is a three-dimensional vector, or in other words:

$$\underline{q} = iq_1 + jq_2 + kq_3$$
(Equation 13-8)

Quaternions have interesting uses in transforming three-dimensional systems (for example in transforming from the coordinate system of a space shuttle to Earth's coordinate system without encountering singularities [the dreaded divide-by-zero]). They also can be used in iterative equations to create strange four-dimensional fractals. Of course, you run into problems when you try to display a four-dimensional figure on a two-dimensional screen. Generally, you compute the data for a three-dimensional slice of the figure and then use the usual methods for projecting this onto the two-dimensional screen.

These quaternions are iterated with different constants. The *RevSolid* quaternion is a solid of revolution because the constant lies on the real axis. Examine Color Plate 39 for a rendering of a Solid of Revolution ($q = -1$). This was a rendering of RevSol2.B with object RevSol2.BO generated by Quater2.C and Smooth .EXE, described later. Figure 13-3 shows sampling occurring in three-dimensional space, moving from front to back (+z to -z) to see when the iteration does not escape, thus converging, saying that you have intersected the quaternion. (Note that q=r+xi+yj+zk with k=0.) Note that the Quater.C program computes from back to front and Quater2.C from front to back, revealing different approximations for the quaternion.

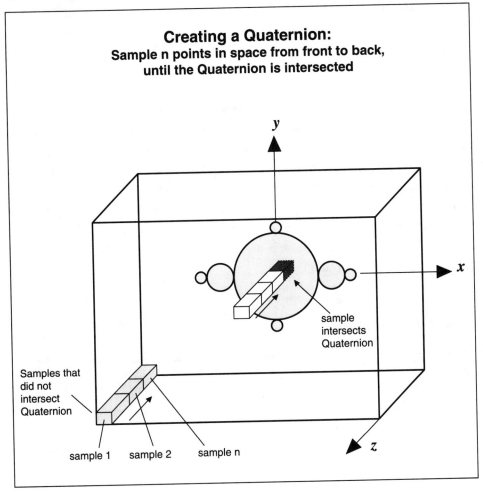

Figure 13-3. Sampling occurring in three-dimensional space

Quaternion Mathematics

Quaternion addition and subtraction can be done on a component-by-component basis just as vectors are added and subtracted. However, quaternion multiplication is somewhat more complicated. Suppose you have two quaternions, *P* and *Q*. The product is

$$
\begin{aligned}
PQ &= p_0q_0 + p_0q + q_0p + i^2p_1q_1 + j^2p_2q_2 + k^2p_3q_3 + \\
&\quad ip_1(jq_2 + kq_3) + jp_2(iq_1 + kq_3) + kp_3(iq_1 + jq_2) \\
&= p_0q_0 + p_0q + q_0p - (p \cdot q) + p \times q
\end{aligned}
$$

(Equation 13-9)

where $p \cdot q$ and $p \times q$ are the vector dot product and vector cross product, respectively, as defined in any text on vector analysis. If you examine this expression closely, you see that it has two scalar terms (which may be summed to give one scalar) and three three-dimensional vector terms (which may be summed to give one three-dimensional vector). The result then consists of a scalar and a three-dimensional vector (which is a quaternion), so that the product of two quaternions is a quaternion. Note that since one of these terms is not commutative ($p \times q = -q \times p$), the quaternion multiplication is also not commutative. Listings 13-7, 13-8, and 13-9 show the quaternion math.

```
typedef double QA[4];
```

Listing 13-7. The BkQDefs.H
```
/*

    BkQuat.H Defines Header File for Quaternion Math Module BkQuat.C
           BkQuat.H = Quaternion prototypes for BkQuat.C
      Copyright 1988,1992 Christopher D. Watkins and Stephen B. Coy
                       ALL RIGHTS RESERVED

*/

extern double SqrFPQ(double x);

extern void QAdd(QA p, QA q, QA r);            /* r=p+q */

extern void QSubtract(QA p, QA q, QA r);       /* r=p-q */

extern void QMultiply(QA p, QA q, QA r);       /* r=p*q */
```

378

```
extern void QDivide(QA p, QA q, QA r);                /* r=p/q */

extern void QSquareRoot(QA q, QA s);

extern void QSquare(QA q, QA r);                      /* r=q^2 */
```

LISTING 13-8. The BkQuat.H

```
/*
```

```
               BkQuat.C = Quaternion Mathematics Module
        Dependencies = BkDefs.H, BkMath.H, BkGraph.H, BkQDefs.H
        Copyright 1988,1992 Christopher D. Watkins and Stephen B. Coy
                        ALL RIGHTS RESERVED
```

```
*/

#include "stdio.h"
#include "dos.h"
#include "conio.h"
#include "math.h"
#include "malloc.h"

#include "BkDefs.H"
#include "BkMath.H"
#include "BkGraph.H"

#include "BkQDefs.H"


double SqrFPQ(double x)
{
  return(x*x);
}



/*
    QAdd        - quaternion addition
    QSubtract   - quaternion subtraction
    QMultiply   - quaternion multiplication
    QDivide     - quaternion division
    QSquareRoot - quaternion square root
    QSquare     - quaternion square
```

```
    Q = R + Ai + Bj + Ck = q[0] + q[1]i + q[2]j + q[3]k
*/

void QAdd(QA p, QA q, QA r)                         /* r=p+q */
{
    r[0]=p[0]+q[0];
    r[1]=p[1]+q[1];
    r[2]=p[2]+q[2];
    r[3]=p[3]+q[3];
}

void QSubtract(QA p, QA q, QA r)                     /* r=p-q */
{
    r[0]=p[0]-q[0];
    r[1]=p[1]-q[1];
    r[2]=p[2]-q[2];
    r[3]=p[3]-q[3];
}

void QMultiply(QA p, QA q, QA r)                     /* r=p*q */
{
    r[0]=p[0]*q[0]-p[1]*q[1]-p[2]*q[2]-p[3]*q[3];
    r[1]=p[0]*q[1]-p[1]*q[0]-p[2]*q[3]-p[3]*q[2];
    r[2]=p[0]*q[2]-p[2]*q[0]-p[3]*q[1]-p[1]*q[3];
    r[3]=p[0]*q[3]-p[3]*q[0]-p[1]*q[2]-p[2]*q[1];
}

void QDivide(QA p, QA q, QA r)                       /* r=p/q */
{
    QA t, s;
    double a;

    q[1]=-q[1];
    q[2]=-q[2];
    q[3]=-q[3];
    QMultiply(p, q, t);
    QMultiply(q, q, s);
    a=1.0/s[0];
    r[0]=t[0]*a;
    r[1]=t[1]*a;
    r[2]=t[2]*a;
    r[3]=t[3]*a;
}
```

```
void QSquareRoot(QA q, QA s)
{
double len, l, m;
double a, b;
QA r;

    len=sqrt(SqrFPQ(q[0])+SqrFPQ(q[1])+SqrFPQ(q[2])); l=1.0/len;
    r[0]=q[0]*1.0;
    r[1]=q[1]*1.0;
    r[2]=q[2]*1.0;
    r[3]=0.0;
    m=1.0/sqrt(SqrFPQ(r[0])+SqrFPQ(r[1]));
    a=sqrt((1.0+r[2])/2.0);
    b=sqrt((1.0-r[2])/2.0);
    s[0]=sqrt(len)*b*r[0]*m;
    s[1]=sqrt(len)*b*r[1]*m;
    s[2]=sqrt(len)*a;
    s[3]=q[3];
}

void QSquare(QA q, QA r) /* r=q^2 */
{
    double a;

    a=2.0*q[0];
    r[0]=SqrFPQ(q[0])-SqrFPQ(q[1])-SqrFPQ(q[2])-SqrFPQ(q[3]);
    r[1]=a*q[1];
    r[2]=a*q[2];
    r[3]=a*q[3];
}
```

Listing 13-9. The BkQuat.C

You need a complete set of functions for performing these operations before you begin any serious programming with quaternions. Such a set of functions is provided in the file BkQuat.C, shown in Listing 13-9. The functions are self-explanatory. By examining them in detail, you should get a good idea of what is involved in each operation. The file BkQuat.C is incorporated within the principal program file Quater.C (or Quater2.C), Listing 13-10, by means of an *include* directive.

```
/*
```

```
                    Quaternion Fractal Generator
          Quater.C = generates rough approximations of Quaternions
                     through the use of the Forward Equation.
                  The program is set up to generate a Quaternion
                        Dragon and a Solid of Revolution
          Copyright 1988,1992 Christopher D. Watkins and Stephen B. Coy
          NOTE : this program performs iteration tests from back to front
                           ALL RIGHTS RESERVED.
                    This software is published, but is NOT
            Public Domain and remains the propery of ALGORITHM, Inc.,
          Christopher D. Watkins and Stephen B. Coy. This software may not be
                 reproduced or integrated into other packages without the
          prior written consent of Christopher D. Watkins and Stephen B. Coy.
              Requires = BkDefs.H, BkGlobs.H, BkMath.H, BkGraph.H, BkZBuf.H,
                              BkQDefs.H, BkQuat.H
```

```
*/
```

```c
#include "stdio.h"
#include "stdlib.h"
#include "dos.h"
#include "conio.h"
#include "math.h"
#include "string.h"

#include "BkDefs.H"
#include "BkGlobs.H"

#include "BkMath.H"
#include "BkGraph.H"
#include "BkZBuf.H"

#include "BkQDefs.H"
#include "BkQuat.H"


/*
```

```
┌─────────────────────────────────────────────────────────────┐
│                                                               │
│           Constants for the Quaternion Generator              │
│                                                               │
└─────────────────────────────────────────────────────────────┘
```

```
    QSetCons - set up constants for quaternion generator
*/

QA q, l;
double DivergenceBoundary;
int MaximumIterations;
double XLeft, XRight;
double YBottom, YTop;
double ZBack, ZFront;


char ObjF1[]="Dragon";

void QSetCons1()
{
   q[0]=0.0;
   q[1]=0.0;
   q[2]=0.0;
   q[3]=0.0;
   l[0]=0.2809;
   l[1]=0.53;
   l[2]=0.0;
   l[3]=0.0;
   DivergenceBoundary=4.0;
   MaximumIterations=100;
   XLeft =-1.3;
   XRight =1.3;
   YBottom=-1.3;
   YTop = 1.3;
   ZBack = 0.0;
   ZFront = 1.3;
}


char ObjF2[]="RevSolid";

void QSetCons2()
{
   q[0]=     0.0;
   q[1]=     0.0;
   q[2]=     0.0;
   q[3]=     0.0;
   l[0]=-1.0;
   l[1]=     0.0;
```

```
   l[2]=      0.0;
   l[3]=      0.0;
   DivergenceBoundary=4.0;
   MaximumIterations=100;
   XLeft =-1.8;
   XRight = 1.8;
   YBottom=-1.8;
   YTop = 1.8;
   ZBack = 0.0;
   ZFront = 1.8;
}


double XScale, YScale, ZScale;
double XOffset, YOffset;

void Parameters()
{
   int tmp;

   textcolor(YELLOW);
   textbackground(BLUE);
   clrscr();
   printf("Quaternion Generator\n\n");
   printf("Equation : f(q)=lambda+q_\n\n");
   printf("lambda : quaternion constant for a particular fractal curve\n\n");
   printf("q : quaternion variable seeded as 0+0i+0j+0k\n\n");
   printf("The fractal surface is realized by examination of the\n");
   printf(" divergence properties of the equation in quaternion space\n\n");

   XScale=(double) Res/(XRight-XLeft);
   XOffset=-XScale*XLeft;
   YScale=(double) Res/(YBottom-YTop);
   YOffset=-YScale*YTop;
   tmp=Res*Scaling;
   ZScale=(double) tmp/(ZFront-ZBack);
}

/*

┌─────────────────────────────────────────────────────────┐
│                                                           │
│                    Function Iteration                     │
│                                                           │
└─────────────────────────────────────────────────────────┘

*/

void Func(QA Q, QA NQ)
{
```

```
   QSquare(Q, Q);
   QAdd(Q, 1, NQ);
}


void Iterate(QA p, int *NumberOfIterations)
{
   QA nq;
   double magnitude;

   Func(p, q);
   *NumberOfIterations=0;
   do
   {
      Func(q, nq);
      ++*NumberOfIterations;
      q[0]=nq[0];
      q[1]=nq[1];
      q[2]=nq[2];
      q[3]=nq[3];

      magnitude=SqrFPQ(nq[0])+SqrFPQ(nq[1]);
   }
   while( (magnitude<DivergenceBoundary) &&
          (*NumberOfIterations!=MaximumIterations) );
}

/*
```

```
                          Scanning Space
```

```
*/


void UpdateHeight(double x, double y, double z)
{
   int PlotX, PlotY, PlotZ;

   PlotX=Round(XScale*x+XOffset);
   PlotY=Round(YScale*y+YOffset);
   PlotZ=Round(ZScale*z);
   Height[PlotX][PlotY]=PlotZ;
}
```

```
QA p;
double X, Y, Z;
int NumOfIters;

void ScanSpace()
{
   double dx, dy, dz;
   int Slice;
   int Done;

   dx=(XRight-XLeft)/(double) Res;
   dy=(YBottom-YTop)/(double) Res;
   dz=(ZFront-ZBack)/(double) Res;

   Slice=0;

   X=XLeft;
   do
   {
      Y=YTop;
      do
      {
         Z=ZBack;
         do
         {
            p[0]=X;
            p[1]=Y;
            p[2]=Z;
            p[3]=0.0;
            Iterate(p, &NumOfIters);

            if(!(NumOfIters<MaximumIterations))
               goto Done;

            Z+=dz;
         }
         while(!(Z>=ZFront));
Done:
         UpdateHeight(X, Y, Z);
         Y+=dy;
      }
      while(!(Y<=YBottom));
      gotoxy(1, 20);
      printf("Slice # %d\n", Slice);
      ++Slice;
      X+=dx;
   }
   while(!(X>=XRight));
}
```

```
/*

┌─────────────────────────────────────────────────────────┐
│ ┌───────────────────────────────────────────────────────┐ │
│ │                      Main Program                       │ │
│ └───────────────────────────────────────────────────────┘ │
└─────────────────────────────────────────────────────────┘

*/

void main()
{
    Res=64;
    MaxHeight=Res;
    HeightBufferScalingFactor();

    Write_RAW_Data = 1;

    /* Create Dragon. */

    ClearHeightBuffer();
    QSetCons1();
    Parameters();
    ScanSpace();
    strcpy(ObjectFile, ObjF1);
    SaveHeightBuffer(ObjectFile);

    /* Solid of Revolution */

    ClearHeightBuffer();
    QSetCons2();
    Parameters();
    ScanSpace();
    strcpy(ObjectFile, ObjF2);
    SaveHeightBuffer(ObjectFile);
}
```
Listing 13-10. Quater.C

Generating Quaternion Fractal Databases

The file Quater.C shown in Listing 13-10 includes the main program and functions for generating databases for quaternion fractals.

The main program is relatively simple. It begins by calling the function *Parameters* to establish some initial parameters. It then sets the maximum height and calls *HeightBufferScalingFactor* to determine the scaling factor for the height values. Next, it calls *ScanSpace* to fill the height array with height values. The program finally calls *SaveHeightBuffer* to save the height data to a disk database file.

The function *Parameters* first sets the text color to yellow and the background to blue. It then clears the display screen and displays ten lines of data about the quaternion generator. Next, it calls *ClearHeightBuffer* to zero the height array. Next it calls the function *QSetCons1*. This function sets up a number of constants needed by the program. Two versions of this function exist–one to generate a shape that is similar to the two-dimensional dragon curves (its data is stored in the file Dragon.RAW [or Dragon.BO if Write_RAW.Data = 0, where you do not want to use Smooth.EXE]) and the other to generate a shape that is similar to two-dimensional Julia sets (stored in the data file RevSolid.RAW). Both files are generated with this program. The *Parameters* function then sets up scale factors in the x, y, and z directions and offsets in the x and y directions.

ScanSpace begins by computing the change on *x* and *y* required for each increment in the height array, and the change in *z* for each increment of height allowed. The function then enters three nested "do" loops, which iterate once for every member of the height array. Within these loops, the function sets up the initial value for the quaternion *P* (at $z = 0$) and then calls *Iterate*. This function repeatedly calls *Func* (which performs one iteration of the quaternion equation) until either the maximum number of iterations is achieved, or the magnitude of the quaternion exceeds a predetermined level (the Divergence Boundary).

Iterate then returns to *ScanSpace*. If the maximum number of iterations was reached, you are done and the proper height value is determined. In this case, you call *UpdateHeight* to place the height data in the proper member of the height array. If the maximum number of iterations was not reached, the function is run again for the nearest *z*. This will continue until the above condition is met. If the maximum number of iterations was not reached you are done and the proper height value is determined. Again, you call *UpdateHeight* to place the height data in the proper member of the height array.

When all of this has been done for one slice of data (a plane), the message "Slice # *nn*", where *nn* is the column (plane) number, is displayed. You then increment *Slice*, set *X* to a new value, and proceed through the loop again, until the entire height array has been filled and the function returns to the main program.

Color Plate 39 shows a quaternion solid of revolution produced by the z-buffering technique found in Quater2.C. Note our description above is of Quater.C computed from back to front, and that Plate 39 is computed from front to back using Quater2.C. RevSol2.B was the rendering file.

Terrain z-Buffer

Generating realistic terrain can be quite a chore. Some types of terrain, however, have a common look to them (such as water, mountains, sand dunes, and so forth). One of the first applications of fractals to computer graphics was in the rendering of coastlines and simulated mountains. These features have the *self-similarity* property that distinguishes fractals from other types of procedural objects.

The procedure for generating a fractal terrain set is a variation of the recursive process for trees described in Chapter 12. You start with a base grid of four points. The midpoint of each side is offset from the mean of the two endpoints by a small random amount. The center point of the square is also offset from the mean of all four corner points. This subdivision now creates four new squares, each of which can be processed in the same way. In our program Terrain.C, we offset the z height value, as opposed to offsetting the xy coordinates. The process continues until all of the grid points in the final output database are filled in. Figure 13-4 shows how this process works.

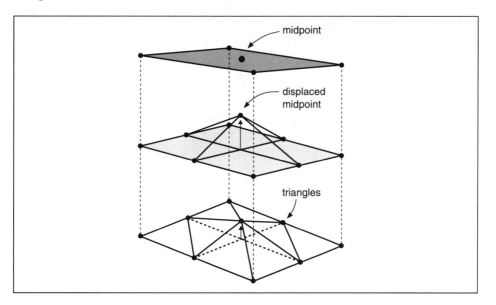

Figure 13-4. Fractal terrain

Terrain.C, shown in Listing 13-11, generates the output file Terrain.RAW You can alter the scale, spacing, and final output size by changing the appropriate parameters at the start of the file.

```
/*
```

```
                    Fractal Plasma Terrain
            Terrain.C = generates fractal plasma terrain
      Copyright 1988,1992 Christopher D. Watkins and Stephen B. Coy
          Requires : BkDefs.H, BkGlobs.H, BkMath.H, BkMath.C,
                        BkGraph.H, BkGraph.C
                         ALL RIGHTS RESERVED
```

```
*/
```

```c
#include "stdio.h"
#include "stdlib.h"
#include "dos.h"
#include "conio.h"
#include "math.h"
#include "string.h"

#include "BkDefs.H"
#include "BkGlobs.H"

#include "BkMath.H"
#include "BkGraph.H"
#include "BkZBuf.H"

#define mcol 63

void Init_Palette_3(Palette_Register Color)
{
  Byte i;

      Color[0].Red=0;
      Color[0].Grn=Round(mcol/85);
      Color[0].Blu=mcol;
      for(i=1; i<=85; i++)
      {
        Color[i].Red=0;
        Color[i].Grn=Round((i*mcol)/85);
        Color[i].Blu=Round(((86-i)*mcol)/85);
```

```
         Color[i+85].Red=Round((i*mcol)/85);
         Color[i+85].Grn=Round(((86-i)*mcol)/85);
         Color[i+85].Blu=0;
         Color[i+170].Red=Round(((86-i)*mcol)/85);
         Color[i+170].Grn=0;
         Color[i+170].Blu=Round((i*mcol)/85);
   }
}

void UpdateHeight(int x, int y, int Color)
{
  Plot(x, y, Color&255);
  Height[Res-x][Res-y]=Color;
}

void NewCol(int xa, int ya, int x, int y, int xb, int yb)
{
  int Color;

  Color=abs(xa-xb)+abs(ya-yb);
  Color=random(Color<<1)-Color;
  Color+=(Get_Pixel(xa, ya)+Get_Pixel(xb, yb)+1) >> 1;
  if(Color<1)
    Color=1;
  else
  {
    if(Color>255)
      Color=255;
  }
  if(Get_Pixel(x, y)==0)
    UpdateHeight(x, y, Color);
}

void SubDivide(int x1, int y1, int x2, int y2)
{
  int x, y, Color;

  if(!((x2-x1<2) && (y2-y1<2)))
  {
    x=(x1+x2)>>1;
    y=(y1+y2)>>1;
    NewCol(x1, y1, x, y1, x2, y1);
    NewCol(x2, y1, x2, y, x2, y2);
    NewCol(x1, y2, x, y2, x2, y2);
    NewCol(x1, y1, x1, y, x1, y2);
    Color=(Get_Pixel(x1, y1)+Get_Pixel(x2, y1)
           +Get_Pixel(x2,y2)+Get_Pixel(x1, y2)+2)>>2;
```

```
      UpdateHeight(x, y, Color);
      SubDivide(x1, y1, x, y);
      SubDivide(x, y1, x2, y);
      SubDivide(x, y, x2, y2);
      SubDivide(x1, y, x, y2);
   }
}


/*
┌─────────────────────────────────────────────────────────┐
│ ┌───────────────────────────────────────────────────────┐ │
│ │                     Main Program                      │ │
│ └───────────────────────────────────────────────────────┘ │
└─────────────────────────────────────────────────────────┘
*/

Palette_Register PalArray;

void main()
{
  ClearHeightBuffer();
  Res=60;
  MaxHeight=6000;
  HeightBufferScalingFactor();
  Write_RAW_Data = 1;
  Init_Graphics(0);
  Init_Palette_3(PalArray);
  Set_Palette(PalArray);
  randomize();

  UpdateHeight( 0, 0, 255);
  UpdateHeight(Res, 0, 1);
  UpdateHeight(Res, Res, 1);
  UpdateHeight( 0, Res, 255);

  SubDivide(0, 0, Res, Res);
  strcpy(ObjectFile, "TERRAIN");
  SaveHeightBuffer(ObjectFile);
  Exit_Graphics();
}
```

Listing 13-11. The Terrain.C program

Smooth.EXE

Okay, now we have a number of .RAW files, and we want to convert them to .BO object files in order for Bob to render them. We set *Write_RAW_File* = 1 because we want smooth databases (*Write_RAW_File* = 0 in the database generator programs would have written out very jagged .BO files). We will post-process the .RAW file. Data entering the Smooth.EXE program looks like this:

```
x1 y1 z1 <- vertex 1 of facet 1
x2 y2 z2 <- vertex 2 of facet 1
x3 y3 z3 <- vertex 3 of facet 1

x1 y1 z1 <- vertex 1 of fact 2
x2 y2 z2 <- vertex 2 of fact 2
x3 y3 z3 <- vertex 3 of fact 2
.
.
.
```

Note that no surface normals are mentioned. This is raw triangular facet data, where only the 3-D coordinates of a facet are defined. In order for our Phong shading algorithm to work, we need surface normals computed for the corners of a triangular facet, thus we can use it with our "patch" primitive. That is exactly what Smooth.EXE does. Normals are computed for the vertices of a given facet by examining the facets that surround the given facet. Examine some "pseudo-output" of Smooth.EXE:

```
patch {
   vertex x1 y1 z1    normal nx1 ny1 nz1
   vertex x2 y2 z2    normal nx2 ny2 nz2
   vertex x3 y3 z3    normal nx3 ny3 nz3
}
```

Notice that normals are computed for all vertices. For example: you have just run CPMMSET and it produced the file CPMMSET1.RAW. You need a .BO file to render, so type

```
SM CPMMSET1
```

This invokes a batch file, SM.BAT, which uses the DOS pipe to run the CPMMSET1.RAW dataset through Smooth.EXE and generate the dataset CPMMSET1.BO.

Yes, it's that simple. Now, just run Bob on the CPMMSET1.B file with CPMMSET1.BO available and voilà—Mount.CPM Mandelbrot!

How to Move Mountains

So far, you have been able to produce several different types of objects and view them with a test view file. But what if you want to move or rotate the object, or change the view position? To do this, you need an interactive utility that allows you not only to create new objects, but also to manipulate them interactively. You need a new tool. You need to meet Ed.

PART IV

CAD Production of Object Databases

Chapter 14: The Three-Dimensional
Database Modeler

The Three-Dimensional Database Modeler

by Bill Tolhurst

Your three-dimensional environment has been taken for granted–until now–almost as though the environment specification were the easy part and rendering it was the hard part. In fact, the opposite is true. The rendering at least proceeds without your intervention, no matter how long it takes. Positioning objects, setting surface characteristics, and building complex models require extensive use of your mathematical, artistic, and, up until this chapter, your typing skills.

While the images included in this book are interesting to view and illustrative in nature, Bob's real value to you is supporting your own experiments in photorealistic rendering. Experimentation is one of the best ways to clarify and reinforce your understanding of the concepts presented in this book.

An examination of the input files used by Bob, though, may be enough to discourage the most enthusiastic readers from attempting database modeling. Although the concepts are not difficult, creation of databases solely through the use of an ASCII text editor can quickly lead to frustration.

Bob, like many other rendering packages, requires complex and fully specified databases to create his masterpieces. This requirement has spawned companies whose sole products are accurate, detailed databases of everything from the human skull to aircraft carriers. Other organizations thrive on creating the tools that are used to create, modify, and manage these databases. Dozens of database-building products are on the market and range in price (and complexity) from less than $30 to more than $3,000.

The sections that follow discuss important features of database creation tools, as well the importance of a hierarchical approach to creating databases. This discussion shows how to apply affine transformations to take the same basic primitives and to scale, rotate, and translate them to make new ones. The rendering package presented in this book includes Ed, a simple database modeler, to assist you in developing your own images. This chapter examines all of Ed's commands and capabilities, as well as a top-level review of Ed's source code.

Like Bob, Ed has been developed for educational and demonstrational purposes only. As a result, error checking is minimal and a simple, unassuming user interface is provided. Since the focus of this book is on methods of photorealistic rendering and not on interactive three-dimensional modeling, not all the features Bob provides are available through Ed. As always, you are encouraged to modify Ed's source code to better suit your particular system and desired models.

Features of a Database Modeler

An effective database modeler must provide several key features if it is to be of any value.

Primitive support and manipulation

While it is possible to define an entire scene from a least common denominator means such as a list of vertices, it would be extraordinarily difficult and tedious to do so. The modeler should provide a straightforward means for creating elements of the scene from collections of predefined graphic elements or primitives. Typically, this creation process is based on several cardinal primitives (such as polygons, spheres, and so on). You should be able to scale, rotate, translate, and characterize (for example, assign a color and texture to) these primitives.

Object support and manipulation

In a scene of even moderate complexity, manipulating individual primitives still is a daunting task. You can have dozens or even thousands of primitives in the scene. In addition, primitives rarely exist on their own, but are collected together to form descriptions of more real-world things like chairs, desks, and cars. Such a collection of primitives is commonly called an "object." A good modeler must provide a means for creating, editing, and placing objects within a scene. The ability to define objects is also integral in creating hierarchical databases, the virtues of which are detailed in the next section.

Database views in human-tolerable time

Another key feature of the modeler is a view of the database under construction so you can review it while it is being built. The fidelity of this view must be traded off against the speed with which the view can be generated. A modeler that produces images nearly identical to that of the renderer, but takes as long to generate, would be of little use. If the result of your work is displayed in "real time" within the modeler, but the image produced by the renderer looks nothing like your previews (for instance, segments of objects are not properly connected or objects are misplaced), then the modeler is equally useless.

A typical compromise is to provide a three-dimensional "wire-frame" view of the database from within the modeler. You form this representation of the database by using lines and arcs to create an accurate outline of the objects in view. The resulting image is similar to a Tinkertoy rendition of the objects. The sides and endpoints are visible, but the rest of the object is not. The wire-frame view provides a means for checking the construction and placement geometry of objects. It also yields interactive display update rates, since far fewer pixels must be processed and displayed than for a more complete view. With this responsiveness, you can quickly see the results of a change in viewing position or an object parameter.

Free movement through the database

When building a model of something, you may find it useful to examine both the item being modeled and the model itself from a number of perspectives. Blueprints for a construction site often include a plan view (which is drawn as if the site were being seen from above) as well as elevation views (drawn from a ground-level perspective).

The capability to move freely throughout the database and evaluate it from several points of view is analogous to the multiple views provided in blueprints. In scenes of even moderate complexity, some objects may be partially or completely obscured from view by others. It may be necessary to "zoom in" to an area for greater level-of-detail examination. In addition, relative scale and placement between objects change with eyepoint position. You often must view three-dimensional models from several perspectives to insure proper placement of objects within the same.

Hiding details of the database

Another useful feature of a modeler is that it effectively removes the requirement of knowing anything about the details of the database file format. When you are artistically inspired to produce graphics, you would rather not worry about trivialities such as whether polygon vertices are delimited by parentheses or curly braces. The modeler performs the formatting automatically so you are not bothered by such details.

The Importance of Hierarchy in Database Construction

As mentioned previously, the construction of the database describing the scene and its elements is the most time-consuming task in producing photorealistic images. As a result, you typically want to avoid "reinventing the wheel."

Suppose you are creating a scene that includes an automobile, perhaps a brand new Hommina-Pow-Zoom VQZ-5000/LE-X. Obviously, you will need to include the four wheels in your scene description. Being the stickler for detail that you are, you take hundreds of accurate measurements from a neighbor's /LE-X and, after a time, you create the ultimate model of a wheel.

Now you certainly would not expect to go through this arduous process again and again to create four separate wheels from scratch. Rather, you would like to create four copies of your original wheel model within the scene. In other words, you would place four "instances" of a wheel "object" at appropriate places within the scene. This instancing approach establishes the means for building a database hierarchy. If collections of objects can themselves be objects, the mechanism exists to support a hierarchy with a practically unlimited number of levels.

You obtain several benefits by approaching your database efforts in a hierarchical fashion, and it is interesting to note that they are similar to the benefits provided through following classic structured programming techniques. These benefits can be summarized as reuse, flexibility, locality, extensibility, and efficiency.

Reuse

As in the example given previously, objects can be used repeatedly within the same scene, or across several scenes.

Flexibility

Since each instance of an object is a separate entity within the scene, each can be independently scaled, rotated, translated, textured, and so forth.

Locality and extensibility

After all your modeling work, what if the manufacturer of the /LE-X recalls them all to be refitted with a different style of wheel utilizing a new hub construction? After gathering new measurement data, you alter the wheel object database to reflect the design changes and all your future models are corrected. Since all the models you have done in the past used instances of the wheel object rather than hard-coded descriptions of the wheel, all of your /LE-X scenes will be correct the next time they are rendered. In this way, you have taken advantage of the localized nature of the data describing the wheel.

Suppose the manufacturer offered a special hub cover as an option. You would not change the standard wheel model, since a given vehicle may or may not have the hub cover. You could, however, make a different model based on the standard wheel that includes the hub cover. Better yet, you could simply model the hub cover as its own object, then create a higher-level object that contains the standard wheel and the hub cover. In either case, you have extended the applicability of your wheel model.

Efficiency

Once an object has been modeled and "debugged," you can use your time more efficiently by creating new objects and integrating objects into new scenes. You can reap further benefits of this approach when you create animation sequences. For example, if you decide to make an animation series using the /LE-X automobile, you must rotate the wheels to provide the illusion of motion. This is a simple matter when the wheels are separate objects, but would be quite difficult if the description of each wheel were integral with the rest of the automobile model.

Bob's Database Hierarchy: Primitives, Objects, and Scenes

Bob supports a database hierarchy consisting of objects, scenes, and primitives. Five types of primitives are recognized by Bob: the polygon, the patch, the sphere, the ring, and the cone. You can use as many of each type of primitive as you need to create objects, or you can use primitives by themselves.

Objects are collections of primitives or other objects, with each object definition stored in a separate object file. By convention, an object file has the .BO file extension.

A scene specifies parameters such as the viewer position within the scene, lighting types and placement, and so on. The scene also includes references to objects that make up the scene and specifies their placement, orientations, and other characteristics for each instance of the objects. This information is stored in a scene file. By convention, a scene file has the .B file extension. Chapter 11 provides a complete discussion of the input file formats.

Ed recognizes the following graphics primitives:

❖ *The polygon primitive.* The polygon primitive uses three or more planar vertices that define a convex surface. Polygons require parameters detailing the number of vertices and world space (x,y,z) positions of each vertex.

❖ *The patch primitive.* The patch primitive is a special case of the polygon. It is limited to three vertices, and requires that you specify an explicit surface normal and position for each vertex. You use patches to define rounded or smooth surfaces. You use the surface normals to soften the edges between surfaces.

❖ *The sphere primitive.* You must include the radius and parameters that give the center in world space (x,y,z).

❖ *The ring primitive.* The ring creates washer and disk shapes (a *disk* is a ring with an inner radius of 0). You describe a ring with parameters that specify its center, surface normal, and the minimum and maximum radius.

❖ *The cone primitive.* The cone primitive creates conic and cylindrical shapes (a *cylinder* is a cone with the same radius at both ends). Cones do not have end caps. Parameters specify the centers of the opening at either end in world space x,y,z, and the radii of the openings. A 0 radius at one end produces a pointed cone.

More thorough discussions of the graphics primitives appear in Chapter 7 and Chapter 11.

Ed: A Simple Database Modeler for Bob

With an understanding of the basics of database modeling and the graphics primitives, you are ready to delve into the mechanics of how to use Ed to create databases.

Starting Ed

To invoke Ed, type **ed <ENTER>** at the DOS prompt. (Be sure you are either in the same subdirectory as Ed.EXE, or that the appropriate subdirectory is in your path.) Ed has no command-line parameters or switches.

Note: As implemented, Ed uses the 1024 X 768, 256-color mode of the SVGA driver. If your system does not support this mode, you must modify and recompile the source code for Ed. Included with the source code for Ed is a file named Edres.DOC. This file documents the changes necessary to use other display resolutions.

Ed's screen

Ed partitions the display screen into three areas. The largest partition, which starts in the upper-left corner, is the Object Display Area. When you load or modify scene and object files, this area shows a wire-frame view of the database under construction. Objects or portions of them are highlighted when they are edited.

To the right of the Object Display is the System Status Area. This area displays important information such as the file currently being manipulated, the eyepoint position and look-angle coordinates, system mode, and so forth.

The lower portion of the screen is the User Dialog Area. When Ed requires additional information (such as the name of the object file you want to load), a prompt appears here. This area also displays user responses and error messages.

Telling Ed what to do

All user input to Ed comes from the keyboard. Ed's commands are single alphabetic characters, and are not case-sensitive. The arrow keys manipulate eyepoint and object position when the system is in Scene mode (see the "System Modes" section beginning on the next page).

System parameters

Ed displays the values for the following system parameters in the System Status Area:

- ❖ *Linear Delta.* Change in x, y, or z position of eyepoint per keystroke.
- ❖ *Angular Delta.* Change in yaw, pitch, or roll of eyepoint position per keystroke. Specified in degrees.
- ❖ *Object Scale Delta.* Scaling factor per keystroke.
- ❖ *Current Eyepoint Position.* Current x, y, z of eyepoint.
- ❖ *Current Eyepoint Look -Angle.* Current yaw, pitch, and roll of eyepoint. Specified in degrees.

To modify the system parameters, press P. Ed lists the system parameters in the Dialog Area, along with the current value and a prompt for you to enter another value. For example

```
Linear Delta  [10.0] :
Angular Delta [1.0]  :
```

If you press ENTER at each prompt, you retain the previous value. Otherwise you type in the new value and press ENTER.

System Modes

Ed has several modes of operation, depending upon what commands have been previously issued or are in process. Ed starts up in Scene mode, which allows you to move the eyepoint position, and add or delete existing objects. You use the object mode to modify existing objects or create new ones. Vertex mode is a subset of Object mode for creating and modifying polygon vertex lists. Studio mode is active when modifying the studio parameters.

Reading and writing scene files

To read an existing scene file into Ed, press the R key while in Scene mode. Ed prompts you for the file name and then loads the file. After you have entered a file name or accepted the current file, Ed loads the file. For complex scenes, the load process can take some time, so be patient with Ed.

To write the current state of your scene file, press W. Ed asks you to accept the current file name or specify another. Ed checks to see if objects have not been saved, and asks you whether to save those it finds.

Moving the eyepoint

You control eyepoint movement by using the arrow keys for left, right, up, and down motion. You control movement along the world space x-axis (in and out of the screen) by using the + (to move in) and - keys. In addition, you control the eyepoint look-angle by combining the CTRL key with the desired directional key (for example, CTRL-UP ARROW pitches the eyepoint look-angle up). The backslash "\" key rolls the eyepoint left, while the forward slash "/" key rolls the eyepoint right.

Selecting objects

You select objects by pressing the TAB key in Scene mode until the desired object is highlighted.

Instancing and deleting objects

You can instance previously defined objects (a previously existing .BO file) into the current scene by pressing the I key while in Scene mode. Ed prompts you in the Dialog Area for the file name of the object, then loads the object from the file and shows it with default placement and scale factor in the Display Area. To remove the highlighted object instance from the scene, press the D key.

Editing the object placement and scale

You change an object's placement within the scene by using the arrow keys to "drag" the object from its current location to another, or using the CTRL-arrow keys to change the object's orientation (for example, rotate the object). When the object has been moved to its new position, press the ENTER key to exit placement editing. To scale an object up, use the < key. To scale it down, use >.

Changing the studio

Ed uses a template (which prompts you for the necessary parameters) to create and modify the studio definition. To enter Studio mode, press S. Ed will display the current values for the studio parameters in the status area.

Editing studio parameters

To edit the studio parameters, press S again. Ed lists the parameters and their current values, allowing you to change them as desired.

Leaving Studio mode

When you have completed making changes to the studio, press ENTER.

Editing objects

Once an object is selected, Ed enters the Object mode to modify the object. You can edit two types of parameters within an object: the object's constructive geometry (its physical dimensions) and its characteristics (color, texture, and so forth). Press the O key to enter Object mode.

Note: Ed "flattens" the database hierarchy when it loads objects. That is, if an object file itself contains other objects, the hierarchical relationship of these two objects is lost, and Ed treats them as two objects of the same level. This necessitates care when editing objects. As a rule, if you have modified an object, save it to a new file name.

Editing object construction

You can alter the construction of an object through the Display and Dialog areas. Ed provides three functions for construction editing: adding primitives, deleting primitives, and modifying existing primitive parameters.

Adding and deleting primitives

To select this function, press the A key. Ed then asks you to identify which type of primitive to add and the values for the primitive parameters.

Use the TAB key to move through the primitives until the desired one is highlighted. Press the D key and you delete the selected primitive.

Modifying primitives

Use the TAB key to move through the primitives until the desired one is highlighted. Press the M key. Ed lists the parameters for that primitive in the Dialog

Area, along with the current value and a prompt for you to enter another value. For example, if you select a circle primitive, Ed displays something like

```
radius [150.5] :
center X    [0.0]       :
```

If you press ENTER at each prompt, you retain the previous value. Otherwise, type in the new value and press ENTER. After all the parameters for the primitive have been reviewed or modified, the results of the change are displayed in the Display Area. Press ENTER and you have completed the modify function.

A special case for polygons

Polygons may have a variable number of vertices. If you want to delete or add vertices to a polygon, press the V key once a polygon primitive has been selected. This places Ed in Vertex mode. While in the Vertex mode, press the A key to add a vertex and the D key to delete a vertex. Exit the Vertex mode by pressing ENTER.

Note: Ed does not perform a convexity check or other means of verifying that polygon primitives are valid. It is your responsibility to make sure the vertices create a convex, planar surface.

Editing object characteristics

Press C in Object mode and Ed displays the current characteristics of the object and allows you to alter the characteristics. Ed lists the characteristics for the object in the Dialog Area, along with the current value and a prompt for you to enter another value. For example, if you select a circle primitive, Ed displays something like:

```
Ambient Red [0.8]:
Ambient Green [0.2]:        :
```

If you press ENTER at each prompt, Ed retains the previous value. Otherwise, type in the new value followed by ENTER.

Note: Ed does not support assigning characteristics to primitives, only to entire objects. Ed does not save object characteristics within the .BO file, but rather places them in the .B file prior to including the object. Also, Ed does not support bump or texture surface characteristics.

Leaving Object mode

When you have finished making changes to the selected object, press ENTER. Ed asks if you want to overwrite the existing object file, create a new one, or abandon the edit. After making your selection, you are returned to Scene mode.

Exiting Ed

To exit Ed, press <ESC>. Ed asks you if you are sure you want to exit. If you confirm the exit, you are returned to the command line.

Note: Ed manipulates the PC graphics adapter and uses dynamic memory allocation during operation. If you terminate Ed by using CTRL-C or CTRL-BREAK, your machine may be left hurt and confused. If Ed does totally lose it, you should reboot the system rather than use other means of ejecting.

Overview of Ed's Source Code

Ed makes liberal use of the mathematics and graphics routines that were introduced in Part I of this book. As such, few new concepts directly related to the focus of this book are introduced within Ed. Perhaps the most value is gained from Ed's source code by using it as an example of how to use these routines to construct new graphics-related applications. Undoubtedly, the least valuable use of the code is as an example of good programming technique. The emphasis of this discussion is to provide a top-level understanding of the code structure and function, and thereby encourage modification and experimentation with Ed.

Conventions in Ed's source code

The following conventions are used in the source code for Ed:

ED<*filename*>	All of Ed's source (.C) and header (.H) files have file names that start with ED.
gv<*varname*>	All global variables used within Ed start with "gv", making them easier to spot within the code. All global variables are declared in Edmain.C prior to the definition of *main( )*.

| GC_<*constname*> | All global constants used within Ed start with "GC_", making them easier to spot within the code. All global constants are declared in Edmain.H. |
| <*varname*>Ptr | All pointers used within Ed have the "Ptr" suffix in their names. This provides a clue about the nature of certain assignment and manipulation operations in the code. |

Fundamental data structures

The structures discussed in this section account for the majority of the flow of data within Ed.

Object Type

Objects in the database are stored in a doubly linked list. This structure is dynamically allocated as objects are added and freed as they are deleted. This structure contains the current position, orientation, scale factor, characteristics (such as color), associated .BO file name, and a pointer to the next object in the list. It also contains a pointer to the first primitive used in defining the object.

Prim Type

Primitives that define each object are stored in a singly linked list and are dynamically allocated. *Prim* contains a "C" union of the individual primitive structures and a pointer to the next primitive in the list.

Poly Type, Patch Type, Sphere Type, Cone Type, Ring Type

These structures contain the parameters for each of the supported primitives.

Vertex Type

Use this structure with polygon primitives to store vertices. This structure contains the position (x,y,z) of the vertex and a pointer to the next vertex in the list.

View Type

This structure contains the eyepoint position, look-angle, and unit change caused by an eyepoint movement command.

Studio Type

This structure contains the parameters that describe the studio.

Global variables

The global variables in this section are included in Ed's source code.

gvObjectListPtr

This is a pointer to the list of objects within the database.

gvViewer

This structure contains the parameters that define the current eyepoint.

Major program elements

The functions included in this section account for the majority of the processing performed within Ed.

main(), Object_Exec(), Studio_Exec(), Vertex_Exec()

main() acts as the Scene mode executive, directing Ed's response to the appropriate function. The other functions act as the executive for the appropriate mode.

Initialize_System()

This function initializes the PC's video system to graphics mode, subdivides the screen into the Display, Status, and Dialog areas, and initializes eyepoint position.

Shutdown_System()

This function frees all remaining dynamically allocated memory, and returns the PC video system to text display mode.

Get_Scene_Cmd(), Get_Object_Cmd(), Get_Studio_Cmd(), Get_Vertex_Cmd()

These routines handle the retrieval and mapping of keyboard command characters to their requisite functions for the various modes of the system. If a valid command key is received, a function index is returned that directs the current executive to invoke the appropriate function.

Move_Viewer()

When a valid eyepoint movement key is received in Scene mode, this function is invoked to modify the eyepoint position and look-angle structure.

Read_Session(), Read_Object()

These functions request the name of the file to load, then parse information from the file and into Ed's data structures.

Write_Session(), Write_Object()

This function writes object data to the specified file name in .BO file format.

Edit_Studio()

This function lists the studio parameters and allows the user to modify them.

Add_Object()

This function adds an object to the database object list.

Delete_Object()

This function removes an object from the database object list.

Edit_Object()

This function lists the object parameters and characteristics, and allows the user to modify them.

Move_Object()

When a valid object movement key is received in Object mode, this function is invoked to modify the object position and orientation.

Draw_View()

This function erases and repaints the Display Area, using the updated eyepoint, object, and parameters. It checks to see that objects are visible or highlighted prior to drawing them. The *Draw_View()* function in turn invokes drawing functions for each of the graphics primitives.

Draw_Polygon(), Draw_Patch(), Draw_Sphere(), Draw_Cone(), Draw_Ring()

These functions draw the appropriate primitive.

Display_Status()

This function displays the current value of the system parameters.

Get_Dialog(), Put_Dialog()

These functions are used to write to and read from Ed's Dialog Area. The *Put_Dialog()* function simply writes a string, while *Get_Dialog()* expects a response and echoes this response on the screen.

Limits of Ed's Output Files

The scene (.B) files that Ed creates are meant to be used to verify placement and orientation of objects within the scene. Ed expects a precise format for its .B files, since he lacks the complex file parsing functions used by Bob. The best way to use Ed's scene files is to copy them first to another file with a .ED extension. Then you will be able to modify the .B file to include lights and other enhancements, yet still be able to re-create the scene in Ed by reading the .ED scene file.

Similarly, Ed's object (.BO) files can contain only primitives. Surfaces, transforms, and other object definitions are not capable of being processed by Ed.

PART V

Image Processing Techniques in Computer Graphics

Chapter 15: Image Processing

Image Processing

Now that Bob has completed an image, you'll need some method for displaying the image on your graphics card. If the card only allows 8-bit display, then the 24-bit image color values must be reduced to a suitable set of 256 colors that produces a reasonable facsimile of the full-color image. Some relatively simple image-processing techniques also can greatly increase the quality of your images. This chapter introduces the techniques and software to perform both of these tasks.

IMG2GIF.C

If you have a 24-bit color card, you may skip this part of the chapter. This section focuses on how 24-bit color images can be converted into 8-bit images through judicious choice of lookup tables and application of some image processing techniques. The image is then suitable for display on an 8-bit color graphical display device (such as an SVGA). The IMG2GIF program converts the .IMG image file that Bob generates into the more or less standard .GIF file format. This particular format is widely used on bulletin boards and by text-processing programs that include graphics. Once in .GIF format, this file can be converted to one of many other formats by using any of a number of freeware and shareware conversion programs.

Once converted, you can view the .GIF file by using your favorite view program. A good viewing program is Bob Montgomery's *VPic*. Look for it on your local BBS. In a pinch, even the public-domain Fractint can be used to view .GIF files. Chapter 16 describes a .IMG to .TGA converter and .TGA viewer.

When running IMG2GIF, you must make two main decisions:

❖ Which 256-color palette to use?
❖ Should the output image be dithered?

Choosing a suitable palette is not always easy. The standard VGA card allows you to view only 256 of the available 262,144 colors. An "average" low-resolution image has about 7,000 colors that must be reduced to the 256 colors. A higher-resolution image may have tens of thousands of colors to represent. The principal method for selecting which colors to view is to assign "similar" colors to the same palette entry. While there are many means for accomplishing this, the following algorithms are implemented by IMG2GIF.

Specifying a palette directly

A palette may be input via a .MAP file. This uses the same format as the .MAP files created and read by Fractint. This option is useful for creating multiple .GIF files with the same palette for animation.

Popularity

The popularity algorithm chooses the palette by picking the 256 colors representing the greatest number of pixels in the image. This is called a *partial histogram* of the image. A histogram is basically an array of counts for a particular color. Figure 15-1 shows an example color histogram. The program scans the entire image

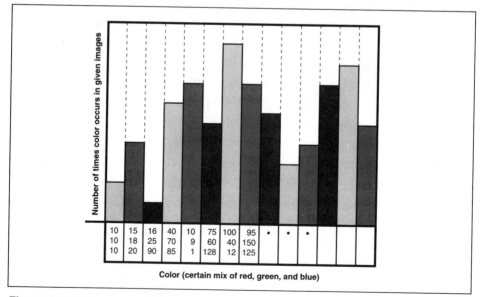

Figure 15-1. Histogram of color

to produce a histogram of all color values. The top 256 colors are used and all the remaining colors in the image are mapped onto the palette using a minimum distance criterion. In other words, the colors are mapped to the nearest one of the popular (top 256) colors.

The popularity algorithm tends to work best on images with a small number of colors. One problem with the algorithm is that small highlights may not be colored correctly. Highlights generally only cover a few pixels, so their colors usually do not have enough representation in the image to be chosen by the popularity algorithm. To help alleviate this problem, the IMG2GIF program forces the corners of the color cube (white, red, green, blue, cyan, magenta, yellow, and black) to be selected as the first eight palette entries. Since most highlights are white, this helps reduce unwanted artifacts in the resulting image.

Median cut

This is the color-space version of the median-cut algorithm described in Chapter 8 for building the internal database tree. (*Color-space* refers to seeing color as a 3-D vector of RGB.) The median-cut algorithm tries to choose a well-balanced set of colors to represent the image. The general idea of the median cut is to choose a palette in which each entry represents about the same number of pixels in the image. This helps to correctly color highlights that a pure popularity algorithm might miss.

The IMG2GIF program also allows you to limit the number of pixels represented by any one color. This, in effect, increases the importance of the colors in highlights and other small regions of the image. With this limit set to 1, every color in the image is given the same weight without regard to the number of pixels it covers.

Fixed palette

The fixed palette option uses a predetermined palette instead of choosing one based on the content of the image. This has the advantage of being much faster. When using either the popularity or median-cut method, IMG2GIF must first build in memory a tree structure that contains every color in the image and contains a count of the number of pixels represented by that color.

After choosing the palette, the colors in the tree must then be mapped onto the colors in the palette. This can slow down IMG2GIF quite a bit. When using a fixed palette, the image colors are mapped directly onto the palette colors by using simple equations that eliminate the need for building the tree structure and the subsequent costly remapping of the image colors to an arbitrary palette. Also, the current version of IMG2GIF only supports a tree containing about 57,000 colors. The fixed palettes supported by IMG2GIF are as follows:

0 : A gray-scale image using 256 gray-scale tones. Because of VGA limitations, this displays as 64 shades on most PC systems.

1 : Divides the color cube into eight shades of red, eight shades of green, and four shades of blue. This generally produces fairly bad images. Blue gets the lower resolution because, in general, the human eye is much less sensitive to the blue. Furthermore, blue is more difficult to focus on edges. Therefore, the loss of blue color resolution is not missed as much.

2 : Divides the color cube into six shades of red, seven shades of green, and six shades of blue. This option gives the best balance of speed versus good color representation. This palette works best with images that have a large number of colors. When combined with dithering, the images are even better.

Dithering for Fun and Profit

Dithering is the process of displaying pixels of differing colors next to each other in such a way as to produce the illusion of more colors. An everyday example of this is your television. The television screen is made up of tiny red, green, and blue dots that vary in intensity. These are the only colors your television actually produces, but your eye combines them to produce the rest of the spectrum.

You can produce quite an acceptable gray image on your graphics display by alternating a pattern of black and white dots. Examine a newspaper photograph with a magnifying glass. Notice that it, too, is simply composed of alternating black and white dots. The concept is easily extended to color. For example, you can create a yellow screen by alternating red and green pixels.

Floyd-Steinberg dithering is one of the original error-diffusion dithering algorithms. Error-diffusion dithering attempts to compensate for a limited palette by ensuring that the sum of the errors in any region of the image is 0, even though the colors at each individual pixel may contain some error. As IMG2GIF scans through the image, it chooses the nearest color for each pixel. The matching color usually is slightly different (in other words, you have introduced an error). The difference between the chosen palette color and the true color is then added to the neighboring pixels which have not yet been scanned. The next pixel is processed in the same manner, except the error term is added to it before choosing the nearest color from the palette. The advantage of Floyd-Steinberg dithering is that it has a "random" look. Generally, it does not produce noticeable patterns in the output image.

Ordered dithering adds a fixed amount to each pixel color based on its location. The sum of these additions over a region of the image is equal to 0. For example, you may subtract 2 from every even-numbered pixel and add 2 to every odd one. Since ordered dithering does not take into account the values of neighboring pixels, it produces fixed patterns in the images that may be distracting in some cases.

Ordered dithering combined with the fixed-palette option has an advantage when you are producing single frames for an animation. During an animation, the background (nonmoving) regions of the image remain constant, whereas Floyd-Steinberg dithering causes the patterns to shift from frame to frame as objects move through the scene. This is caused by the differences along the edges of the moving objects. Figure 15-2 shows some ordered dithering patterns.

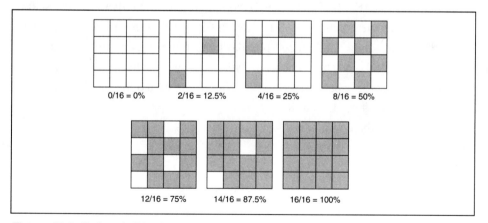

Figure 15-2. Ordered dithering patterns

The random-noise option enables you to add white noise to an image. As odd as this sounds, this kind of randomization can improve the appearance of some types of images. In some cases, this may help as much as dithering. It can also be used in conjunction with either of the dithering options. You can obtain interesting effects by increasing the range of the noise. Images converted with a large amount of noise tend to take on a distinctly grainy look.

While this effect may look interesting, it is not particularly useful to have such a large range. The default range for the noise is ±8 on a 0..255 range. This value is used because it seems to look good in most cases. Random noise has the advantage of being constant from image to image. In other words, the same random amount is added for the same pixel positions. This means that smooth areas in a series of images do not shimmer during animation.

Color Plate 14 shows an image with no processing, an image with ordered dithering, an image with Floyd-Steinberg dithering, and an image with added noise.

Creating the .GIF file

The default palette-choosing algorithm is the popularity method. The command you use to run IMG2GIF is as follows:

```
img2gif [-m #] [-f #] [-p palfile] [-d] [-o] [-r [#]] file
```

where [-m #] chooses median cut and limits each color to represent at most # pixels (# defaults to 64K). [-f #] chooses fixed palette # (# defaults to 0, gray scale). [-p palfile] reads the palette out of the file Palfile.MAP. If this file does not exist, the palette is chosen by median cut, popularity, or fixed, depending on what other flags are set. After the palette is chosen it will then be written to the file Palfile.MAP. [-d] chooses Floyd-Steinberg dithering. [-o] chooses ordered dithering. [-r #] chooses random noise ± # (# defaults to 8).

For example, the command

```
Img2Gif -f 2 -d test
```

converts Test.IMG to Test.GIF using fixed palette 2 and Floyd-Steinberg dithering. Assuming that test.map does not exist, the commands

```
Img2Gif -m -p test test1
Img2Gif -m -p test test2
Img2Gif -m -p test test3
Img2Gif -m -p test test4
```

first convert *test1* using median cut to choose the palette. The palette is saved to Test.MAP. *Test2*, *test3*, and *test4* are also then converted using the palette in Test.MAP.

Generally, you obtain the best results by using the -m -d flags as in

```
Img2Gif -m -d test.
```

For images that tend to be fairly monochromatic, the -m -d -r 4 combination works well. Adding the small amount of random noise helps break up some of the banding. On the down side, the random noise also adds to the .GIF file size since it is difficult to compress random noise. To get good-looking gray-scale images, try the -f 0 -r combination.

Technical Notes on IMG2GIF.C

The median-cut algorithm implements as a two-pass algorithm—one to construct the histogram of colors and one to convert the image. Once the first pass is completed, the palette can be determined. For .GIF output, you want the 256 colors that "best" represent the colors in the image. To do this, first define a bounding box around all of the colors in the histogram. This becomes the initial list of boxes. Eventually you want one box for each entry in the color palette (256 boxes).

For as many times as you need a new color entry,

1. Pick the largest box, where "largest" is determined by the total count of the colors in the box.
2. Find the longest axis (the greatest variation between the minimum and maximum of red, green, or blue) of this box and split the box in half across this axis.
3. Create two new lists, divided along the color axis you just chose, and compute the bounding boxes for the pixels in each list.
4. Repeat the process until you have 256 boxes.

Once you have 256 boxes, the color-palette entry for each box is computed as the average color of all of the pixels in the box. Note that by changing how "largest" is defined (total colors instead of total count, which is currently implemented as the "count limit" command-line flag), you can tune how the program actually picks the colors. So far, the only thing you have determined is that no single method seems to work best on all images.

Look at the code and note that the eight corners of the color cube are forced to be in the palette always. This helped during debugging of some earlier code and was not changed. It does come in handy occasionally if you want to ensure that at least one palette entry is black or white for other drawing programs. Also, some VGA cards give strange results in 800 x 600 x 256 mode if the background color is not black.

Looking at the data structures used, you can also see a definite DOS influence. A fairly typical practice with color-quantization algorithms is to clip the 8-bit RGB data to 5-bit RGB data to reduce the internal table sizes. Since VGA cards are capable of displaying 6 bits each of RGB, you want to retain as much of the resolution as possible. However, this immediately leads to memory problems.

The 5 bits give you a possible 32K colors. If you want to keep track of counts and palette-mapping information, you can assume 4 bytes per color, resulting in 4 * 32 * 32 * 32 = 128K of data. This is not too hard to fit into the 640K limit of DOS. Keeping 6 bits of information means you have 256K possible colors. But 4 bytes per color point requires 1MB of storage.

Working around this problem while trying to keep within the standard DOS memory model, you can use a two-dimensional array of linked lists. The two-dimensional array is 64 x 64 and represents the red and green components of the colors. Each node in the linked list then holds a blue value. You find a color by using the red and green values to index into the two-dimensional array of linked list headers and then follow the linked list down until you find the correct blue node. With this structure, you can store about 50K colors in normal DOS memory. Since most images have far fewer colors, you usually will not run into any limits with this and will reap the full benefit of using 6-bit information for each of the color components.

File Formats

The information included in this section will help you write your own image-manipulation utilities compatible with the Bob and Vivid formats. Experiment with these and share any interesting results.

Bob's .IMG file format

This is the format of the files output by Bob and the format that Bob expects for texture maps you might use in your images. The images are stored 24 bits per pixel with a simple run-length encoding scheme to help keep the size down. The run-length encoding works by replacing a repetitive string of the same color with a count value (number of pixels of this color) and the color value. "Runs" of the same color are not allowed to continue beyond the end of a scan line. This avoids having to deal with nasty wraparound problems. The format consists of a 10-byte header followed by the image data. The 16-bit numbers in the header are stored most-significant byte first.

<2-bytes>	x size of image
<2-bytes>	y size of image
<2-bytes>	first scanline, usually 0
<2-bytes>	last scanline, usually y size - 1
<2-bytes>	number of bitplanes, always 24
<image data>	

The image data format looks like this:

<1-byte>	a repeat count for the following color
<1-byte>	blue, 0..225
<1-byte>	green, 0..255
<1-byte>	red, 0..255

This is repeated as many times as necessary to complete the image. Basically, your program reads (or writes) pixels until the current scan line is complete. It starts fresh on the next line.

Note: Runs do not wrap from one scan line to the next. This helps simplify postprocessing. In some of Bob's anti-aliasing modes, an extra scan line is output to the file. This may eventually be changed, but for now the best thing to do is to always use the information in the header rather than looking for the end of the file.

Palette .MAP file format

This is the format used for palette files and was chosen to be compatible with Fractint. The file is in plain ASCII text and consists of 256 lines, with each containing the red, green, and blue value for that palette entry. The RGB values are integers in the range 0..255.

Image Improvement

The Filter.C program can help extract information from an image to which you normally would not have access. Listing 15-1 shows the simple three-by-three convolution filter program. In convolution, the filter array (3 x 3) will process the pixels around the pixel that you are computing, based on the filter, to give you your new pixel value. The only thing slightly tricky about it is the way it uses an index pointer to keep track of which scan line is the center one for the three-by-three filtering computations.

The program allocates room for three scan lines in memory. After a scan line is filtered, instead of moving up two lines of data and reading in the new one, it just increments the index pointer and reads the new line in over the old one. This saves considerable data shuffling and ends up being fairly quick. Color Plate 15 shows some of the effects the filtering program can generate. This plate shows an unfiltered image, an averaged image, an image that has horizontal edges highlighted, and a Laplacian edge-detected image.

```
/*

    3x3 Image Filtering Program
    Filter.C = 3x3 Filter Image Processing Program
    Copyright 1988,1992 Christopher D. Watkins and Stephen B. Coy
    ALL RIGHTS RESERVED

    filter - filter an image using a user defined 3x3 filter.

    Modified to read stdin and stdout ie
        filter -f ave.flt -o foo.img <bar.img
            -f filter def
            -i input file (stdin default)
            -o output file (defaults to stdout)

    filter files have extension .flt and are of the form
```

```
        1 2 3
        4 5 6
        7 8 9
        div
*/

#include <stdio.h>
#include <stdlib.h>
#include <fcntl.h>

#define MSDOS

#ifdef MSDOS
        #define READ_MODE        "rb"
        #define WRITE_MODE       "wb"
#else
        #define READ_MODE        "r"
        #define WRITE_MODE       "w"
#endif

unsigned char   *inbuf[3][3];    /* index, rgb */
unsigned char   *outbuf[3];      /* rgb */

int     xres, yres;
int     weights[3][3], divisor;

main(int ac, char **av)
{
        FILE    *infp, *outfp, *filtfp,
                *open_input_file(), *open_output_file();
        char    filter_file[256], input_file[256], output_file[256];
        int     i, j, y;

        /* if no args present, remind user of command line args */
        if(ac == 1) {
                usage(av[0]);
        }

        /* init strings for file names */
        filter_file[0] = '\0';
        input_file[0] = '\0';
        output_file[0] = '\0';

        /* loop through and process command line args */
        for(i=1; i<ac; i++) {
                /* check first character, must be a '-' */
                if(av[i][0] != '-') {
                        fprintf(stderr, "Error, unknown command line argument
                                %s\n\n", av[i]);
```

```
                              usage(av[0]);
                    }
                    switch(av[i][1]) {
                         case 'f' :
                              i++;
                              strcpy(filter_file, av[i]);
                              break;
                         case 'i' :
                              i++;
                              strcpy(input_file, av[i]);
                              break;
                         case 'o' :
                              i++;
                              strcpy(output_file, av[i]);
                              break;
                         default :
                              usage(av[0]);
                              break;
                    }         /* end of command line switch statement */
          }

     filtfp = fopen(filter_file, "r");
     if(!filtfp) {
          fprintf(stderr, "Error opening filter definition file %s.\n",
               filter_file);
          exit(1);
     }
     fscanf(filtfp, "%d %d %d", &weights[0][0], &weights[1][0],
          &weights[2][0]);
     fscanf(filtfp, "%d %d %d", &weights[0][1], &weights[1][1],
          &weights[2][1]);
     fscanf(filtfp, "%d %d %d", &weights[0][2], &weights[1][2],
          &weights[2][2]);
     fscanf(filtfp, "%d", &divisor);

     /* open files, read/write headers, get image resolution */

     infp = open_input_file(input_file);
     outfp = open_output_file(output_file);

     fprintf(stderr, "Image size %dx%d\n", xres, yres);

     /* allocate space for input/output buffers */
     for(i=0; i<3; i++) {
          for(j=0; j<3; j++) {
               inbuf[i][j] = (unsigned char *)malloc(xres *
                         sizeof(char));
               if(inbuf[i][j] == NULL) {
                    fprintf(stderr, "Error allocating input
```

```
                                   buffer memory. Aborting.\n");
                          exit(1);
                     }
             }
             outbuf[i] = (unsigned char *)malloc(xres * sizeof(char));
             if(outbuf[i] == NULL) {
                     fprintf(stderr, "Error allocating output buffer memory
                             Aborting.\n");
                     exit(1);
             }
        }

        read_scan(infp, 0);     /* get first scan line */
        read_scan(infp, 1);     /* get second scan line */

        write_scan(outfp, inbuf[0]);    /* output first scan line */

        for(y=1; y<yres-1; y++) {
                fprintf(stderr, "%5d%c", y, 13);
                read_scan(infp, (y+1)%3);        /* get bottom scan line */

                filter(y%3);

                write_scan(outfp, outbuf);
        }
        fputc('\n', stderr);

        write_scan(outfp, inbuf[y%3]);  /* output last scan line */

        fclose(infp);
        fclose(outfp);

}       /* end of main() */

/*

        usage() — If the user executes the program with no arguments
                or has an error in the arg list then print out
                instructions.  Note that this function exits.
*/

usage(char *prog_name)
{
        fprintf(stderr, "Copyright 1988,1992 Christopher D. Watkins and
                Stephen. B. Coy\n");
        fprintf(stderr, "Usage: %s [-f <filt_file>] -i <input_file> -o
                <output_file>\n\n", prog_name);
        fprintf(stderr, "    -f causes the specified filter input file to be
                used.\n");
        fprintf(stderr, "    Filter input files should have an extension
```

```
                    of .flt\n");
        fprintf(stderr, "      If no input and/or output files are
specified, standard\n");
        fprintf(stderr, "      input/output is assumed.\n");

        exit(1);
}       /* end of usage() */

/*
        open_input_file() - opens the specified file for input and reads
                the header info.  If no file name is given then stdin is
                assumed.  For MSDOS this must be forced into binary mode
                before use.
*/

FILE *open_input_file(char *filename)
{
        FILE    *fp;
        if(filename[0] != '\0') {
                fp = fopen(filename, READ_MODE);
                if(!fp) {
                        fprintf(stderr, "Error opening file %s for input.\n",
                                filename);
                        exit(1);
                }
        } else {
                fp = stdin;
#ifdef MSDOS
                setmode(fileno(fp), O_BINARY);
#endif
        }

        /* read header */

        xres = fgetc(fp) * 256;
        xres += fgetc(fp);

        yres = fgetc(fp) * 256;
        yres += fgetc(fp);

        fgetc(fp); fgetc(fp);   /* wasted bytes */
        fgetc(fp); fgetc(fp);
        fgetc(fp); fgetc(fp);

        return fp;

}       /* end of open_input_file() */

/*
```

```
        open_output_file() - opens the specified file for output and writes
                the header info.  If no file name is given then stdout is
                assumed.  For MSDOS this must be forced into binary mode
                before use.
*/

FILE *open_output_file(char *filename)
{
        FILE     *fp;

        if(filename[0] != '\0') {
                fp = fopen(filename, WRITE_MODE);
                if(!fp) {
                        fprintf(stderr, "Error opening file %s for output.\n",
                                filename);
                        exit(1);
                }
        } else {
                fp = stdout;
#ifdef MSDOS
                setmode(fileno(fp), O_BINARY);
#endif
        }

        /* write header */

        fputc(xres/256, fp);
        fputc(xres%256, fp);

        fputc(yres/256, fp);
        fputc(yres%256, fp);

        fputc(0, fp); fputc(0, fp);
        fputc(0, fp); fputc(0, fp);
        fputc(0, fp); fputc(24, fp);

        return fp;

}       /* end of open_input_file() */

/*
        read_scan() - Reads a single scan line from the input file.
*/

read_scan(FILE *fp, int index)
{
        int     cnt, r, g, b, i;

        i = 0;
```

```
        while(i < xres) {
                cnt = fgetc(fp);
                if(cnt == EOF) {
                        fprintf(stderr, "Error, unexpected end of file
                                reached.\n");
                        exit(1);
                }
                r = fgetc(fp);
                g = fgetc(fp);
                b = fgetc(fp);
                while(cnt-) {
                        inbuf[index][0][i] = r;
                        inbuf[index][1][i] = g;
                        inbuf[index][2][i] = b;
                        i++;
                }
        }
}       /* end of read_scan() */

/*
        write_scan() - Writes a single scan line to the output file.
*/

old_write_scan(FILE *fp, char *buf[3])
{
        int     i;

        for(i=0; i<xres; i++) {
                fputc(1, fp);     /* kludge count to 1 */
                fputc((int)buf[0][i], fp);
                fputc((int)buf[1][i], fp);
                fputc((int)buf[2][i], fp);
        }
}       /* end of write_scan() */

write_scan(FILE *fp, char *buf[3])
{
        int     i,              /* which pixel? */
                total,          /* how many left in scan? */
                count,          /* current run total */
                or, og, ob,     /* current run color */
                r, g, b;        /* next pixel color */

        i = 0;
        total = xres;
        or = buf[0][i];
        og = buf[1][i];
        ob = buf[2][i];
        i++;
```

```
        do {
                count = 1;
                total--;
                while(1) {
                        r = buf[0][i];
                        g = buf[1][i];
                        b = buf[2][i];
                        i++;
                        if(r!=or || g!=og || b!=ob || count>=254 || total<=0) {
                                break;
                        }
                        total--;
                        count++;
                }
                if(fputc(count, fp) == EOF) {
                        fprintf(stderr, "Error writing to disk.  Must be out of
                                space.\n");
                        exit(1);
                }
                fputc(ob, fp);
                fputc(og, fp);
                fputc(or, fp);

                or = r;
                og = g;
                ob = b;

                if(total==1) {              /* if at last pixel */
                        fputc(1, fp);
                        fputc(buf[0][xres-1], fp);
                        fputc(buf[1][xres-1], fp);
                        fputc(buf[2][xres-1], fp);
                        total--;
                }
        } while(total>0);

}       /* end of write_scan() */

/*
        filter() - Applies the filter to a scan line.  Uses the index
                to determine which scan line in the buffer is the
                "center" one.
*/

filter(int index)
{
        int     i, j, k, sum, offset;

        /* catch first and last pixels on scan line */
```

```
    for(i=0; i<3; i++) {
        outbuf[i][0] = inbuf[index][i][0];
        outbuf[i][xres-1] = inbuf[index][i][xres-1];
    }

    if(index == 0) {
        offset = 1;
    } else if(index == 1) {
        offset = 0;
    } else {
        offset = 2;
    }

    for(j=0; j<3; j++) {                  /* for each color */
        for(i=1; i<xres-1; i++) {         /* for each pixel not on edge
*/
            sum = 0.0;
            for(k=0; k<3; k++) {
                sum +=  inbuf[k][j][i-1] *
                weights[0][(k+offset)%3] +
                        inbuf[k][j][i] * weights[1]
                        [(k+offset)%3] +
                        inbuf[k][j][i+1] * weights[2]
                        [(k+offset)%3];
            }
            sum = sum/divisor;
            if(sum<0) {
                sum = -sum;
            }
            if(sum>255) {
                sum = 255;
            }
            outbuf[j][i] = sum;
        }
    }
}   /* end of filter() */
```

Listing 15-1. The 3x3 Filter Program

The following are a few of the supplied file filter types and their functions:

Average.FLT	Simple blurring filter
Horizntl.FLT	Highlights horizontal edges
Lmr.FLT	Local mean-removal (also called a high-pass filter)
Vertical.FLT	Highlights vertical edges

Diaglapl.FLT   Diagonal Laplacian

Unity.FLT   Unity filter

The *Average* filter blurs an image. It averages pixel values of surrounding pixels with the pixel you are computing, thus causing that pixel to "absorb" some of the characteristics of the surrounding pixels. You use the *Horizntl* filter to highlight horizontal edges in an image, which gives an embossed look to an image. The *Lmr* local mean-removal filter is a high-pass filter. This filter actually sharpens an image by removing many of the lower-frequency components. The *Vertical* filter highlights vertical edges, and produces the same eerie effect as the horizontal filter. The *Laplac* Laplacian edge-detection filter actually brings out detail in an image by significantly increasing the contrast of the image. The *Diaglapl* filter and the *Unity* filters are included for you to experiment with, and to provide a basis for you to develop your own filters.

Note that when you are developing your own filters, the nine elements of your three-by-three filter should sum up to 0 or 1 (thus using a divisor of 1 shown as the tenth element of your filter file). If the sum of these nine elements is greater than 1, as it is in the *Average* filter, then normalization must occur. This happens with the tenth element—the divisor. The filter program processes a three-by-three window of pixels. Each pixel value (for each pixel of red, green, and blue) is multiplied by the corresponding coefficient in the filter and the results summed. The sum is then divided by the divisor you specify as the tenth element in the filter file. Usually, you set the divisor to be equal to the sum of the filter coefficients to keep the average color intensity the same. The exception is if the coefficients sum to 0 (such as the edge detecting filters). In that case, you should use a divisor of 1.

Figures 15-3 through 15-9 examine the actual numbers that make up the filters.

```
1 1 1
1 1 1
1 1 1
9
```

Figure 15-3. Blurring (average) filter

```
0 -1 0
0  2 0
0 -1 0
1
```

Figure 15-4. Horizontal highlighting filter

```
-1 -1 -1
-1  9 -1
-1 -1 -1
1
```

Figure 15-5. Sharpening (local mean-removal) filter

```
 0 0  0
-1 2 -1
 0 0  0
1
```

Figure 15-6. Vertical highlighting filter

```
 0 -1  0
-1  4 -1
 0 -1  0
1
```

Figure 15-7. Laplacian edge-detection filter

```
          -1 0 -1
           0 4  0
          -1 0 -1
            1
```

Figure 15-8. Diagonal Laplacian filter

```
           0 0 0
           0 1 0
           0 0 0
            1
```

Figure 15-9. Unity filter

Image Display

Chapter 16 discusses how to display images on screen. In addition, Chapter 16 explains how to use a 24-bit card to get more colors than you could ever possibly see.

Graphics Hardware Drivers

Chapter 15 presented some image-processing techniques for improving image quality and, more importantly, showed how to reduce the 24-bit color image produced by Bob to an SVGA-displayable 8-bit format. The .GIF file format is used because of its wide availability and fast display programs.

This chapter presents some utilities for displaying images on the STB Systems PowerGraph SVGA card using 8-bit color. For those readers who have a 24-bit color card, this chapter provides a program to convert Bob's 24-bit .IMG files into the 24-bit color .TGA Targa 2 file format.

The SVGA card is one of many inexpensive, high-performance graphics cards. Table 16-1 depicts the varieties of graphics modes in which the card can operate. The *mode* number shown in the first column is passed to the *Init_Graphics()* call described in Chapter 3 to set the display resolution and place the card in graphics mode. Most of the code in this book uses mode 19 (320 x 200), mode 46 (640 x 480), or mode 56 (1024 x 768). Generally, your SVGA documentation provides the information necessary for making any changes to the code (such as the assignment of mode numbers).

Mode	Type	Resolution Characters	Resolution Pixels	Colors	Horizontal Frequency
0,1	Text	40 x 25	320 x 200	16	31.5 KHz
2,3	Text	80 x 25	640 x 200	16	31.5 KHz
4,5	Graphics	40 x 25	320 x 200	4	31.5 KHz
6	Graphics	80 x 25	640 x 200	2	31.5 KHz
7	Text	80 x 25	720 x 350	4	31.5 KHz
8	Text	132 x 25	1056 x 350	16	31.5 KHz
10	Text	132 x 44	1056 x 616	16	31.5 KHz
13	Graphics	40 x 25	320 x 200	16	31.5 KHz
14	Graphics	80 x 25	640 x 200	16	31.5 KHz
15	Graphics	80 x 25	640 x 350	2	31.5 KHz
16	Graphics	80 x 25	640 x 350	16	31.5 KHz
17	Graphics	80 x 30	640 x 480	2	31.5/38.0 KHz
18	Graphics	80 x 30	640 x 480	16	31.5/38.0 KHz
19	Graphics	40 x 25	320 x 200	256	31.5 KHz
34	Text	132 x 44	1056 x 616	16	31.5 KHz
35	Text	132 x 25	1056 x 350	16	31.5 KHz
36	Text	132 x 28	1056 x 400	16	31.5 KHz
41	Graphics	100 x 43	800 x 600	16	35.5/45.0 KHz
45	Graphics	80 x 25	640 x 350	256	31.5 KHz
46	Graphics	80 x 30	640 x 480	256	31.5/38.0 KHz
48	Graphics	100 x 43	800 x 600	256	35.5/45.0 KHz
55	Graphics	128 x 54	1024 x 768	16	35.5/48/57 KHz
56	Graphics	128 x 54	1024 x 768	256	35.5/48/57 KHz
106	Graphics	100 x 43	800 x 600	16	35.5/45.0 KHz
120	Graphics	80 x 25	640 x 400	256	31.5 KHz

Table 16-1. Display Modes for PowerGraph ERGO Extended VGA

The GIFView.C program is a display program for .GIF files. It uses the mathematics and graphics modules found in the Watcom compiler. Note that the decoding of the LZW file compression of the .GIF file is much simpler than the encoding process. Thus, displaying the files is fast and easy, whereas the initial encoding generally takes much longer. This program is provided for your information so you can access .GIF files through your own program. As mentioned in Chapter 15, the *VPic* program is a flexible, general-purpose display program with many options for creating playback sequences, manipulating the palette, and so forth. The GIFView.C program provides a basic capability on which you can expand.

24-Bit Color

The principal advantage of using the 24-bit color cards is that you see what you produce. You need not go through the color-reduction step necessary for 8-bit displays. Thus, you see the file exactly as it has been rendered. This is necessary for any detailed examination of the file. With the complex lighting models in Bob, you can produce scenes that have elaborate patterns of light and shadow. The color-reduction methods of Chapter 15 always seem to lose some of the detail of the scenes, especially in low light situations. A 24-bit color card is essential for being able to see the detail. Note that all production-oriented computer graphics use 24-bit color cards for final image display to ensure the accuracy of whatever is to be printed or filmed.

The 24-bit color file Targa 2 format is the "target" output format. Again, several display programs are available for Targa files and they can be easily exchanged with others who want to see the pictures you have produced. The program IMG2TGA.C shown in Listing 16-1 performs the basic conversion. The run-length encoded .IMG file is expanded and written out as the single 24-bit color value per pixel format of the Targa file.

```
/*

        IMG to TGA conversion
   IMG2TGA.C = IMG to TGA 24-bit color conversion
 Copyright 1988,1992 Christopher D. Watkins and Stephen B. Coy
        ALL RIGHTS RESERVED

        img2tga — converts .img format files to 24 bit
                uncompressed Targa files.
*/

#ifdef MSDOS
        #define READ_MODE       "rb"
        #define WRITE_MODE      "wb"
#else
        #define READ_MODE       "r"
        #define WRITE_MODE      "w"
#endif

#include <stdio.h> #include <stdlib.h>

main(int ac, char **av)
{
```

```
int          xres, yres;              /* image size */
FILE         *ifp, *ofp;              /* input and output file
                                           ptrs */
char         infile[256], outfile[256];
int          i, x, y, total, count, red, grn, blu;

if(ac != 2) {
            printf("Usage: img2tga <file_root>\n");
            exit(0);
}

strcpy(infile, av[1]);
strcat(infile, ".img");
ifp = fopen(infile, READ_MODE);
if(!ifp) {
            fprintf(stderr, "Error opening file %s for
                      input.\n",
            infile);
            exit(1);
}

strcpy(outfile, av[1]);
strcat(outfile, ".tga");
ofp = fopen(outfile, WRITE_MODE);
if(!ofp) {
            fprintf(stderr, "Error opening file %s for out-
                      put.\n",
            outfile);
             exit(1);
}

/* Read .img header.  Get resolution and toss the rest. */

xres = fgetc(ifp)<<8;
xres += fgetc(ifp);
yres = fgetc(ifp)<<8;
yres += fgetc(ifp);

fgetc(ifp);
fgetc(ifp);
fgetc(ifp);
fgetc(ifp);
fgetc(ifp);
fgetc(ifp);

/* write .tga header */
```

GRAPHICS HARDWARE DRIVERS

```
        fputc(0, ofp);
        fputc(0, ofp);
        fputc(2, ofp); /* type 2 targa file */
        for(i=3; i<12; i++) {
            fputc(0, ofp);
        }
        fputc(xres&0xff, ofp);
        fputc(xres/256, ofp);
        fputc(yres&0xff, ofp);
        fputc(yres/256, ofp);
        fputc(24, ofp); /* bits per pixel */
        fputc(32, ofp); /* image descriptor */

        printf("image size : %d x %d\n", xres, yres);

        for(y=0; y<yres; y++) {          /* for each scan line */
                /* let user know we're awake */
                if(y%10 == 0) {
                    printf("%c%4d", 13, y);
                }
                total = xres;
                while(total>0) {
                            count = fgetc(ifp);
                            total -= count;
                            red = fgetc(ifp);
                            grn = fgetc(ifp);
                            blu = fgetc(ifp);
                            for(i=0; i<count; i++) {
                                    fputc(red, ofp);
                                    fputc(grn, ofp);
                                    fputc(blu, ofp);
                            }
                }
        }

        /* wave goodbye */

        fclose(ifp);
        fclose(ofp);

        exit(0);

}       /* end of main() */
```

Listing 16-1. IMG2TGA.C

The program View.C in Listing 16-2 is essentially the same as ViewGIF, except for the 24-bit color card. It reads the .TGA file one line at a time, packing the data into a buffer, and then writes it out to the display. The program can also handle 15-bit color .TGA images as well, although these are not used in Bob.

```
File: view.c
Purpose: Provide a simple demo of the true-color mode. To use,
type "trueview filename [/I | /mode_num]", where mode_num is:
      19 - 320x200, 32768 colors
      45 - 640x350, 32768 colors
      47 - 640x400, 32768 colors
      46 - 640x480, 32768 colors*
      48 - 800x600, 32768 colors
      62 - 640x480, 16.8M colors**

      * = Standard default mode
      ** = 24-Bit default mode
The filename is assumed to be an uncompressed Targa file
(type 2) and will be displayed in the selected mode. If
no mode selection is made then the applicable default
mode will be used.

If the "/I" switch is used then information about the
file will be displayed.
```

```c
#include <stdio.h>
#include <stdlib.h>
#include <string.h>
#include <conio.h>
#include <fcntl.h>
#include <dos.h>

#define MAIN_COMPILE 1

#include "true.h"

#define    OFF      0            /* Standard stuff.           */
#define    FALSE    0
#define    ON       1
#define    TRUE     1
```

```
typedef struct {
    char *mode_switch;        /* Mode switch argument */
    int mode_num;             /* equivalent Mode # */
    int dac_req;              /* Minimum Dac Type requirement for mode */
    int x_res;                /* X Resolution of screen */
    int y_res;                /* Y Resolution of screen */
    int bits_per_pixel;       /* Bits per pixel */
    int hicolor;              /* HiColor Mode Bios call required */
    } MODE;

static MODE mode_table [] =

{
    "/19",0x13,2,320,200,16,1,    /* Mode 19 - 320x200, 32768 colors */
    "/45",0x2d,1,640,350,16,1,    /* Mode 45 - 640x350, 32768 colors */
    "/47",0x2f,1,640,400,16,1,    /* Mode 47 - 640x400, 32768 colors */
    "/46",0x2e,1,640,480,16,1,    /* Mode 46 - 640x480, 32768 colors */
    "/48",0x30,2,800,600,16,1,    /* Mode 48 - 800x600, 32768 colors */
    "/62",0x2e,3,640,480,24,3     /* Mode 62 - 640x480, 16.8M colors */
} ;


#define NMODES  (sizeof(mode_table)/sizeof(MODE))


/* Standard default Mode 46 - 640x480, 32768 colors */

static MODE default_mode_table [] =
{
    "/46",0x2e,1,640,480,16,TRUE
} ;

static MODE *mode_ptr;          /* Pointer for Mode parameters */


typedef struct {
    int image_type;           /* Image Type (must be 2 for RGB TrueColor) */
    int image_xorg;           /* Bottom Left X coordinate of image */
    int image_yorg;           /* Bottom Left Y coordinate of image */
    int image_width;          /* Width of image in pixels */
    int image_height;         /* Height of image in pixels */
    int image_bpp;            /* Bits per pixel (must be 16 or 24) */
    int image_descriptor;     /* Image Descriptor */
    } IMAGE;

static IMAGE image_info [1]; /* storage for image information */
static IMAGE *image_ptr;
```

445

```
char *info_switch1 = "/i";           /* Command Line switch for Info */
char *info_switch2 = "/I";           /* Command Line switch for Info */
char *default_mode = "/46";          /* Default Mode switch */
char *default24_mode = "/62";        /* Default 24-Bit Mode Switch */

static FILE *fptr;
static unsigned char image_buf[1920];

/* Prototypes */

int main(int argc, char *argv[]);
int set_mode_parms(char *mode_sel);
int open_targa_file(char *filename, int iflag);
void image_to_et4000(void);
```

```
┌─────────────────────────────────────────────────────────────┐
│┌───────────────────────────────────────────────────────────┐│
││                  Function: main(argc, argv) *               ││
│└───────────────────────────────────────────────────────────┘│
└─────────────────────────────────────────────────────────────┘
```

```
main(int argc, char *argv[])

{
     int dac_type;              /* storage for hardware DAC type */
     int saved_mode;            /* storage for saved VGA mode */
     int mode_switch_flag;      /* Mode switch on command line
                                   indicator */
     int file_info_flag;        /* Info switch on command line
                                   indicator */

     mode_ptr = default_mode_table;
     mode_switch_flag = FALSE;
     file_info_flag = FALSE;

     if (argc == 1) {           /* Display Help Menu if no filename */

     printf ("\n\r");
     printf ("\n\r");
     printf ("\n\r");
     printf ("TRUEVIEW Targa File Viewer Version 1.0 2-3-92");
     printf ("\n\r");
     printf("Cardinal Technologies, Inc.");
     printf ("\n\r");
     printf ("\n\r");
     printf("Demo Program for TRUE-COLOR Modes");
     printf ("\n\r");
     printf("Usage: TRUEVIEW [d:path] filename [/I | /Mode].");
     printf ("\n\r");
```

```
        printf ("\n\r");
        printf("Where filename is an uncompressed Targa RGB file.");
        printf ("\n\r");
        printf("Where /I is to display targa file information only.");
        printf ("\n\r");
        printf("Where /Mode is one of the following numbers:");
        printf ("\n\r");
        printf ("\n\r");
        printf(" 19 - 320x200, 32768 colors");
        printf ("\n\r");
        printf(" 45 - 640x350, 32768 colors");
        printf ("\n\r");
        printf(" 47 - 640x400, 32768 colors");
        printf ("\n\r");
        printf(" 46 - 640x480, 32768 colors*");
        printf ("\n\r");
        printf(" 48 - 800x600, 32768 colors");
        printf ("\n\r");
        printf(" 62 - 640x480, 16.8M colors**");
        printf ("\n\r");
        printf ("\n\r");
        printf(" * = Standard default mode ");
        printf ("\n\r");
        printf(" ** = 24-Bit default mode ");
        printf ("\n\r");
        printf ("\n\r");
        printf ("\n\r");
        printf ("\n\r");
        exit(0);

    }

if (argc > 3) {          /* check if illegal argument count */

                    printf("\n\rInvalid Parameters\n\r");
                    exit(0);
    }

set_mode_parms(default_mode);   /* set default mode parameters */

if (argc == 3) {                /* if possible switch on command line */

                    if (!strcmp(argv[2], info_switch1)) {

                            file_info_flag = TRUE;

                    } else if (!strcmp(argv[2], info_switch2)) {
```

447

```
                                file_info_flag = TRUE;

                } else {

                                if(!(mode_switch_flag =
                                    set_mode_parms(argv[2]))) {


                                                printf("\n\rInvalid
                                                Parameter\n\r");
                                                exit(0);
                                }
                }
        }

        if (!open_targa_file(argv[1],file_info_flag)) {

                exit(0);

        }

        if (mode_ptr->bits_per_pixel != image_ptr->image_bpp) {

                if (mode_switch_flag == TRUE) {


                                printf("\n\rRequested Mode does not
                                        support File Image\n\r");
                                fclose(fptr);
                                exit(0);

                } else if (image_ptr->image_bpp == 24) {

                                set_mode_parms(default24_mode);

                } else {

                                printf("\n\rFile Image not supported
                                        by Hardware\n\r");
                                fclose(fptr);
                                exit(0);

                }
        }

        dac_type = get_vga_type();       /* Check if hi-color DAC pre-
                                             sent */
```

```
        if (dac_type < mode_ptr->dac_req) {

                printf("\n\rHicolor Hardware Support not present:");
                printf("\n\r Dac Type %d found", dac_type);
                printf("\n\r Dac Type %d required",
                        mode_ptr->dac_req);
                printf ("\n\r");
                fclose(fptr);
                exit(0);

        }

        saved_mode = get_vga_mode();    /* Save present VGA Mode  */

        if (!set_vga_mode(mode_ptr->mode_num, mode_ptr->hicolor)) {

                printf("\n\rCould not set (%d) mode.", mode_ptr-
                        >mode_num);
                printf("\n\r");
                fclose(fptr);
                exit(0);

        }

        image_to_e..t4000();       /* Output File Image */

        getch();

        set_vga_mode(saved_mode, FALSE);

/*

        printf("\n\rMode Switch: %s", mode_ptr->mode_switch);
        printf("\n\rMode: 0x%x",mode_ptr->mode_num);
        printf("\n\rDac type required: %d", mode_ptr->dac_req);
        printf("\n\rX Resolution: %d", mode_ptr->x_res);
        printf("\n\rY Resolution: %d", mode_ptr->y_res);
        printf("\n\rbbp: %d", mode_ptr->bits_per_pixel);
        printf("\n\r");
*/

        return(0);

}
```

```
/*

┌─────────────────────────────────────────────────────────────────┐
│ ┌───────────────────────────────────────────────────────────────┐ │
│ │   Function: set_mode_parms(char *mode_sel)                      │ │
│ │   Purpose:  Sets VGA Mode parameters from /Mode switch on       │ │
│ │             command line or from internal default mode switches.│ │
│ │   Returns:  TRUE for mode found in mode table, FALSE for        │ │
│ │             mode not found in table.                            │ │
│ └───────────────────────────────────────────────────────────────┘ │
└─────────────────────────────────────────────────────────────────┘

*/

int set_mode_parms(char *mode_sel)

{
    int i;
    int mode_flag;

    mode_ptr = default_mode_table;
    mode_flag = FALSE;

    for (i = 0; i < NMODES; i++) {

        if (!strcmp(mode_sel, mode_table[i].mode_switch)) {

            mode_ptr->mode_switch = mode_table[i].mode_switch;
            mode_ptr->mode_num = mode_table[i].mode_num;
            mode_ptr->dac_req = mode_table[i].dac_req;
            mode_ptr->x_res = mode_table[i].x_res;
            mode_ptr->y_res = mode_table[i].y_res;
            mode_ptr->bits_per_pixel = mode_table[i].bits_per_pixel;
            mode_ptr->hicolor = mode_table[i].hicolor;
            mode_flag = TRUE;
            break;
        }
    }
    return(mode_flag);
}
```

```
/*
```

```
        Function:  open_targa_file(filename, iflag)
        Purpose:   Opens requested targa file and stores header
                   information. If iflag is set then header information
                   is displayed and file is closed.
        Note:      The only checking done is to ensure that the Image
                   Type field = 2 for uncompressed True-Color image.
                   If wrong image type then file is closed.
        Returns:   File open status; TRUE for file is open, FALSE for
                   file closed or unable to open.
```

```
*/

int open_targa_file(filename,iflag)

    char *filename;
    int iflag; /* Open File for Information Only Flag */
{
    unsigned int buf[18/2];    /* Targa File Header = 18 Bytes */
    char fname[80];

    strcpy (fname, filename);

    image_ptr = image_info;

    if ((strstr(fname, ".TGA") == NULL) && (strstr(fname, ".tga")
        == NULL))

        strcat(fname, ".TGA");

    fptr = fopen(fname, "rb");

    if (fptr == NULL) {

        printf ("\n\r %s Input file not found.\n\r",fname);
        return(FALSE);

    }

    /* Read targa header. */
    if (!fread((void *)buf, 18/2, sizeof(int), fptr)) {

        printf ("\n\rError reading Input file.\n\r");
        return(FALSE);

    }
```

```
        /* store header information
        */ image_ptr->image_type = (buf[1] & 0xff);
        image_ptr->image_xorg = buf[4];
        image_ptr->image_yorg = buf[5];
        image_ptr->image_width = buf[6];
        image_ptr->image_height = buf[7];
        image_ptr->image_bpp = (buf[8] & 0xff);
        image_ptr->image_descriptor = ((buf[8] >> 8) & 0xff);


        if (iflag == TRUE) {     /* if iflag set display info and close file */

            printf("\n\r\n\rFILE: %s", filename);
            printf("\n\rImage Type: %d", image_ptr->image_type);
            printf("\n\rImage X Origin: %d", image_ptr->image_xorg);
            printf("\n\rImage Y Origin: %d", image_ptr->image_yorg);
            printf("\n\rImage Width: %d", image_ptr->image_width);
            printf("\n\rImage Heigth: %d", image_ptr->image_height);
            printf("\n\rBits per Pixel: %d", image_ptr->image_bpp);
            printf("\n\rImage Descriptor: %d", image_ptr->image_descriptor);
            printf("\n\r");
/*
            printf("\n\rMode Switch: %s", mode_ptr->mode_switch);
            printf("\n\rMode: 0x%x",mode_ptr->mode_num);
            printf("\n\rDac type required: %d", mode_ptr->dac_req);
            printf("\n\rX Resolution: %d", mode_ptr->x_res);
            printf("\n\rY Resolution: %d", mode_ptr->y_res);
            printf("\n\rbbp: %d", mode_ptr->bits_per_pixel);
            printf("\n\r");
*/
            fclose(fptr);
            return(FALSE);

        }

        if (image_ptr->image_type != 2) {        /* ensure image type 2 */

            printf ("\n\rInput file not RGB Type 2.\n\r );
            fclose(fptr);
            return(FALSE);

        }

return(TRUE); }
```

```
/*
```

```
        Function: image_to_et4000()
        Purpose:  Transfers file Image Data to ET4000 display memory.
                  It is assumed that the file is opened and that fptr
                  is pointing to start of Image data. The file is
                  closed at the end of the transfer. No checking is
                  done during the transfer.
        Note:     If the Image Data is wider than the Display then the
                  image is clipped on the right. It is also assumed
                  that the ordering of the image data starts from the
                  bottom left. (Image Descriptor not used).
```

```
*/
```

```c
void image_to_et4000(void)

{
    int i; int width;      /* width of image data in bytes */
    int height;            /* height of image in scanlines */
    int xres;              /* current x resolution of display */
    int bytes_per_pixel;   /* bytes per pixel */
    int bytes_per_line;    /* #bytes transfered to ET4000 for each scanline */

    xres = mode_ptr->x_res;

    /* calculate bytes per pixel */
    bytes_per_pixel = mode_ptr->bits_per_pixel / 8;

    /* calculate #image bytes to read per scanline */
    width = image_ptr->image_width * bytes_per_pixel;

    height = image_ptr->image_height - 1;


    if (image_ptr->image_width > xres) {    /* clip image if necessary */

        bytes_per_line = xres * bytes_per_pixel;

    } else {

        bytes_per_line = width;

    }
```

```
    for (i = 0; i <= height; i++)            /* transfer image data */
        {
        if (fread((void *)image_buf, width, sizeof (char), fptr))
            {
            write_vga_scanline(0, i, xres, bytes_per_pixel,
                                        bytes_per_line, image_buf);
            }
        else
            {
            break;
            }
        }
    fclose(fptr);
}
```

Listing 16-2. View.C

The End of Bob

You can now display the resulting images on the card that fits your needs and budget. You should try to generate some of the example files provided on your disk. Then you can create your own databases, change the lighting, turn on depth of field, and see just how long you can wait for a picture. Above all, have some fun with Bob.

Chapter 17 explores life after Bob by looking into the present and the future.

PART VII

Looking Beyond this Text

Chapter 17: Beyond Bob

Beyond Bob

The field of computer graphics has expanded in many directions with great numbers of people researching various techniques for improving image quality, fidelity with the real world, and visualization of complex data sets. Many problems (such as realistic human animation) have yet to be solved. Bob is a tool for the realistic visualization of a wide variety of data sets and scene environments. While Bob appears to be the ultimate in three-dimensional graphic rendering programs, even he has his limits (among them implementation in the DOS environment). Even removing that onerous restriction leaves much that can be improved upon and enhanced. In addition, many areas (such as the creation of animated sequences) are simply outside the scope of a program such as Bob.

Even within the limitations of Bob, you can produce some extremely impressive pictures. Color Plates 42 and 45 show how the Phong-shaded triangles can (with enough modeling effort) produce striking images of people, both inside (the skull and the heart) and out (the face). Plate 38 of the Mandelbrot set illustrates how Bob can visualize things that can only exist in a computer-generated environment. You can create the realistic scenes displayed in Plate 44 as well as the surrealistic scenes in Plate 46.

As discussed in Chapter 14, these realistic models require a sophistication and complexity that go beyond the techniques available within the modeling tool represented by Ed. Since so many options need to be explored, these models also require considerable artistry when you create scenes such as those previously mentioned. Including the more sophisticated effects such as focus, depth-of-field, and realistic shadows can require an enormous amount of computing resources. As you generate more complex images, your patience surely will be tested.

Production Graphics

It seems as though just about every movie and every television commercial these days uses some sort of computer-generated imagery. Most of the higher-quality movies and commercials use ray-traced imagery in one form or another. This is especially true when it is necessary to merge computer-generated objects into real scenes. The defining difference between low and high quality is the way the computer-generated objects interact with the scene lighting. Care is taken to see that the objects cast the correct shadows and properly blend in with the rest of the scene. Only the ray tracing approach allows this kind of precise modeling.

Production animation requires the following two basic components:

- ❖ Fast, flexible, and highly interactive modeling tools to create and modify the environment.
- ❖ Accurate and flexible scene-rendering software.

The distinguishing feature of many production companies is the ability to produce rapidly a scene that is appealing to the customer. This requires tools that can be manipulated by an artist (such as a set designer or animator) rather than by a programmer. Designing these tools and providing intuitive interfaces to them requires considerable design effort and testing. The integration of live models with animated imagery requires even more effort, as any Disney executive can attest.

Some of the databases that appear in the color plates (such as the human heart) were not generated by any of modeling tools or programs presented in this book. Instead, the data was acquired by other means (such as three-dimensional digitizers and magnetic wands). More sophisticated model-conversion programs then transform these databases into a format suitable for Bob to render. As mentioned, Bob does not provide all of the features you might want in a rendering package. The remainder of this chapter presents some other features and areas of research that either Bob cannot support or simply are not practical in the PC environment.

Animation

Bob does not perform animation, at least not in any convenient sense. You can create animation sequences by setting up batch files in which a series of .B files generate each successive frame of an animation. But the animation aspects are not an integral part of the renderer, as they are in a package designed for animation.

Animation is defined as the process of emulating a continuous motion sequence. When presented rapidly enough, a series of still frames is perceived as continuous, smooth motion. For computer animation, you specify the position and orientation of the observer and all of the moving objects on a frame-by-frame basis. Each frame of the sequence is rendered and stored in the output file until ready for final playback. Many of the issues and problems of animation (especially on the PC) are discussed in *Programming in 3 Dimensions* (M&T Books, 1992). Consider some of the more advanced issues which a production project must deal with.

Wagon wheels

An animation sequence introduces the problem of *temporal aliasing*. Just as spatial aliasing causes problems in the quality of imagery, temporal aliasing can produce equivalent problems in an animation sequence. The basic situation is the same as in rendering the scene. You sample the motion at discrete points in time and at a finite rate. If the motion is too rapid, it is sampled incorrectly and odd artifacts result.

The classic example of this is watching the wagon wheel spokes in old cowboy movies. Movie scenes are recorded at 24 frames per second. When the wheels are turning rapidly, the camera undersamples the rotation and motion appears awkward (such as appearing to rotate backward). This same effect can occur with any type of motion in which changes occur more rapidly than the frame rate can effectively sample.

Motion blur

The "wagon wheel" problem can be solved, at least partially, by the temporal equivalent of anti-aliasing. The technique is commonly referred to as *motion blur*. The idea is to cast some rays at different points in time than other rays. For example, suppose the time between successive frames is $dt = 1/24$ seconds. The ray for the first pixel is cast with everything in position at time $t = 0$. The ray for the second pixel is cast at time $t = dt/2$. The third ray is cast at time $t = dt/3$, and so forth. This is exactly the same as the jitter solution for anti-aliasing, except now the jitter offsets the ray in time instead of in pixel position.

In order to minimize the amount of extra computing, most systems combine motion blur with the anti-aliasing algorithm. Thus, the subpixel rays simultaneously are offset in time and in position. The term *distributed ray tracing* was coined by Rob Cook in a 1984 SIGGRAPH paper that described this notion of combining multiple special effects with anti-aliasing. You can use this technique to combine the depth-of-field computation (in which extra rays are cast for the finite aperture) with the anti-aliasing computation. Thus, you have minimized the additional computational cost because few extra rays are cast. Their positions are simply chosen differently.

A motion-blurred wagon wheel now appears as a blur rather than as individual spokes. You have traded off the aliasing artifacts for lower-resolution in time. You can no longer discern quite as fine and rapid a motion as you can in the case without motion blurring. However, you cannot trust the result in the image that is not subjected to anti-aliasing.

Texture troubles

Remember that anti-aliasing is important when using texture mapping. The problem is worse in an animated sequence. The reason, of course, is that now the actual texture map intersections vary slightly from frame to frame in the animation. Any aliasing problems are compounded and appear as "crawlies," or random dot motion, in the texture. These effects are magnified even more when using surface normal perturbation with fuzz or wave textures. Production animation systems must take great pains to eliminate these effects or the quality suffers greatly. The problem with animated text is that the sponsor always wants the label to be readable.

You can produce nifty effects by animating the texture map parameters. For instance, you can simulate moving waves by simply changing the phase term in the wave texture. Or, you can move the point of origin of the wave. With the noise textures, you can change the phase or offsets to produce eerie animated marble textures.

Real-Time Ray Tracing

Ray tracing algorithms never have been used in any type of real-time animation system because the computer horsepower simply is not available to perform the sorting operations (that is, building the hierarchical tree and determining the nearest object for each ray) quickly enough. Standard projective rendering programs have the advantage in that they need only sort the object lists (farthest to nearest) one time per frame. If you use only one level of recursion, a ray tracer could do the same thing, but then you lose the improved image quality and realism of ray tracing. One of the real hopes for ever achieving this goal is parallel computing. Remember, each pixel is processed independently, and thus the image calculation can be spread across several processors that have access to the same scene description. As the cost of these types of machines decreases, you can expect to see more attempts to run ray tracing in near real-time. However, note that you always can saturate any ray tracing computation by increasing the recursion level, computing depth-of-field effects, and adding more complicated shadow and lighting computations.

Advanced Lighting

One of the more intense areas of research these days concerns sophisticated lighting models. Chapter 9 mentioned that Bob's lighting model makes quite a few approximations about how a surface is actually lit. For instance, Bob uses a 1/distance fall-off in light intensity from a light source when, in fact, light intensity falls off as 1/distance^2. The reason for using this was simple—better looking results.

Also not modeled in Bob is the effect of large diffuse surfaces such as a wall in a room. If the wall is painted red, objects in the room take on a slight red tinge from the diffuse light bouncing off the wall. Bob would handle this only if you were to set the ambient light level to red. Things would become most confusing (and incorrect) if you used a red, green, and blue wall. Generally, objects near those walls are slightly color-tinged by the light bouncing off the wall. This phenomenon is referred to as *diffuse interreflection*, and is one of the many physical effects Bob does not even attempt to model accurately.

Radiosity

The physical modeling of the interaction of light and surfaces within a scene is called *radiosity*. This type of modeling attempts to create a complete physical model of how light reflects throughout a scene. It is based on the theory of radiative heat transfer between surfaces. An object surface receives light not only from the light sources and specularly reflective objects, but also from the diffuse illumination of surfaces. In the example of the red wall, a radiosity model actually computes the entire diffuse light contribution from the entire wall reflecting onto the surface. Note that this is far more complex than modeling a mirrored surface.

With a mirror, you only looked for specular reflections, and only needed to cast a single ray. With a radiosity solution, you must integrate the contribution from all of the diffuse surfaces within a scene. Additionally, a radiosity approach makes no particular assumption about the ambient and diffuse lighting of a scene.

All the light contributions are computed as integrated contributions rather than single-point evaluations. This applies to specular as well as diffuse components. Recall that the specular contribution in Bob came only from the light sources. A full radiosity solution also includes specular effects of diffuse surfaces reflecting off as well.

For even a simple scene such as a typical office, this is an extensive computation. You may think that Bob can take an inordinate amount of time to render a scene. Radiosity solutions can try the most powerful supercomputers because execution time is more accurately measured in days rather than minutes.

Even more approximation

Because of the long compute times, even purists have been driven to develop approximations and shortcuts for radiosity solutions. The key to using these heuristics is that for a static scene with no highly reflective objects, you only need to compute the diffuse contributions of the surfaces once. The contribution depends only on the geometry of the objects, not on the particular lighting within the scene. This contribution is expressed in terms of effective light intensity from the surfaces involved, and so can be used for the diffuse contribution directly. This is ideal for a z-buffered ray tracing approach in that the diffuse contribution can be computed and stored at the same time as the z-buffering occurs. Once this diffuse intensity map is created, you may then add new light sources to the scene with much less difficulty. Only the contributions caused by this light source need be considered. All the others have been accounted for. It is still time-consuming, but much less so than recomputing the entire scene.

Why radiosity?

The advantage of a radiosity solution is that it can make a scene appear much more like its real-life counterpart by providing more details in shadowed areas and correctly depicting the effects of indirect lighting. This is particularly useful to an architect who wants to know what type of lighting and what intensity he should use in the new office building he is designing. A radiosity solution provides the flexibility of being able to add new light sources at will (such as a desk lamp) and literally being able to turn it on and off and see the effect. Shadowing effects are more accurate in a radiosity solution as well. The real advantage, however, is that it provides a test bed for fully understanding and testing theories of how light propagates through a scene.

Real Three-Dimension

Another area of research is the production of stereo images to produce a three-dimensional look. This can be quite impressive. The idea is simple: you generate two separate images, each with the viewpoint slightly offset to correspond to the separation of your eyes. Each image is therefore a *stereo pair*.

An image-rendering program makes this relatively easy to do, at the cost of the extra computation. The trick is to present the two images to each eye separately. Your brain does the rest by putting the images together to create the illusion of depth. The simplest trick has been the use of three-dimensional glasses containing one red lens and one green lens. One stereo image presented is then colored red, the other green. With the glasses on, each eye perceives only one of the images and you have a terribly colored, but still three-dimensional, effect. Many other techniques are available for stereo imaging, including the use of polarized lenses and LCD lenses that turn one lens on and the other off at 60 frames per second. These techniques all suffer from artifacts of either unacceptable loss of intensity, color, or resolution, or they are too expensive. In either case, this is another area where things undoubtedly will only get better.

Where to Now?

Bob is the result of the efforts of several programmers, large quantities of Jolt Cola, and patient families. You may be the kind of person who wants to know even more about computer graphics than presented in this book. This chapter has touched on only a few of the other areas of computer graphics. A few other sources of information about the field include the following:

Association for Computing Machinery (ACM)
11 West 42nd Street
New York, NY 10036

ACM/SIGGRAPH (Special Interest Group on Computer Graphics)

Computer Graphics (annual conference proceedings)

IEEE Computer Graphics and Applications (magazine)
10662 Los Vaqueros Circle
Los Alamitos, CA 90720

Graphics:

Advanced Graphics Programming in C and C++, Roger T. Stevens and Christopher D. Watkins, M&T Books, 1992.

Programming in 3 Dimensions, Christopher D. Watkins and Larry Sharp, M&T Books, 1992.

Fractals:

Advanced Fractal Programming in C, Roger T. Stevens, M&T Books, 1990.

Fractal Programming in C, Roger T. Stevens, M&T Books, 1989.

List of Files on Diskettes and How They are Connected

After the standard installation process has completed, you should have six subdirectories off the \BOB directory on your hard drive. These subdirectories are as follows:

1. C:BOB\SAMPLE
2. C:BOB\PROC
3. C:BOB\PROCZBUF
4. C:BOB\MODELER
5. C:BOB\RT
6. C:BOB\TOOLS

Listed below are the contents of each of the subdirectories and how the programs in them work together with other files to perform a given function.

Directory of C:\BOB

```
SAMPLE    <DIR>         <- the six
subdirectories

PROC      <DIR>
PROCZBUF  <DIR>
MODELER   <DIR>
RT        <DIR>
TOOLS     <DIR>

PKUNZIP   EXE   23528  <- file
extraction utility

INSTALL   BAT   2716   <- installa-
tion batch for Disk 1
```

```
README          6640   <- a readme
file (helpful hints)

RUNME1ST  BAT   645    <- a batch
file that must be invoked any time
you want to use any of the software
found with this book

PLANETS   GIF   57893  <- an 8-bit
color image generated by BOB - the
ray tracing program

DOS4GW    EXE   202376 <- the DOS
memory extender required by all pro-
grams compiled with the Watcom com-
piler. It must be in the path
statement.

INSTALL2  BAT   582    <- installa-
tion batch for Disk 2
```

Directory of C:\BOB\SAMPLE
(Compile with Borland at present)

(Sample Programs to show use of math and graph modules)

```
BKDEFS    H     1621   <- the math-
ematics and graphics

BKGLOBS   H     1213   modules used
with the programs
```

BKMATH   C   13367   found in
this subdirectory.

BKMATH	H	3998	
SVGA256	BGI	6335	
BKGRAPH	C	12099	
BKGRAPH	H	2749	
CRYSTAL	C	4700	<- fractal

crystal growth program

CRYSTAL	DSK	1696	
CRYSTAL	PRJ	5787	
CRYSTAL	EXE	60581	
PLANTS	C	3573	<- fractal

plant/coral generation program

PLANTS	DSK	1694	
PLANTS	PRJ	5798	
PLANTS	EXE	59153	
STARS-3D	C	4616	<- 3-D

starfield program

STARS-3D	DSK	1698	
STARS-3D	PRJ	5824	
STARS-3D	EXE	63476	
3D-3PORB	C	6849	<- 3-D 3-

particle orbit simulator

3D-3PORB	DSK	1698	
3D-3PORB	PRJ	5766	
3D-3PORB	EXE	59177	
RUNALL	BAT	37	<- batch

that executes all of the .EXE files
in this subdirectory

Directory of C:\BOB\PROC
(Compile with Watcom at present or Borland if you make project files)

(these programs generate .BO files for the ray tracer when used as a DOS pipe)

TREES	C	4239	<- recursive

tree generation program

TREES	EXE	25192	
TREES_C	BAT	78	

TORUS	C	4764	<- torus

generation program

TORUS	EXE	30172	
TORUS_C	BAT	78	
TILEPUZL	C	3700	<- tile puz-

zle generation program

TILEPUZL	EXE	25526	
TILEPU_C	BAT	84	
SPHRFLAK	C	3066	<- sphere-

flake object generator

SPHRFLAK	EXE	25020	
SPHRFL_C	BAT	84	
SPONGE	C	1916	<- Menger

Sponge generator

SPONGE	EXE	24872	
SPONGE_C	BAT	80	
HEXER	C	1929	<- hex pat-

tern sphere floor generator

HEXER	EXE	24734	
HEXER_C	BAT	78	
RUNALL	BAT	205	<- batch

that executes all of the .EXE files
in this subdirectory

Directory of C:\BOB\PROCZBUF
(Compile with Borland at present)

(these programs generate .RAW files for the SMOOTH.EXE program found in this subdirectory. The SMOOTH.EXE program generates a .BO file for the ray tracer when SM.BAT is invoked so that piping is done)

BKDEFS	H	1621	<- the math-

ematics and graphics modules used
with the programs found in this subdirectory.

BKGLOBS	H	1213	
BKMATH	C	1336	
BKMATH	H	3998	
SVGA256	BGI	6335	

BKGRAPH	C	12099	
BKGRAPH	H	2749	
BKQDEFS	H	1034	<-

quaternion math modules

BKQUAT	C	3043	
BKQUAT	H	1364	
BKZBUF	C	5184	<- z-

buffer database modules

BKZBUF	H	1407	
BKQUAT	C	3043	
BKQUAT	H	1364	
PLOTEQN	C	3727	<- equa-

tion database generator

PLOTEQN	DSK	1742	
PLOTEQN	PRJ	6121	
PLOTEQN	EXE	114506	
OCEAN	C	3633	<- ocean

database generator

OCEAN	DSK	1760	
OCEAN	PRJ	6119	
OCEAN	EXE	114751	
CPM-MSET	C	3653	<- 3-D

Mandelbrot Set database generator

CPM-MSET	DSK	1767	
CPM-MSET	PRJ	6124	
CPM-MSET	EXE	115319	
CPM-JSET	C	3904	<- 3-D

Julia Set database generator

CPM-JSET	DSK	1747	
CPM-JSET	PRJ	6144	
CPM-JSET	EXE	115463	
QUATER	C	6927	<-

quaternion database generator (B to F)

QUATER	DSK	1848	
QUATER	PRJ	6412	
QUATER	EXE	117721	
QUATER2	C	6927	<-

quaternion database generator (F to B)

QUATER2	DSK	1851	
QUATER2	PRJ	6413	

QUATER2	EXE	117723	
TERRAIN	C	3807	<-plasma

terrain database generator

TERRAIN	DSK	1865	
TERRAIN	PRJ	6123	
TERRAIN	EXE	118547	
SM	BAT	311	<- batch

file for piping with

SMOOTH.EXE   (we bring
in .RAW files and write out BO
files)

SMOOTH	EXE	29610	
RUNALL	BAT	2546	<- batch

that executes all of the .EXE files
in this subdirectory

Directory of C:\BOB\MODELER
(Compile with Borland at present)

(ED the object and scene modeling tool - uses and
creates .B and .BO files)

BKDEFS	H	1621	<- the

mathematics and graphics modules
used with the programs found in this
subdirectory.

BKGLOBS	H	1213	
BKMATH	C	13367	
BKMATH	H	3998	
SVGA256	BGI	6335	
BKGRAPH	C	12099	
BKGRAPH	H	2749	
EDCMD	C	4602	
EDDIA	C	4227	
EDEDIT	C	26846	
EDFILE	C	18807	
EDGRAPH	C	18307	
EDKEY	H	2010	
EDMAIN	C	5754	
EDMAIN	H	5700	
EDMOVE	C	3420	
EDOBJECT	C	7163	
EDOCMD	C	4289	

```
EDOEXEC    C    4025
EDOMODE    H    2321
EDPRIM     C    5655
EDPROTOS   H    6499
EDSCMODE   H    2298
EDSTAT     C    5444
EDSTCMD    C    2169
EDSTEXEC   C    2307
EDSTMODE   H    1748
EDSYS      C    5081
EDVCMD     C    2319
EDVERTEX   C    4456
EDVEXEC    C    2835
EDVMODE    H    1811
ED         DSK  2466
ED         PRJ  9629
ED         DOC  12651   <- documen-
tation for ED (as seen in CH14)

EDRES      DOC  2997  <- notes for
changing screen resolution

ED         EXE  11435  <- Ed - the
Object Modeler

STUDIO     B    450    <- sample
studio section of .B file

TEST       BO   52     <- sample
.BO object file
```

Directory of C:\BOB\RT

(BOB requires at least a .B file. It may also need
.BO, .BS, .IMG, .MAP, and .BC files based on
the given .B file)

```
SRC        <DIR>       <- source
code for BOB

SCNS       <DIR>       <- scene .B
files

OBJS       <DIR>       <- object
.BO files
```

```
MAPS       <DIR>       <- bit map
.IMG files

BKGS       <DIR>       <- back-
ground .MAP files

COLS       <DIR>       <- color .BC
files

SRFS       <DIR>       <- surfaces
(no surfaces-placeholder)

BOB        EXE  116215 <- Watcom
compiled version of BOB

TEST       BAT  47     <- Batch
file using quick render mode to pre-
view your scene before a full render
```

Directory of C:\BOB\RT\SRC (Compile with Borland (BOBBOR_C.BAT) or Watcom (BOB____C.BAT) - note, reduce the level of recursion to 8 in Config.H for compilation with Borland, also note that you will be able to generate few of the images without the DOS memory extender and compilation with Borland - the Watcom .EXE is given on this disk.)

```
BOUND      C    6278
CLIP       C    5538
CONE       C    6901
DATA       C    3777
ERROR      C    1847
FILE       C    2827
INTER      C    5309
MAIN       C    6029
MEMORY     C    2184
NOISE      C    4894
PARSE      C    34785
PIC        C    5404
POLY       C    5173
PQUEUE     C    2655
PREPROC    C    12086
RING       C    3917
SCREEN     C    29854
```

SHADE	C	12910
SHADOW	C	7825
SPHERE	C	4471
STATS	C	3009
TEXTURE	C	10724
TOKENS	C	8036
TRACE	C	3117
TRI	C	7342
VECTOR	C	7848
VERSION	C	1355
WAVE	C	2334
YYSTUFF	C	4509
CONFIG	H	2558
DEFS	H	10089
EXTERN	H	3274
PIC	H	1276
PROTO	H	6674
TOKENS	H	4472
BOBBOR_C	BAT	47
BOB____C	BAT	72

Directory of C:\BOB\RT\SCNS

(.B scene files - used by BOB to define the scene
-> these relate to cover images and to book plates)

HEX2	B	1332
CRYPT1	B	1067
VENUS3	B	1660
POOL6	B	11245
LIGHT	B	2509
CHESS4	B	8371
POOLTBL2	B	2472
GALLERY	B	5770
PLANETS	B	2125
ANTALIOF	B	2515
ANTALION	B	2539
PROGRS1A	B	2530
PROGRS1B	B	2589
PROGRS1C	B	2677
PROGRS1D	B	2807
PROGRS2	B	3743
CLIP1	B	2755
CLIP2	B	2045
CLIP3	B	1934
CLIP4	B	1786
CLIP5	B	1732

CLIP6	B	1816
CLIP7	B	1357
CLIP8	B	1923
CLIP9	B	1859
AMP	B	2024
TERMS	B	2028
BOX	B	3259
FOCUS	B	1567
CAUSTIC	B	1367
BLEND1	B	2346
BLEND2	B	2381
BLEND3	B	2504
BLEND4	B	2555
WOOD	B	1732
AXIS	B	3275
ICE2	B	2236
FLOOR3	B	5169
COL1	B	1769
BOX1	B	2665
LAKESIDE	B	2573
POOL5	B	11246
F117	B	1541
DICE1	B	2147
TILES1	B	1902
BASIN1	B	2823
SPONGE	B	1306
PLOTEQN1	B	1216
OCEAN	B	1207
CPMMSET1	B	1210
DRAGON	B	1182
REVSOLID	B	1184
DRAGON2	B	1183
REVSOL2	B	1183
TERRAIN	B	1214
M&T	B	2495
FACES	B	2088
STACK	B	1801
DUCKS	B	2457
HEART	B	1552
RACE	B	1792
BKG2	B	1801
BOBSTUFF	B	2611
PLOTEQN2	B	1216
PLOTEQN3	B	1216
PLOTEQN4	B	1216
CPMMSET2	B	1210
CPMJSET1	B	1210

CPMJSET2	B	1210
TOR2	B	1493

Directory of C:\BOB\RT\OBJS

(.BO object files - referenced by .B files, where a special object is called)

BLOCK	BO	1100
BOBLOGO	BO	23440
BOBLOGO2	BO	9874
BOX	BO	132497
CLIPS	BO	125
COLUMN	BO	4859
COLUMN2	BO	3504
SCULPT	BO	625
DIE2	BO	10123
F117	BO	50826
HEART	BO	339253
ICE	BO	90321
CRYPT	BO	1666
CRYPTSEC	BO	1407
POOLBALL	BO	9398
CHALK	BO	1012
BALLS2	BO	885
SOLID	BO	86
STICK	BO	1141
STRIPE	BO	450
BASIN	BO	1871
DUCK	BO	172257
TEAPOT	BO	326065
CUBE	BO	724
DODECA	BO	1809
ICOSA	BO	1806
OCTA	BO	740
TETRA	BO	394
VENUS	BO	291802
HOTROD	BO	326082
VETTE	BO	179572
MANSFACE	BO	168915
NEFERTT	BO	259627
SKULL2	BO	259831
M	BO	1846
&	BO	985
T	BO	1112
BISHOP	BO	117783
KING	BO	149581

KNIGHT	BO	99388
PAWN	BO	71557
QUEEN	BO	134578
ROOK	BO	62205

Directory of C:\BOB\RT\MAPS

(.IMG bitmap files - referenced by .B files, where a special image texture map is called)

ALGORITH	IMG	45638
BRICK	IMG	124314
CCDM27	IMG	97842
CCDM31	IMG	50794
CCDMOON	IMG	175490
CCDSATRN	IMG	88290
CNN	IMG	176650
PALERMO	IMG	44562
PATTERN	IMG	230
PLANETS2	IMG	110202
SHUTTLE	IMG	293458
VIVID1	IMG	150258
BALL1	IMG	6834
BALL2	IMG	7786
BALL3	IMG	8306
BALL4	IMG	7430
BALL5	IMG	7738
BALL6	IMG	7750
BALL7	IMG	7030
BALL8	IMG	8210
BALL10	IMG	13850
BALL11	IMG	12410
BALL12	IMG	13390
BALL13	IMG	13906
BALL14	IMG	13026
BALL15	IMG	13338

Directory of C:\BOB\RT\BKGS

(.MAP background files - referenced by .B files, where a special background is called)

GREYS	MAP	2998
SKY	MAP	2490

Directory of C:\BOB\RT\COLS

(.BC color files - referenced by .B and .BO files, where a predefined color definition is used)

```
COLOR      BC     3612
```

Directory of C:\BOB\RT\SRFS

(.BS surface files - not used)

```
SRFS       TX     69
```

Directory of C:\BOB\TOOLS

```
IMG2GIF    <DIR>
IMG2TGA    <DIR>
VIEWGIF    <DIR>
VIEWTGA    <DIR>
FILTER     <DIR>
GIF2IMG    EXE    30644    <- exe-
```
cutables that fall into the path created by RUNME1ST.BAT (the source code for each of these programs is given in the subdirectories found just above)

```
IMG2GIF    EXE    48298
IMG2TGA    EXE    24544
TGA2IMG    EXE    25288
GIFVIEW    EXE    64494
VIEW       EXE    23460
FILTER     EXE    29968
AVERAGE    FLT    24
DIAGLAPL   FLT    31
HORIZNTL   FLT    27
LAPLAC     FLT    34
LMR        FLT    33
UNITY      FLT    24
VERTICAL   FLT    31
```

Directory of C:\BOB\TOOLS\IMG2GIF (Compile with Watcom at present)

(utilities for conversion between .IMG and .GIF image file formats)

```
GIF____C   BAT    172
ERRS       H      415
STD        H      343
DECODER    C      12293
GIF2IMG    C      4771
GIF2IMG    EXE    30644
IMG2GIF    C      44349
IMG2GIF    EXE    48298
```

Directory of C:\BOB\TOOLS\IMG2TGA (Compile with Watcom at present)

(utilities for conversion between .IMG and .TGA image file formats)

```
TGA____C   BAT    160
IMG2TGA    C      2732
IMG2TGA    EXE    24544
TGA2IMG    C      3746
TGA2IMG    EXE    25288
```

Directory of C:\BOB\TOOLS\VIEWGIF (Compile with Watcom at present)

(utility for viewing .GIF image files on an SVGA adapter (TSENG4000))

```
GIFV___C   BAT    31
ERRS       H      415
STD        H      343
DECODER    C      12293
GIFVIEW    C      3943
GIFVIEW    EXE    64494
```

Directory of C:\BOB\TOOLS\VIEWTGA (Compile with Borland at present)

(utility for viewing .TGA image files on the Cardinal 7000 24-bit color card)

```
TRUE        ASM   7285
TRUE        H     483
VIEW        C     13292
ASSEMBLE    BAT   23
VIEW        DSK   678
VIEW        PRJ   5237
VIEW        EXE   23460
```

Directory of C:\BOB\TOOLS\FILTER (Compile with Watcom at present)

(filter utility, requires .IMG file format in and out. Use with FILT.BAT - FILT infile outfile - you set a given filter in the batch file)

```
FILTER_C    BAT   80
FILTER      C     8391
FILTER      EXE   29968
AVERAGE     FLT   24
DIAGLAPL    FLT   31
HORIZNTL    FLT   27
LAPLAC      FLT   34
LMR         FLT   33
UNITY       FLT   24
VERTICAL    FLT   31
FILT        BAT   130
```

.BO files not found on the disks (these must be generated with the database generators):

```
PROC

TREES       BO
T16_16P     BO
TILES       BO
SPHFLK3     BO
SPONGE      BO FOR SPONGE B
HEXGRID2    BO
```

```
PROCZBUS

PLOTEQN1    BO
PLOTEQN2    BO
PLOTEQN3    BO
PLOTEQN4    BO
OCEAN       BO
CPMMSET1    BO
CPMMSET2    BO
CPMJSET1    BO
CPMJSET2    BO
DRAGON      BO
REVSOLID    BO
DRAGON2     BO
REVSOL2     BO
TERRAIN     BO
```

Bibliography

Akeley, Kurt, and Jermoluk, Tom, "High Performance Polygon Rendering," *Computer Graphics* (SIGGRAPH '88 Procedings) 22 (August 1988):239-246.

Blanton, Keith, "Image Extrapolation for Flight Simulator Visual Systems," AIAA Conference, 1988.

Blanton, Keith, "The Design of Videodisc Based Interactive Simulation Visual Systems," SCS Eastern Simulation Conferences, 1988.

Bouville, C., "Bounding Ellipsiods for Ray-Fractal Intersection." SIGGRAPH '85, 19 (1985):45-52.

Carpenter, L. "Computer Rendering of Fractal Curves and Surfaces." *Computer Graphics* (1980): 109 ff.

Demko, S., Hodges, L., and Naylor, B., "Construction of Fractal Objects with Iterated Function Systems." SIGGRAPH '85, 19 (1985): 271-278.

Dewdney, A.K., "Computer Recreations: Exploring the Mandelbrot Set." *Computer Graphics* 20 (1985):16 ff.

Escher, M.C., *The World of M.C.Escher*. New York: H.N. Abrams, 1971.

Feigenbaum, M.J., "Quantitative Universality for a Class of Non-Linear Transformations." *Journal of Statistical Physics* 19 (Jan 1978): 25-52.

Finlay, Mark, "Fractal Terrain Image Synthesis for Simulation Using Defense Mapping Agency Data," SPIE Technical Symposium on Optics, Electro-Optics, & Sensors - Orlando, FL, 1987.

Finlay, Mark, "Computer Generated 3-D Infrared Background Imagery Model," Report to U.S. Army Missile Command, 1983.

Foley, James, van Dam, Andries, Feiner, Steven, and Hughes, John. *Computer Graphics Principles and Practice.* Addison Wesley, 2nd ed., 1990.

Fournier, Alain, Reeves, William, "A Simple Model of Ocean Waves." *Computer Graphics* 20 (1986): 75-84.

Glassner, Andrew S., *An Introduction to Ray Tracing,* Academic Press, Ltd., 1989.

Gouraud, H., "Continuous Shading of Curves Surfaces." *IEEE Transactions on Computers* 20 (June 1971: 623-628.

Mastin, G.A., Watterberg, P.A., and Mareda, J.F., "Fourier Synthesis of Ocean Scenes." *IEEE Computer Graphics and Application* (March, 1987): 16-24.

Musgrave, F. Kenton, "Uses of Fractional Brownian Motion in Modelling Nature." SIGGRAPH '91, Course 14 Notes, pp 5-34.

Peitgen, H.O., and Richter, P.H., *The Beauty of Fractals.* Berlin: Springer-Verlag, 1986.

Peitgen, H.O., and Saupe, D., *The Science of Fractal Images.* Berlin: Springer-Verlag, 1988.

Peachey, Darwin, "Modeling Waves and Surf," *Computer Graphics* 20 (1986): 65-74.

Phong, Bui Tuong, "Illumination for Computer Generated Pictures" *Communications of the ACM* 18 (June 1975: 311-317.

Prusinkiewicz, Przemyslaw, and Hammel, Mark, "Automata, Languages, and Iterated Function Systems." SIGGRAPH '91, Course 14 Notes, pp 115-143.

Rushmeier, Holly E., "Extending the Radiosity Method to Transmitting and Specularly Reflecting Surfaces." Master's Thesis, Cornell University, 1986.

Saupe, Dietmar, "*Simulation und Animation von Wolken mit Fraktalen* (German Language)," GI-19. *Jahrestagung I.* Berlin: Springer-Verlag, 1989.

Watkins, Christopher D., Stevens, Roger T. *Advanced Graphics Programming in Turbo Pascal.* San Mateo, CA: M&T Publishing Co., 1990.

Watkins, Christopher D., Stevens, Roger T. *Advanced Graphics Programming in C and C++.* San Mateo, CA: M&T Publishing Co., 1991.

Watkins, Christopher D., Sharp, Larry E. *Programming in 3 Dimensions: 3-D Graphics, Ray Tracing, and Animation* San Mateo, CA: M&T Publishing Co., 1992.

Watt, Alan, *Fundamentals of Three-Dimensional Computer Graphics.* Addison-Wesley Publishing Co., 1989.

Whitted, Turner, "Managing Geometric Complexity with Enhanced Procedural Models." SIGGRAPH '86, Vol. 20, No. 4, (1986) pp. 189-195.

Index